# The Database Experts' Guide to FOCUS

# The Database Experts' Guide to FOCUS

Joseph DeVita, PhD

Intertext Publications
McGraw-Hill Book Company
New York, N.Y.

Library of Congress Catalog Card Number 88-80273

Copyright © 1988 by Multiscience Press, Inc. All rights reserved. Printed in the United States of America. Except as permitted under the United States Copyright Act of 1976, no part of this book may be reproduced or distributed in any form or by any means, or stored in a database or retrieval system without the prior written permission of the publisher.

10 9 8 7 6 5 4 3 2 1

ISBN 0-07-016604-8 (paperback)
ISBN 0-07-016609-6 (hardcover)

Intertext Publications/Multiscience Press, Inc.
McGraw-Hill Book Company
1221 Avenue of the Americas
New York, NY 10020

FOCUS is a trademark of Information Builders Inc.

# Contents

| | | |
|---|---|---|
| Preface | | xi |
| Chapter 1 | **Applications Development With FOCUS: An Introduction** | 1 |
| | Fourth-Generation Programming Languages | 1 |
| | What is FOCUS? What is a Fourth-Generation Language? | 2 |
| | FOCUS: For the Casual Programmer or Data Processing Professional | 5 |
| | How to Use This Book | 8 |
| | Supplemental Aids to Learning Focus | 10 |
| | Database Management With FOCUS | 11 |
| | FOCUS Reporting Requests — Printing and Summing Data From the Sales File | 21 |
| | FOCUS File Structure | 27 |
| Chapter 2 | **Basics of Designing FOCUS Applications** | 31 |
| | File Design | 32 |
| |     MASTER File Description | 32 |
| | Example 1: Vendor Contract Bids | 33 |
| | Cross-referencing Between FOCUS Files | 37 |
| | Unique Segments | 41 |
| | External Files: Sequential and Tape Files | 44 |
| | Avoiding Overflow Conditions | 47 |
| | COBOL Files | 48 |

| Chapter 3 | Working in the FOCUS Environment: The Basics of Report Writing | 49 |
|---|---|---|
| | FOCUS in the VM/CMS Operating System | 49 |
| | Status Inquiry and Default Settings | 50 |
| | Working in the VM/CMS Operating System | 51 |
| | The Basics of Report Requests — A Sample Application | 54 |
| | The Offline and Online Commands | 58 |
| | Using the BY Phrase | 60 |
| | Counting Records | 62 |
| | The Verb PRINT | 69 |
| | Some Limitations of PRINT Verb | 70 |
| | The TABLEF Command | 70 |
| | Multiverb TABLE Requests | 71 |
| | Screening Conditions | 73 |
| | Using the DEFINE Instead of IF Conditions | 75 |
| | Other Screening Considerations | 76 |
| | | |
| Chapter 4 | Techniques for Customizing Reports | 79 |
| | Define and Compute Statements | 80 |
| | Rounding Error | 83 |
| | Other DEFINE Techniques | 84 |
| | Concatenate | 85 |
| | Decode | 87 |
| | The COMPUTE Statement | 88 |
| | Column Positional Notation | 90 |
| | The LAST Command | 92 |
| | Direct Calculations on Verb Objects | 93 |
| | Formatting Customized Reports | 95 |
| | Formatting Headings, Footings, Etc. | 99 |
| | Direct Operations Performed | 101 |
| | Subheading and Subfooting | 102 |
| | Performing Subtotals and Other Calculations | 104 |
| | Additional Considerations for Preparing Reports | 108 |

| Chapter 5 | Designing Procedures for Reporting: Two Case Studies | 113 |
|---|---|---|
| | Organizing the FIles to Contain Detailed and Summary Data | 114 |
| | Application 1: Income Tracking System for Servicing Deals | 115 |
| | Managing FOCEXECS with Dialogue Manager | 118 |
| | Other Considerations for the "Driver" FOCEXEC | 124 |
| | Short Path Segments | 129 |
| | Report 2 | 129 |
| | Report 3 | 138 |
| | Report 4 | 144 |
| | Programming Style: Reusing FOCUS Techniques | 146 |
| | Supplying Values as Dialogue Manager Variables | 151 |
| | Example 2: Daily Price History for Mortgage Securities | 153 |
| | Indexed Fields and Efficiency Considerations | 156 |
| | Report 1: Price Spreads for Securities With the Same Label-Between Pairs of Coupons | 158 |
| | Using JOINS to Reference Data in Other Files | 170 |
| | Report 2: Price Spread Report Between Labels | 175 |
| Chapter 6 | Maintaining FOCUS Files | 185 |
| | Creating a Transaction File | 192 |
| | Matching Transaction Values to Database Records | 194 |
| | Modifying Unique Segments | 201 |
| | The FIXFORM Statement — Using an Input Transactions File | 202 |
| | Considerations When Using Transaction Files | 203 |
| | Suppressing System Messages | 204 |
| | The Sort Order of the Transaction Records | 204 |
| | A Sample Input Transactions File | 205 |

|  |  |  |
|---|---|---|
| | FIXFORM Transaction Field Formats | 209 |
| | Record-by-Record Processing | 210 |
| | Logging Transactions | 214 |
| | Using SAVE Files as Transaction Files | 216 |
| | Transaction Files With Records in Internal Format | 218 |
| | An Example of Using Internal Format Records | 220 |
| | Conditional Fields | 223 |
| | Validating Transaction Values | 225 |
| | Logging Invalid Transactions | 228 |
| | Other Validate Features | 230 |
| **Chapter 7** | **FIDEL: Generating Interactive Data Entry Screens** | **235** |
| | FIDEL CRT Data Entry in Dialogue Manager | 239 |
| | Terminating Data Entry in FIDEL or -CRTFORM | 240 |
| | Formatting a FIDEL Screen | 240 |
| | Display and Turnaround Fields | 243 |
| | Clearing the Screen | 246 |
| |     CLEAR/NOCLEAR Option | 246 |
| | Using Multiple CRTFORMS | 247 |
| |     The LINE Option | 247 |
| **Chapter 8** | **Using Case Logic in Modify Procedures** | **249** |
| | Considerations When Using Case Logic With CRTFORMs | 252 |
| | Branching to Cases Using the IF and GOTO Statements | 253 |
| | Examples of Case Logic | 256 |
| | Example 1: Allowing the Operator to Confirm Data Entry | 256 |
| | Example 2: Processing FIXFORM Transactions Based on Values of a Field | 257 |
| | Example 3: Multiple Record Processing (Repeating Groups) | 260 |

| | | |
|---|---|---|
| Chapter 9 | **Designing FOCUS Applications:**<br>**Case Studies** | **277** |
| | Working With the End User | 277 |
| | Basic Utilities for Implementing FOCUS<br>  Procedures | 278 |
| | The USE Command | 279 |
| | Debugging Features and Checking for Errors | 281 |
| | Setting Up TEMP Space | 283 |
| | Example 1: Member Enrollment Application | 284 |
| | Example 2: Sales Tracking and Analysis System | 287 |
| |    Report 1 | 292 |
| |    Report 2 | 294 |
| |    Report 3 (The MATCH FILE Command) | 296 |
| |    Using the MATCH Command | 297 |
| | Example 3: Client Mailing List System | 308 |
| | Example 4: Project Tracking System | 314 |
| | Example 5: Security Trading System | 321 |
| |    Determining Net Position | 327 |
| | Example 6: Working With External Files;<br>  Audit Trail Reports | 340 |
| |    COBOL to FOCUS Format Conversion | 344 |
| |    Creating an Audit Trail for a Modify<br>     Procedure | 348 |
| | Example 7: Executing FOCEXECS<br>Interactively; CMS EXECS | 353 |
| | Example 8: Processing Employee Expense<br>Vouchers | 358 |
| Appendix | **Using FOCUS in the Operating Systems:**<br>**VM/CMS, MVS/TSO, PC/DOS, VAX/VMS** | **373** |
| | Operating FOCUS Under VM/CMS | 374 |
| |    Setting Up the Environment | 374 |
| |    FOCUS Databases and MASTER<br>     Descriptions | 375 |
| |    External Files | 376 |
| |    Space Requirements | 377 |
| |    CMS EXECS | 378 |

| | |
|---|---:|
| Rebuilding FOCUS Files | 380 |
| Operating FOCUS Under MVS/TSO | 380 |
|    Setting Up the Environment | 380 |
|    Issuing TSO Commands From Within FOCUS | 383 |
|    Interrupting FOCUS Programs | 384 |
|    FOCUS Databases, MASTER Descriptions, and FOCEXECS | 385 |
|    Using CLISTS | 387 |
|    Space Requirements | 388 |
|    REBUILD and REORG | 389 |
| FOCUS in the VAX/VMS Environment | 389 |
|    Setting Up the Environment | 389 |
|    FOCUS Databases, FOCEXECS, and MASTER Descriptions | 392 |
|    The USE Command | 393 |
|    External Files | 395 |
|    Other FOCUS VAX Considerations | 397 |
| FOCUS in the PC/DOS Environment | 398 |
|    Setting Up the Environment | 398 |
|    FOCUS Databases, FOCEXECS, and MASTER Descriptions | 400 |
|    The USE Command | 401 |
|    External Files | 403 |
|    Other PC/DOS FOCUS Considerations | 405 |
| **Index** | **407** |

# Preface

A major goal being considered today by many large organizations is how to effectively utilize our human resources in the light of developments in new technology. Our own individual requirements, hopefully, should be compatible with that goal. For example, many of us wish to improve our quality of life by spending less time with routine jobs. The new, powerful computer hardware and software can help us realize such achievements. The general public now has access to these powerful computers. If the use of the new computer technology can bring about such gains, how do we motivate more people to learn how to apply it?

Fortunately, we are a people who enjoy sharing our discoveries with others. This book describes how to use an important fourth generation computer programming language, FOCUS. The major reason FOCUS is important is because it offers the ability to develop database applications without a great deal of programming. It is intended for anyone who needs to be conversant with user-friendly software for database applications. This group includes professional managers who need more powerful computer tools, and college students who are learning how to program.

As a database consultant, I have seen how FOCUS has been used in a wide variety of applications. I have also found that many organizations have developed innovative approaches in working with end users, training programmers, and managing their databases. However, there is still a great need to educate more end users about the development of FOCUS applications. That is one of my goals in writing this book. I have tried to demonstrate the basic techniques of working with FOCUS by presenting real applications, and describing business problems which are given solutions here. I have covered most of the important capabilities of FOCUS, so that the novice may have a comprehensive guide to how the techniques are used. As you work with FOCUS applications, you will obtain more and more insight into how FOCUS programs are developed, and how databases are designed. People learn the FOCUS language by setting up their own databases and writing their own programs. This book recognizes that fact by providing plentiful examples and applications in the last chapter.

I would like to take this opportunity to give credit to others who have shared their experiences using FOCUS with me. Whenever I had questions about a FOCUS technique, they always seemed to be available for discussions. I will name a few from this long list: Naum Bukherovich, Michael Colen, Norman Dee, Jonathan Fisher, Barry Rindner, and Jerry Varney. I am also thankful to my wife Cindy and boys Chris and Tim for their support, and for helping me keep at it to finish this book. My love and respect for my parents is always important since they have given me everything they've had.

Chapter

# 1

# Applications Development With FOCUS: An Introduction

### Fourth-Generation Programming Languages

FOCUS is usually described as a fourth-generation programming language (or 4GL) because it consists of procedures and commands developed from FORTRAN — a third-generation language. It is also referred to as a "database" language, because data records are organized in FOCUS files which have a special database structure. We shall make no attempt to assign a particular definition of the FOCUS language. Since FOCUS is a data processing tool, the purpose of this book shall be to describe how the tool is used in application. Also, as with any tool, we shall describe how it can best be learned by programmers and endusers. A major goal of this book will be to clarify for the novice FOCUS user the basic techniques which are available in FOCUS for report writing, file maintenance, and developing entire applications. We shall cover how the basic techniques are used in real applications so that you can refer to these examples when starting your own applications.

## What is FOCUS? What is a Fourth-Generation Language?

FOCUS is a programming language which was developed in the 1970s to increase the programmer's productivity in developing applications. The language consists primarily of simple commands, which are composed of FORTRAN instructions. These FORTRAN instructions are transparent to the user, since the user only needs to know how to use the FOCUS commands.

FOCUS was developed by the company Information Builders Inc. (IBI) as a tool for application development. IBI has continually succeeded in showing the user community that the language has a well-designed mixture of commands, whose structure is easy to learn, and whose functionality can handle almost any application. The FOCUS language is not a patchwork of procedures and modules which have been poorly designed. It has maintained its integrity by staying with commands which were designed properly from the start. The commands, written with FORTRAN code, each have a simple, specific purpose — to perform basic applications tasks such as listing records, summing records, defining new fields on records, extracting records into more manageable files, etc. Some data processing managers, who have never worked with FOCUS, might say that it means "Fool Our Computer Users." I hope to show that FOCUS has techniques to offer many kinds of computer users. I prefer to think of it as meaning

F or O ur C omputer USers.

Over the past ten years, data processing has taken a lot of criticism from endusers, who seem to require more timely access to information and analysis. As hardware and firmware technology and costs have improved dramatically, the cost of developing applications software has certainly not come down. Data is still not easily available to administrative, sales, and technical staff, nor is it easily available to other management. Meanwhile, approximately 60% of the total yearly business expenditures on computers goes to fixing and updating existing third-generation programs written in COBOL. See High Technology magazine, April 1986, "Programming Without Tears." Data processing managers must somehow find ways to maintain this existing code, while satisfying new requests for applications development. This is not easy when there is a lot of turnover in most programming groups due to the high salaries being offered.

Certainly, an increasing number of users are turning to personal computers to obtain better control of their data, and to even develop applications themselves. This may be the solution for simple data manipulation and inquiry. Hovever, larger-scale applications still require programming and customized databases. The question is how to implement these applications using the best hardware and software technologies available. This comes down to a question of managerial skill, training, and organized initiatives. This should be the goal of any organization — to provide the incentives for its people to learn the best tools and technologies so that their customers are better served, and that the work becomes easier.

In the rest of this chapter, we shall outline how the fourth-generation language FOCUS can be used to implement and manage a large variety of programming applications. We shall discuss the important aspects of the FOCUS database structure from the point of view of the programmer and enduser. Hopefully, after reading this chapter, you will know the basic capabilities of the language, and the range of applications they are used for.

How do FOCUS and other fourth-generation database languages improve the productivity of the applications programmer? FOCUS combines a few easily understood commands with a database methodology for organizing the data. As we shall see, the commands required to specify processing are so much simpler and so much more powerful than the language of traditional programming languages. There is a sacrifice which has to be made to obtain these simple procedures — the programmer has less control over how the data is output in reports, and how the data should be organized for various FOCUS procedures. However, this restriction on controlling the data also contributes to the ease of use of the language. By working with the procedures and performing the same tasks over and over again, the techniques are learned very quickly. The language constantly reinforces the user in understanding how the commands are used. This is how people learn almost anything. Doctors learn how to perform operations by repeatedly watching how it is done, and then by practicing operations with the assistance of others. Architects and builders may understand the theoretical constraints of designing structures, but it is their actual work in the field which determines what they will learn. Similarly, lawyers are brought up with the concept of learning through case studies, and evaluating a case based on precedent. Similarly, we claim that FOCUS techniques encourage repetition, which reinforces the learning process. Furthermore, the learning process is made even easier because programmers can help each other when it is needed. Because of the small number of commands and standard formats of reports and procedures, it is not uncommon for programmers to work together in designing the procedures for an application, or when debugging various procedures. There are more opportunities for teamwork and communication among individuals since experience and insight can be shared. With more traditional programming languages, such as COBOL or FORTRAN, there are an unlimited number of procedures which can be written with no standard format. This makes it difficult to assist each other when problems come up, or when a new application must be designed. We shall say more about this often overlooked aspect of fourth-generation languages, since it may well be their most important feature.

According to Focus Research in West Hartford, Conn., which tracks the market for software, in 1985 about 20% of the IBM mainframe sites in the U.S. used a fourth-generation language. FOCUS accounts for half of all new sales. Also, while there was no increase in the number of sites using other data-management software, the number of sites using fourth-generation database software increased over 20% from 1985 to 1986. The potential looks to be enormous since these new languages can also be used in non-data processing (end-user) departments. Personal computer users can now run FOCUS, as can non-IBM mainframe users. (FOCUS is available for the DEC VAX.)

As the costs of hardware go down, there will be a greater demand for new software applications. Many people also will want to deal with data when they need it, rather than waiting for access to a programmer in the data-processing department. What is needed is a breakthrough not only in the software technology, but also in the way in which we manage this technology. If you read between the lines of this chapter, you will see that the major opportunities are in working with endusers, and understanding the applications that are really needed. This is not a problem of technology, but one of organization and management style.

FOCUS provides a new methodology for handling the tasks most important to the programmer. It offers a tool that:

1. Makes available to the user those techniques which accomplish common tasks — such as formatting tabular reports, sorting data, storing data, selecting data based on screening conditions.

2. Helps the user and programmer work together with the problem definition. The data can be organized in terms meaningful to the user.
3. Organizes and stores data in files which can be related to each other, and processed together.
4. Permits the entry and modification of data either interactively, from existing files, or using extracts from other database systems.
5. Provides facilities for validating data before it is stored, and for insuring the security and integrity of the database.
6. Simplifies the execution of procedures from simple menus, or commands which allow the user to supply parameters and options at run time.
7. Permits the easy preparation of standard reports, and allows requests for ad hoc reports to be quickly satisfied.

## FOCUS: For the Casual Programmer or Data Processing Professional

One of the goals of this book is to show that FOCUS has been used as a complete applications development tool. From this point of view, FOCUS is intended for the data processing professional. However, in a large number of cases, the casual programmer, who has some knowledge of programming terms (such as fields, records, files), can write his or her own requests for extracting data, entering data, and developing simple reports. In some cases, the user will have little time or inclination to learn some FOCUS commands, or to write programs. However, almost all users will obtain enough familiarity with FOCUS, so that they recognize the type of applications which are best handled by FOCUS. At best, the user will be better able to understand the language of the programmer, and what is generally involved in setting up a new application. By knowing what the tool can do, the user can assist the programmer in designing a system. At the least, the fear of dealing with unknown tools should be eliminated.

The basic tasks which can be performed in the FOCUS environment are:

1. The TABLE command for sorting records, and extracting data, and formatting reports. Reports can be viewed interactively using the many features of the HOT SCREEN facility.

2. A complete database management system which supports hierarchical and relational file structures, integrated data dictionary, utilities for describing and rebuilding the structure, and access to external non-FOCUS files.
3. Processing transactions interactively, or from extracted records, using the MODIFY command. MODIFY allows for validating records, creating LOG files, building data entry screens with FIDEL, performing computations on data fields.
4. Controlling the execution of FOCUS procedures using DIALOGUE MANAGER which allows one program (FOCEXEC) to be used in a number of different ways. The user may select options at run time using dialogue manager variables.
5. Two editing tools which facilitate the coding and testing of programs (TED) and the quick manipulation of data stored in a FOCUS file (SCAN).
6. Integrated financial modeling language appropriate for generating "spreadsheet" reports, and which accomodates almost all regular reporting features.
7. Interactive color graphics integrated with a report generator.
8. Complete integrated statistical package.
9. An interactive spreadsheet facility, FOCCALC, which contains much of the capability of LOTUS 123.
10. Host Language Interface which allows for procedures written in other languages to access a FOCUS database.

In addition, FOCUS can work well with other programming languages, and even with other database products. Reporting commands can be used with other relational databases such as IDMS, ADABAS, DB2, etc. It is quite practical to let FOCUS access data from a number of database systems, and to present it in summary form to management. This is also an area which is always being improved by Information Builders.

Before we introduce the basics of designing applications with FOCUS, something more should be said about the nature of FOCUS, and other fourth-generation languages as a programming tool. Regardless of how "user-friendly" a language claims to be, there will be times when a programmer is required. Except for simple inquiry or reporting, the casual user is bound to run into problems whether he is using FOCUS or some other 4GL. In these cases, he will need a more experienced programmer to solve the problem. However, as the user sees how these problems are solved, he will be gaining the confidence to tackle more and more applications. The major difference between the casual FOCUS user, and FOCUS programmer is the amount of practice which they have had with the various techniques. In my experience, this is the test of a "user-friendly" language — the amount of practice we get in using the various techniques. Whether we are developing a report or updating a database, FOCUS allows you to use the same techniques over and over. Since we are using a few simple techniques to perform major functions, we are working less — which is a goal of any technology.

Three other points are usually made with respect to user-friendliness. I will not try to debate the pros and cons of these points, simply because I don't know that these points are relevant to programming. The first point is that a 4GL should have a "natural" syntax in its commands. Does this simply mean that verb objects should come after verbs, that screening conditions contain no complicated expressions, etc.? What do human beings consider to be natural with respect to programming? Does the language need to use key words and methods in a consistent way time after time? The FORTRAN language is very consistent in its use of syntax but casual users would probably not say it is user-friendly. On the other hand, the English language has a number of inconsistent rules, pronunciations, etc., but most of us have no problem using it in our day-to-day lives. One might say that English is user-friendly. The second point has to do with documentation. The FOCUS 5.0 Users Manual is not a tutorial manual for beginners. It contains useful information about all the FOCUS features, which you can refer to when you forget how to use a technique. The beginner may have a difficult time finding things in the manual — probably because he doesn't know what he is looking for. Once you start developing FOCUS applications, you will become more interested in some techniques than others. For example, if you write code to extract data into SAVE files, you probably will not be too interested in the MODIFY command. Therefore, you should scan the users manual in order to know where to find interesting topics, or features which you think you will use in your next application. There's little chance of knowing everything about FOCUS unless you are using the techniques quite often.

The last point on user-friendliness is whether FOCUS is a procedural or non-procedural language. The degree to which FOCUS is procedural is relative. I prefer to think in terms of how the commands are "bundled" or "modularized." FOCUS allows you to be free of performing detailed instructions on data — such as reading a record, opening and closing files, accumulating totals, etc. FOCUS allows you to concentrate on performing a common request, like printing a report in standard format, or building a data entry screen. These requests can be performed in any order and in this respect are non-procedural. However, as you will see, each request is composed of key words and commands which should follow a particular order. The real power of FOCUS comes from using the same procedures and application "modules" over and over again so that each new application becomes easier to design.

## How to Use This Book

FOCUS is a rewarding tool for those who experiment with it, and those who are willing to ask questions when getting started. There is a TV commercial for a technology company, which describes its purpose: "to find information, to use the information, and to move the information somewhere else."

This is a good way to think of the goal of FOCUS. If you want to program applications with FOCUS, you will need to know the kinds of techniques available to handle various tasks. To a large extent, this will depend on what you've used before, or on what you may have seen elsewhere. The same is true if you are an enduser. You should be familiar with what FOCUS can and cannot do so that you can be comfortable with how an application will be designed. The more you know about how the database is organized, or how one file is related to another, the more use you will be able to get from the system. You will also be able to share your insights to FOCUS applications with other potential users and assist them in starting their own applications.

The purpose of this book is to demonstrate what you really need to know to write FOCUS applications. It identifies the fundamentals, and tries to use them in a number of examples. Ideally, each FOCUS technique should be explained by more than one example so that your understanding may be reinforced several times. However, this is not easy to do in a single book on FOCUS. What we have done is to organize the basic concepts on reporting, file maintenance, and dialogue manager so that the casual FOCUS user has a source of reference for how the basics are used in real applications. All the chapters in the book have been designed from the point of view of the novice FOCUS programmer. The material has been organized so that the novice may obtain an explanation of the basic techniques, along with demonstrations of how the techniques are used in real applications. By presenting a large number of examples, we have tried to take out the guess work in determining when to use various features. The experience we offer in each section should be supplemented with the more detailed experience you gain in your own applications. As you gain experience in writing FOCUS programs, you will probably want to use the techniques in different ways. At this point, it is best to use the FOCUS 5.0 manual as a source of reference for particular commands and procedures.

The examples are based on real applications which I have encountered as a FOCUS consultant. The examples, hopefully, will be of interest to you even though I have removed the more interesting, proprietary aspects. Please keep in mind that the sample programs are intended to expose you to the process of obtaining results using the basic techniques. Our emphasis is on explaining the nature of an application, and what is accomplished by each section of code. Unfortunately, we do not have the time to discuss every line of code. Some of the code may even be unnecessary or contain minor errors in the naming of fields. This should not prevent you from learning how a particular technique was used.

The material covered in this book is as follows:

Chapter 1: Intended for novices; the basics of the structure of FOCUS files is presented by describing the relationships between data in a file. An introduction to extracting and reporting data is also presented.

Chapter 2: Intended for novices; the details of setting up MASTER descriptions and designing FOCUS databases are presented. An explanation and examples of parent-child relationships, cross-referencing, and HOLD (external) files are presented.

Chapter 3: The basic concepts of report requests and data extraction are outlined with numerous examples. The reader is shown how to work in the FOCUS environment, and how to organize files and programs in VM/CMS.

Chapter 4: The basic TABLE request techniques are combined with more powerful techniques which expand the range of FOCUS reporting.

Chapter 5: Two case studies are described which show how reporting techniques are implemented in real applications. The basics of dialogue manager are presented in these examples, as well as other useful techniques.

Chapter 6: Techniques for maintaining FOCUS files are described for the novice and database designer. Insight is offered into how some of the MODIFY features should be used. Numerous examples are described.

Chapter 7: FIDEL interactive screen formatting is presented for use in MODIFY applications and in Dialogue Manager.

Chapter 8: An introduction to CASE logic — with practical examples.

Chapter 9: Eight FOCUS applications are presented — which cover most of the techniques used by an applications developer.

If you are an experienced FOCUS user, you realize that FOCUS techniques lend themselves to an unlimited variety of applications — these cannot be easily demonstrated in one book. Our goal has been to provide enough examples and commentary so that the new FOCUS programmer can understand the essential techniques, and gather some insight into designing databases, reports, and maintenance procedures. Although it is not possible to describe every line of code in these examples, the examples should provide something of value for all levels of FOCUS users. If you can understand how the techniques are used in a few examples, you should be able to apply them to your own applications. The examples should also be of interest to endusers, managers, and instructors, who need to be aware of developments in software technology. Hopefully, anyone who needs to interact with a programmer will have an easier job doing so if he or she understands what the tools can accomplish and how an application can be best organized.

## Supplemental Aids to Learning Focus

Depending on your requirements for developing systems, there should be facilities for training FOCUS users and programmers readily available in the organization. Information Builders provides a number of facilities, including courses and hotline, to satisfy much of your training needs. It is comforting to know that as your needs become more sophisticated, more sophisticated capabilities and resources are readily available.

You may also obtain assistance from me on FOCUS problems in this book, or on your own applications, by writing me at:

11 Van Buren Street, Pearl River, New York 10965.

You may also write me for information on obtaining the following (for a small charge):

1. Diskette containing the programs and sample database described in Chapter 9 for the Trade Inventory System. The report programs described in the example may be accessed using a simple online menu. Several other reports are also presented. You may also use the programming code to test other features of FOCUS.
2. Diskette containing a documentation program, which enables you to easily document any FOCUS system by describing the usage of FOCUS fields and commands in each program. The documentor, which is menu-driven, also describes the data in the FOCUS files, and the relationships between segments. It provides for a professional, comprehensive, approach for analyzing the use of fields and data included in any FOCUS application. The reports are useful in many documentation tasks. Figure 1-1 describes the format of several documentor reports.

## Database Management With FOCUS

The ability to organize data records into a file structure which describes the natural relationships between the data is essential to enhancing the performance of the FOCUS programmer. The basic structure of a FOCUS file is the concept of the parent-child relationship or the "one-to-many" relationship. In addition, FOCUS provides the ability to relate records in one file with those in another based on a field which is common to the records in both files. In this sense, FOCUS has many of the properties of relational database products.

```
System: TRADERS INVENTORY ( INV )                                          Page:    1

Date   : 11/19/87   Time:  11.03.59
======================================================================================
Program   Lines  Table  Prompt  Match  Define  -SET  Modify  Case Reports  Hold  Save  Include
--------------------------------------------------------------------------------------
ARCLOOK      1     0      1       0      0       0     0         0          0     0      0
ARCTAN      37     5      0       1      3       0     0         0          3     1      0
CONDPOS      5     1      0       0      0       0     0         0          0     0      0
CONDUSUM    24     3      0       2      0       0     0         0          4     0      0
GETDATE      3     0      0       0      3       0     0         0          0     0      0
GRPREP      42     1     10       0      1      19     0         0          0     0      0
INVADD      43     0      0       0      0       0     1        10          0     0      0
INVENT      16     0      0       0      0      13     0         0          0     0      1
INVLABLD    27     0      0       0      0       0     1         5          2     0      0
INVMOD      79     0      0       0      0       0     1        17          0     0      0
INVOPTAD    46     0      0       0      0       0     1         8          0     0      0
INVOPTUP    48     0      0       0      0       0     1        10          0     0      0
NETPOS      37     2      4       0      1      18     0         0          1     0      0
NETREP      31     3      1       0      1       1     0         0          1     0      0
NETVOL      24     1      0       1      4       2     0         0          2     0      2
OPTPOS      25     2      3       0      1      10     0         0          1     0      0
OPTVOL      52     2      1       4      4       2     0         0          5     0      7
PROFILE      1     0      0       0      0       0     0         0          0     0      1
SEETRD      23     1      6       0      1       3     0         0          0     2      0
TSY         22     1      0       3      2       0     0         0          4     0      0
VOLATIL      7     0      1       0      0       5     0         0          0     0      1
VOLDATE      4     1      0       0      0       1     0         0          0     1      0
VOLPRI      12     1      0       0      1       0     0         0          1     0      7
```

**Figure 1-1  Documentation program sample.**

```
WHOLPOS      5    1    0    0    0    0    0    0    0    0    0
WHOLSUM      5    1    0    0    0    0    0    0    0    1    0
===========================================================================
           619   26   27   11   23   77    5   50    8   22    4   19
===========================================================================


System : TRADERS INVENTORY ( INV )
.FEX   : INVOPTUP                                          Page:   1

Date   : 11/19/87  Time: 11.03.59
===========================================================================
Line                    F O C U S   S T A T E M E N T          Command
----                                                           -------
00001
00002
00003   SET MSG = OFF
00004   MODIFY FILE INVENT                                     MODIFY
00005   LOG DUPL MSG OFF
00006   LOG NOMATCH MSG OFF
00007   LOG INVALID MSG OFF
00008   CHECK 1
00009   COMPUTE                                                COMPUTE
00010   PFKEY/A4 =;
00011   XPORT/A4=' ';XLABEL/A4=' ';XMD/A6=' ';XCOUP/A6=' ';
00012   XSDAT/A6=' ';
00013
00014   GOTO CASE1
00015
00016   CASE CASE1                                             CASE
```

**Figure 1-1 (continued) Documentation program sample.**

```
FILENAME=SALES  ,SUFFIX=FOC,$
SEGNAME=SALESEG,SEGTYPE=S2,$
   FIELDNAME=PRODUCT,PROD,A3  ,$
   FIELDNAME=REGION ,REGN,A2  ,$
   FIELDNAME=UNITS,UNITS,I5,$
   FIELDNAME=UNITPRICE,PRICE,D8.2,$
   FIELDNAME=BRAND       ,BRAND,A4   ,$
   FIELDNAME=MANAGER  ,MGR   ,A10  ,$
```

Figure 1-2   MASTER file description.

The key element of a FOCUS file is the segment — the simplest type of FOCUS file consists of one segment. The segment consists of any number of records with the same layout of fields. You describe the segment by entering the names of the fields, and field formats into a MASTER file description. The MASTER file for one FOCUS file is shown in figure 1-2. The records contain data on the annual unit sales of products sold by a company. The data has been organized by product code and by sales region. They are known as the key fields in the segment. Besides the fields PRODCODE and REGION, the records in the segment contain the following other fields:

AMOUNT: the number of units of product sold.
PRICE: the unit price of the product in the sales region.
BRAND: the brand or product group to which the product code belongs.
MANAGER: the last name of the manager of the sales region.

FOCUS files are intended primarily as a way to organize the data so that reports can be obtained, and the data analyzed. The other purpose of FOCUS files is to describe how the data is related to the application. In this product file, we have decided to use the fields PRODUCT and REGION to uniquely define the records in the file. No two records can have the same product code and region code. This should make sense to you, since the units sold in each record depend on the product and the region. We assume that the input data, which has been accepted into the FOCUS file, has been summarized for the year. If there are 50 regions and 10 products, then there is a maximum of 500 records in the file. If some products have not been sold in some regions, then there will be less than 500 records. Some examples of records in the file are shown below:

```
FILENAME=SALES   ,SUFFIX=FOC,$
SEGNAME=PRODSEG,SEGTYPE=S1,$
   FIELDNAME=PRODUCT,PROD,A3  ,$
   FIELDNAME=UNITPRICE,PRICE,D8.2,$
   FIELDNAME=BRAND       ,BRAND,A4   ,$
SEGNAME=REGSEG  ,PARENT=PRODSEG,SEGTYPE=S1,$
   FIELDNAME=REGION ,REGN,A2  ,$
   FIELDNAME=UNITS,UNITS,I5,$
   FIELDNAME=MANAGER    ,MGR   ,A10  ,$
```

Figure 1-3   Two segment MASTER file description.

| PRODUCT | REGION | UNITS | PRICE | BRAND | MANAGER |
|---|---|---|---|---|---|
| 101 | 02 | 5000 | 2.50 | 1001 | SMITH |
| 102 | 02 | 2000 | 1.25 | 1001 | SMITH |
| 103 | 04 | 1000 | 1.00 | 1001 | JONES |
| 108 | 04 | 5000 | 3.00 | 1002 | JONES |
| 201 | 08 | 2000 | 1.00 | 1005 | KIRBY |
| 202 | 05 | 5500 | 1.75 | 1005 | ELLIS |
| 101 | 05 | 1500 | 2.50 | 1001 | ELLIS |
| 103 | 04 | 4200 | 1.00 | 1001 | JONES |
| 105 | 08 | 2800 | 3.50 | 1002 | KIRBY |
| 201 | 06 | 1000 | 1.00 | 1005 | MACK |

Although this is not the actual order of the records, it shows that the annual sales units have been obtained for each product and region. Also, the brand associated with each product is identified on the record, as well as the price of the product, and the manager of each region.

The MASTER file description is the basis for understanding how the data has been organized, and how it may be used. There usually is more than one way of describing a MASTER for an application. If there are complex relationships between the data, then care should be taken in designing the MASTER. In this case, you can take advantage of the capability of defining segments of related fields as a means to identify the relationships. In the above MASTER, the file has been set up as a single-segment file. This simply indicates that the records in the file are all of one type. Most FOCUS files can be set up with a single segment. An example of a MASTER with more than one segment is shown in figure 1-3. This MASTER may be a more natural way of describing the relationships between the data fields. The top segment, PRODSEG, uniquely identifies the fields related to products, while the CHILD segment, REGCODE, uniquely identifies the fields related to the annual units sold in each region. There are several points to be made about the hierarchical structure of this MASTER description. This parent-child segment structure can be used when you have several instances of data in the child that are related to one instance in the parent. For example, for product 101, there are several regions which have annual sales units for that product. Similarly, product 201 also has several regions with annual sales units.

Each segment contains data fields which are related to the other fields in the segment. For example, the unit price is related to the product, as is the brand code. Note that in the single segment version, it is not clear whether the unit price may also be dependent on the region. The only way to know this, for the single segment version, is to know the application, or where the data comes from. This may not be obvious for users and programmers who need to access data from the file. Another problem with the single-segment version is the redundant data stored in the records. For example, the following two records contain the unit price and brand code for the product 101.

```
PROD REGION UNITS PRICE BRAND MANAGER
101  02      5000  2.50  1001  SMITH
101  05      4000  2.50  1001  JAMES
```

With a single segment file, the records may contain redundant data. Since product 101 has one price and one brand code, we should not have to repeat this information on more than one record. This not only increases the amount of data that must be stored in the file, but it increases the likelihood that incorrect data may be entered into the system. In a system with many thousands of records, this redundant data could degrade the performance of FOCUS in accessing records. However, in relatively small files like this one, the effect is insignificant.

The parent-child relationship shown in figure 1-4 is a natural way to relate segments in the same file, when you have several instances of data in the child that are related to one instance of the parent. Notice that the single instance of data for product 101 will have several region codes associated with it. Notice also that an alternate way to describe the multiple segment file is with region code as the top segment, and the product codes in the child segment. Furthermore, a child segment can have descendant segments of its own. The

```
STRUCTURE OF FOCUS FILE SALES  ON 10/30/87 AT 11.48.24
            PRODSEG
   01         S1
       **************
      *PRODUCT       **
      *UNITPRICE     **
      *BRAND         **
      *              **
      *              **
       **************
     **************
          I
          I
          I
          I  REGSEG
   02     I   S1
           **************
          *REGION        **
          *UNITS         **
          *MANAGER       **
          *              **
          *              **
           **************
         **************
```

Figure 1-4    Structure diagram — shows one-to-many relationships.

descendants of a descendant segment have a many-to-one relationship with their parent, just as the first descendant segment has a many-to-one relationship with its parent ("root") segment. In the MASTER in figure 1-5, a third segment describes the units sold in each month of the year. In this case, we assume that the sales data has been summarized by month, instead of the entire year. Since the months have a many-to-one relationship with each region, the monthly sales are placed in a descendant segment of the region segment. The monthly sales are contained in the field UNITS.

As you can see, the MASTER file is the key to describing the relationships between the data. Once it has been set up, the data may be entered or "loaded" into the FOCUS file using procedures discussed in Chapter 5. Then, any of the reporting features can be used with the file. Before continuing our discussion of the structure of FOCUS files, you should be aware of the following. The reporting features used to create a report depend very little on whether a file is single-segment

```
FILENAME=SALES  ,SUFFIX=FOC,$
SEGNAME=PRODSEG,SEGTYPE=S1,$
   FIELDNAME=PRODUCT,PROD,A3  ,$
   FIELDNAME=UNITPRICE,PRICE,D8.2,$
   FIELDNAME=BRAND       ,BRAND,A4   ,$
SEGNAME=REGSEG ,PARENT=PRODSEG,SEGTYPE=S1,$
   FIELDNAME=REGION ,REGN,A2 ,$
   FIELDNAME=MANAGER   ,MGR  ,A10 ,$
SEGNAME=DATESEG,PARENT=REGSEG,SEGTYPE=SH1,$
   FIELDNAME=DATE,MONTH,A4YM,$
   FIELDNAME=UNITS,UNITS,I5,$
```

**Figure 1-5  Sales MASTER with additional child segment.**

or multisegment. In many reporting applications, the programmer may use the same techniques for screening records, summing records, defining new fields, etc. on single segment or multisegment files. Furthermore, if the FOCUS file contains a large number of records, a common practice is to first extract a subset of the records into a HOLD file. The reports may then be formatted using the data in the HOLD file.

For example, assume that records are to be selected if the annual sales units of a product in a region exceed 10,000. The records which qualify will be extracted into a HOLD file, and used for further processing — such as reports, graphical analysis, etc. The following procedure may first be used to extract the records into a HOLD file.

```
TABLE FILE SALES
PRINT UNITS PRICE
BY PRODUCT BY REGION
IF UNITS GT 10000
ON TABLE HOLD
END
```

The next part of the procedure is to create two reports, with the first report printing the records sorted by region code, and the second report sorting the records by product. Since we are interested only in records with units exceeding 10,000, we are first going to extract the qualified records into a HOLD file. The two reports can be obtained in less time, since FOCUS will be able to process a fewer number of records. Figure 1-6 shows the entire procedure for creating the two

```
TABLE FILE SALES
PRINT UNITS PRICE
BY PRODUCT BY REGION
IF UNITS GT 10000
ON TABLE HOLD
END

TABLE FILE HOLD
"ANNUAL SALES - BY PRODUCT "
" "
PRINT UNITS PRICE
BY PRODUCT BY REGION
ON PRODUCT SUBTOTAL
END

TABLE FILE HOLD
"ANNUAL SALES - BY REGION   "
" "
PRINT UNITS PRICE
BY REGION BY PRODUCT
ON REGION   SUBTOTAL
END
```

**Figure 1-6    Extracting records into a HOLD file.**

reports. Alternatively, these reports could have been generated without extracting the records into a HOLD file. The first approach is more efficient if the SALES FOCUS file contains a large number of records (several thousand records may be considered a large file).

The point of this example is to introduce the idea of preprocessing the data for subsequent storage and manipulation. Any FOCUS file can be preprocessed in this way, with HOLD files to contain a smaller, more manageable set of data. The HOLD file itself is not a FOCUS file. It is an external file, with a MASTER description, which can be used in FOCUS reporting procedures. Looking at the MASTER description for the HOLD file, in figure 1-7, notice its similarity to the MASTER of the SALES FOCUS file:

1. The HOLD file contains a single segment.
2. The segment contains the original field names, as in the SALES MASTER.
3. The fields for BRAND and MANAGER, in the SALES file, do not appear in the HOLD file because they were not mentioned in the TABLE request.

```
FILE=HOLD              ,SUFFIX=FIX
SEGNAME=HOLD
FIELDNAME   =PRODUCT      ,E01        ,A03       ,A04      ,$
FIELDNAME   =REGION       ,E02        ,A02       ,A04      ,$
FIELDNAME   =UNITS        ,E03        ,I05       ,I04      ,$
FIELDNAME   =UNITPRICE    ,E04        ,D8.2      ,D08      ,$
```

Figure 1-7    MASTER description for a HOLD file.

The original structure of the SALES file, as a multisegment file, is useful only to remind us of the relationship between the product and region data. After the HOLD file is created, this relationship becomes obscured as the HOLD contains a single segment. Nevertheless, almost any report can be created from this HOLD file.

There are very few restrictions when setting up a MASTER description for a FOCUS file. The FILE must be named, and a suffix FOC used to indicate that it is a FOCUS file. The different SEGMENTS within the file must be identified as well as specifying the key fields, the sort order of the key fields (low-to-high or high-to-low), and the relationship its parent segment (if any). Finally, the fields within each segment must be identified along with its alias name and usage format. In any segment, the SEGTYPE specifies the number of key fields and their sorting order. For example, PRODSEG has a SEGTYPE = S1, indicating that the first field PRODUCT is the key field. The segment REGCODE also has SEGTYPE = S1, indicating that the field REGION is the key field. The order of the other fields in each segment is arbitrary for FOCUS files. Before any data is entered into the file, the fields may be positioned in any order. Field names can contain up to 12 characters, as can the alias name. The alias can be used interchangeably with the field name in any FOCUS command.

The FORMAT element in the MASTER tells FOCUS about the data type, and how the data will be formatted on reports. The formats contain the data type — alphanumeric, integer, floating decimal, packed decimal, etc. — and the length of the field. The format may also include editing options, such as floating dollar sign, date formats, etc., used when the values are displayed in a report.

FOCUS has a number of ways to describe relationships between data. For example, the records in one file may be related to the records in another file using the FOCUS cross-reference technique. In the SALES file, assume that the price data and brand data for each product are contained in another FOCUS file, whose MASTER is shown in figure 1-8. In this case, we can remove the fields BRAND

```
FILENAME=BRANDS   ,SUFFIX=FOC,$
SEGNAME=BRANDSEG,SEGTYPE=S1,$
   FIELDNAME=PRODUCT,PROD,A3   ,FIELDTYPE = I , $
   FIELDNAME=UNITPRICE,PRICE,D8.2,$
   FIELDNAME=BRAND        ,BRAND,A4    ,$
   FIELDNAME=DESCRIPTION,DES,A20   ,$
```

**Figure 1-8   Storing product data in another file.**

and PRICE from the SALES file, and obtain them by JOINING the field PRODUCT in SALES with the field PRODUCT in the BRAND file. The JOIN command, which can be used in any program, is

```
JOIN PRODUCT IN SALES TO ALL PRODUCT IN BRAND AS JOIN1
```

In the BRAND file, FOCUS has created an indexed field, with an index table of data values and internally stored locations. Using a JOIN, FOCUS matches the value for the field named PRODUCT in the SALES file to the field named PRODUCT in the BRAND file by using the index for the PRODUCT field in the BRAND file. FOCUS maintains these indexes automatically and invisibly. When a file is cross-referenced, you may obtain access to all segments in the file — not only the single segment which is cross-referenced. Therefore, you have great flexibility in organizing your data into several FOCUS files, and to link them when necessary.

There are other ways to relate segments in different files. For example, any number of files, including HOLD files, can be related to each other using the FOCUS MATCH FILE procedure, if they have one or more fields in common. MATCHING is especially useful when reports require the creation of a subset of records that have been derived from two or more files. The MATCH command seeks to match records according to specified fields which are common to the two files. See example 2 in Chapter 9 for a detailed discussion of the MATCH command.

## FOCUS Reporting Requests — Printing and Summing Data From the Sales File

The most important aspect in FOCUS is the user-friendly reporting language. Reports may be quickly prepared using the standard options available in the TABLE command. The standard techniques include:

1. Summing and sorting records in numerous ways.
2. Formatting standard columnar reports with heading, footing, subtotals, and other formatting options.
3. Computing new fields from existing fields.
4. Screening of records.
5. Performing direct numerical operations such as average, count, min, max.
6. Saving extracted records as sequential or binary format files.

The TABLE command has a very simple structure.

```
TABLE FILE SALES
PRINT (SUM) field1 field2 ...
BY sortfield1 by sortfield2 ...
IF screenfield1 eq value
IF screenfield2 eq value
END
```

Without special formatting, this is what all reporting and data extraction commands look like. Even with formatting of page headings, column headings, subtotals, etc., the form of the TABLE command does not change much. With such a simple technique available for manipulating and displaying data, the FOCUS user can spend more time understanding the relationships between the data, and enhancing the application.

A report request can be made in two ways:

1. Entered with the editor as a named, executable FOCUS procedure (called a FOCEXEC) and named as a file. You invoke the request by executing the FOCEXEC name.
2. Entered directly without an editor. The request is checked line-by-line by the system as you enter it, then executed immediately after you type the last line of the request (END or RUN).

Let's write a report using the second method. This request will show the use of the verb PRINT. The request will print all data values in

Applications Development With FOCUS: An Introduction 23

the TOP (PRODSEG) SEGMENT of the SALES FOCUS file with MASTER shown in figure 1-3.

To begin,

    TYPE: **FOCUS**
    PRESS: **ENTER key**
    RESULT: **FOCUS appears**
    TYPE: **TABLE FILE SALES**
    PRESS: **ENTER key**

To write the necessary request statement, the fields in the top segment are used with the PRINT verb:

    TYPE: **PRINT PRODUCT BRAND PRICE**
    PRESS: **ENTER key**
    TYPE: **BY PRODUCT NOPRINT**
    PRESS: **ENTER key**
    TYPE: **END**
    PRESS: **ENTER key**
    RESULT: **The report statistics message (below) appears:**

**NUMBER OF RECORDS IN TABLE = 50 LINE = 50**
**PAUSE..PLEASE ISSUE CARRIAGE RETURN WHEN READY**

To display the actual report produced:

    PRESS: **ENTER key**
    RESULT: **The report shown in figure 1-9 is displayed.**

Up to 17 report lines are displayed on the terminal at one time. If more lines are present, the bottom righthand corner of the screen contains the word MORE . You display the next page by pressing the PF8 KEY to scroll down (the PF7 KEY to scroll up, PF11 to scroll right, PF10 to scroll left). Notice that field name headings identify each column of the report. Columns are printed in the order specified in the PRINT statement.

After viewing the report, remove it from the screen as follows:

    PRESS: **ENTER key**
    RESULT: **FOCUS appears**

1 PAGE      1

```
PRODUCT   BRAND   UNITPRICE
-------   -----   ---------
  101     1001         2.50
  102     1001         1.25
  103     1001         1.00
  104     1001          .55
  105     1002         3.50
  106     1002          .50
  107     1002          .50
  108     1002         3.00
  201     1005         1.00
  202     1005         1.75
  203     1005         2.00
  204     1005          .50
  205     1005         1.75
  301     1006         1.50
  302     1006         1.20
  303     1006         1.75
  304     1006         1.75
```

**Figure 1-9  Output for TABLE request.**

In the next chapters, we shall describe the reporting techniques by creating small FOCEXECS stored in files instead of entering the commands interactively (as shown above).

Note, the above report could have been created by executing a FOCEXEC containing the following:

```
TABLE FILE SALES
PRINT PRODUCT BRAND PRICE
BY PRODUCT NOPRINT
END
```

The report is sorted by product code. To sort by another field, use the FOCUS BY command:

```
TABLE FILE SALES
PRINT PRICE
BY BRAND BY PRODUCT
END
```

The lines on the report will be sorted first by brand code, then by product code. FOCUS allows sorting on any field in the MASTER, as well as DEFINED fields (see next chapter). The BY fields are called SORT fields, as they indicate the order of sorting. The SORT fields always appear in the first columns of the report. As shown in the report below, duplicate sort values are not repeated. For example, for brand 1001, there are sales of several products. But, the brand 1001 appears only once.

```
BRAND  PRODUCT  PRICE
-----  -------  -----
1001   101       2.50
       102       1.25
       103       1.00
       104        .55
1002   105       3.50
```

We can use the PRINT verb to display the records in each segment of the SALES file. Records from the child segments will not be displayed if the TABLE request does not include a field from those segments. If a field from a child segment is included, then all the records in that segment will also be displayed. In this way, FOCUS keeps the segments "separate" unless you need to use them together. For example,

```
TABLE FILE SALES
PRINT BRAND PRODUCT UNITS
BY REGION
IF BRAND EQ 1001
END
```

The report looks like:

```
REGION  BRAND  PRODUCT  UNITS
------  -----  -------  -----
01      1001   101      5100
        1001   102      3500
        1001   103      4400
02      1001   101      6200
        1001   103      4800
```

```
          1001  105      1100
03        1001  101      4100
 . . .
 . . .
```

We have also demonstrated above how TABLE request may use selection criteria for accepting records to be used in the report. The IF statement will restrict any verb operation such as PRINT or SUM to specific records in the file whose field(s) has specific values. More than one IF statement can be used in a request. Suppose we wish to print the units sold of product 101 in all regions in the months 8601 or 8606. This request is written as follows:

```
TABLE FILE SALES
PRINT PRODUCT UNITS
BY REGION
BY MONTH
IF MONTH EQ 8601 OR 8606
IF PRODUCT EQ 101
END
```

While the verb PRINT displays the requested fields, as they appear in individual records of the file, the verb SUM (or WRITE) adds together the data values stored for numeric fields (then prints the total on a report). The fields to be summed are written as objects of the verb. For example, to sum units of product 101 sold for each region, and display them in numeric order by region code, the request is:

```
TABLE FILE SALES
SUM UNITS
BY REGION
IF PRODUCT EQ 101
END
```

The BY phrase:

1. Follows verb objects.
2. Indicates the criteria by which the quantities are summed.
3. Prints the lines of the report by alphabetic or numeric order depending on the values of the field named in the BY phrase.

This field is also called a SORT field. The figure below shows the report created from the above request:

```
REGION  UNITS
------  -----
01      10500
02      11150
03      22020
04       8500
05       7950
....
....
```

## FOCUS File Structure

Once a MASTER description is created, the FOCUS reporting techniques can make simple the creation of various types of reports. In the next chapter, we shall demonstrate how the techniques for formatting, subtotalling, etc. are used in several applications. Almost all the reporting techniques are short, simple, and repetitive. Furthermore, FOCUS reporting techniques include the capability of creating new, temporary fields in a file with the DEFINE. The DEFINE can be used in simple ways, or can help create more complicated reports. The example in figure 1-10 shows how it is possible to produce MAILING LABELS across a page using the DEFINE command.

There are numerous ways to make a FOCUS file more efficient with respect to reporting and file maintenance. However, casual FOCUS users and programmers are not likely to deal with efficiency considerations, since the the number of records in their FOCUS files will not be large. For those users, the FOCUS files should be structured as simply as possible using only a few segments to show major parent-to-child relationships between the data. On the other hand, the design of large FOCUS files should depend on the type of reports and record retrieval which is required. In general, you should try to have a file structure which is going to allow you to access information in the manner you want, in the most efficient way possible. This subject is treated in advanced courses on FOCUS INTERNALS offered by IBI. The FOCUS manual Chapter 4 Section 6.2.2 discusses some of the considerations. We will present an introduction to the internals of

28  The Database Experts' Guide to FOCUS

```
-PROMPT &HM.I2.HOW MANY LABELS ACROSS DO YOU WISH.
-CMS FI OFFLINE DISK MAILING  LABELS A (LRECL 133 RECFM FB BLKSIZE
133

SET LINES=999999,PAGE=OFF,MSG=ON ,NODATA=' '
OFFLINE


DEFINE FILE MAIL
NAME/A40     = FIRST_NAME || (' ' | LAST_NAME);
ADDRESS/A50 = CITY || (', ' | STATE) || (' ' ] ZIP);
CLMS/I4 WITH NAME = IF  CLMS EQ &HM THEN 1
    ELSE   CLMS + 1;
RWS/I4 WITH NAME = IF CLMS EQ 1 THEN RWS + 1 ELSE    RWS;
BL/A5 WITH NAME   =' ';
END

TABLE FILE MAIL
SUM NAME AS '' OVER
STREET    AS '' OVER ADDRESS AS ' '
OVER BL AS ''
OVER BL AS ''
OVER BL AS ''
OVER BL AS ''
BY RWS AS '' NOPRINT ACROSS CLMS AS '' NOPRINT
END

-LEAVE5
OFFLINE CLOSE
-EXIT
```

Figure 1-10    Program to generate mailing labels.


FOCUS file structures, and some guidelines to follow when designing large FOCUS files.

The speed with which you screen records is determined by the information that appears in the root (top) segment. If FOCUS can determine that a record should be selected based on the information stored in the root segment, then there is no need to read the descendant segments. This will save considerable processing time if there are many records in the descendant segment. Therefore, you should place in the root segment fields on which you know you will perform screening tests. However, it is impossible to design a file so that all the fields you may screen on are located in the root segment. Sometimes you may want to consider using the ALTERNATE FILE VIEW feature for accessing records in a segment that is deep in the segment hierarchy. As described in the FOCUS manual Chapter 4 Section 6.2.2, an alternate file view can be requested at any time, and on any segment in a file (except for a cross-referenced segment).

A major consideration for increasing the speed in which many records can be retrieved for reports is the size of the root segment. You can maximize the number of records read at one time by minimizing the size of the root segment. Notice that this is counter to the above rule which places screening fields in the root segment. If a root segment contains only the key fields, then FOCUS will have faster access to more records. Therefore, a good file design should have as few fields as possible in the root segment — perhaps only key fields and fields used often in screening. One way to isolate key fields is to place related fields in a UNIQUE segment. A unique segment (SEGTYPE = U) contains fields having a one-to-one relationship with its parent. They are described in the FOCUS manual Chapter 4 Section 2.2.3. For example, say the fields in the top segment are to be NAME, ADDRESS, DEPT, HIRE-DATE, etc. As shown below, by placing only NAME in the top segment, and the rest in a unique segment, the size of the top segment is greatly reduced.

```
NAME 300 bytes    | NAME 32 bytes
ADDRESS           | 4 bytes (pointer)
DEPT              | 4 bytes (description)
...               |
...               | UNIQUE SEGMENT
...               | ADDRESS
...               | DEPT
...               | ...
...               | ...
```

Using the UNIQUE segment, the size of the root segment is reduced from about 300 bytes to 40 bytes. This should be done if you don't need to see the employee's address and department every time you access his name. Notice that a cross-reference file may also be used to store data related to the employee.

You should know that FOCUS structures files internally as "pages" of storage. A FOCUS file contains at least one page for each segment. The number of records in a segment which can fit into one page depends on the size in bytes of the fields in the segment. Each page has about 3972 bytes available. Furthermore, each record contains not only the fields, but also "pointers" (4 bytes) and descriptors (4 or 8 bytes). The more records which can be contained in a single page, the more efficient the processing. The more pages the CPU processor needs to access on a request, the longer it takes. This is an important consideration for large files when deciding the number of fields to appear in each segment. Other considerations, which we shall not discuss here, regarding efficient file design include:

1. Indexing fields.
2. Handling missing data.
3. Reducing overhead of storing "pointers" (which are required to identify the record's parent, descendant, and chain to other records).

Chapter

# 2

# Basics of Designing FOCUS Applications

Most of the time spent in using FOCUS is related to

1. Understanding what the user expects from the application.
2. Designing the FOCUS files and the relationships between files.
3. Implementing programs which produce reports or extract data.
4. Deciding how the parts of a program fit together and how the program is executed.

Notice that file maintenance and update is not considered a time-consuming step and is not included in this list. This is because file maintenance procedures are usually designed once for any file. Once it is implemented correctly, the procedure changes very little. Also, many maintenance programs depend on where the input records are coming from — which can be looked at as a problem in data extraction. However, much time can be spent with file maintenance if complicated data manipulation is required or if elaborate data entry procedures using FIDEL screens must be designed.

We will emphasize here the basic concepts related to file design, reporting, and program execution. Item 1, understanding what the user wants, will be treated in a separate section at the beginning of the last chapter. A number of examples or cases will be developed in this chapter, from which sample programs will be taken. Our plan is to discuss how the basic FOCUS tools are applied in common situations. It is important to understand these FOCUS concepts that are used most of the time in developing new applications. Similarly, it is also important to understand the "kinds" of problems or situations which FOCUS handles best. We shall refer to the concepts as FOCUS tools and the problem types as FOCUS applications. Much will be said about the nature of these tools and applications which distinguishes FOCUS from third-generation programming languages. In Chapter 1, we outlined the best ways for you to learn and use FOCUS in your organization. If you are a novice to FOCUS, you should try to simplify your understanding of the basic concepts by studying the situations in which they are used. By knowing how to handle various situations, you will effectively be learning the "building blocks" of the language. We will try to help you by taking every opportunity to categorize the problems solved with FOCUS procedures. However, this book will only be able to present the most common and general problems that are handled by FOCUS procedures. The more subtle and peculiar situations can only be learned through trial and error as you work with particular applications. Also, we will refer you to the FOCUS users manual to learn the detailed aspects of various FOCUS features.

## File Design

### MASTER File Description

A FOCUS file (or database) is simply a collection of variable names with data values (or fields) whose format is described by a MASTER file. You may think of a FOCUS file as a "sequential file of data records with pointers which permit quick retrieval of data." The actual data records are arranged in a special "internal" order in which records are sometimes related to other records by pointers. However, this internal order is unimportant to most FOCUS users, as FOCUS reporting commands make this transparent to the user. The basic way to "look at" or retrieve the data is through the reporting command TABLE. Since the data is stored in internal format, you cannot read the data directly from the editor.

```
FILENAME = CONTRACT         ,SUFFIX = FOC
SEGNAME  = VBIDSEG          ,SEGTYPE=S1,$
  FIELDNAME = VENDNO         ,,A8 ,$

SEGNAME  = VENDSEG , CRFILE = VENDOR , CRKEY = VENDNO,
   PARENT= VBIDSEG , SEGTYPE = KU,$

SEGNAME  = CONTSEG          ,SEGTYPE=S1, PARENT = VBIDSEG,$
  FIELDNAME = CONTRACT,, A6,$
  FIELDNAME = VDOL     ,, D9,$
  FIELDNAME = PODATE   ,, I6YMD,$
  FIELDNAME = SELECT   ,, I1,$
  FIELDNAME = NOBID    ,, I1,$
  FIELDNAME = COMMENT  ,, A40,$
```

Figure 2-1    MASTER file for contract bids.

As shown in figure 2-1, the MASTER description file has a simple layout.

## Example 1: Vendor Contract Bids

A FOCUS file is used to keep track of Vendor bids on contracts to supply printed forms to a company. Several vendors bid on each contract offered throughout the month. Sometimes a contract will be awarded to a vendor without accepting bids from other vendors (i.e., "no-bid" contracts). The purpose of this application is to keep track of the number of contracts bid and awarded throughout the year.

The MASTER file description is a text file which you type in using a system editor, such as XEDIT, or using the FOCUS editor TED. The MASTER describes the fields in the FOCUS file, and the relationships between groups of fields. The basic declaration for each field looks like:

FIELD=CONTRACT,ALIAS=CONT,FORMAT=A6,  $

Field declarations are required for every field in your database. The field name and alias name can be used interchangeably in FOCUS commands. They identify the data items in a file. The alias name is usually a shortened abbreviation for the field name, and is optional.

The FORMAT attribute identifies the field as alphanumeric, integer, floating point decimal, double precision, or packed. There is also a special format for dates. Numeric fields may be summed or used in arithmetic calculations, while alphanumeric fields cannot. The format also specifies the length of the field. For example, a format of A8 for VENDNO describes an alphanumeric field that is 8 characters long. A format of I6 means an integer field with up to 6 digits. A format of D10.2 means a double precision decimal number of up to 10 digits. Two of these are decimal places. The FOCUS manual Chapter 4 section 7 describes the acceptable values for the FORMAT attribute. The FORMAT is important since it describes how the field's values will be displayed or printed on a report. In addition to the type and length of the field, the FORMAT also may include an editing operation (up to 5) that is performed on the data before it is displayed. For example, the field PODATE is a 6-digit integer field. Additionally, the YMD edit option causes the 6 digits to display in the form YY/MM/DD. For example, the value 861125 prints as 86/11/25.

Fields with date formats are stored in a fashion to allow you to perform calculations on them, as well as give you some flexibility in displaying them. The date format allows entered dates to be stored as a single numeric value, representing the elapsed number of days from a base date — DEC 31, 1900. However, you never see the dates displayed as elapsed time from the base date.

FORMATS may be changed in the MASTER file, even after data has been stored in the FOCUS file. The length part of I,F,D, and P formats may be changed. The decimal part of the length may be changed for F or D, but not P. The length of A format data may not be changed without using the REBUILD feature. The edit options may be changed at any time.

As discussed in Chapter 1, each segment of a FOCUS file should contain data which is related to each other. If there is a "one-to-many" relationship between the data, then you may represent this as a "parent-child" relationship between segments. The FOCUS file, as described by the MASTER, is a "single-path" file with two "real" segments (named VBIDSEG and CONTSEG) and one "virtual" segment (named VENDSEG). Segment VBIDSEG contains only one field, VENDNO, and is called the "root" segment because it is the top segment. It is also called the "parent" segment to its "child" segment CONTSEG. This notation is used merely to show that there are many child records for each parent. During the year a vendor will bid on more than one contract. For example, the single value of data for

## Basics of Designing FOCUS Applications 35

```
FILENAME = CONTRACT           ,SUFFIX = FOC
SEGNAME  = VBIDSEG            ,SEGTYPE=S2,$
  FIELDNAME = VENDNO             ,,A8   ,$
  FIELDNAME = CONTRACT,, A6,$
  FIELDNAME = VBID      ,, D9,$
  FIELDNAME = PODATE    ,, I6YMD,$
  FIELDNAME = VSEL      ,, I1,$
  FIELDNAME = NOBID     ,, I1,$
  FIELDNAME = COMMENT   ,, A40,$
```

**Figure 2-2  Single segment version of Contract Bid file.**

VENDNO 11111111 will have several contracts associated with it, as shown in the list below.

vendor 11111111
contracts bid: 100001, 100004, 100005, 100011, etc.

Note, there is one instance of the parent segment (VENDNO) and four instances of the child segment that all relate to vendor 11111111.

In general, most applications will have "natural" parent-child relationships between data fields which should be built into the layout of the MASTER file. As you have seen, FOCUS files with two or more segments could have also been designed with one segment only. For small files this is especially true since there is little savings in space or CPU when using parent-child relationships. However, you do give up showing the natural parent-child relationship between the data to be stored. The MASTER file descriptions for the single-segment version of our database is shown in figure 2-2.

FOCUS is able to achieve rapid access of data records from large files because of its internal use of "pointers" which identify the child records for each parent record. So, for fairly large files (over 10,000 records), it pays to use multiple segments to describe the parent-child relationship between the data. The other important thing to remember about segments is that a segment usually has one or more "key fields" which identifies each unique record in the segment. The values of the key field or key fields in a record will not be duplicated in other records of that segment. The number of key fields is denoted by the segment type in the MASTER description. The type S1 in the VBID-SEG segment means there is only one key field VENDNO in the segment, while type S1 in the CONTSEG segment means CONTRACT is the key field. In the MASTER with a single segment, the type S2

```
FILENAME=CAR,SUFFIX=FOC
SEGNAME=ORIGIN,SEGTYPE=S1
  FIELDNAME=COUNTRY,COUNTRY,A10,FIELDTYPE=I,$
SEGNAME=COMP,SEGTYPE=S1,PARENT=ORIGIN
  FIELDNAME=CAR,CARS,A16,$
SEGNAME=CARREC,SEGTYPE=S1,PARENT=COMP
  FIELDNAME=MODEL,MODEL,A24,$
SEGNAME=BODY,SEGTYPE=S1,PARENT=CARREC
  FIELDNAME=BODYTYPE,TYPE,A12,$
  FIELDNAME=SEATS,SEAT,I3,$
  FIELDNAME=DEALER_COST,DCOST,D7,$
  FIELDNAME=RETAIL_COST,RCOST,D7,$
  FIELDNAME=SALES,UNITS,I6,$
SEGNAME=SPECS,SEGTYPE=U,PARENT=BODY
  FIELDNAME=LENGTH,LEN,D5,$
  FIELDNAME=WIDTH,WIDTH,D5,$
  FIELDNAME=HEIGHT,HEIGHT,D5,$
  FIELDNAME=WEIGHT,WEIGHT,D6,$
  FIELDNAME=WHEELBASE,BASE,D6.1,$
```

Figure 2-3  Example of single path file.

denotes that the two fields VENDNO and CONTRACT are the key fields in the file.

The segment type also describes the logical order of the records in a segment. It indicates how FOCUS organizes the records internally using the values of the key fields. Segtype S1 means that FOCUS stores the records based on the values of the one key field sorted low-to-high. Segtype SH1 organizes the records based on the values of the key field sorted high-to-low. This segtype has no effect on how you will write a TABLE command to extract records from the file — since you specify the fields on which the records in the report will be sorted. However, it is usually faster to retrieve records if the segtype sort order coincides with the order in which data is retrieved.

In designing the segments and fields which you will include in the MASTER for a FOCUS file, it is important to start off with a simple structure and then add segments as they are needed (for other reports or applications). "Single path" files, are the simplest for reporting purposes since all the fields can be retrieved with a simple TABLE command. An example of a single path file with more than two segments is shown in figure 2-3.

Notice that every segment except the top has a parent segment.

```
FILENAME=MULTIPAT,SUFFIX=FOC,$
SEGNAME=EMPSEG,SEGTYPE=S1,$
   FIELDNAME=EMPKEY,,A5,$
   FIELDNAME=EMPNAM,,A20,$
   FIELDNAME=ADDRL1,,A40,$
   FIELDNAME=ADDRL2,,A40,$
SEGNAME=JOBHIST,PARENT=EMPSEG,SEGTYPE=S1,$
   FIELDNAME=BEGDATE,,I6YMD,$
   FIELDNAME=JOBCODE,,A3,$
   FIELDNAME=JOBTITLE,,A40,$
SEGNAME=EDUC,PARENT=EMPSEG,SEGTYPE=S2,$
   FIELDNAME=SCHCODE,,A5,$
   FIELDNAME=DEGREE,,A4,$
```

Figure 2-4   A multiple path FOCUS file.

"Multipath" files refer to those in which a segment can have more than one child segment. Perhaps, there is additional data needed whose records describe a "one-to-many" relationship with the records in the top segment (or in some other segment). It is convenient to think of each parent-child path as consisting of fields from one type of record. The fields from each path can be retrieved together with an ordinary TABLE command. While the data fields in each path are related to each other, the fields in one path may not be related to the fields in the other path. Figure 2-4 shows a multi-path FOCUS file. Also refer to the FOCUS 5.0 manual, p.4–17, for examples of multipath files.

## Cross-referencing Between FOCUS Files

One of the most powerful features of FOCUS is the ability to combine the records from segments in different FOCUS files. Using cross-referencing, the fields of a segment from a "cross-referenced" file can be considered part of a segment from another FOCUS file. The segments in one FOCUS file become "virtual" segments in another FOCUS file. When the cross-referenced segment is described in the MASTER description of the main file, this is known as "static" cross-referencing — since the linkage to the cross-reference file is a permanent one. This technique is simply another way to relate different records. There are many applications where you will need to combine information from more than one FOCUS file. For example, in person-

```
FILENAME=PERSON  ,SUFFIX=FOC
 SEGNAME=EMP , SEGTYPE=S1
  FIELDNAME=EMP_ID        ,ALIAS=EID    ,FORMAT=A9      ,$
  FIELDNAME=LAST_NAME     ,ALIAS=LN     ,FORMAT=A15     ,$
  FIELDNAME=FIRST_NAME    ,ALIAS=FN     ,FORMAT=A10     ,$
  FIELDNAME=HIRE_DATE     ,ALIAS=HDT    ,FORMAT=I6YMD   ,$
 SEGNAME=DEPTINFO,SEGTYPE=S1,PARENT=EMPINFO
  FIELDNAME=DEPARTMENT    ,ALIAS=DPT    ,FORMAT=A10     ,$
  FIELDNAME=DATEDPT       ,ALIAS=DDPT   ,FORMAT=I6YMD   ,$
  FIELDNAME=DEPT_SAL      ,ALIAS=DSAL   ,FORMAT=D12.2M  ,$
  FIELDNAME=DEPT_LEVEL    ,ALIAS=DLEV   ,FORMAT=A3      ,$
 SEGNAME=CRSEG,CRFILE=FILE,CRKEY=EMP_ID ,PARENT=EMP ,SEGTYPE=KU ,$
```

Figure 2-5    MASTER file with cross-referencing.

nel applications, the main FOCUS file might contain salary, level, title, and department information for each department in which an employee has worked. A cross-reference file might contain the employee's address, phone number, Social Security Number, etc. Figure 2-5 shows the PERSON FOCUS file MASTER description — including cross-reference segments.

In the Vendor Bid example, we added a cross-reference segment which has detailed information on each vendor. Figure 2-6 shows the MASTER with this segment.

The segtype of the new segment is KU, for "keyed unique." This is a "virtual segment" because the records in this segment are not in the CONTRACT FOCUS file, but in another FOCUS file VENDOR. The records in VENDOR are related to the CONTRACT file through the "cross-reference key" VENDNO (vendor number). For each vendor number, there is a unique (one) record in the VENDOR file related to it. For retrieval purposes, the fields on the VENDSEG segment are considered part of the VBIDSEG segment in CONTRACT. As mentioned, the VENDOR file is itself a FOCUS file, and has a MASTER description file (shown in figure 2-7). Notice that the MASTER contains a field VENDNO which has a FIELDTYPE=I. This "indexed" field is necessary for the file to be cross-referenced from the CONTRACT file.

The other segtypes which indicate "virtual" segments are:

SEGTYPE KM — keyed multiple; indicates that the cross-reference file has several records of data associated with a single data ele-

```
FILENAME  = CONTRACT            ,SUFFIX = FOC
SEGNAME   = VBIDSEG             ,SEGTYPE=S1,$
 FIELDNAME = VENDNO              ,,A8 ,$

SEGNAME   = VENDSEG , CRFILE = VENDOR , CRKEY = VENDNO,
   PARENT= VBIDSEG , SEGTYPE = KU,$

SEGNAME   = CONTSEG             ,SEGTYPE=S1, PARENT = VBIDSEG,$
 FIELDNAME = CONTRACT,,  A6,$
 FIELDNAME = VDOL      ,, D9,$
 FIELDNAME = PODATE    ,, I6YMD,$
 FIELDNAME = SELECT    ,, I1,$
 FIELDNAME = NOBID     ,, I1,$
 FIELDNAME = COMMENT   ,, A40,$
```

**Figure 2-6   Contract file with cross-referencing.**

ment in the main file. The syntax of the KM segment in the MASTER is:

```
SEGNAME=PROJSEG,SEGTYPE=KM,
 PARENT=EMPINFO,CRFILE=PROJFILE,
CRKEY=EMP_ID,$
```

SEGTYPE KL (or KLU) — keyed through linkage; when you cross-reference a segment from another file, you can also retrieve any segment which is a child or parent segment of the cross-referenced segment. KL indicates there are multiple occurrences of child segment, while KLU indicates there is singly occurring child segment or the parent of the cross-referenced segment. The syntax of the KL or KLU segment is:

```
SEGNAME=name,SEGTYPE=KL,
 PARENT=parent ,CRFILE=filename,
CRSEGNAME=segname,$
```

where:

**name:** is the name of the cross-reference segment in the main file.
**segtype:** is either KL or KLU.
**parent:** is the segment's parent in the cross-reference file.
**filename:** is the name of the cross-refernce file.

```
FILENAME = VENDOR , SUF = FOC
 SEGNAME = VENDSEG, SEGTYPE = S1,$
   FIELD = VENDNO    ,          ,A08, FIELDTYPE = I,$
   FIELD = VENDNAME  ,VNAME     ,A20,$
   FIELD = VENDCAT   ,VCAT      ,A1 ,$
   FIELD = ADDR1     ,ADDR1     ,A20,$
   FIELD = CITY      ,CITY      ,A10,$
   FIELD = STATE     ,STATE     ,A2 ,$
   FIELD = CONTACT   ,CONTACT   ,A20,$
```

Figure 2-7    Vendor — cross-reference file.


**segname:** is the name of the cross-reference segment in the cross-reference file (not necessary if it is the same as SEGNAME).

Note, that the names of the fields in KU, KM, KL, or KLU segments are usually the same as the fields in the cross-reference file. However, they may be renamed by specifying the fields in the segment.

The FOCUS manual Chapter 4 section 3.1 and 3.2 contains a discussion of these cross-reference segment types. As an example of using KM segments, consider the PERSON FOCUS file. Suppose there existed a PROJECT FOCUS file that keeps track of the projects employees had done or were doing. The MASTER description of the PROJECT file is shown in figure 2-8.

The top segment of the file contains the projects which have been done by employees in the company. The segment is keyed by the field PROJNO, or project number. The field EMPNO, which identifies the employee assigned to the project, is the same ID number as the employee ID in the PERSON file.

If we want to see a list of the projects worked on by employees in the PERSON file, we can create a cross-reference to the PROJECT file, based on the field EMP_ID. Since there are potentially many project records in the PROJECT file for each employee id, this should be a multiple cross-reference. The MASTER description of the PERSON file with a multiple cross-reference to the PROJECT file is shown in figure 2-9. This can be compared with the KU segment EMPCRSEG in the PERSON file, which is a keyed unique segment. There is only one record in the EMPFILE cross-reference file for each employee id in the PERSON file.

Cross-referencing is an important way to connect FOCUS files. This connection can be built into the MASTER description when the main

```
FILENAME=PROJECT,SUFFIX=FOC
SEGNAME=PROJSEG, SEGTYPE=S1
  FIELDNAME=PROJNO      ,ALIAS=PROJ    ,FORMAT=A9           ,$
  FIELDNAME=REQUESTOR   ,ALIAS=REQ     ,FORMAT=A10          ,$
  FIELDNAME=DESCRIPT    ,ALIAS=DES     ,FORMAT=A20          ,$
  FIELDNAME=DATEREQ     ,ALIAS=DATE1   ,FORMAT=I6YMD        ,$
  FIELDNAME=DATEEND     ,ALIAS=DATE2   ,FORMAT=I6YMD        ,$
  FIELDNAME=EMP_ID      ,ALIAS=EID     ,FORMAT=A9, FIELDTYPE = I, $
```

**Figure 2-8   File used as a KM segment in Person file.**

file is designed. This allows the segments in many files to be accessed together for reporting purposes. Note that cross-referenceing can also be accomplished using the technique called JOINS, which is nearly identical to the STATIC cross-referencing method. JOINS will be discussed in the next section.

When designing a KU segment, the field name or alias of the cross-reference key must be the same as the name of the indexed field in the cross-referenced file. Their formats also must be the same. (For D or P format, the fields need not be the same width, only the same type.) The KU segment should be included in the MASTER when the FOCUS file is designed and before data records are loaded into the file. Even if the cross-referenced file has only a MASTER description, but the FOCUS file has not yet been created, you can refer to it in the MASTER description of the host file. The KU segment, if initially omitted, can be added at any time using the REBUILD- REORG option (see FOCUS manual Chapter 12 section 7).

Cross-referencing is important to the design of FOCUS files because it is also a convenient way to access information which is common to many records of a FOCUS file. Figure 2-10 shows the PERSON MASTER containing several KU segments. Having a KU segment for department information saves you the trouble of entering and revising department information for every record in the PERSON file. Instead, you can maintain a list of departments and department information in a separate file, named DPTFILE.

### Unique Segments

Another important type of segment are unique segments, an example of which is shown in figure 2-11.

```
FILENAME=PERSON  ,SUFFIX=FOC
SEGNAME=EMPINFO, SEGTYPE=S1
  FIELDNAME=EMP_ID        ,ALIAS=EID   ,FORMAT=A9      ,$
  FIELDNAME=LAST_NAME     ,ALIAS=LN    ,FORMAT=A15     ,$
  FIELDNAME=FIRST_NAME    ,ALIAS=FN    ,FORMAT=A10     ,$
  FIELDNAME=HIRE_DATE     ,ALIAS=HDT   ,FORMAT=I6YMD   ,$
SEGNAME=DEPTINFO,SEGTYPE=S1,PARENT=EMPINFO
  FIELDNAME=DEPARTMENT    ,ALIAS=DPT   ,FORMAT=A10     ,$
  FIELDNAME=DATEDPT       ,ALIAS=DDPT  ,FORMAT=I6YMD   ,$
  FIELDNAME=DEPT_SAL      ,ALIAS=DSAL  ,FORMAT=D12.2M  ,$
  FIELDNAME=DEPT_LEVEL    ,ALIAS=DLEV  ,FORMAT=A3      ,$
SEGNAME=EMPCRSEG, CRFILE=EMPFILE, CRKEY=EMP_ID ,PARENT=EMPINFO ,
  SEGTYPE=KU ,$
SEGNAME=PROJSEG, CRFILE=PROJECT, CRKEY=EMP_ID ,PARENT=EMPINFO ,
  SEGTYPE=KM ,$
```

Figure 2-9   Person file — with KM segment.

In the personnel application, assume the file needs to contain information on the graduate school attended by its employees. For a large number of employee records, this might require considerably more space in the file. Also, the size of the top segment would increase by several fields if these fields were added to it. For large files, the size of the root segment should be made as small as possible in order to improve the efficiency (and speed) of retrieving records. The unique segment is a way to separate the fields in the graduate school segment from the root segment. Unique segments reduce the size of its parent segment, since FOCUS reserves space for the additional fields only if the parent contains a unique record. If the additional fields are instead placed in its parent segment, then FOCUS must allocate space in every parent record. When placed in a unique segment, these fields are treated logically as if they were in its parent segment. (There can only be one unique segment record for each parent record.) Although unique segments are treated in reports as being in their parent segment, they are maintained differently as will be shown in the chapter on file maintenance.

Note some of the fields in any segment can always be separated out into a unique segment. However, this should be done only for large files — for speed considerations or to reduce the size of the file. In the example, if no data values were ever entered into the graduate school unique segment for some employees, then no storage space in the file would be used for those employees. For this reason, a unique segment

```
FILENAME=PERSON  ,SUFFIX=FOC
SEGNAME=EMPINFO, SEGTYPE=S1
  FIELDNAME=EMP_ID        ,ALIAS=EID       ,FORMAT=A9       ,$
  FIELDNAME=LAST_NAME     ,ALIAS=LN        ,FORMAT=A15      ,$
  FIELDNAME=FIRST_NAME    ,ALIAS=FN        ,FORMAT=A10      ,$
  FIELDNAME=HIRE_DATE     ,ALIAS=HDT       ,FORMAT=I6YMD    ,$
SEGNAME=DEPTINFO,SEGTYPE=S1,PARENT=EMPINFO
  FIELDNAME=DEPT_CODE     ,ALIAS=DPT       ,FORMAT=A10      ,$
  FIELDNAME=DATEDPT       ,ALIAS=DDPT      ,FORMAT=I6YMD    ,$
  FIELDNAME=DEPT_SAL      ,ALIAS=DSAL      ,FORMAT=D12.2M   ,$
  FIELDNAME=DEPT_LEVEL    ,ALIAS=DLEV      ,FORMAT=A3       ,$
  FIELDNAME=DEPT_TITLE    ,ALIAS=DTIT      ,FORMAT=A10      ,$
SEGNAME=EMPCRSEG,CRFILE=EMPFILE,CRKEY=EMP_ID ,PARENT=EMPINFO ,
SEGTYPE=KU ,$
SEGNAME=DPTCRSEG,CRFILE=DPTFILE,CRKEY=DPT    ,PARENT=DEPTINFO,
SEGTYPE=KU ,$
======================================================================

FILENAME=EMPFILE   ,SUFFIX=FOC
SEGNAME=EMPCRSEG, SEGTYPE=S1
  FIELDNAME=EMP_ID        ,ALIAS=EID       ,FORMAT=A9       ,FIELDTYPE =
I, $
  FIELDNAME=LAST_NAME     ,ALIAS=LN        ,FORMAT=A15      ,$
  FIELDNAME=FIRST_NAME    ,ALIAS=FN        ,FORMAT=A10      ,$
  FIELDNAME=ADDRESS       ,ALIAS=ADDRESS,FORMAT=A20         ,$
  FIELDNAME=CITY          ,ALIAS=CITY      ,FORMAT=A10      ,$
  FIELDNAME=STATE         ,ALIAS=STATE     ,FORMAT=A2       ,$
  FIELDNAME=PHONEHOME     ,ALIAS=PHONE     ,FORMAT=A3       ,$
======================================================================

FILENAME=DPTFILE   ,SUFFIX=FOC
SEGNAME=DPTCRSEG, SEGTYPE=S1
  FIELDNAME=DEPT_CODE     ,ALIAS=DPT       ,FORMAT=A10      ,FIELDTYPE =
I, $
  FIELDNAME=DEPT_NAME     ,ALIAS=DNAME     ,FORMAT=A20      ,$
  FIELDNAME=DEPT_MGR      ,ALIAS=MGR       ,FORMAT=A20      ,$
  FIELDNAME=BUDGET_CODE   ,ALIAS=BUD       ,FORMAT=A4       ,$
  FIELDNAME=SECRETARY     ,ALIAS=SECS      ,FORMAT=A20      ,$
  FIELDNAME=LOCATION      ,ALIAS=LOC       ,FORMAT=I2       ,$
```

Figure 2-10   Person file and cross-reference files.

requires considerably less space than a regular segment if no data has been entered into the unique segment for many parent records. A FOCUS file may contain any number of unique segments.

```
FILENAME=PERSON  ,SUFFIX=FOC
SEGNAME=EMPINFO, SEGTYPE=S1
  FIELDNAME=EMP_ID        ,ALIAS=EID    ,FORMAT=A9      ,$
  FIELDNAME=LAST_NAME     ,ALIAS=LN     ,FORMAT=A15     ,$
  FIELDNAME=FIRST_NAME    ,ALIAS=FN     ,FORMAT=A10     ,$
  FIELDNAME=HIRE_DATE     ,ALIAS=HDT    ,FORMAT=I6YMD   ,$
SEGNAME=DEPTINFO,SEGTYPE=S1,PARENT=EMPINFO
  FIELDNAME=DEPARTMENT    ,ALIAS=DPT    ,FORMAT=A10     ,$
  FIELDNAME=DATEDPT       ,ALIAS=DDPT   ,FORMAT=I6YMD   ,$
  FIELDNAME=DEPT_SAL      ,ALIAS=DSAL   ,FORMAT=D12.2M  ,$
  FIELDNAME=DEPT_LEVEL    ,ALIAS=DLEV   ,FORMAT=A3      ,$
SEGNAME=GRAD,SEGTYPE=U,PARENT=EMPINFO
  FIELDNAME=GRADSCHOOL    ,ALIAS=GS     ,FORMAT=A10     ,$
  FIELDNAME=DATE_ENTERED,ALIAS=DE       ,FORMAT=I6YMD   ,$
  FIELDNAME=MAJOR         ,ALIAS=MJ     ,FORMAT=A10     ,$
  FIELDNAME=DEPT_TITLE    ,ALIAS=DTIT   ,FORMAT=A10     ,$
SEGNAME=EMPCRSEG,CRFILE=EMPFILE,CRKEY=EMP_ID ,PARENT=EMPINFO ,SEG-
TYPE=KU ,$
SEGNAME=DPTCRSEG,CRFILE=DPTFILE,CRKEY=DPT    ,PARENT=DEPTINFO,SEG-
TYPE=KU ,$
```

Figure 2-11  Person file with unique segment.

## External Files: Sequential and Tape Files

FOCUS has the capability to easily create reports and extract data from various kinds of sequential disk and tape files using the same commands and procedures which work with FOCUS files. We'll first give an overview of working with disk files on the VM operating system. (You should refer to Appendix 1 for a discussion of the differences in operating systems). We'll also discuss the basics in handling tapes. As you will see, in order to use FOCUS with these files, they must have a MASTER description which describes the fields on each record.

Most external files which you'll work with are called HOLD files. They are created by FOCUS programs which need to extract data records into files which are easier to work with than FOCUS files. You will see HOLD files are used in various steps of a program to simplify the format of the data (i.e., the sort order of the records, the number of fields, the field formats) and to simplify calculations which require the records to be sorted or aggregated.

You don't have to create a MASTER description for a HOLD file since it is created by FOCUS when the file is produced. Other sequen-

## Basics of Designing FOCUS Applications 45

```
FILE=EXTFILE          ,SUFFIX=FIX
SEGNAME=EXTFILE
FIELDNAME    =PRPOOL       ,E01      ,A8       ,A08    ,$
FIELDNAME    =PROGRAM      ,E02      ,A2       ,A02    ,$
FIELDNAME    =POOL         ,E03      ,I6       ,A06    ,$
FIELDNAME    =TYPE         ,E04      ,A3       ,A03    ,$
FIELDNAME    =COUPON       ,E05      ,D6.3     ,A06    ,$
FIELDNAME    =ISSUE        ,E06      ,A6YMD    ,A06    ,$
FIELDNAME    =MATURITY     ,E07      ,A6YMD    ,A06    ,$
FIELDNAME    =ORIGINAL     ,E08      ,D13.2    ,A13    ,$
FIELDNAME    =WAM          ,E09      ,I4       ,A04    ,$
FIELDNAME    =WAC          ,E10      ,F7.3     ,A07    ,$
FIELDNAME    =ZIP_CODE     ,E11      ,I5       ,A05    ,$
FIELDNAME    =PTKEY        ,E12      ,A5       ,A05    ,$
FIELDNAME    =YEAR         ,E13      ,I2       ,A02    ,$
FIELDNAME    =JANUARY      ,E14      ,D10.8    ,A10    ,$
FIELDNAME    =FEBRUARY     ,E15      ,D10.8    ,A10    ,$
FIELDNAME    =MARCH        ,E16      ,D10.8    ,A10    ,$
FIELDNAME    =APRIL        ,E17      ,D10.8    ,A10    ,$
FIELDNAME    =MAY          ,E18      ,D10.8    ,A10    ,$
FIELDNAME    =JUNE         ,E19      ,D10.8    ,A10    ,$
FIELDNAME    =JULY         ,E20      ,D10.8    ,A10    ,$
FIELDNAME    =AUGUST       ,E21      ,D10.8    ,A10    ,$
FIELDNAME    =SEPTEMBER    ,E22      ,D10.8    ,A10    ,$
FIELDNAME    =OCTOBER      ,E23      ,D10.8    ,A10    ,$
FIELDNAME    =NOVEMBER     ,E24      ,D10.8    ,A10    ,$
FIELDNAME    =DECEMBER     ,E25      ,D10.8    ,A10    ,$
```

Figure 2-12   MASTER file for an external sequential file.


tial files and tape files require a MASTER description, which resembles the MASTER for FOCUS files.

In figure 2-12, the MASTER description is shown for a sequential file of records containing alphanumeric text.

The records have been entered manually using the editor. But they could have come from a program (FOCUS,FORTRAN, etc.) which can generate alphanumeric (text) records. Because of the time required to write a program which creates external files, or to input the data from the editor, many new FOCUS applications do not use external files. However, they have been found to be useful in situations where:

1. Reporting is needed for large files which have been generated from other Fortran or Cobol programs.

2. Cobol-generated tape files require reporting or quick analysis of its data.
3. Data files need to be edited or the data manipulated (for input to other programs or procedures).
4. Error reports, log reports, or audit trails are required using sequential files generated from FOCUS file maintenance procedures.

You should refer to example 7 in the last chapter, which describes how to setup a MASTER description for an audit trail external file.

Most external files (other than HOLD files) will contain ordinary sequential records in alpha (text) format. However, when external files are generated from COBOL programs (or other programs), the records may contain "internal" formats such as packed or integer. An external file is given a MASTER description file whose name must correspond to that given in a filedef or allocation. In VM/CMS, an example of a FILEDEF is:

```
FILEDEF WORKCEN DISK WORKCEN DATA A (RECFM FB LRECL 100
```

This tells FOCUS the location of the physical records. The filedef can be issued in a FOCEXEC program or in an exec. (Refer to Appendix A for the external file descriptions used in TSO, VAX, DOS.)

The MASTER file contains, for each field, the field name, alias name, usage format, and actual format. The field name and alias name are interchangeable in FOCUS programs. In HOLD files, the alias has a special notation for the fields in the file. The first field's alias is E01, the second field is E02, etc. These aliases are created automatically when the HOLD file is created in a program. As you will see, the alias name is particularly useful in HOLD files where two fields have the same field name — in these cases, the alias should be used to distinguish one field from another in various requests. (For example, in a TABLE request, when summing and counting the values of a field, the resulting values are given the same field name in a HOLD file). Also, note that the field name and alias can be changed in the MASTER at any time. This is not the case for field names in FOCUS files, where under certain conditions they cannot be changed. (See FOCUS 5.0 manual, Chapter 4 section 7).

The usage and actual format are both needed in external files, while in FOCUS files only a "usage" format is assigned each field. The "actual format" of fields in a FOCUS file is transparent to the user and irrelevant in most cases). In external files, the actual format describes the actual physical description of the values in each record. For example, if the file contains regular ebcdic (or text) characters, then the actual format will be alpha (A) (or zoned decimal — which is rare). If the file were generated from a program, then other formats are possible.

Usage format is more important, since it describes how the field will be used in FOCUS programs. This format may be changed in the MASTER at any time according to the usage required by various programs. For example, if you need a program simply to list the values of certain fields or to sort the records, you may assign alphanumeric usage formats to every field. Since there are no numerical calculations required, the fields do not need numerical usage formats. This will save a lot of time if you need to create a MASTER file from scratch.

The numerical usage formats for fields in external files are:

Integer (eg.I5,)
Floating Pt. (eg.F8.2)
Packed (eg.P8.2)
Double Precision (eg.D8.2)

They are used in programs in exactly the same way as the formats of fields in FOCUS files.

## Avoiding Overflow Conditions

A major problem you might run into with numerical usage formats is if the width of the format is too small to accommodate the number of digits in a value. For example, if the value of field with format P7.3 in some record is

1455.222,

You will get an overflow condition (i.e. '********' on the report) when you try to print the value (or use it in a DEFINE, COMPUTE, or TABLE ). This is because P7.3 has room for only three digits before the decimal (the decimal takes up one space). In this case, change the format to at least P8.3. You will get an overflow condition if you sum the values of a field and the result is too large for the format of the field.

Another problem with numerical usage formats is that they are mistakenly used to determine the position of the decimal point for values which appear in the file as a string of digits. For example, a field whose value is 99876 in a record, cannot be assigned a format of D6.3 (expecting to get the value 99.876). The value of the number is 99,987 — which gives an overflow condition when printed with a D6.3 usage format.

Another potential problem may be due to round off when summing values or performing calculations. An important thing to note is that fields with packed (P) formats will truncate the insignificant decimals on each record, while fields with double precision format (D) will maintain the precision of the number. Therefore, if a high degree of accuracy in the resulting computation is required, the usage format should be D. Note that the format of a field may be redefined using a DEFINE request.

## COBOL Files

An important application with external files is handling files generated from COBOL programs. The data records in the output file are written in formats described by the record layout in the COBOL program. COBOL uses the PICTURE clause to indicate the actual format of each field. The records in the file are stored in binary format, and cannot be considered alphanumeric text data.

First, you need to know what the record layout is (by looking at the COBOL program). You will also need to know a little about the types of COBOL record formats.

In example 6 included in the last chapter, we shall describe two important aspects of creating a MASTER description for a COBOL file:

1. Translating COBOL internal formats to FOCUS actual and usage formats using the COBOL format translation table shown in the FOCUS manual Chapter 3 section 2.3.
2. How to handle more than one type of record in a COBOL file — using the RECTYPE field described in the FOCUS manual Chapter 3 section 6.

Chapter

# 3

# Working in the FOCUS Environment: The Basics of Report Writing

## FOCUS in the VM/CMS Operating System

One of the big advantages in using FOCUS is that programs can be written and tested very quickly. Many times code can be copied from other existing programs after making minor adjustments to it. All FOCUS code is interpreted as it is executed — rather than compiled. Therefore, the modified code can be tested out in seconds in the FOCUS environment without having to go through a compilation procedure.

In order to take advantage of these features, one should be adept in using the other tools of his machine's operating system such as the file management system. These features are especially important on the mainframe since there is more to manage such as printers, readers, libraries, disk space, CPU, etc.

We will discuss the basics of writing and testing programs in the VM/ CMS operating system (found in many IBM mainframe environments). In Appendix 1, we will point out the major differences between CMS and other operating systems such as MVS, VAX, and PC-DOS. Obviously, we cannot cover the details in using the operating system environment. But, you will understand the details after some use in different situations.

Once a FOCUS file has been created and loaded with data (see Chapter 5 on file maintenance), you will be able to extract the data in the form of reports, or extract files. We will present several cases in this chapter to demonstrate the basics of report writing and writing FOCEXEC programs. But first, we will give an overview of the CMS operating system and FOCUS environment.

To get into the FOCUS environment, simply enter (from the operating system environment) the command.

```
FOCUS
```

Once in the FOCUS environment, the system will respond with the FOCUS banner and prompt:

```
FOCUS VERSION 5.2
>>
```

In mainframes, this command has been set up by system operations. It starts the FOCUS environment so that you may execute FOCUS programs and various status inquiry routines. It also automatically does things like erase files which FOCUS must reuse for work space, sorting, etc. You can leave FOCUS and get back into the CMS operating system by typing

```
FIN
```

## Status Inquiry and Default Settings

FOCUS allows you to query for information during your FOCUS session. By entering ?, you will see a list of information which is available. The FOCUS manual Chapter 12 section 10 describes how each query command is used. Figure 3-1 shows the default settings in a typical FOCUS environment.

You usually do the following in the FOCUS environment:

1. Execute programs (called FOCEXECS) which you've already coded to handle some application.

```
FOCUS   5.0.2V   <CP/A>   CREATED 06/14/87   7883.02
>
>
>
>
? set

PARAMETER SETTINGS

LINES/PRINT       57
LINES/PAGE        66
WIDTH            130
MODE             CMS
TEMP DISK          A
BINS              60
PRINT         ONLINE
PAUSE             ON
MESSAGE           ON
PAGE-NUM          ON
ALL.             OFF
NODATA             .
SESSION MONITOR   ON
FOCSTACK SIZE     8K
INDEX TYPE       NEW
SHADOW PAGES     OFF
SCREEN            ON
```

**Figure 3-1**  Default settings for FOCUS parameters.

2. Perform ad hoc reporting or data extraction, issuing commands interactively one by one.

There are other things you can do from FOCUS such as rebuild/reorganize FOCUS files, perform graphical analysis, etc. However, these are done infrequently. We will not be discussing how to execute FOCUS commands one by one in the interactive environment. As you experiment with this, you will discover how to quickly perform ad hoc requests — getting results in seconds.

## Working in the VM/CMS Operating System

Before we demonstrate how to work in the FOCUS environment, we will discuss the basic issues you should know related to the VM/CMS operating system. The operating systems TSO, PC-DOS, AND VAX-VMS are discussed in Appendix 1.

VM/CMS, like the other operating systems, allows you to manage your files (i.e., programs, FOCUS files, exec files, etc.) so that applications can be designed, tested, and maintained in an organized manner. You can think of it as an elaborate "bookkeeping" system. It allows you to link to other disks to see where various FOCUS files reside. All files are named by :

FILENAME FILETYPE FILEMODE

For example, FOCUS files are usually named with a filetype of FOCUS, while FOCUS programs are usually named with a filetype of FOCEXEC. MASTER description files have a filetype of MASTER. Examples of file names are:

VENDBID FOCUS A
VENDOR FOCUS C
VENRPT1 FOCEXEC A
VENRPT2 FOCEXEC A
VENDOR MASTER

For an application, you should be consistent in assigning file names to files so that they can be easily organized as having a common prefix and are related to the same application. In CMS, the filemode indicates in which virtual disk the file resides. Unless you are linked to other IDs, the filemode will be 'A' indicating that your file is on the A disk. (This disk has a logical unit number of 191.)

At times, you will need to run programs or use Focus files which are on another ID. In CMS, you must link to the ID and then determine the filemode of the files. The command

QUERY DISK (or Q DISK)

can be issued to see the disks you are linked to. It is also useful for seeing the amount of space (blocks, % full, etc.) available on your A-disk (and on other linked disks). Do not regularly run FOCUS programs when your A disk is above 95% full, since FOCUS requires some space for sorting and work areas.

## Working in the FOCUS Environment: The Basics of Report Writing 53

If you have two FOCEXECS by the same name on two disks, say the A and C disks, you can execute (in FOCUS) the program on the C disk by including the name of the file in single quotes;

```
EX 'VENDREP FOCEXEC C'
```

CMS has powerful commands for assisting you in building and testing programs. In particular, the commands for COPY, RENAME, etc. are often used to copy "sections" of code from one program to another (saving considerable time in writing new programs when applications use similar code). Also, the system editor (XEDIT in most CMS installations) is invaluable for developing programs and maintaining them. (I recommend using XEDIT instead of the FOCUS editor TED for most applications; XEDIT has a few features which are not in TED — such as merging lines, setting zones for replace commands, etc.)

The following CMS commands are considered the basic tools for organizing the day to day work of the programmer:

- FLIST (or LISTFILE): for listing all or selected files from disk(s). The "wild card" feature is used to list all files with a given file name, filetype, etc. eg.

```
FLIST * FOCEXEC A
FLIST VEND* LISTING A
FLIST *RPT FOCEXEC B
```

  The files can be sorted by date, size, etc. They can also be copied, erased, and renamed, using commands on the FLIST screen.
- BROWSE: for looking through a file, especially reports, to examine its content and format. File lines extending beyond the width of the screen can be browsed easily using PF keys for scrolling.
- COPY/RENAME: for copying/renaming files on your disk. Copy also can be used to copy files from another linked disk.
- COMPARE: for comparing the contents of two files; used to determine if two programs, data files, etc. are the same.
- ERASE: for deleting files from a disk
- VMBLIST: for restoring files from the system backup in order to recover a prior copy of the file.

- SPOOL CONSOLE: for turning on the console spool which will keep a record of messages sent to the screen in the execution of a program or procedure (useful for debugging or to obtain a log of a FOCUS session). See also the FOCUS SESSION MONITOR in the FOCUS manual Chapter 12 section 5.

Another important CMS tool is EXEC language (and the recently developed REXX language), which allows the programmer executing to write procedures which combine executing FOCUS programs with executing other steps. This is particularly useful in situations where the output of a program is required as an input to another program. Procedures which have more than one step and which run in "batch" mode use EXEC language to control the execution of various steps. As a designer of FOCUS systems, you do not have to be an expert in the use of EXECS. But you should know enough about them so that you can copy simple execs written by others and adapt them to your application. Example 7 in the last chapter describes an exec procedure which invokes a FOCEXEC, and manipulates files.

## The Basics of Report Requests — A Sample Application

We will now demonstrate the basics of working with the FOCUS language and especially writing programs (called FOCEXECS). Before you create reports using FOCUS, you must have:

1. A FOCUS file with data.
2. A corresponding MASTER file description.

In the following reporting examples, we will deal with the CONTRACT FOCUS file, which contains information on the contracts bid by a number of vendors. Typically, a contract will be bid on by more than one vendor, and the one coming in with the lowest bid will get the contract. The purpose of the system is to keep track of the contracts awarded throughout the year to each vendor. Monthly and quarterly reports are required which summarize the percent of contracts and contract dollars awarded to each vendor. The MASTER description for the CONTRACT file is shown in figure 3-2.

In order to write reports, you should be familiar with the names and formats of fields in the MASTER file description. The data in the

```
FILENAME = CONTRACT          ,SUFFIX = FOC
   SEGNAME  = VBIDSEG         ,SEGTYPE=S1,$
      FIELDNAME = VENDNO       ,,A8 ,$

   SEGNAME  = VENDSEG , CRFILE = VENDOR , CRKEY = VENDNO,
      PARENT= VBIDSEG , SEGTYPE = KU,$

   SEGNAME  = CONTSEG          ,SEGTYPE=S1, PARENT = VBIDSEG,$
      FIELDNAME = CONTRACT,, A6,$
      FIELDNAME = VDOL     ,, D9,$
      FIELDNAME = PODATE   ,, I6YMD,$
      FIELDNAME = SELECT   ,, I1,$
      FIELDNAME = NOBID    ,, I1,$
      FIELDNAME = COMMENT  ,, A40,$
```

Figure 3-2   Contract MASTER file.

CONTRACT file is stored in two segments — with the vendor numbers in the root segment, and the information on each contract bid in the child segment. (Note: The field NOBID indicates whether the contract was bid by only one vendor.)

The fastest way to test some of the basics of FOCUS is with a simple FOCEXEC (i.e., program) which has been written and ready to execute. Since there is only a small number of commands and syntax in the FOCUS language, it usually is easy to understand what the code does. In this sense, FOCUS is "self-documenting." It is easy to add code to the FOCEXEC to test various other features while keeping the functionality of the program intact.

When coding a FOCEXEC, the code on each line may be placed anywhere between columns 1 and 80. Comment lines should always start with -* in columns 1 and 2. The following FOCEXEC reports the dollar amount of contracts awarded each vendor from January '86 to June '86.

```
DEFINE FILE CONTRACT
YRMN/A4 = EDIT(PODATE,'9999$$');
END

TABLE FILE CONTRACT
SUM VDOL
BY YRMN AS 'MONTH'
BY VENDNO
```

```
IF YRMN FROM 8601 TO 8612
IF SELECT EQ 1
END
```

This program can be entered in a CMS file BIDREP1 FOCEXEC A. The FOCUS file CONTRACT is named CONTRACT FOCUS A and its MASTER file is named CONTRACT MASTER A. The report is generated by getting into FOCUS and executing the FOCEXEC:

```
EX BIDREP1
```

The resulting report will be displayed, unless there is an error in syntax (in which case, execution will stop and an error message displayed). If an error occurs and you are still in the TABLE request environment, you can enter the command 'QUIT' to get out of the request. Note that the alias name of a field can be used instead of the fieldname in the TABLE request. The request contains two screening conditions:

1. For indicating the range of months.
2. For including those vendors selected for each contract.

With respect to terminology:

- VDOL is the verb object;
- VENDNO and YRMN are sort fields.

FOCUS is able to compute the code and execute it quickly. If there are no errors in the logic and syntax of the code, the report will appear on the screen.
You can hit 'enter' after you see the message

```
PAUSE... PLEASE ISSUE CARRIAGE RETURN WHEN READY
```

If the FOCEXEC contains additional TABLE requests, the results will be displayed on the screen with pauses in between reports. Figure 3-3 displays the report created by BIDREP1.
FOCUS also displays the number of lines generated:

```
NUMBER OF RECORDS IN TABLE = 100 LINES = 100
```

```
1 PAGE      1

MONTH   VENDNO      DOLLARS
-----   ------      -------
8602    11111111       1500.
        22222222          0.
        33333333          0.
        44444444          0.
        55555555          0.
        66666666          0.
        77777777          0.
        88888888          0.
        99999999          0.
8603    11111111          0.
        22222222       3800.
        33333333       1600.
        44444444       2600.
        55555555       2600.
        77777777          0.
        88888888          0.
8604    11111111          0.
        22222222          0.
        33333333          0.
        44444444       3600.
        55555555       3600.
        66666666       1800.
        77777777          0.
        88888888          0.
        99999999          0.
8605    11111111          0.
        22222222       7200.
        33333333          0.
        44444444          0.
        77777777       1800.
        88888888       1800.
8606    22222222          0.
        33333333       2600.
        44444444       1600.
        55555555       3600.
8607    55555555       3500.
        66666666       2500.
        88888888       2500.
        99999999       2500.
8608    88888888       2500.
        99999999          0.
8609    66666666       8000.
        99999999          0.
```

Figure 3-3   Contract amounts awarded to vendors each month.

You may also determine the number of lines in the report after viewing the report by issuing the command:

? STAT

The number of lines retrieved is shown as are a number of other statistics which may or may not be relevant to the last request issued.

## The Offline and Online Commands

It is an easy matter to print the report, instead of showing it on the screen. In the FOCEXEC, add a line , OFFLINE, which indicates that the printed report is to be directed to an OFFLINE device instead of displayed on the console screen. If the FOCEXEC contains other TABLE requests, each report will begin on separate pages of the OFFLINE printer.

After viewing the report on the screen (note: see FOCUS manual Chapter 2 section 13 for using the 'HOT SCREEN' capability ), the FOCEXEC is also finished and control returns to FOCUS (and the prompt FOCUS appears). You may see the report again on the screen by entering

RETYPE

or send the report to the printer by entering

OFFLINE
RETYPE

The command ONLINE is the opposite of OFFLINE — it sends reports to the console screen. They can be issued at any time to send the report to the screen for viewing. Note that you can issue the SET commands (SET PRINT ONLINE or SET PRINT OFFLINE) as separate commands which have the same effect as ONLINE and OFFLINE.

The format of the report in figure 3-4 shows the default format of standard FOCUS reports. We will show how other features of the TABLE command permits you to enhance this format to create almost any type of report.

1. VENDOR REPORT - LIST OF AMOUNTS AWARDED


2. MONTH    VENDOR              DOLLARS
   -----    --------            --------
3. 8602     EMPIRE               1500.
            QUAKER                  0.
            SANDER                  0.
            COLORA               1700.

4. *TOTAL MONTH 8602
5.                               3200

   8603     EMPIRE                  0.
            QUAKER               3800.
            SANDER               1600.
            COLORA               2600.
            PENNCO               2600.
            LEBANON                 0.
            ALEXANDER               0.

*TOTAL MONTH 8603
                                10600

   8604     EMPIRE                  0.
            QUAKER                  0.
            SANDER                  0.
            COLORA               3600.
            PENNCO               3600.
            CENTURY              1800.

*TOTAL MONTH 8604
                                 9000

6. TOTAL                        22800
------------------------------------------

1. PAGE HEADING
2. COLUMN HEADINGS
3. ALL REQUESTED VALUES ARE RETRIEVED FOR EACH MONTH
4. A SUMMARY LINE APPEARS FOR THE MONTH
5. SUBTOTALS ARE PRINTED FOR EACH NUMERIC FIELD
6. A GRAND TOTAL IS PRODUCED AT THE END OF REPORT

Figure 3-4    Basic features in a FOCUS report.

## Using the BY Phrase

In the TABLE request, the sort verbs determine how the output records are sorted. Note that a report request can sort on any field in the MASTER (and even on DEFINED fields). The default sort order is low-to-high (for alphabetic as well as numeric fields) but the order can be made high-to-low using the word HIGHEST before the sort verb; eg., BY HIGHEST YRMN.

The sort verbs play an important part in the TABLE request for other things besides sorting. They control:

1. How numerical fields are summed; i.e., the level of aggregation
2. Where subtotals, subheading, subfootings, and recap calculations are performed
3. Formatting features such as page-break, fold-line, skip-line, etc.
4. How direct operations on verb objects (such as MIN., MAX., AVE.) are performed

Using the SUM verb, FOCUS can sum the numerical values in each record. It sums the values of the object fields by aggregating the values over each value of the sort field(s). The first BY FIELD is sometimes called the 'major' sort field, and it determines the first field over whose values the aggregation is made. Similarly, the second BY field determines the next field over which the aggregation is made. The last BY field is the last field over which the aggregation is done. Note that the summed values appearing on the report are generated for each value of the last (innermost) BY field. You can use up to 32 BY fields in a TABLE request. The total number of fields in the request is 95.

The following report request sums contract dollars awarded by vendor category, by month (the field VENDCAT appears in the VENDOR cross-reference file):

```
DEFINE FILE CONTRACT
YRMON/A4=EDIT (PODATE, '9999');
DOLLARS/F6=IF SELECT EQ 1 THEN VDOL ELSE 0;
END

TABLE FILE CONTRACT
SUM DOLLARS
BY VENDCAT
```

```
1 PAGE       1


VENDCAT  MONTH    DOLLARS
-------  ------   -------
A        8602      3200.
         8603     11000.
         8604      7800.
         8605     12300.
         8606     25800.
B        8602      7800.
         8603     12600.
         8604     17800.
         8605     17300.
         8606     34700.
C        8602     21800.
         8603     15600.
         8604     26400.
         8605     37500.
         8606     38710.
```

Figure 3-5   Contract dollars awarded in each vendor category.


```
BY YRMON AS 'MONTH'
IF YRMON FROM 8601 TO 8606
END
```

Notice that the field DOLLARS is a DEFINED field — so that it is equal to the contract dollars (VDOL) if the contract was awarded to a vendor, otherwise it is zero. The report is shown in figure 3-5 and gives the dollar amount of contracts awarded in each of the three vendor categories. In this report, the dollars amounts are aggregated according to vendor category. By changing the BY fields, the aggregation can be performed in a different way. One can sum the total dollars awarded (to all vendors) in each month by using the TABLE request:

```
TABLE FILE CONTRACT
SUM DOLLARS
BY YRMON AS 'MONTH'
IF YRMON FROM 8601 TO 8612
END
```

FOCUS recognizes the verb WRITE (or ADD) as a synonym for SUM — it has the same effect in a TABLE request. You may want to use it if one of the verb objects is an alphanumeric field.

For example,

```
TABLE FILE CONTRACT
WRITE VENDNAME DOLLARS
BY YRMON AS 'MONTH'
BY VENDNO
IF YRMON FROM 8601 TO 8612
END
```

The verb object VENDNAME is an alphanumeric field (from the VENDOR file). FOCUS recognizes alpha fields as verb objects, and does not try to 'sum' them as it does the numeric fields. FOCUS assumes there is only one value of the alphanumeric field for each BY field, and displays the last value of the alpha field found for each BY field value. The above TABLE request produces the report in figure 3-6.

We mentioned that a TABLE request can sort on any field, in any order. The sort fields appear to the left of the printed page, and the lines of the report are sequenced by these fields. An example of this is

```
TABLE FILE CONTRACT
SUM DOLLARS
BY VENDCAT
BY HIGHEST DOLLARS BY VENDNO
IF YRMON EQ 8601
END
```

As shown in figure 3-7, the dollars are shown in each category sorted in order of the highest dollars awarded for each vendor in the month of 8601.

## Counting Records

FOCUS only has three verbs which are used in a TABLE request. Besides SUM (or WRITE), there is PRINT and COUNT. The verb COUNT is used in reports when you need to count the number of records in the file. When used with BY fields, the number of records

```
1 PAGE        1

MONTH   VENDNO      VENDNAME              DOLLARS
-----   ------      --------              -------
8602    11111111    EMPIRE                1500.
        22222222    QUAKER                   0.
        33333333    SANDER                   0.
        44444444    COLORA                   0.
        55555555    PENNCO                   0.
        66666666    CENTURY                  0.
        77777777    LEBANON                  0.
        88888888    ALEXANDER                0.
        99999999    SCOTTPRESS               0.
8603    11111111    EMPIRE                   0.
        22222222    QUAKER                3800.
        33333333    SANDER                1600.
        44444444    COLORA                2600.
        55555555    PENNCO                2600.
        77777777    LEBANON                  0.
        88888888    ALEXANDER                0.
8604    11111111    EMPIRE                   0.
        22222222    QUAKER                   0.
        33333333    SANDER                   0.
        44444444    COLORA                3600.
        55555555    PENNCO                3600.
        66666666    CENTURY               1800.
        77777777    LEBANON                  0.
        88888888    ALEXANDER                0.
        99999999    SCOTTPRESS               0.
8605    11111111    EMPIRE                   0.
        22222222    QUAKER                7200.
        33333333    SANDER                   0.
        44444444    COLORA                   0.
        77777777    LEBANON               1800.
        88888888    ALEXANDER             1800.
8606    22222222    QUAKER                   0.
        33333333    SANDER                2600.
        44444444    COLORA                1600.
        55555555    PENNCO                3600.
8607    55555555    PENNCO                3500.
        66666666    CENTURY               2500.
        88888888    ALEXANDER             2500.
        99999999    SCOTTPRESS            2500.
8608    88888888    ALEXANDER             2500.
        99999999    SCOTTPRESS               0.
8609    66666666    CENTURY               8000.
        99999999    SCOTTPRESS               0.
```

Figure 3-6  Report showing vendor name and contract dollars.

1 PAGE     1

```
VENDCAT   DOLLARS   VENDNO     DOLLARS
-------   -------   ------     -------
A          4500.    66666666    4500.
           3800.    22222222    3800.
           3700.    22222222    3700.
           3600.    44444444    3600.
           3500.    22222222    3500.
                    66666666    3500.
           2600.    44444444    2600.
           2500.    66666666    2500.
           1800.    66666666    1800.
           1600.    44444444    1600.
           1500.    11111111    1500.
              0.    11111111       0.
                    22222222       0.
                    44444444       0.
                    66666666       0.
B          3600.    55555555    3600.
           3500.    55555555    3500.
           2600.    33333333    2600.
                    55555555    2600.
           1600.    33333333    1600.
              0.    33333333       0.
                    55555555       0.
C          2500.    88888888    2500.
                    99999999    2500.
           1800.    77777777    1800.
                    88888888    1800.
              0.    77777777       0.
                    88888888       0.
                    99999999       0.
```

**Figure 3-7   Contract dollars sorted high to low.**

for each value of the inner BY field is counted. You may also think of COUNT as counting the number of records in a segment of the file. In the CONTRACT file, we can count the number of contracts awarded each vendor in each month (instead of summing the dollars awarded). The TABLE request looks like:

```
TABLE FILE CONTRACT
COUNT VDOL
BY YRMON AS 'MONTH'
```

```
1 PAGE      1


                VDOL
MONTH  VENDNO   COUNT
-----  ------   -----
8602   11111111   1
8603   22222222   1
       33333333   1
       44444444   1
       55555555   1
8604   44444444   1
       55555555   1
       66666666   1
8605   22222222   2
       77777777   1
       88888888   1
8606   33333333   1
       44444444   1
       55555555   1
8607   55555555   1
       66666666   1
       88888888   1
       99999999   1
8608   88888888   1
8609   66666666   2
```

**Figure 3-8   Counting contracts awarded.**

```
BY VENDNO
IF SELECT EQ 1
IF YRMON FROM 8601 TO 8612
END
```

The report is shown in figure 3-8.
The screening condition

```
IF SELECT EQ 1
```

has been added to assure us that only those contracts awarded to a vendor are counted. If the screening condition is removed, then every contract bid on by a vendor will be counted.

```
FILENAME=DPTSTORE   ,SUFFIX=FOC,$
SEGNAME=REGSEG,SEGTYPE=S1,$
   FIELDNAME=REGION  ,REGN,A2  ,$
   FIELDNAME=REGMGR  ,RMGR  ,A10  ,$
SEGNAME=STORSEG,PARENT=REGSEG,SEGTYPE=S1  ,$
   FIELDNAME=STORE,STORE,A3,$
   FIELDNAME=DOLLARS,DOLLARS,I5,$
   FIELDNAME=UNITS,UNITS  ,I5,$
```

Figure 3-9   DPTSTORE MASTER file.


COUNT is useful in counting the total number of records in a file or the number of records for each different value of some field. For example, to count the number of vendors in each vendor category, use the TABLE request:

```
TABLE FILE CONTRACT
COUNT VENDNO
BY VENDCAT
END
```

The report would show:

```
         COUNT
VENDCAT  VENDNO
-------  ------
A           11
B            6
C            5
```

Note that the title on the report has the word COUNT. This can be renamed to any column title using AS 'title.'

When counting the number of records for each value of a sort field, it is sometimes important to know how the file is structured in order to be sure you get exactly what you expect. (If there are redundant values of fields in more than one record, you may not get the result you want.) In the next example, there is a parent-child relationship between the fields REGION and STORE. Assume the segments are described as in figure 3-9.

A count of the number of stores in each region is requested as:

```
FILENAME=DPTSTORE ,SUFFIX=FOC,$
SEGNAME=REGSEG,SEGTYPE=S1,$
    FIELDNAME=REGION ,REGN,A2 ,$
    FIELDNAME=REGMGR ,RMGR ,A10 ,$
SEGNAME=DATESEG,PARENT=REGSEG,SEGTYPE=S2 ,$
    FIELDNAME=DATE,MONTH,A4YM,$
    FIELDNAME=STORE,STORE,A3,$
    FIELDNAME=DOLLARS,DOLLARS,I5,$
    FIELDNAME=UNITS,UNITS ,I5,$
```

Figure 3-10   DPTSTORE MASTER — with different child segment.

```
TABLE FILE DPTSTORE
COUNT STORE
BY REGION
END
```

The report appears as:

```
       COUNT
REGION STORE
------ -----
EAST     55
NORTH    12
SOUTH    27
WEST     40
```

If the FOCUS file has a different structure, permitting multiple occurrences of STORES for each REGION, the result may be interpreted so clearly. This is because FOCUS counts the number of records for each value of the sort field. The MASTER in figure 3-10 gives an example where there may be multiple occurrences of the values of STORES for each REGION.

The verb COUNT is often used with SUM to count the number of records retrieved in obtaining the sum. For example, we can count the number of contracts awarded each vendor together with the total dollars awarded using the TABLE request:

```
TABLE FILE CONTRACT
SUM VDOL AND COUNT
BY YRMN AS 'MONTH'
```

1 PAGE     1

```
DATE   VENDOR     DOLLARS   COUNT
----   -------    -------   -----
8701   11111111    1,500      1
       22222222    8,900      3
       55555555   11,300      3
       66666666   15,500      4
8702   11111111   10,300      3
       33333333   12,900      3
       44444444   25,300      5
8703   11111111    5,550      1
       22222222   10,400      2
       33333333   11,850      2
       77777777   13,900      3
       88888888   21,650      3
8704   11111111   22,500      3
       44444444   23,300      3
       55555555   13,200      2
       66666666   14,100      2
       88888888   15,200      4
       99999999   16,300      4
```

Figure 3-11    Using SUM and COUNT together.

```
BY VENDNO
IF YRMN FROM 8601 TO 8612
IF SELECT EQ 1
END
```

or alternatively, using CNT. as a direct operation on VDOL,

```
TABLE FILE CONTRACT
SUM VDOL AND CNT.VDOL
BY YRMN AS 'MONTH'
BY VENDNO
IF YRMN FROM 8601 TO 8612
IF SELECT EQ 1
END
```

The report is shown in figure 3-11.

## The Verb PRINT

The FOCUS verb PRINT displays individual records from a file. (Note: The verb LIST is nearly identical to PRINT). PRINT is used simply to show the values of verb objects in each record of the FOCUS file or external file. As with the verb SUM, output records can be sorted by any fields. The records printed can be formatted into various types of reports. In the CONTRACT example, a report which shows the contract numbers and contract dates bid on by each vendor can be requested as:

```
TABLE FILE CONTRACT
PRINT CONTRACT PODATE
BY VENDNO
END
```

No numerical summing operation is done on the records — the individual records themselves are displayed. For this reason, PRINT is a good way to look at the data in the records of your file. It is important to know the structure of your FOCUS file when using the PRINT command. FOCUS will print the records in the segment which contains the requested field(s). Occurrences of records in children segments will not be shown unless a field from a children segment is requested. For example, in the DPTSTORE file whose structure looks like figure 3-9, there are four regions and each region has a number of department stores (represented by its child records).

The request

```
TABLE FILE DPTSTORE
PRINT REGION
END
```

shows only four records. While the request

```
TABLE FILE DPTSTORE
PRINT REGION STORE
END
```

gives 134 records (the number of child records in the STORE segment).

Be careful when using the PRINT command against large files —
FOCUS will print all the records in a child segment if a field from that
segment is requested. This usually will require a lot of processing
time (and a lot of paper printed) for large files. Note that you can
abort such a request if it was inadvertently made by entering

HX (OR FX).

This may be used to abort almost any TABLE request (or
FOCEXEC) while it is running — without leaving the FOCUS environment.

**Some Limitations of PRINT Verb**

There are times you should not use PRINT in TABLE requests (in
favor of SUM or WRITE) even though you are displaying individual
records in the file. This is because you cannot always use some of the
features of the TABLE command with PRINT. Some of these features
(which will be described in later sections) are:

1. Direct operations on fields such as AVE, SUM, CNT, FST.
2. TABLE requests which use the ACROSS feature to format the report
3. Some requests which use the MATCH command to combine records in more than one file.

**The TABLEF Command**

In large FOCEXECS involving several steps of extracting records and
aggregating records (using HOLD files), the last TABLE step which
formats the report may use the PRINT command if no further summing of records is required. For such FOCEXECS, all the sorting and
computations can usually be performed before the last TABLE request. When working with large files which have already been sorted
or do not require sorting, you may use the TABLEF command instead
of the TABLE command. The TABLEF command is a fast way to
retrieve and report records if no sorting is required. The command is
used to print records without sorting them. However, BY fields may
be included in order to use formatting features such as SKIP-LINE,

UNDER-LINE, SUBFOOT. See the FOCUS manual Chapter 2 section 12.2 for other considerations.

## Multiverb TABLE Requests

The TABLE command allows more than one set of verbs to operate on the object fields in a multiverb request. The object fields can be summed at a summary level and then again at a more detailed level. In the example below, the first SUM verb aggregates the field DOLLARS by vendor category while the second SUM verb aggregates DOLLARS by each vendor. The report appears in figure 3-12.

```
TABLE FILE CONTRACT
SUM DOLLARS
BY VENDCAT
BY YRMON AS 'MONTH'
SUM DOLLARS
BY VENDCAT
BY YRMON
BY VENDNO
IF YRMON FROM 8601 TO 8612
END
```

The report shows the dollars summed for each category followed by the sum for each vendor. Note that the second set of BY fields includes the first set (as this is required by FOCUS). Therefore, the first verb request aggregates the data in more summary form than the second verb request.

Another application of multiverb TABLE requests is when individual records need to be aggregated (summed) and also printed on the same report. For example, a report is to contain the sum of contract dollars and list of contract numbers which were awarded. A multiverb request for this is:

```
TABLE FILE CONTRACT
SUM VDOL
BY VENDNO
BY YRMN AS 'MONTH'
PRINT CONTRACT VDOL
BY VENDNO
```

```
1 PAGE       1

VENDCAT  MONTH  DOLLARS  VENDNO    DOLLARS
-------  -----  -------  ------    -------
A        8602    1500.   11111111   1500.
                         22222222      0.
                         44444444      0.
                         66666666      0.
         8603    6400.   11111111      0.
                         22222222   3800.
                         44444444   2600.
         8604    5400.   11111111      0.
                         22222222      0.
                         44444444   3600.
                         66666666   1800.
         8605    7200.   11111111      0.
                         22222222   7200.
                         44444444      0.
         8606    1600.   22222222      0.
                         44444444   1600.
         8607    2500.   66666666   2500.
         8609    8000.   66666666   8000.
B        8602       0.   33333333      0.
                         55555555      0.
         8603    4200.   33333333   1600.
                         55555555   2600.
         8604    3600.   33333333      0.
                         55555555   3600.
         8605       0.   33333333      0.
         8606    6200.   33333333   2600.
                         55555555   3600.
         8607    3500.   55555555   3500.
C        8602       0.   77777777      0.
                         88888888      0.
                         99999999      0.
         8603       0.   77777777      0.
                         88888888      0.
         8604       0.   77777777      0.
                         88888888      0.
                         99999999      0.
         8605    3600.   77777777   1800.
                         88888888   1800.
         8607    5000.   88888888   2500.
                         99999999   2500.
         8608    2500.   88888888   2500.
                         99999999      0.
         8609       0.   99999999      0.
```

Figure 3-12  Multi-verb report request.

```
1 PAGE      1


VENDOR     MONTH     DOLLARS    CONTRACT   DOLLARS
-------    -----     -------    --------   -------
11111111   8701       1,500     100001      1,500
           8702      10,320     200001      5,300
                                200004      3,700
                                200005      1,300
           8703       5,500     300007      5,500
           8704      22,500     400001      8,000
                                400004      8,000
                                400006      3,100
                                400011      3,400
22222222   8701       8,900     100006      3,500
                                100011      2,500
                                100012      2,900
           8703      10,400     300005      2,300
                                300006      3,700
                                300007      4,400
```

**Figure 3-13   Summing and listing records.**


```
BY YRMN
IF SELECT EQ 1
END
```

As mentioned, the second verb request must include the sort fields in the first verb request. Also, FOCUS requires that the PRINT verb must be the last verb in the TABLE request. The report appears in figure 3-13.

### Screening Conditions

When a TABLE command is requested, every record in the FOCUS file is considered acceptable and is retrieved for printing or summing. If you need to restrict the records retrieved based on conditions on the values of a field(s), FOCUS allows a number of different screening conditions. The 'IF' screening conditions look like:

```
IF fieldname RELATION literal
```

```
1 PAGE      1


VENDNO     MONTH    CONTRACT    DOLLARS
------     -----    --------    -------
11111111   8602     100001      1500.
33333333   8603     100008      1600.
44444444   8606     100019      1600.
66666666   8604     100006      1800.
77777777   8605     100011      1800.
88888888   8605     100016      1800.
```

Figure 3-14    Screening records.

The acceptable relations are shown in the FOCUS manual Chapter 2 section 4.2. TABLE requests can contain a number of screening conditions. They should appear in the TABLE request after the sort verbs (and usually just before END statement). If a request contains more than one screening condition, then a record is included only if all the conditions are satisfied. Also, more than one condition should not refer to the same field. The most frequent screening conditions are based on selecting records in which a field has certain values or a range of values. For example, print the contract and contract dollars awarded each vendor if the contract dollar amount is less than $2,000.

```
TABLE FILE CONTRACT
PRINT CONTRACT VDOL
BY VENDOR
BY YRMON AS 'MONTH'
IF DOLLARS LT 2000
IF SELECT EQ 1
END
```

In figure 3-14, the report shows only those contracts with dollar amounts less than $2,000. Similarly, the condition can depend on the equality between a field and literal value. For example, show the contracts and contract dollars awarded to vendors 111111 and 222222 in the month May 1986.

```
TABLE FILE CONTRACT
PRINT CONTRACT DOLLARS
BY VENDOR
```

```
1 PAGE     1


VENDNO      MONTH   CONTRACT    DOLLARS
------      -----   --------    -------
11111111    8605    100001       1500.
                    100003       2800.
22222222    8605    100001       5500.
                    100003       3400.
```

Figure 3-15   Screening records.


```
BY YRMON AS 'MONTH'
IF VENDOR EQ 111111 OR 222222
IF YRMON EQ 8605
IF SELECT EQ 1
END
```

The report appears in figure 3-15. Notice that the word 'OR' connects both values in the condition.

The IF conditions supply test conditions which must be passed before data is selected for a report. When used with the verb SUM, values are included in the summation only when the record in the file meets the selection criteria.

### Using the DEFINE Instead of IF Conditions

There are many situations where a record will be included if either one condition or some other "if" condition is satisfied. For example, print all contracts if

1. Awarded to class A vendors, OR,
2. The dollar amount is at least $25,000.

This is best handled using a DEFINE, whereby each record is checked if either of the above conditions is satisfied. E.g.

```
DEFINE FILE CONTRACT
FLAG/I1 = IF VENDCAT EQ A OR VDOL GE 25000 THEN 1
ELSE 0;
END
```

```
TABLE FILE CONTRACT
PRINT CONTRACT VENDOR VENDCAT
IF FLAG EQ 1
END
```

## Other Screening Considerations

There is no restriction on the format of the field for a GT,LT screening condition. For example, if the field PRODUCT is an alpha field (eg. 'A4' format), the following conditions are valid:

```
IF PRODUCT GT A101
IF PRODUCT FROM A101 TO B101
```

If a literal contains embedded blanks then it must be enclosed in single quotes ' '.

```
IF VENDNAME EQ 'CRAZY EDDIE'.
```

An important feature of screening conditions is 'wild card' or 'masked' screening — where alphanumeric fields can be tested against literals containing any character in certain positions. The '$' symbol denotes the position in the literal of the masked character, as shown below,

```
IF PRODUCT EQ X$$$
```

This means a record passes the screen if the value of PRODUCT contains 'X' in the first position and any characters in the other positions. The second, third, and fourth characters are 'masked' by the "$." Its presence means to skip the test on that character. Notice that the condition

```
IF PRODUCT IS '$$$$'
```

is equivalent to no test at all since any character passes the test in each of the four positions. (This condition is useful in some applications where a screening value supplied by the user may be $$$$ to indicate that any code is acceptable.)

1

```
MONTH   VENDNO    DOLLARS
-----   ------    -------
8602    77777777   27500.
        99999999   35000.
8603    33333333   27100.
        55555555   45000.
        88888888   33600.
8604    11111111   25200.
        22222222   30400.
        44444444   35000.
        66666666   31800.
8605    11111111   43200.
        22222222   27800.
        77777777   34100.
```

**Figure 3-16   Screening based on report totals.**


Another kind of screening does not screen out individual records, but instead eliminates output lines (or records) from the report whose total for a field (after accumulating it for sort values) fails to pass a test condition. The syntax for a screen on a total for a field is:

```
IF TOTAL fieldname relation literal
```

The fieldname must be one of the fields which is summed or counted in the verb request. For example,

```
TABLE FILE CONTRACT
SUM DOLLARS
BY YRMON AS 'MONTH'
BY VENDOR
IF TOTAL DOLLARS GT 25000
END
```

If the total dollars awarded to a vendor in a month exceeds 25,000, then it is displayed. The request displays on the report (figure 3-16) only lines containing dollars exceeding 25,000.

Chapter

# 4

# Techniques for Customizing Reports

This chapter continues with the basics of report writing. Usually, before the final report or extracted file can be obtained, it is necessary to add additional fields temporarily to the file so that the data can be used to show different results. This is done using the DEFINE command. The defined fields behave as the other fields in the file. They allow almost any kind of expression to be performed on the values in each record of the file. There are six basic ways of creating new values in each record:

1. Arithmetic Expressions
2. Date Expressions
3. Alphanumeric Expressions
4. Logical Expressions
5. Compound Expressions — using IF statements
6. Functions

With a little imagination, there is almost nothing that the programmer cannot do with DEFINES. We shall also describe how a similar technique, COMPUTE, is used to create new fields which hold the results of a calculation in a TABLE request.

## Define and Compute Statements

The basics of the TABLE request have already been covered allowing you to create simple reports from FOCUS files or external files. The major difference between these simple requests and more sophisticated reporting procedures are the steps sometimes needed to extract the data into HOLD files (where a fewer number of records is faster to work with), and to define additional fields whose values depend on the values of other fields. We will next discuss the use of the DEFINE and COMPUTE for creating new fields. Note that FOCUS has another important command, RECAP, for computation which we will discuss in the next section on report formatting. The last chapter will present applications of using those features in the examples. The CONTRACT file will be used in the following examples. See the MASTERs in figures 2-6 and 2-7.

The DEFINE and COMPUTE can be used with FOCUS files or external files. The DEFINE statement has a simple structure:

```
DEFINE FILE filename

field1/format=expression ;
field2/format=expression ;
END
```

Figure 4-1 shows how a defined field is represented on each record of a FOCUS file. For the CONTRACT file, a new field BUDGET is defined as follows:

```
DEFINE FILE CONTRACT
BUDGET/F6 = IF VENDCAT EQ 'A' THEN 1.5 * VDOL ELSE
2.0 * VDOL;
END
```

Notice that the field receives a value on every record in the file.

Programs use DEFINES to create new fields from the values of other fields. These new fields, once defined, have a value for every record in the file. They behave like any other field in the MASTER; they can be used in TABLE commands as verb objects, sort fields, etc. (Note: A database field can also be defined to change its format or values).

Techniques for Customizing Reports 81

| VENDCAT | VENDNO | BID | BUDGET |
|---------|----------|------|--------|
| A | 11111111 | 1500 | 2250 |
| A | 11111111 | 1700 | 2550 |
| A | 11111111 | 1800 | 2700 |
| A | 11111111 | 1700 | 2550 |
| A | 11111111 | 1500 | 2250 |
| A | 11111111 | 1600 | 2400 |
| A | 22222222 | 2500 | 3750 |
| A | 22222222 | 1700 | 2550 |
| A | 22222222 | 4600 | 6900 |
| B | 33333333 | 2500 | 5000 |
| B | 33333333 | 1700 | 3400 |
| B | 33333333 | 2800 | 5600 |
| B | 33333333 | 2700 | 5400 |
| B | 33333333 | 3500 | 7000 |
| B | 33333333 | 2600 | 5200 |
| B | 33333333 | 1600 | 3200 |
| B | 33333333 | 2600 | 5200 |
| B | 33333333 | 5600 | 11200 |
| A | 44444444 | 2500 | 3750 |
| A | 44444444 | 2700 | 4050 |
| A | 44444444 | 4800 | 7200 |
| A | 44444444 | 1700 | 2550 |
| A | 44444444 | 3500 | 5250 |
| B | 55555555 | 2500 | 5000 |
| B | 55555555 | 2700 | 5400 |
| B | 55555555 | 4800 | 9600 |
| B | 55555555 | 3500 | 7000 |
| B | 55555555 | 3600 | 7200 |
| B | 55555555 | 2600 | 5200 |
| B | 55555555 | 1600 | 3200 |
| B | 55555555 | 3600 | 7200 |

Figure 4-1    Representing defined fields in each record.

DEFINES can contain definitions for a large number of fields (note: LIMITATIONS on FOCUS commands can be obtained by referring to the index at the end of the FOCUS 5.0 manual). They can be placed anywhere in a FOCEXEC, but are usually placed just before the TABLE command. Once a field is defined it remains defined throughout the entire FOCUS session. It can be used repeatedly in a single FOCEXEC and by other FOCEXECS which are executed in the same FOCUS session. However, all the DEFINED fields are cleared when another DEFINE is issued on the same file. You can issue the

| VENDCAT | VENDNO   | BID  | RECEIVE | DIFF | INDEX |
|---------|----------|------|---------|------|-------|
| A       | 11111111 | 1500 | 2050    | 550  | .367  |
| A       | 11111111 | 3000 | 4000    | 1000 | .333  |
| A       | 11111111 | 5500 | 5100    | -400 | 0     |
| A       | 22222222 | 5100 | 6000    | 900  | .176  |
| A       | 22222222 | 6500 | 6400    | -100 | 0     |
| B       | 33333333 | 5200 | 10000   | 4800 | .941  |
| B       | 33333333 | 3000 | 3500    | 500  | .167  |
| B       | 44444444 | 2000 | 3000    | 1000 | .500  |
| B       | 44444444 | 8500 | 10000   | 1500 | .176  |
| B       | 44444444 | 9000 | 10000   | 1000 | .111  |

Figure 4-2  Representing defined fields in each record.

?DEFINE command at any time to check which fields have been previously defined.

The same DEFINE (especially large DEFINES) may often be used in more than one FOCEXEC to define the same fields used in different reports. FOCUS allows you to store this code in a file and then include it in other FOCEXECS. This feature is done through the INCLUDE command — a dialogue manager feature.

You can think of a field in a DEFINE as another field located in each record of the file. Its values are calculated from the values of other fields on a record by record basis — before any sorting or summing of records occurs. In the record shown in figure 4-2, two new fields DIFF and INDEX has values which are calculated from the dollars bid and the actual contract amount (fields VDOL and VRCV). DIFF is the difference between the original bid for the contract and actual amount spent on the contract. (Assume that another field VRCV has been added to the CONTRACT file.) INDEX is the fraction by which the actual contract amount exceeds the original bid.

The two fields are created in the following DEFINE

```
DEFINE FILE CONTRACT
DIFF/P8.3= VRCV-VDOL;
INDEX/P6.2= IF DIFF GT 0 THEN DIFF/VBID ELSE 0;
END
```

The values are calculated on a record-by-record basis and the values are used in a TABLE request. FOCUS allows almost any kind of calculation to be done on numerical fields using the arithmetic operations and the arithmetic functions described in the FOCUS 5.0

manual. Alphanumeric fields and date fields (see Chapter 2) can also be manipulated in a number of ways using various functions and routines.

FOCUS allows conditional (IF...THEN...ELSE) logic in DEFINE expressions. For example:

```
DEFINE FILE CONTRACT
LABEL/A7 = IF VDOL GT 20000 THEN 'CLASS1' ELSE
           IF VDOL GT 10000 THEN 'CLASS2' ELSE
           IF VDOL GT 5000 THEN 'CLASS 3' ELSE
           'CLASS4';
END
```

The DEFINE normally uses very few incremental CPU resources when the TABLE request is invoked. For large multisegment files, unnecessary DEFINES may result in extra CPU. If you can use a simple screening condition instead of a defined field, then do so — since it is more efficient. Also, you should avoid defining fields for child segments if the TABLE request refers only to fields in the parent segment.

The DEFINE offers a very flexible way to manipulate the data to obtain new fields which can be used in various steps of a report program. There are little restrictions on the fields which can be used in a DEFINE statement. A defined field can also have the same value of a constant number or alpha string on every record. With FOCUS files, the fields should not be on different paths leading from a parent segment to a child segment since the data values are not logically related to the same record. Since DEFINES operate on every record of a file, you may not always want to use it on large files — if you can first aggregate the records into a fewer number of records. Using HOLD files and COMPUTES in TABLE request is usually a good way to perform the calculation on a fewer number of records.

The expression for each defined field may extend to more than one line — with a semicolon at the end of the statement. Like other FOCUS code, each line cannot go beyond column 80.

## Rounding Error

You should be aware that there is rounding in calculations for defined fields having packed format. For example, P10.2 format will result in defined values having precision to only two decimal places. Therefore, summing many precise values in a TABLE request could result in considerable 'rounding error' in the final result. On the other hand, fields defined with double precision format will have no rounding of values. The format D10.2 results in values stored precisely, but the result of the TABLE request will be displayed with only two decimal places. In short, you can get different results in the summed values if you change the format of a field from double precision to packed.

## Other DEFINE Techniques

There are three other features of DEFINES which are used often in report requests. They apply primarily to alphanumeric ('A') fields — allowing their values to be assigned from the values of other alphanumeric fields:

1. Masking out characters from values, using the EDIT command.
2. Concatenating characters from the values of more than one field.
3. Assigning values to a field using the DECODE command.

For example, in the CONTRACT file, assume a report is needed which sums the contract dollars each month by the type of service performed — identified in the contract number by the first two characters.

  100051 — the type of service is 10 — printing forms
  200041 — the type of service is 20 — graphic art
  500045 — the type of service is 50 — advertising

A new field TYPE is defined as follows:

```
DEFINE FILE CONTRACT
TYPE/A2=EDIT (CONTRACT, '99$$$$');
YRMON/A4=EDIT (PODATE, '9999');
DOLLARS/F8.3=IF SEL EQ 1 THEN VDOL ELSE 0;
END
```

The TABLE request which follows to sum the dollars by TYPE is:

```
TABLE FILE CONTRACT
SUM DOLLARS
BY TYPE AS 'SERVICE PERFORMED'
BY YRMON AS 'MONTH'
IF YRMON FROM 8601 TO 8612
END
```

The new field is used for sorting and aggregating, since a sum is needed for each of its values. In the DEFINE, the '99' indicates that only the first two characters of each number is assigned. The '$$$$' at the end are not necessary. They indicate that the last four characters are masked. This command is useful for obtaining any string of characters from a larger string, since the '9' can be placed anywhere in the string. For example, if the value of the field is 100-15-1248 then the value of the field SSN1 is 100151248, when the following mask is used.

```
DEFINE FILE PERSON
SSN1/A9=EDIT (SSN, '999$99$9999');
END
```

The mask feature allows the values of alphanumeric fields (or strings) to be appended to each other — while inserting other text as needed. For example, to add hyphens between the numbers of Social Security id, such as SSN = 100151248,

```
DEFINE FILE PERSON
SSN1/A11 = EDIT (SSN,'999-99-9999');
END
```

## Concatenate

The concatenate feature allows alphanumeric fields and text to be appended to each other to create new fields. The single bar (I) keeps trailing blanks which may be at the end of each field, while (II) removes trailing blanks.

In the next example, the MASTER shown in figure 4-3 tracks test scores for a group of students.

The new field GRADEIT indicates the test number and a PASS/FAIL grade. We also require another new field (FULLNAME)

```
      FILENAME = STUDENT                ,SUFFIX = FOC
      SEGNAME  = NAMESEG                ,SEGTYPE=S1 ,$
        FIELDNAME = STUDENT_NUM         ,CNUM       ,I04,FIELDTYPE=I, $
        FIELDNAME = LASTNAME            ,LNAME      ,A10              , $
        FIELDNAME = FIRSTNAME           ,FNAME      ,A08              , $
        FIELDNAME = CITY                ,CITY       ,A30              , $
        FIELDNAME = BIRTH_DATEM         ,BDATEM     ,I2               , $
        FIELDNAME = BIRTH_DATED         ,BDATED     ,I2               , $
        FIELDNAME = BIRTH_DATEY         ,BDATEY     ,I2               , $
SEGNAME=TESTSEG,PARENT=NAMESEG,SEGTYPE=S1,$
  FIELDNAME=TESTNUM,TEST  ,A6   ,$
  FIELDNAME=SCORE,SCORE,I3,    $
  FIELDNAME=COMMENT    ,COMMENT, A20, $
```

**Frame 4-3    Student MASTER file.**


to contain the last name and first name of the student — separated by a comma. The DEFINE is:

```
DEFINE FILE STUDENT
NAME/A20 = LASTNAME || ',' || FIRSTNAME ;
GRADE/A5 = IF SCORE GE 65 THEN '-PASS' ELSE '-FAIL';
GRADEIT/A11 = TESTNO | GRADE ;
END
```

The field GRADEIT will contain values which look like:

```
GRADEIT
-------
TEST1-PASS
TEST2-FAIL
TEST3-FAIL
TEST4-PASS
TEST10-PASS
```

The concatenate will not work with numeric fields. Notice that the format width of the new fields should be large enough for the widths of the appended fields. If it is too small, the result will be truncated on the trailing right characters. This should not give a FORMAT ERROR — although versions of FOCUS on the VAX and PC have been known to give syntax errors.

## Decode

The third feature DECODE is useful for the same reasons as the MASK and concatenate. It permits you to define new fields needed for sorting, for line names on reports, for headings on a report page, for matching values with fields in other files, etc.

DECODE assigns values to a field based on the particular values of another field. There are two different ways to use it:

1. Specify in a DEFINE the values for a field and the decoded values of the new field.
2. Specify in a flat file the values of a field and the decoded value.

A third way, which we will not go into now, is to create a HOLD file or SAVE file in your FOCEXEC which contains the values and decoded values. (SAVE files are created in a TABLE request just like HOLD files.)

Consider an example from the Income Tracking System which is described in the next chapter. Each type of deal income has a two-digit code. 'M1' for management deal, 'A1' for agent, 'L1' for lender, etc. — these may be thought of as the type of service performed. The field TYPE (with format A2) can be decoded into its proper name for display in reports. This is shown below:

```
DEFINE FILE INCOME
DEALTYPE/A20=DECODE TYPE (M1 MANAGEMENT A1 AGENT L1
LENDER LE 'LETTER OF CREDIT')
END
```

(Note: Blanks in the value require ' ' around it — as in 'LETTER OF CREDIT.')

The coded pairs must be separated from each other by either a blank or comma. In the next example, a flat file is used to contain the coded pairs.

```
DEFINE FILE INCOME
DEALTYPE/A20=DECODE TYPE (DEALNAME ELSE ' ');
END
```

DEALNAME is a DDNAME of a CMS file containing the values and decode values on separate lines (shown in figure 4-4). The FILEDEF which should be included in the FOCEXEC looks like:

```
-CMS FILEDEF DEALNAME DISK DNAMES DATA A
```

where, DNAMES DATA is the CMS file containing the decode values. This file may contain other data on each line in addition to the decode values — since it will be ignored.

The below TABLE request demonstrates using the new field as a sort field. The report prints the deals and income amounts for each type of service:

```
TABLE FILE INCOME
PRINT DEALNO DNAME FEEAMT
BY DEALTYPE
END
```

When a decode list needs to be used in more than one FOCEXEC, it is best to place the list in a file and reference the file in each program. Whenever a new value is added to the file it will be available to all of the programs — creating an easier maintenance task.

## The COMPUTE Statement

It is worth mentioning again that you should learn to use DEFINE STATEMENTS — like other aspects of FOCUS — by trying out things in your own programs or by observing how others have used them in programs, which can be explained to you. This also is a good way to understand some of the differences in usage between similar commands — such as the DEFINE and COMPUTE.

The COMPUTE command has exactly the same syntax in defining expressions for new fields as the DEFINE. However, it is USED WITHIN THE TABLE REQUEST to create fields which will appear as columns on the report, or which will be used to compute other fields. The COMPUTE uses the resulting values of other fields after all sorting and summing takes place.

In the CONTRACT example, suppose a report must compute next year's projected dollar amount for each vendor based on the total dollars awarded in contracts for the year. Assume that the projection fac-

```
A  AGENT
C  COMMITMENT
E  EVALUATOR
H  HEDGE
L  LIQUIDITY
M  MANAGEMENT
O  OTHER
P  PLACEMENT
R  RISK
S  'SWAP FEE'
T  TENDER
U  UNDERWRITING
AA 'ACCR ADJ '
AD ADVISORY
AR ARRANGEMENT
A2 'AGENT 2'
A7 'ACCR ADJ 2 '
A8 'ADVISORY 2'
A9 'ARRNGMNT 2'
CE CEILING
CL CLEARANCE
CO COLLATERAL
C1 'CEILING 2'
C2 'COMMITMENT 2'
C8 'COLLATERAL 2'
C9 'CLEARANCE 2'
DR DRAWDOWN
D9 'DRAWDOWN 2'
EX 'EXP  RESERVE'
E2 'EVALUATOR 2'
E9 'EXP RESRVE 2'
IN INTEREST
IV INVESTMENT
I9 'INTEREST 2'
I8 'INVESTMENT 2'
LE 'LETTER OF CREDIT'
LG LEGAL
LI 'LINE OF CREDIT'
L2 'LIQUIDITY 2'
L7 'LEGAL 2'
L8 'LINE OF CR 2'
L9 'LETTER OF CR'
M2 'MANAGEMENT 2'
OP 'OPBD RESERVE'
O2 'OTHER 2'
O9 'OPBD RSRVE 2'
PR PROFIT
```

Figure 4-4  Sample records in a DECODE file.

tor depends on the vendor category. For example, 'A' vendors have a factor of 1.1, 'B' vendors have a factor of 1.5, etc. The following request may be used:

```
TABLE FILE CONTRACT
SUM VDOL VCAT AND COMPUTE
NEXTYEAR/P8.3 = IF VCAT EQ 'A' THEN 1.1 * VDOL ELSE
IF VCAT EQ 'B' THEN 1.5*VDOL ELSE IF VCAT EQ 'C' THEN
1.7 * VDOL ;

BY VENDOR
IF YRMN FROM 8601 TO 8612
END
```

The verb object VDOL is first summed for each vendor and the result is used in the COMPUTE. Note that the verb object VCAT is an alphanumeric field. FOCUS will not sum alphanumeric fields, so its value is returned for each vendor. Also, it is not necessary to include VCAT as a verb object. Any field in the MASTER description or in another COMPUTE or DEFINE can be included in a COMPUTE. (Even if the field is not specified as a verb object, FOCUS will treat it as if were one — but it will not be displayed in the report.)

The COMPUTE, like the DEFINE, can be extended over many lines as long as it ends with a semicolon. The column heading for the computed field defaults to the name of the field and can be replaced by the specifying of column headings such as in:

```
COMPUTE
NEXTYEAR/P8.3 = 1.1*DOLLARS; AS '1987,PROJECTION';
```

The printing of a computed field can be suppressed by using the NOPRINT feature after the semicolon. If you use the NOPRINT option, or if the column heading is changed, you must repeat the phrase 'AND COMPUTE' before the next computed field.

## Column Positional Notation

Several important features of TABLE requests are worth mentioning here, since they will be useful in special COMPUTE situations.

```
-CMS FI OFFLINE DISK COMPUT1 LISTING A (RECFM UA LRECL 133
OFFLINE

DEFINE FILE CONTRACT
YRMN/A4 = EDIT (PODATE,'9999$$');
DOLLARS/F6.0 = IF SELECT EQ 1 THEN VDOL ELSE 0;
END

-* COMMENT - START TABLE REQUEST
TABLE FILE CONTRACT
SUM DOLLARS BY YRMN AS 'MONTH'
SUM DOLLARS AND COMPUTE
PCTDOL/P8.2 = 100 * (C2/C1);
BY YRMN BY VENDNAME
END
```

**Figure 4-5   Example of column positional notation.**

Verb objects can be referred to in COMPUTES using notation which identifies the column position of the object among the other objects. This is a fast way to refer to objects which may appear in a multiverb request. The notation is as shown in figure 4-5. The sort fields are not counted as columns C1, C2, etc.

In the CONTRACT example, a report request shows the dollars awarded to each vendor as a percentage of the total dollars awarded each month. One way of doing this is to use a multiverb request — the first request summing the dollars for the month — the second SUM summing the dollars for each vendor, as well as month.

```
TABLE FILE CONTRACT
SUM VDOL BY YRMON
SUM VDOL AND COMPUTE
PCTDOL/P8.2=100*(C2/C1)
BY YRMON
BY VENDOR
END
```

'C2' indicates the value of VDOL in second SUM — since it is the second verb object. The verb object VDOL is also summed for each vendor. The first verb object 'C1' is summed for each month. This notation is necessary here in order to distinguish between the two objects which have the same name.

## The LAST Command

An important feature of TABLE requests is the use of the command LAST in COMPUTES. The LAST command is similarly useful in DEFINES if the file has already been sorted. As you have seen, FOCUS performs DEFINE and COMPUTE computations using the values on each record. By using the LAST command, it is possible to obtain a new field from the values on more than one record. In the following request, the LAST allows a three-month moving average to be calculated on the total contract dollars awarded.

```
TABLE FILE CONTRACT
SUM DOLLARS AND COMPUTE
DOLL1/P8.3=DOLLARS;
DOLL2/P8.3=LAST DOLL1;
DOLL3/P8.3=LAST DOLL2;
MOAVE/P8.3=DOLL1+DOLL2+DOLL3/3;
BY YRMON
IF YRMON FROM 8601 TO 8612
END
```

The LAST before DOLL1 refers to the computed value of DOLL1 for the previous value of the sort field YRMON (i.e., the total dollars in the previous month). Similarly, the LAST DOLL2 refers to the value of DOLL2 in the previous month (or the total dollars two periods ago).

The LAST indicates to use the value on the previous record of the report. Consider another example,

```
TABLE FILE CONTRACT
SUM VDOL
AND COMPUTE
RATIO/P8.2=IF VENDOR EQ LAST VENDOR THEN
VDOL/(LAST VDOL) ELSE 0;

BY VENDOR
BY YRMON
IF RATIO GE 1.5
IF YRMON FROM 8601 TO 8612
END
```

The ratio of contract dollars to the previous month's contract dollars is calculated for each vendor, for each month. The record is shown on the report if the ratio exceeds 1.5 (e.g., the report shows months where contract dollars went up by more than 50%).

Because 'LAST' may refer to a field which is a sort field (such as VENDOR in the above example), it allows for very flexible aggregations and counting. An example of assigning a line number to a report line according to each time a sort field changes is shown.

```
TABLE FILE CONTRACT
SUM VDOL AND COMPUTE
LINENO/I4=IF VENDOR EQ LAST VENDOR THEN LAST LINENO
ELSE LAST LINENO+1;

BY VENDOR
BY CONTRACT
IF YRMON EQ 8601
END
```

LINE NO is simply a count which is incremented by one only when the vendor sort field changes.

Other situations in which 'LAST' is helpful is for:

1. Cumulative total (e.g., year to date)
2. Constructing indices over time (e.g., investment rates of return).

## Direct Calculations on Verb Objects

FOCUS also allows direct calculations on verb objects to be placed in each COMPUTE expression. For example, the direct calculations AVE., SUM., CNT., MIN., MAX., etc. can be performed and the result substituted in a COMPUTE statement. For example, the average size of a contract may be computed for each month ( the verb must be SUM or COUNT, not PRINT):

```
TABLE FILE CONTRACT
SUM VDOL AND COMPUTE
DELTA/P8.3 = VDOL/AVE.VDOL ;
BY VENDOR
```

```
BY YRMON
IF YRMON FROM 8601 TO 8612
IF SELECT EQ 1
END
```

The AVE. is a direct operation which FOCUS can perform on verb objects. It is calculated at the lowest sort level, by summing the dollars for the month and dividing by the number of contracts (the count) awarded for the month. Note: The above TABLE request is equivalent to the following, in which the column positions of the verb objects are used:

```
TABLE FILE CONTRACT
SUM VDOL AVE.VDOL AND COMPUTE
DELTA/P8.3=C1/C2;

BY VENDOR
BY YRMON
IF YRMON FROM 8601 TO 8612
IF SELECT EQ 1
END
```

The operation is performed on the verb object. As will be shown in a later section, direct operations may also be used for fields in the heading, footing, subfooting, etc.

FOCUS allows using the 'WITHIN' option to specify over what sort field to perform the calculation. As an example, MAX.VDOL is the highest contract amount awarded to a vendor in the year. The result will be displayed along with the total contract amount awarded each month. (Assume that the field YEAR has been defined from the field YRMON.)

```
TABLE FILE CONTRACT
SUM VDOL MAX.VDOL WITHIN YEAR
BY VENDOR
BY YEAR
BY YRMON
IF YRMON FROM 8601 TO 8612
IF SELECT EQ 1
END
```

More than one WITHIN may be used in the same TABLE request — on different verb objects.

## Formatting Customized Reports

The last step in coding a TABLE request to create a report is laying out the formatting details. Most of the time you should be able to copy these details from one program to another. This is one of the things which makes FOCUS easy, and quick to use. Most of the time the user will be flexible in deciding what the report format will look like. The programmer should give suggestions on what the report should look like based on:

1. The programs which have already been done in the past, and which are similar to the request
2. What you think the user really needs to see on the report — based on your experience working in the user's area.

Unless absolutely convinced that a much different format is required, try to implement simple formats. Also, keep in mind that you might reuse your code over and over — thus, try to design your code so that it is easy to copy. Novice programmers will find that the ability to reuse sections of code is essential to keeping FOCUS easy to learn.

We will go over some features which should demonstrate FOCUS's flexibility in designing reports. You may not ever need some of these features, but it's good to know they are there. It is recommended that you study examples of customized FOCUS reports found in programs available to you, or in the examples in the last chapter. Also, refer to the FOCUS 5.0 manual Chapter 2 for a more elaborate treatment of the features.

Formatting a report consists of:

1. Using the SET command to control such things as the number of lines per page, page numbering, panel size (page width), etc.
2. Laying out the columns (verb objects) and sort fields — including computed fields and sort fields which may not be printed on the report.

3. Specifying column headings using the 'AS' after each field (or by removing the column headings and reformatting them in the page headings).
4. Specifying other data and text required in the HEADING and FOOTING.
5. Specifying other data and summaries required between each sort break (or rows of the report) such as SUBHEADING, SUBFOOTING, SUBTOTALS, RECAPS.

The columns of the report are displayed in a standard format:

1. The sort fields usually occupy the leftmost part of the page — although a sort field may be suppressed using a NOPRINT — such as in

```
SUM DOLLARS
BY VENDOR NOPRINT
BY VENDNAME
BY YRMON
```

2. The width of each column is determined by the width of the field format (e.g., P10.3 has a width of 10 spaces) — unless the column heading is larger than this width. For example, the verb object DOLLARS in

```
PRINT DOLLARS AS 'AMOUNT AWARDED'
```

will occupy a column of 14 spaces even if the format of DOLLARS is P10.2. If no column heading is specified, then the name of the field is the column heading. Note, that a blank column heading can be assigned to any column in the report using the ' ' to denote a blank. For example,

```
PRINT DOLLARS AS ' '
```

3. FOCUS places two spaces between each column of the report unless overridden by positional markers. See the FOCUS 5.0 manual for examples with position markers. Also, if the columns will not fit in 133 spaces (the maximum size of a printed page), then FOCUS will attempt to fit it in 133 spaces by using one space between columns.

```
ELEMENTS OF A TABLE REQUEST:


TABLE FILE SALES

" MONTHLY SALES SUMMARY: "  <------ REPORT HEADING
" "

SUM   CASES DOLLARS  <------ VERB AND VERB OBJECTS

BY MONTH    <------ SORT FIELDS
BY PRODUCT

IF MONTH FROM 8601 TO 8606   <------ SCREENING PHRASE

ON MONTH UNDER-LINE SUBFOOT   <------ CONTROL CONDITIONS
" TOTAL CASES: <ST.CASES "
" TOTAL DOLLARS: <ST.DOLLARS "

END
```

Figure 4-6    Formatting a report — the basic elements.


4. The sort fields (like any other field) occupies a column on the report unless suppressed using a NOPRINT.
5. Each report page generated by a TABLE request is numbered starting with PAGE 1 — this may be overridden using the SET PAGE option or the TABPAGENO feature.

These standard features may be sufficient in many cases, but when not, there are many ways to enhance the layout. You should be aware of the techniques used by other programmers to format various reports, and then experiment with these techniques so that you understand what works and what doesn't work. Figure 4-6 outlines the elements of a FOCUS report and the code used for each feature.

FOCUS automatically positions the verb objects in the order specified in the request. You may also specify the column position of a verb object or sort field using the IN feature. Verb objects may be placed over each other by placing the word 'OVER' in front of a verb object as follows:

```
TABLE FILE PERSON
PRINT NAME OVER PHONE
BY DEPTCODE
END
```

The report looks like:

```
DEPT
----
101      NAME:  JOHN SMITH
         PHONE: 777-1111
         NAME:  MARY DOE
         PHONE: 777-2222
         NAME:  TOM JONES
         PHONE: 333-1111
         NAME:  PETER BEST
         PHONE: 444-2222
```

Sometimes, a report will require special techniques or "tricks" to create a particular format. For example, the DEPT name and phone number should appear next to the employee names and phone numbers. It should appear only on the first line of each list of employees. This requires a technique to suppress printing the department name and phone number after the first line.

```
JOHN SMITH  DEPT: ENGINEERING  PHONE: 555-3333
0555-1155
MARY DOE
555-4444
. . . . .
JOHN MACK   DEPT: GRAPHICS     PHONE:555-1111
0555-2345
FRED DOE
555-4444
. . . . .
```

In cases where the columns are formatted differently on each row, you will need to define or compute new fields with the appropriate values. In this case, you should use a COMPUTE to set up new fields for department name and phone number. These should be blank after the first sort line.

```
TABLE FILE PERSON
PRINT DEPTNAME NOPRINT DEPTPHONE NOPRINT AND COMPUTE
NEWDEPT/A20=IF DEPTCODE EQ LAST DEPTCODE THEN ' ' ELSE
DEPTNAME; NOPRINT
NEWPHONE/A10=IF DEPTCODE EQ LAST DEPTCODE THEN ' '
ELSE DEPTPHONE; NOPRINT
AND
EMPNAME AS ''
NEWDEPT AS ''
NEWPHONE AS '' OVER
EMPHONE AS ''
BY DEPTCODE AS NOPRINT
END
```

The department name is non-blank only when the value of department code changes. Also, the report is sorted by department code — although it is not printed on the report.

## Formatting Headings, Footings, Etc.

The next major formatting topic we will cover is headings, footings, subheadings, etc. These items are not required in the TABLE request. However, there are very few customized reports which don't include some of these features. Certain reports may even require formatting with only HEADINGS, or SUBHEADINGS — and no verb objects.

The most common of these features is the report HEADING. This is where text such as report title, column headings, etc., is included which will be displayed at the top of each report page. In the TABLE request, the HEADING should be placed before the verbs, verb objects, and sort fields. For example, in the CONTRACT example, the report in figure 4-7 displays the dollars awarded to each vendor for months 8601 to 8612. A separate page is required for each month — with a HEADING appearing on each page.

The TABLE request is:

```
1 PAGE        1

      VENDOR CONTRACT DOLLARS
           1986 ACTIVITY
           MONTH: 8602

VENDNAME                  DOLLARS
--------                  -------
ALEXANDER                      0.
CENTURY                        0.
COLORA                         0.
EMPIRE                      1500.
LEBANON                        0.
PENNCO                         0.
QUAKER                         0.
SANDER                         0.
SCOTTPRESS                     0.

*TOTAL 8602                 1500.

  PAGE        2

      VENDOR CONTRACT DOLLARS
           1986 ACTIVITY
           MONTH: 8603

VENDNAME                  DOLLARS
--------                  -------
ALEXANDER                      0.
COLORA                      2600.
EMPIRE                         0.
LEBANON                        0.
PENNCO                      2600.
QUAKER                      3800.
SANDER                      1600.

*TOTAL 8603                10600.

  PAGE        3

      VENDOR CONTRACT DOLLARS
           1986 ACTIVITY
           MONTH: 8604

VENDNAME                  DOLLARS
--------                  -------
ALEXANDER                      0.
```

**Figure 4-7   Example of report headings.**

```
TABLE FILE CONTRACT
HEADING CENTER
"VENDOR CONTRACT DOLLARS"
"1985 ACTIVITY"
"MONTH: YRMON"
" "
SUM DOLLARS
BY YRMON NOPRINT
BY VENDOR
IF YRMON FROM 8501 TO 8512
ON YRMON SUBTOTAL PAGE-BREAK
END
```

The HEADING is displayed on the top of every report page. The control-condition PAGE-BREAK determines when a new page starts. For each value of YRMON, there is a separate page. (Note: If there is no PAGE-BREAK condition, then the SET LINES parameter determines the number of lines per page.)

Any fields can appear in the HEADING, such as YRMON, by placing it in < >. (The open left caret does not preserve trailing blanks in an alphanumeric field.) If the field is not a sort field ('BY' field), it may appear in the HEADING. In this case, the first line of data created by PRINT or SUM will supply the value of the field in the HEADING.

## Direct Operations Performed

Some reports require a direct calculation such as AVE., MAX., MIN., CNT., etc., to be performed on a field, and also displayed in the HEADING (or FOOTING). This can be done using the direct operation as a prefix to the field. For example,

```
TABLE FILE CONTRACT
HEADING
"CONTRACT ACTIVITY"
"VENDOR:"

"TOTAL NUMBER OF CONTRACTS: <TOT.PONUM"
"TOTAL CONTRACT DOLLARS: <TOT.DOLLARS"

SUM DOLLARS NOPRINT
```

```
BY VENDOR PAGE-BREAK
IF YRMON EQ 8601
END
```

Any field referenced in the heading, which is not a sort field, will be treated as if they were verb objects. The value of the field in the first line of the report is displayed in the HEADING, while the value on the last line of the page is displayed in the FOOTING. Notice that the above report will have only a heading. No lines or columns will be printed because of "NOPRINT." This is called a "letter-type" report because the report resembles a letter's format.

Sometimes, HEADINGS and FOOTINGS require precise formatting with respect to the column positioning and number of lines. This is always a trial-and-error process using the formatting techniques below:

1. Spot markers: for positioning the next character in the nth column from the start of the line (<n TEXT), or, n spaces from the last non-blank character (<+n TEXT).
2. Line skipping: for skipping n lines before the next character is positioned (</n TEXT).

Long lines of text in a HEADING can be easily handled by using two consecutive lines, such as in:

```
"THIS REPORT LINE HAS LOTS OF TEXT AND/OR DATA IN IT -
ON THIS DATE JAN 10, 1986"
```

The quotes are left out intentionally, since FOCUS will combine a maximum of two lines into one. (This applies to formatting lines in SUBFOOT, SUBHEAD also.)

### Subheading and Subfooting

The next topic important to formatting is the use of SUBHEADINGS, and SUBFOOTINGS. Above and below each line of the report, one can place text and data to create summary lines. These lines are formatted the same way HEADINGS are formatted, but they are controlled by the sort control fields. The syntax is:

```
ON fieldname SUBHEAD
"text and/or data — line 1"
"text and/or data — line 2"
...
```

For example,

```
TABLE FILE CONTRACT
SUM DOLLARS
BY VENDOR
BY YRMON
ON VENDOR NOPRINT AND SUBHEAD
"ACTIVITY FOR VENDOR"
" "
END
```

Before each sort break on VENDOR, a line will show the text and data in the subheading. The subheading may be centered or formatted using placement markers controlling column position and line skipping.

DIRECT OPERATIONS on database fields or computed fields may be placed in the subfooting and subheading. The operation is controlled by the sort field. The field is treated as if it were a verb object, but need not be a verb object. Arithmetic operations can be used in the SUBFOOT, and also in the SUBHEAD — with the exception of the prefix ST. (for subtotaling) which cannot be used in the subheading. If the SUBFOOTING contains a numeric field (with no direct operation), the value displayed is the value which would appear on the last line before the sort break.

```
TABLE FILE CONTRACT
SUM DOLLARS
BY VENDOR
BY YRMON
ON VENDOR SUBFOOT
"VENDOR:"
"TOTAL DOLLARS:<ST.DOLLARS"
"NUMBER OF CONTRACTS:<CNT.DOLLARS"
END
```

```
MONTH     DOLLARS
-----     -------
8701         1500
8702        10320
8703         5500
8704        22500

* VENDOR: 11111111
TOTAL DOLLARS:  39820
NUMBER OF CONTRACTS: 14

8701         8900
8703        10400

* VENDOR: 22222222
TOTAL DOLLARS:  19300
NUMBER OF CONTRACTS: 8
```

Figure 4-8    Subfooting containing direct calculation.

The total number of contracts is directly counted for each vendor and shown in the subfooting. The report also shows the subtotal of DOLLARS for each vendor. See figure 4-8. The FOCUS manual Chapter 2 section 5.1 describes the direct operations for fields, which may be used in the headings and footings.

## Performing Subtotals and Other Calculations

Subtotals can also be performed whenever a sort field changes. The subtotal of one or more fields is shown in the same column as the field. To subtotal all object fields, the syntax is simple

```
ON sortfield SUBTOTAL, or BY sortfield SUBTOTAL
```

To subtotal only a particular field use

```
ON sortfield SUBTOTAL fieldname
```

For example,

```
TABLE FILE CONTRACT
SUM DOLLARS
BY VENDOR
BY YRMON
ON VENDOR SUBTOTAL
END
```

The report is shown in figure 4-9.
In figure 4-9, the subtotal line is labeled

*TOTAL DOLLARS.

To remove this label from the report, use

ON VENDOR SUBTOTAL AS ' '

(a blank is enclosed between single quotes).
The verb PRINT may also be used when obtaining subtotals. The command SUB-TOTAL can be used instead of SUBTOTAL when subtotals are to be suppressed for the higher sort fields.
FOCUS also has the features COLUMN-TOTAL and ROW-TOTAL for obtaining a total of each numeric field at the end of the report (or across each row). For example,

```
SUM DOLLARS
BY VENDOR
BY YRMON
IF YRMON EQ 8601 OR 8602 OR 8603
ON TABLE COLUMN-TOTAL
```

There are two other calculations which can be performed at the sort-breaks:

1. SUMMARIZE
2. RECAP

SUMMARIZE is nearly the same as SUBTOTAL. However, where SUBTOTAL totals all columns of the report, SUMMARIZE will total those fields which are verb objects. SUMMARIZE will not total COMPUTED fields, but instead determine the summary values using the

```
1 PAGE        1


MONTH    DOLLARS
-----    -------
8602          0.
8603          0.
8604          0.
8605       1800.
8607       2500.
8608       2500.

*TOTAL ALEXANDER
           6800.

8602          0.
8604       1800.
8607       2500.
8609       8000.

*TOTAL CENTURY
          12300.

8602          0.
8603       2600.
8604       3600.
8605          0.
8606       1600.

*TOTAL COLORA
           7800.

8602       1500.
8603          0.
8604          0.
8605          0.
```

Figure 4-9    Report with subtotals.


subtotals of the fields, and the calculation performed in the COM-
PUTE. For example,

```
SUM DOLLARS FORECAST AND COMPUTE
RATIO/D8.2=(DOLLARS — FORCST)/DOLLARS;
BY VENDOR
BY YRMON
```

```
ON VENDOR SUMMARIZE
END
```

For each vendor, the SUMMARIZE line will look like:

```
RATIO       TOTAL DOLLARS TOTAL FORCST

.2500         20000         15000
```

where RATIO is not a subtotal, but determined by the COMPUTE relationship using the subtotal for DOLLARS and FORECAST.

The RECAP command is used differently than the SUBTOTAL or SUMMARIZE. With RECAP, new calculations can be performed using the subtotals of any field or report column. The results are shown directly underneath the content line after the sort-break. For example,

```
TABLE FILE CONTRACT
SUM DOLLARS FORCAST
BY VENDOR
BY YRMON
ON YRMON RECAP
RATIO/D8.2=1-(DOLLARS/FORCAST); as 'FORECAST RATIO'
IF VENDOR EQ 1111111
IF YRMON FROM 8601 TO 8603
END
```

The values of the fields in the RECAP computation refer to the subtotals of each field at each sort-break.

Note that only fields which appear as verb objects can be used in a RECAP. Alphanumeric fields which appear as verb objects (e.g., SUM or WRITE VENDNAME) are not "summed" by FOCUS, and can be used in a RECAP (its value on the last content line before the sort break is used).

Fields defined by RECAPS can be displayed in the SUBFOOT. In this case, the RECAPS normally shown after the sort breaks are automatically suppressed. RECAPS cannot be used in SUBHEADS.

```
TABLE FILE CONTRACT
SUM DOLLARS FORECAST
BY VENDOR
```

```
BY YRMON

ON VENDOR RECAP
RATIO/D8.2=FORECAST/DOLLARS;
NEXT/D8.2=RATIO+.05;
NEWAMT/D10.2=NEXT * DOLLARS;
ON VENDOR SUBFOOT
"PROJECTION FOR VENDOR <VNAME"
"FORECAST FACTOR IS <RATIO "
"FORECAST DOLLARS IS <NEWAMT"
END
```

See figure 4-10.

In the above figure, the vendor subtotals are used in the calculation for NEWAMT.

The use of SUBFOOTS, SUBHEADS, etc., permits almost any format of report to be created. You should learn how other programmers have used them to format reports, and use their techniques as a guide. Refer to the FOCUS manual Chapter 2 section 8.9 for more information on using data and positioning text in the headings and footings.

## Additional Considerations for Preparing Reports

When using the formatting techniques, you should also be aware of the following features. These may help you to debug a program or to make fast adjustments to an existing program.

1. The verb, verb objects, and sort fields can be placed on the same line of a FOCEXEC; but for better legibility, use more than one line. Screening (IF) conditions usually follow on separate lines. Operations such as PAGEBREAK, SKIP-LINE, UNDERLINE, SUBTOTAL, usually follow the 'IF' conditions. SUBFOOT and SUBHEAD operations are last.
2. Operations like PAGEBREAK, etc., also can be placed with the BY statement. For example,

```
BY YRMON NOPRINT UNDER-LINE SUBTOTAL
```

```
1 PAGE     1

VENDNAME                 MONTH   DOLLARS    FORECAST
--------                 -----   -------    --------

CENTURY                  8604    1800.      1873.6
PROJECTION FOR VENDOR CENTURY
FORECAST FACTOR IS       1.09
FORECAST DOLLARS IS      1962.00

COLORA                   8603    2600.      2655.2
                         8604    3600.      3673.6
PROJECTION FOR VENDOR COLORA
FORECAST FACTOR IS       1.07
FORECAST DOLLARS IS      6634.00

EMPIRE                   8602    1500.      1536.8
PROJECTION FOR VENDOR EMPIRE
FORECAST FACTOR IS       1.07
FORECAST DOLLARS IS      1605.00

PENNCO                   8603    2600.      2655.2
                         8604    3600.      3673.6
PROJECTION FOR VENDOR PENNCO
FORECAST FACTOR IS       1.07
FORECAST DOLLARS IS      6634.00

QUAKER                   8603    3800.      3855.2
PROJECTION FOR VENDOR QUAKER
FORECAST FACTOR IS       1.06
FORECAST DOLLARS IS      4028.00

SANDER                   8603    1600.      1655.2
PROJECTION FOR VENDOR SANDER
FORECAST FACTOR IS       1.08
FORECAST DOLLARS IS      1728.00
```

Figure 4-10   Displaying recaps in the subfooting.

3. Dialogue manager control statements can be placed on (separate) lines in a TABLE request to branch around verb objects, sort fields, subfoot lines, etc. (See a later section for using dialogue manager statements.) Dialogue manager variables also may appear in lines of a TABLE request. Their values will be substituted when the FOCEXEC is executed. For example, if the

variable &FIELD1 is set to have value "DOLLARS," this will be substituted in the TABLE request as shown:

```
-SET &FIELD1 = IF &OPT EQ 'D' THEN 'DOLLARS'
-ELSE 'UNITS' ;
TABLE FILE CONTRACT
SUM &FIELD1
BY YRMON
BY VENDOR
END
```

4. When using special TABLE features such as multiverb requests, direct operations on fields, formatting with ACROSS, formatting with financial modeling language (see FOCUS 5.0 manual Chapter 11),etc., it is best to perform your request using FOCUS files with relatively small and simple segments. Multipath files, joined files, etc., should be simplified by first extracting the data into HOLD files.
5. Formatting features such as SUBTOTALS, SUBFOOTS, RECAPS, UNDER-LINES, etc., do not appear in HOLD files or SAVE files (only verb objects, sort fields, and COMPUTED fields appear in HOLD files). This is good to know if you need to quickly change a TABLE request to produce a HOLD file instead of a report.
6. When working with fairly large files, you can usually check or test the TABLE request by first inserting "IF RECORDLIMIT EQ ___" as a screening condition. This will limit the report to a small number of records.
7. The FOCUS manual Chapter 2 section 10 describes how to handle files which you suspect may have missing data values on some records. During report generation, you may not want to include records with missing data values into SUM and COUNT operations or in direct operations such as AVE., MAX., MIN. The section also describes how to retrieve "short-path" segments — segment instances with missing descendents.

There are other considerations related to reporting and the TABLE request which will be presented in the examples which follow. Most of these considerations deal with organizing your FOCEXEC in a manner which simplifies extracting the final report. Also, in the last chapter, we will demonstrate other special facilities which are useful in various reporting situations. These include:

1. Presorting external files with syncsort and formatting the report with TABLEF.
2. Designing audit trail reports using external files and logged transactions.
3. Using dialogue manager to control how a FOCEXEC is executed, and to pass parameters at execution time. Invoking FOCEXECS from other FOCEXECS.
4. Techniques for combining records from more than one file, and reporting from multipath FOCUS files. (eg. MATCH procedure, JOINING files, alternate file views).

Chapter

# 5

# Designing Procedures for Reporting: Two Case Studies

In the previous chapters, we presented the basics of FOCUS reporting by listing the techniques used in simple TABLE requests. Although you need to remember a few basic commands, there are a number of different situations which require the same techniques. The techniques may not have exactly the same code, but they will manipulate the data in similar ways.

The kind of techniques you use depend on

1. The finished report format required
2. The relationships between data in the FOCUS file.

If the FOCUS file is designed with consideration of how the data will be retrieved, you will need relatively simple and concise procedures for formatting the reports. In this chapter, we will present several case studies which illustrate "typical" procedures for generating custom reports. The intent is to show how the features of the TABLE request are used together. The only way to learn the techniques is to see how they are used in real applications. If you understand how the language was used in one application, you will get an idea of how a similar situation can be handled. We shall also show

```
FILENAME=CAR,SUFFIX-FOC
SEGNAME=ORIGIN,SEGTYPE=S1
  FIELDNAME=COUNTRY,COUNTRY,A10,FIELDTYPE=I,$
SEGNAME=COMP,SEGTYPE=S1,PARENT=ORIGIN
  FIELDNAME=CAR,CARS,A16,$
SEGNAME=CARREC,SEGTYPE=S1,PARENT=COMP
  FIELDNAME=MODEL,MODEL,A24,$
SEGNAME=BODY,SEGTYPE=S1,PARENT=CARREC
  FIELDNAME=BODYTYPE,TYPE,A12,$
  FIELDNAME=SEATS,SEAT,I3,$
  FIELDNAME=DEALER_COST,DCOST,D7,$
  FIELDNAME=RETAIL_COST,RCOST,D7,$
  FIELDNAME=SALES,UNITS,I6,$
SEGNAME=SPECS,SEGTYPE=U,PARENT=BODY
  FIELDNAME=LENGTH,LEN,D5,$
  FIELDNAME=WIDTH,WIDTH,D5,$
  FIELDNAME=HEIGHT,HEIGHT,D5,$
  FIELDNAME=WEIGHT,WEIGHT,D6,$
  FIELDNAME=WHEELBASE,BASE,D6.1,$
```

Figure 5-1 Example of single path file.

how Dialogue Manager statements are used to generalize programs, and allow the operator to supply specific values at run time.

As mentioned, the techniques needed to create reports depend on the relationships between the data in the records of the FOCUS file. The simplest relationship is when the file can be described by a single path from the parent ROOT segment to a child segment to its child segment, etc., as shown in figure 5-1.

In this case, any field or group of fields can be easily summed and sorted by any other field. This type of file layout is favored for easy reporting — and it should be the most common situation you encounter. Note that the number of segments included in this "single-path" file is irrelevant to the techniques needed to extract the report. (However, the number of segments does affect the speed in retrieving data from a large file.) In cases where the record segments do not lie in a single path, special techniques such as file views, file matching, etc., might be needed to refer to fields together in a single TABLE request.

## Organizing the Files to Contain Detailed and Summary Data

Many FOCUS applications are designed to satisfy the requirements for capturing the data at a detailed level and reporting at varying levels of detail. If there are a large number of records in the detailed data base, you may want to summarize the data periodically (e.g., monthly) and load the summarized data into other data files which can be used for reporting. Thanks to FOCUS's simple file maintenance procedures, the creation of "summary" or "spin-off" files is always something that the programmer should consider. Typical applications which involve aggregating detailed records into summary files are:

1. Organization manpower and expense estimates and budgets — e.g., detailed cost center expenses are summarized into "key" categories (advertising, sales, clerical) by department, by division.
2. Accounts Receivable and General Ledger — e.g., receivables for each transaction are summarized into the various General Ledger accounts for posting. Calculating and posting monthly income received and accrued.
3. Employee expense voucher reporting — e.g., employee expenses recorded on each voucher are summarized monthly by division by department.
4. Manufactured parts inspection and quality control — e.g., reject and accept records for each inspected part are summarized for the work centers which manufacture the parts.
5. Sales to the trade of consumer products reported monthly — e.g., figures are summarized by key account, by sales region, by product group, etc.

Summarizing large files into smaller files can usually be accomplished monthly with a minimum of work (and sometimes can be done in an overnight batch procedure — to limit its effect on daily CPU utilization). This will allow key reports to be generated from the smaller files — resulting in simpler programs and faster retrieval times.

## Application 1: Income Tracking System for Servicing Deals

The first application is intended to describe how the features of FOCUS reporting are used to develop reports, which describe the types and amount of fees received from clients. These reports require programs which use some of the basic techniques described in Chapter 3 for TABLE, DEFINE, and COMPUTE. There are several aspects of FOCUS to be treated which were only briefly described in Chapter 3. These include:

1. Cross-Reference (KU) segments
2. Dialogue Manager statements.
3. ONLINE/OFFLINE display options.
4. Short-path segments.

We shall not describe how the data was input to the FOCUS file, since file maintenance is covered in the next chapter. (Data entry via FIDEL is covered for this application in Chapter 9.) The programs have been written for the CMS operating system, but are nearly identical for the TSO, VAX, or PC FOCUS environment.

The DEALS FOCUS file has a simple segment structure as shown in the MASTER description in figure 5-2.

It is a single-path file (i.e., each segment has at most one child segment) with three segments MAIN, DEALINFO, FEETYPE. Note that although segment MAIN has two child segments, one of the segments DEALINFO is a unique segment (SEGTYPE=U). Unique segments (which occur only once for each parent record) are considered part of its parent segment; therefore, the file has a single-path structure. The file also has a cross-reference segment PRODUCT; this indicates that a cross-reference file PRODUCT contains additional information on each product code such as full name, and other characteristics. Note that the segtype KU is called keyed unique, and is another form of unique segment. For reporting purposes, the product segment in the cross-reference file, may be considered part of its parent segment MAIN. So, any field in the product segment is available through the DEALS file — for use in TABLE requests and DEFINE statements.

This application is typical of FOCUS applications designed for simple management reporting such as business tracking, administrative bookkeeping, project management, etc. This particular application is an income tracking system. A bank, for example, receives fee income from clients for helping to arrange financing on major public projects. Each project financed for a client is referred to as a deal. Clients pay fees on either a one-time basis or on a periodic basis. The purpose of the system is to record the fees due and received for each deal; the system should also compute and report the amount of income

```
FILENAME = DEALS, SUF = FOC
 SEGNAME = MAIN, SEGTYPE = SH1,$
   FIELD = DEAL         ,DNUM         ,I05, FIELDTYPE = I,$

 SEGNAME = DEALINFO, PARENT = MAIN, SEGTYPE = U,$
   FIELD = ISSUER       ,ISSUER       ,A27   ,$
   FIELD = STATE        ,ISSU_ST      ,A2    ,$
   FIELD = UNITCODE     ,UCODE        ,A2 ,   TITLE='UNIT',$
   FIELD = PROD_CODE    ,PCODE        ,A04,   TITLE='PROD,CODE',$
   FIELD = ISSUE_SIZE   ,SIZE         ,D12S , TITLE='DEAL AMOUNT',$
   FIELD = CLOSE_DATE   ,CDATE        ,I6YMD, TITLE='DEAL,CLOSE,DATE',$
   FIELD = MATURITY     ,MDATE        ,I6YMD, TITLE='DEAL,MATURITY,
DATE',$ $

 SEGNAME = PRODUCT, CRFILE = PRODUCT, CRKEY = PCODE,
PARENT=DEALINFO,
           SEGTYPE = KU,$

 SEGNAME = FEE_TYPE, PARENT = MAIN, SEGTYPE = S1,
   FIELD = FEE_TYPE     ,FTYPE        ,A2,    TITLE='FEE,TYPE',$
   FIELD = FEE_FREQ     ,FREQ         ,I3,    TITLE='FEE,FREQ',$
   FIELD = FEE_EXP_DT   ,EXPDATE      ,I6YMD, TITLE='FEE EXP, DATE',$
   FIELD = FEEDUE       ,MFD          ,A12,   TITLE='MONTHS,FEES DUE',$
   FIELD = FEEAMT       ,FAMT         ,D12.2, TITLE='FEE,AMOUNT',$
   FIELD = NXT_DUE_DT   ,NEXTDATE     ,I6YMD, TITLE='NEXT DUE,  DATE',$
   FIELD = LST_FEEAMT   ,LASTFEE      ,D12.2 ,TITLE='LAST FEE,
AMOUNT',$
   FIELD = LST_DUE_DT   ,LASTDATE     ,I6YMD, TITLE='LAST DUE,  DATE',$
   FIELD = LST_REC_DT   ,LASTRCVD     ,I6YMD, TITLE='LAST RCVD,
DATE',$
   FIELD = ACCRUAL_COD  ,ACC_CODE     ,A2,    TITLE='ACCT,CODE',$
   FIELD = DAY_DUE      ,DAYDUE       ,I2,    TITLE='DAY,DUE',$
   FIELD = COMMENT      ,COMMENT      ,A40,$
```

Figure 5-2  MASTER description for DEALS FOCUS file.

taken each month on each type of fee. The income reported in a month is based on cash/accrual accounting calculations:

1. If the fee is a one-time fee, it is taken as income (on a cash basis) in the month in which it is actually received.
2. If the fee is paid periodically (e.,g. one, two, or three times per year), then the income is taken every month based on the amount accrued for one month. For example, if a $20,000 fee is received three times a year, then the amount is accrued over a

four-month period. Therefore, the monthly amount accrued as income is $20,000 divided by four, or $5000.

The system has been designed to track when the next payment is due and when the last payment was received. It is not intended to maintain a history of the fees received or of the amounts taken as income each month. An important part of the system, obviously, is data entry of deal and fee information. This will not be presented here.

The segment DEALINFO contains the relevant information about each DEAL, such as issuer (or client requesting the financing), issue size (amount of financing), the closing date of the deal, the date the deal matures, the financial product type, etc. The unit code indicates the type of project being financed (e.g., the unit codes may represent HOUSING, HIGHER EDUCATION, HEALTH CARE, etc.). There may be more than one type of fee associated with each deal. Therefore, the file has been designed with a child segment containing information on each fee. The key field is FEE_TYPE.

We will demonstrate how the FOCUS reporting features are used for online inquiry and to create management reports. The report names are shown in the sample menu in figure 5-4. The reports can be obtained by executing a "driver" FOCEXEC which contains the menu, or by executing the FOCEXECS from native FOCUS.

The "driver" FOCEXEC DEALREP is shown in figure 5-3. It is written mostly with dialogue manager statements which passes control to a particular FOCEXEC to be executed — depending on the option selected in the menu.

A brief discussion of Dialogue Manager Statements follows.

## Managing FOCEXECS with Dialogue Manager

Dialogue manager has two basic functions:

1. To control which "sections" of FOCUS code should be executed according to various options selected at run time by the operator.
2. To substitute values at run time, as variables in FOCUS statements, which determine certain conditions such as screening conditions, formatting options, etc.

```
-************************************************************
-* PURPOSE : DEALS REPORT MENU DRIVER
-************************************************************
SET MSG=OFF
-SET &MSG = '                                              ';
-SET &OPT = ' ';
ONLINE
-RUN

-TOP
-CRTFORM LINE 1
-" <.R. "
-"
 ==================================================================="
-"                              REPORTS MENU
<D.&DATE"
-"
 ==================================================================="
-"<.W. "
-" 1 => DEAL DATA PROFILE       "
-" 2 => AGED TRIAL BALANCE      "
-" 3 => INCOME BY DEAL          "
-" 4 => INCOME SUMMARY          "
-" 5 => MANAGEMENT SUMMARY      "
-" 6 => PRODUCT LISTING         "
-" "
-"                              <39 X => EXIT TO MASTER MENU
<.C. "
-"<.B. "
-"
 ==================================================================="
-" SELECTION =======><T.&OPT><0X
-"
 ==================================================================="
-"<.HD.&MSG"

-RUN
-SET &MSG = ' ';
-RUN
-IF &OPT EQ 'X' GOTO DONE ;
-IF &OPT EQ 1   GOTO DEAL1 ;
-IF &OPT EQ 2   GOTO DEAL2 ;
-IF &OPT EQ 3   GOTO DEAL3 ;
-IF &OPT EQ 4   GOTO DEAL4 ;
-IF &OPT EQ 5   GOTO DEAL5 ;
-IF &OPT EQ 6   GOTO DEAL6 ;
```

Figure 5-3  Driver program for income tracking system report.

```
-GOTO INVAL
-DEAL1
EX DEAL1
-RUN
-GOTO   TOP
-DEAL2
EX DEAL2
-RUN
-GOTO   TOP
-DEAL3
EX DEAL3
-RUN
-GOTO   TOP
-DEAL4
EX DEAL4
-RUN
-GOTO   TOP
-DEAL5
EX DEAL5
-RUN
-GOTO   TOP
-DEAL6
EX DEAL6
-RUN
-GOTO   TOP
-RUN

-INVAL
-SET &MSG = '* INVALID SELECTION ... RETRY!';
-GOTO TOP

-ERRMSG
-RUN
-SET &MSG = '* REPORT COMPLETED!';
-GOTO TOP

-DONE
FIN
```

Figure 5-3   (continued) Driver program for income tracking system report.

By supplying values to the program when it is executed, one program can handle different reporting tasks and requirements. For example, the elements of a TABLE request can be dialogue manager variables, and their values assigned at run time.

### Designing Procedures for Reporting: Two Case Studies

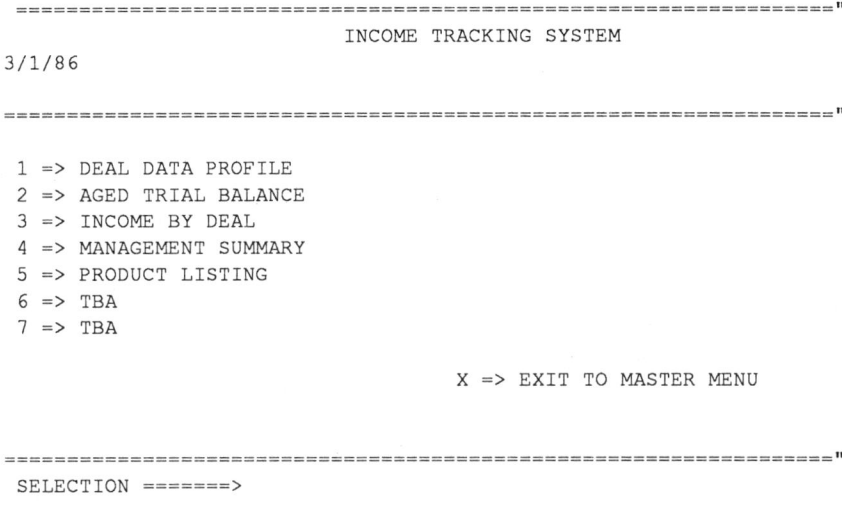

Figure 5-4   Reports menu for income tracking system.

This allows you to change:

1. The sort fields, verb objects
2. The screening conditions
3. The name of the FOCUS file
4. The formatting lines such as column headings, subheadings, etc.

In any FOCEXEC containing dialogue manager (&) variables, FOCUS will not execute regular FOCUS commands (i.e., non-dialogue manager statements) until the values of the variables in the command are determined. The values of the variables are usually supplied by the operator at run time — via prompt statements, or automatic prompts (if no PROMPT statement exists). The values can be supplied in other ways:

1. By reading values from a flat file.
2. In SET and DEFAULT statements.
3. As parameters passed in the execute (EXEC) statement.

Refer to the examples in Chapter 9 for a description of how these features are used.

You should also understand how FOCUS resolves the variables before executing the regular FOCUS commands. This involves the automatic process of placing commands in a "stack;" the FOCUS manual Chapter 6 Section 1.6 describes this in detail. FOCUS searches line by line for any dialogue manager variables. If the variable has no value supplied, FOCUS will prompt the operator to enter a value. FOCUS does this until the end of the TABLE command is reached. It then places the entire command in a STACK, where it is executed when the statement -RUN is encountered. FOCUS then proceeds to the next line, so that other TABLE requests are completed and executed in the same way. Other FOCUS commands such as DEFINE, MODIFY, MATCH, JOIN, are processed in the same way.

FOCUS also checks each line for other dialogue manager statements, such as -IF or -SET, which are executed immediately. SET statements provide important flexibilty, since they can define values of variables based on values of other variables. For example,

```
-PROMPT &FILE.A1.ENTER TYPE OF REPORT (S,D).
-SET &WHATFILE = IF &FILE EQ 'S' THEN 'SUMMARY' ELSE
'DETAIL' ;
...
...
TABLE FILE &WHATFILE
...
...
END
```

The value of &FILE is supplied by the operator at execution time. (See FOCUS 5.0 manual Chapter 6 sections 3.9 to 3.11 for an explanation of supplying values using PROMPT.) When the -SET statement is executed, the value of &WHATFILE will be assigned. The first line of the TABLE request will become:

TABLE FILE SUMMARY

or

TABLE FILE DETAIL

The maximum number of dialogue manager variables available within a FOCEXEC is 256. The variables store a character string or numbers and can be placed anywhere in a FOCEXEC. When used in SET statements, there is no need to place single quotes (' ') around text values unless the text contains blanks. For example, the following are valid SET statements:

```
-SET &UNITCODE = IF &CODE EQ C2 THEN A222 ELSE A111;
-SET &UNITCODE = IF &CITY EQ 'NEW YORK' THEN A555
-ELSE A111;
-SET &UNITCODE = Z111 ;
```

Local variables are identified by a single ampersand (&) preceding the name of the variable. They remain in effect throughout a single FOCEXEC. The values are not passed on to to other FOCEXECS containing the same variables. Global variables differ from local variables in that their value remains current throughout the FOCUS session. All FOCEXECS which include a particular global variable will receive the supplied value until you exit from FOCUS. There are also 21 system variables whose values are provided automatically by FOCUS wherever they are requested. A list of system variables is found in the FOCUS manual Chapter 6 Sections 3.4 and 3.5.

In the DEALREP FOCEXEC, the value of the variable &OPT is requested using a dialogue manager -CRTFORM. Note that the variable &MSG is supplied near the top of the FOCEXEC with a -SET. &MSG is placed in the -CRTFORM only to supply information (e.g., &MSG displays an error message if an invalid option is selected). The D., in D.&MSG, indicates a display variable only, whose value cannot be changed. (Variables can be displayed and changed using the T. prefix). Also, the statement

```
-SET &OPT=' ';
```

determines the width of the variable &OPT as one character; only one blank will be displayed on the screen for this variable.

Branching is accomplished by the dialogue manager IF statements; the form of the IF statement can be simple, as in the DEALREP FOCEXEC, or can contain compound expressions such as

```
-IF &OPTION EQ S THEN GOTO SUMMARY ELSE IF
-&OPTION EQ D THEN GO TO DETAIL ELSE
-GOTO DONE;
```

In DEALREP, the IF statements determine which label to branch to. When the program branches to the appropriate label (-DEAL1, -DEAL2, etc.), the corresponding FOCEXEC will be executed to create the report which was requested.

When a FOCUS EXEC command is found, FOCUS will first stack the commands from the FOCEXEC and then execute them. To be sure that the stacked commands are executed, there is a -RUN on the next line. After the focexec is executed, control returns to the DEALREP focexec. The statement -GOTO TOP sends the program back to the start of the -CRTFORM (and the menu is displayed again). The -EXIT at the end of DEALREP is like a -RUN, but it takes you out of the FOCEXEC and returns you to the FOCUS environment (or to the calling FOCEXEC).

## Other Considerations for the "Driver" FOCEXEC

There are a number of commands which might be placed in a "driver" FOCEXEC, such as DEALREP, to control various aspects of the other FOCEXECS. These features, once activated, remain in effect until cleared or until leaving FOCUS. Some of these features are:

1. USE commands.
2. SET commands.
3. FILEDEFS for OFFLINE files, DECODE files, external files, etc.
4. JOIN commands.
5. DEFINE commands.
6. Selecting printer locations.
7. Setting values for global dialogue manager variables.
8. Creating HOLD and SAVE files.

A particularly useful command for viewing how dialogue manager statements and variables are resolved in a FOCEXEC is the &ECHO command. By placing -SET &ECHO = ALL; near the top of a FOCEXEC, each line of code is displayed on the screen as it is executed. In this way, you may observe where branching occurs, how values are assigned to dialogue manager variables, and what FOCUS commands are executed.

The first report is the Deal Inception report. The DEAL1 FOCEXEC shows the information relevant to each deal in the FOCUS file — including the issuer's name, issue size, closing date, the fee amounts, next due date, etc. The FOCEXEC is shown in figure 5-5. The output is in figure 5-6.

This FOCEXEC illustrates the use of the DECODE feature and EDIT feature in a DEFINE command. The TABLE request shows several formatting techniques to format the columns of the report.

The DECODE is used to convert the two digit codes for UNIT_CODE and FEETYPE into full names. Two types of the DECODE statements are shown:

1. UNAME/A10=DECODE UCODE (H1 'HOUSING 1' H2 'HOUS-
   ING 2'
   H3 'HOUSING 3' GM 'GEN MKT'
   HE 'HIGH EDUC' HC 'HEALTH CARE'
   ELSE ' ';

2. FCD/A20=DECODE FEETYPE (FEECODE ELSE ' ');

In the first method, each two-digit code is followed by its decoded value; each pair can be separated by a blank or comma; if UCODE is not one of the values listed, a value of ' ' (blanks) is given to the field UNAME. In the second method, the values of FEETYPE and its decoded values for the field FCD are not listed in the FOCEXEC, but are contained in a separate file such as the one shown in figure 5-7. This file is known as a "decode table."

Each pair appears on a separate line, and up to 40 decode pairs are possible. If the decoded value contains embedded blanks, then it must be enclosed in single quotes. To get around the limitation of 40 lines, more than one DECODE file can be used. For example,

FCD1/A20=DECODE FEETYPE (FEECODE1 ELSE ' ');
FCD2/A20=DECODE FEETYPE (FEECODE2 ELSE ' ');
FCD/A20= IF FCD1 NE ' ' THEN FCD1 ELSE FCD2;

A second file, FEECODE2, may contain the codes not included in file FEECODE1. In cases where many FOCEXECS reference the same DECODE list, it is easier to keep the list in a file. The file should have a FILEDEF, by assigning a DDNAME to the file name (eg. FEECODE DATA A):

```
-* PROGRAM DEAL1 FOCEXEC - DEAL INCEPTION REPORT
-*
-CMS FI FEECODE DISK FEECODE DATA A (RECFM FB LRECL 80

OFFLINE
SET ALL = ON
SET NODATA = ' '
SET MESSAGE = OFF
SET PAGE-NUM = OFF
-RUN

-DEFAULT  &OPT = 'V'
-SET &MSG = ' ';
-SET &PRO = 'DEAL1' ;
-RUN
-TOP
-CRTFORM
-"         <.W. PUBLIC FINANCE DEAL TRACKING SYSTEM - REPORTS
- <65 <.Y.D.&DATE  "
-"<65 <.Y.D.&TOD "
-" <.TURQ.  TYPE OF REPORT: DEAL INCEPTION REPORT  "
-"      OUTPUT OPTION: <.W.T.&OPT (P)RINT (V)IEW (E)XIT "
-" "
-"</2 "
-"</1 <.Y.D.&MSG <70 <.Y.D.&PRO"

-IF &OPT EQ 'P' GOTO TBLFILE ;
-IF &OPT EQ 'V' GOTO TBLFILE ;
-IF &OPT EQ 'E' GOTO DONE ;
-GOTO TOP

-TBLFILE
-CRTCLEAR

-RUN
-*
DEFINE FILE DEALS
NFEE/D10.2SN = NEXTFEE ;
FCD/A20= DECODE FTYPE (FEECODE ELSE ' ' );
UNAME/A10  = DECODE UCODE(H1 'HOUSING I' H2 'HOUSING II'
                    H3 'HOUSING 3' GM 'GEN MARKET'
                    HE 'HIGH EDUC' HC 'HEALTH CAR'
                    SL 'STUD LOAN' OB 'OB PRE 83 '
                    ML 'ML PRE 83' CL 'CL PRE 83 ' ELSE ' ');
ICODE/A10  = EDIT(ISSUER,'9999999999');
END
```

Figure 5-5    FOCEXEC for Deal Inception report.

```
-RUN
-IF &OPT NE 'V' GOTO PRINT1;
ONLINE
-RUN
-PRINT1
-*
TABLE FILE DEALS
HEADING
"PROG: &PRO   <98 REPORT DATE: <112 &DATE "
" <112 &TOD  "
"<1 PUBLIC FINANCE FEE TRACKING SYSTEM "
"<1 DEALS INCEPTION REPORT "
" "
PRINT ICODE   AS 'ISSUER' UNAME AS 'UNIT' IN +2
   SIZE     AS 'ISSUESIZE' IN +2
   COMPUTE X_CDATE/A8= IF CDATE GT 0 THEN
   EDIT(CDATE,'$$99')|'/'|
   EDIT(CDATE,'$$$$99')|'/'|EDIT(CDATE,'99') ELSE ' ' ;
   AS 'CLOSEDATE' IN +1
   FREQ   AS 'FEEFREQ'
   FCD    AS 'FEETYPE'    NFEE AS 'FEEAMT'
   COMPUTE X_NEXTDATE/A8= IF NEXTDATE GT 0 THEN
   EDIT(NEXTDATE,'$$99')|'/'|
   EDIT(NEXTDATE,'$$$$99')|'/'|EDIT(NEXTDATE,'99') ELSE ' ';
   AS 'DUEDATE' IN +1
   COMPUTE X_LASTRCVD/A8= IF LASTRCVD GT 0 THEN
   EDIT(LASTRCVD,'$$99')|'/'|
   EDIT(LASTRCVD,'$$$$99')|'/'|EDIT(LASTRCVD,'99') ELSE ' ' ;
   AS 'RECVDATE' IN +1
   COMPUTE X_DEALSUM/A8= IF DEALSUM GT 0 THEN
   EDIT(DEALSUM,'$$99')|'/'|
   EDIT(DEALSUM,'$$$$99')|'/'|EDIT(DEALSUM,'99') ELSE ' ' ;
   AS 'DEAL RCVD' IN +1

BY DEAL AS 'CODE'
END
-RUN

OFFLINE
-IF &OPT EQ 'P' GOTO MSG;
-RUN
-GOTO TOP
-MSG
-SET &MSG = '          THE REPORT HAS BEEN SENT TO PRINTER ';
-GOTO TOP
-DONE
```

**Figure 5-5** (continued) FOCEXEC for Deal Inception report.

```
SET ALL = OFF
SET NODATA = .
SET MESSAGE = ON
SET LINES = 57
-EXIT
```

**Figure 5-5** (continued) FOCEXEC for Deal Inception report.

```
-CMS FILEDEF FEECODE DISK FEECODE DATA A (RECFM FB
LRECL 80)
```

The EDIT command is used for two purposes in this DEFINE (COMPUTE):

1. A new field ICODE is assigned values given by the first ten characters of the field ISSUER; the report is to show the first ten characters of ISSUER instead of its full 27 characters — to save space.
2. Several date fields are created which show dates in M/D/Y format, instead of the Y/M/D formats of the fields in the FOCUS file. For example, the field X_CDATE is in M/D/Y format and is defined from the field CDATE as follows:

```
X_CDATE/A8 = EDIT (CDATE,'$$99$$)|'/'|
    EDIT (CDATE,'$$$$99)|'/'|
    EDIT (CDATE,'99$$$');
```

The EDIT command is used to "mask" out the month, day, year from the six character field CDATE; they are then concatenated to '/' to produce an eight-character value in M/D/Y format. The other date fields in the DEFINE use the same technique. FOCUS has no function to convert a YMD format into an MDY format. FOCUS has a number of features to handle fields with date formats — as described in the FOCUS 5.0 manual Chapter 4 Section 8. For example, fields with formats YMD, eg. CDATE/I6YMD, are displayed as YY/MM/DD.

In the TABLE request, the records are displayed using the PRINT command. The lines on the report are sorted by DEAL number. Spacing between columns is set up using positional notation (e.g., IN +2); New column headings are assigned for each verb object.

Another basic feature is the use of ONLINE/OFFLINE. At the start of the FOCEXEC, a -CRTFORM is used to prompt for the output option. If the operator selects "P," the report will be printed to the line printer (i.e., output device); if 'V' is selected, the report will be viewed online at the terminal. This is controlled by the use of ONLINE/OFFLINE.

At the start of the FOCEXEC, the command OFFLINE is found. The report obtained from the TABLE request will be sent offline unless the 'view' option is selected. In that case, the statement ONLINE is executed before the TABLE request, and the report is displayed online. Note the dialogue manager statement,

```
-IF &OPT NE 'V' GOTO PRINT1;
```

will cause the ONLINE command to be skipped if &OPT equals "P." After the report is shown online, the mode is reset to OFFLINE before returning to the label -TOP.

## Short Path Segments

The last important feature in this FOCEXEC is the command at the start

```
SET ALL=ON
```

This is to handle "short path" segments. Some deals may have no information on fees when the report is requested. In this case, there will be no FEETYPE segment for the deal. In order to be able to retrieve deal information from the parent segment (MAIN) when there is no child segment, the SET command for ALL=ON is required. The default setting in any FOCUS session is ALL=OFF, for which short path segments are not retrieved in a TABLE request. See the FOCUS 5.0 manual Chapter 2 Section 10.2, on handling missing segment instances. Notice in the report shown in figure 5-6, deal number 101 contains no fee information — only information on the deal. This record would not have been retrieved if the setting was ALL = OFF.

## Report 2

The second report from the menu is the AGED TRIAL BALANCE, which shows those deals which are late with their first fee payment.

```
PROG: DEAL1                                                                                              REPORT DATE:  09/30/87
                                                                                                                       22.16.07
PUBLIC FINANCE FEE TRACKING SYSTEM
DEALS INCEPTION REPORT

CODE  ISSUER        UNIT         ISSUESIZE   CLOSEDATE  FEEFREQ  FEETYPE             FEEAMT    DUEDATE   RECVDAT
----  ------        ----         ---------   ---------  -------  -------             ------    -------   -------
 50   IRVINE                   100,000,000   12/16/83      0     OTHER 2
 51   HAYWARD                   35,000,000   08/22/84     12     LIQUIDITY        10,787.67   05/30/87  04/17/8
 52   LOS ANGELE                21,000,000   10/24/84     12     LIQUIDITY                    05/30/87  04/29/8
 53   LOUISIANA-                38,672,000   12/09/83      0     ACCR ADJ
      LOUISIANA-                38,672,000   12/09/83      0     INVESTMENT
      LOUISIANA-                38,672,000   12/09/83      0     OTHER
      LOUISIANA-                38,672,000   12/09/83      0     REMARKETING
      LOUISIANA-                38,672,000   12/09/83      2     TENDER           71,043.75   07/01/87  01/22/8
 55   NEW MEXICO    HIGH EDUC   41,730,000   04/13/83      1     COMMITMENT                             04/14/8
      NEW MEXICO    HIGH EDUC   41,730,000   04/13/83      0     OTHER
      NEW MEXICO    HIGH EDUC   41,730,000   04/13/83      0     OTHER 2
 56   CALIFORNIA    HIGH EDUC  100,000,000   05/08/84      4     LETTER OF CREDIT                       01/02/8
      CALIFORNIA    HIGH EDUC  100,000,000   05/08/84      0     LETTER OF CR
      CALIFORNIA    HIGH EDUC  100,000,000   05/08/84      0     OTHER                                  12/17/8
      CALIFORNIA    HIGH EDUC  100,000,000   05/08/84      0     OTHER 2
 57   MAC           GEN MARKET 250,000,000   04/12/84      1     LETTER OF CREDIT                       04/12/8
 58   DETROIT       GEN MARKET  54,200,000   08/29/84      4     LETTER OF CREDIT 118,400.00  04/01/87  04/30/8
      DETROIT       GEN MARKET  54,200,000   08/29/84      0     OTHER
 59   ARLINGTON     GEN MARKET  22,300,000   09/27/84      4     LETTER OF CREDIT  47,958.35  06/01/87  03/03/8
 61   PUERTO RIC    GEN MARKET 100,000,000   10/18/84      0     COMMITMENT
      PUERTO RIC    GEN MARKET 100,000,000   10/18/84      0     COMMITMENT 2
      PUERTO RIC    GEN MARKET 100,000,000   10/18/84      4     LIQUIDITY                              02/25/8
      PUERTO RIC    GEN MARKET 100,000,000   10/18/84      0     OTHER
 62   TEXAS EAST    HIGH EDUC   60,000,000   09/12/85      1     COMMITMENT      129,375.00   09/01/87  09/01/8
```

**Figure 5-6   Deal Inception report.**

| | | | | | | | | |
|---|---|---|---|---|---|---|---|---|
| | TEXAS EAST | HIGH EDUC | | 60,000,000 | 09/12/85 | 0 | OTHER | | |
| | TEXAS EAST | HIGH EDUC | | 60,000,000 | 09/12/85 | 0 | OTHER 2 | | |
| 63 | SANTA CLAR | | | 13,000,000 | 01/14/85 | 12 | LIQUIDITY | 4,140.41 | 05/30/87 04/13/8 |
| 64 | ADAMS COUN | | | 7,500,000 | 02/14/85 | 12 | LIQUIDITY | 2,343.75 | 05/30/87 04/22/8 |
| 65 | ATLANTIC C | GEN MARKET | | 39,000,000 | 02/01/84 | 0 | ARRANGEMENT | | 05/01/8 |
| 66 | TAMPA ELEC | GEN MARKET | | 100,000,000 | 01/01/84 | 0 | ARRANGEMENT | | 05/01/8 |
| 67 | SOUTHERN C | GEN MARKET | | 100,000,000 | 02/09/84 | 0 | ARRANGEMENT | | 05/01/8 |
| 68 | KENTUCKY U | GEN MARKET | | 70,000,000 | 02/16/84 | 0 | ARRANGEMENT | | 05/01/8 |
| 69 | BEXAR | | | 30,000,000 | 07/01/80 | 12 | LETTER OF CREDIT | 9,970.02 | 05/15/87 04/15/8 |
| 71 | PUERTO RIC | | | 400,000,000 | 05/22/85 | 4 | COMMITMENT | 119,005.05 | 04/01/87 04/01/8 |
| | PUERTO RIC | | | 400,000,000 | 05/22/85 | 0 | OTHER | | |
| 73 | BREVARD | | | 146,450,000 | 02/01/81 | 0 | ACCR ADJ | | |
| | BREVARD | | | 146,450,000 | 02/01/81 | 2 | LETTER OF CREDIT | 628,087.50 | 08/01/87 02/02/8 |
| 74 | MISSISSIPP | | | 125,000,000 | 12/21/83 | 0 | ACCR ADJ | | |
| | MISSISSIPP | | | 125,000,000 | 12/21/83 | 2 | LETTER OF CREDIT | 36,292.05 | 06/01/87 12/01/8 |
| 76 | NYS DORM | HIGH EDUC | | 85,000,000 | 07/10/85 | 4 | COMMITMENT | | 11/13/8 |
| | NYS DORM | HIGH EDUC | | 85,000,000 | 07/10/85 | 0 | OTHER | | |
| 77 | SAN FRANCI | | | 30,000,000 | 06/03/85 | 12 | LIQUIDITY | 9,554.79 | 05/30/87 04/16/8 |
| 81 | DENTON-2 | | | 14,920,000 | 12/01/80 | 0 | ACCR ADJ | | |
| | DENTON-2 | | | 14,920,000 | 12/01/80 | 2 | COLLATERAL | 16,056.25 | 05/01/87 11/03/8 |
| | DENTON-2 | | | 14,920,000 | 12/01/80 | 2 | EVALUATOR | 11,141.25 | 05/01/87 11/03/8 |
| 82 | DENTON-1 | | | 24,655,000 | 11/01/82 | 2 | LETTER OF CREDIT | 94,140.00 | 06/01/87 12/01/8 |
| 83 | DENVER-HUT | | | 29,537,352 | 09/27/84 | 0 | ACCR ADJ | | |
| | DENVER-HUT | | | 29,537,352 | 09/27/84 | 2 | INVESTMENT | 22,112.81 | 03/01/87 10/22/8 |

**Figure 5-6  (continued) Deal Inception report.**

```
A  AGENT
C  COMMITMENT
E  EVALUATOR
H  HEDGE
L  LIQUIDITY
M  MANAGEMENT
O  OTHER
P  PLACEMENT
R  RISK
S  'SWAP FEE'
T  TENDER
U  UNDERWRITING
AA 'ACCR ADJ '
AD ADVISORY
AR ARRANGEMENT
A2 'AGENT 2'
A7 'ACCR ADJ 2 '
A8 'ADVISORY 2'
A9 'ARRNGMNT 2'
CE CEILING
CL CLEARANCE
CO COLLATERAL
C1 'CEILING 2'
C2 'COMMITMENT 2'
C8 'COLLATERAL 2'
C9 'CLEARANCE 2'
DR DRAWDOWN
D9 'DRAWDOWN 2'
EX 'EXP   RESERVE'
E2 'EVALUATOR 2'
E9 'EXP RESRVE 2'
IN INTEREST
IV INVESTMENT
I9 'INTEREST 2'
I8 'INVESTMENT 2'
LE 'LETTER OF CREDIT'
LG LEGAL
LI 'LINE OF CREDIT'
L2 'LIQUIDITY 2'
L7 'LEGAL 2'
L8 'LINE OF CR 2'
L9 'LETTER OF CR'
M2 'MANAGEMENT 2'
OP 'OPBD RESERVE'
O2 'OTHER 2'
O9 'OPBD RSRVE 2'
PR PROFIT
```

**Figure 5-7    Decode table in file FEECODE DATA.**

We assume that the first fee has not been received if the field (with alias) LASTRCVD is 0. (If a fee has been received, then LASTRCVD will contain the date received.) This report may be run on any day to show the late fees. The FOCEXEC DEAL2 is shown in figure 5-8, and the report in figure 5-9.

For fees that are late, the report shows the deal, the amount of the fee and whether the fee is 0–30 days late, 30–60 days late, 60–90 days late, or over 90 days late. Several new fields need to be defined which can be used to create the columns on the report. This is a useful technique for grouping records into categories based on the value of some field. First, the number of days late is defined as:

```
DDAYS/I6=YMD(CDATE, &YMD);
```

where, CDATE is the closing date of the deal; &YMD is a system variable containing today's date.

The date function YMD calculates the duration between two dates if the dates are stored in year-month-day format. (You should refer to the FOCUS 5.0 manual Chapter 2 Section 6.4.2 for a treatment of date expressions and fields with date format.)

The field DTYPE is defined to indicate whether a fee is less than 30 days late (DTYPE=1), 30–60 days late (DTYPE=2), 60– 90 days (DTYPE=3), over 90 days (DTYPE=5). If the fee is less than 30 days late, the field DUE30 is set equal to the fee amount. (NEXTFEE contains the value of the fee amount due.) Note, if DTYPE is not equal to 1, the value of DUE30 will be 0. Similarly, the fields DUE60, DUE90, and DUE999 are defined.

As in report 1, the DECODE is used to get the full name for the unit and feetype. ONLINE/OFFLINE is used in a similar way to view the report online or print it offline.

In each report page, some of the column headings occupy two lines. This is done by separating the text of the column heading with commas.

For example,

```
PRINT DUE30 AS '0 TO,30 DAYS'
      DUE60 AS '30 TO, 60 DAYS'
```

```
-* PROGRAM DEAL2 FOCEXEC - AGED TRIAL BALANCE
-CMS FI FEECODE DISK FEECODE DATA A (RECFM FB LRECL 80

OFFLINE
SET MESSAGE = OFF
SET PAGE-NUM = OFF

-RUN
-DEFAULT  &OPT = 'V'
-SET &MSG = ' ';
-SET &PRO = 'DEAL2' ;
-SET &TODAY = '        ';
-RUN

-TOP
-CRTFORM
-"        <.W. PUBLIC FINANCE DEALS TRACKING SYSTEM - REPORTS
-  <65 <.Y.D.&DATE "
-"<65 <.Y.D.&TOD "
-" <.TURQ. TYPE OF REPORT: AGED TRIAL BALANCE "
-"      OUTPUT OPTION: <.W.T.&OPT (P)RINT (V)IEW (E)XIT "
-" "
-" "
-"</2 "
-"</1 <.Y.D.&MSG <70 <.Y.D.&PRO"

-IF &OPT EQ 'E' GOTO DONE ;
-IF &OPT EQ 'P' GOTO TBLFILE ;
-IF &OPT EQ 'V' GOTO TBLFILE ;
-GOTO TOP

-TBLFILE
-CRTCLEAR

-RUN
-*
DEFINE FILE DEALS
DDAYS/I6= YMD(CDATE,&YMD) ;
DTYPE/I1 = IF DDAYS LE 30 THEN  1  ELSE
           IF DDAYS LE 60 THEN  2  ELSE
           IF DDAYS LE 90 THEN  3  ELSE 5 ;
NEXTFEE/I8N = NEXTFEE ;
DUE30/I8N  = IF DTYPE EQ 1 THEN NEXTFEE ELSE 0;
DUE60/I8N  = IF DTYPE EQ 2 THEN NEXTFEE ELSE 0;
DUE90/I8N  = IF DTYPE EQ 3 THEN NEXTFEE ELSE 0;
DUE999/I8N = IF DTYPE EQ 5 THEN NEXTFEE ELSE 0;
UNAME/A10  = DECODE UCODE(H1 'HOUSING I' H2 'HOUSING II'
```

Figure 5-8   FOCEXEC for Aged Trial Balance.

```
                    H3 'HOUSING 3'  GM 'GEN MARKET'
                    HE 'HIGH EDUC'  HC 'HEALTH CAR'
                    SL 'STUD LOAN'  OB 'OB PRE 83 '
                    ML 'ML PRE 83'  CL 'CL PRE 83 ' ELSE ' ');
ICODE/A10    = EDIT(ISSUER,'9999999999');
FCD/A20= DECODE FTYPE (FEECODE ELSE ' ' );
FCODE/A5 = EDIT(FCD,'99999');
END
-RUN

-IF &OPT NE 'V' GOTO PRINT1;
ONLINE
-RUN
-PRINT1
-*
TABLE FILE DEALS
HEADING
"PROG: &PRO   <98 REPORT DATE: <112 &DATE "
" <112 &TOD    "
"<1 PUBLIC FINANCE DEALS TRACKING SYSTEM "
"<1 AGED TRIAL BALANCE "
" "
PRINT ICODE AS 'ISSUER' UCODE AS 'UNIT' IN +1 PNAME AS 'PRODUCT'
IN +1
     SIZE    AS 'ISSUESIZE' IN +1 CDATE AS 'CLOSEDATE' IN +1
     FCODE AS 'TYPE' NEXTFEE AS 'FEEAMT' NEXTDATE AS 'DUEDATE' IN +1
     DUE30 AS '  0 TO,30 DAYS' IN +1 DUE60 AS '31 TO,60 DAYS' IN +1
     DUE90 AS '61 TO,90 DAYS' IN +1
BY DEAL AS 'DEAL'
IF LASTRCVD EQ 0

FOOTING
"<67 UNIT TOTAL <TOT.NEXTFEE <100 <TOT.DUE30 <113 <TOT.DUE60
 <122 <TOT.DUE90 "
END
-RUN

OFFLINE
-IF &OPT EQ 'P' GOTO MSG;
-RUN
-GOTO TOP
-MSG
-SET &MSG = '         THE REPORT HAS BEEN SENT TO PRINTER ';
-GOTO TOP
-DONE
SET MESSAGE = ON
-EXIT
```

**Figure 5-8**  (continued) FOCEXEC for Aged Trial Balance.

```
PROG: DEAL2                                                                    REPORT DATE:  10/01/85
PUBLIC FINANCE DEALS TRACKING SYSTEM                                                         22.42.06
AGED TRIAL BALANCE

                                                                              0 TO      31 TO
DEAL  ISSUER        UNIT  PRODUCT     ISSUESIZE  CLOSEDATE  TYPE   FEEAMT  DUEDATE    30 DAYS   60 DAYS
----  ------        ----  -------     ---------  ---------  ----   ------  -------    -------   -------
  62  TEXAS EAST    HE    LIQUIDITY   60,000,000  85/09/12  COMMI $ 129,375 87/09/01 $ 129,375 $      0
 113  TEXAS WEST    HE    LIQUIDITY   45,000,000  85/09/12  COMMI    97,031 87/09/01    97,031        0
 128  KANSAS        HO    LIQUIDITY   11,500,000  85/09/19  LIQUI    22,522 87/07/15    22,522        0
 129  ARKANSAS-1    HO    RATE RISK  175,000,000  85/08/21  TENDE   465,935 87/08/01         0  465,935
 131  FLORIDA-PA    HO    LIQUIDITY   47,300,000  85/08/30  LIQUI    10,213 87/05/30         0   10,213
 277  MICHIGAN      HE    LIQUIDITY   25,000,000             COMMI   89,062 86/12/14    89,062        0
 278  HARBOR COV    HO    RATE RISK    7,600,000  85/10/01  LIQUI     7,125 87/04/01     7,125        0
 287  NEW JERSEY    GM    RATE RISK    4,100,000  85/09/06  REVAL    33,600 87/05/01    33,600        0
      NEW JERSEY    GM    RATE RISK    4,100,000  85/09/06  REVAL    19,465 87/05/31    19,465        0
 364  SHEARSON H    HO    RATE RISK               85/08/16  HEDGE   838,500                  0  838,500
      SHEARSON H    HO    RATE RISK               85/08/16  REVAL   211,782 87/05/01         0  211,782
      SHEARSON H    HO    RATE RISK               85/08/16  REVAL   195,643                  0  195,643
 365  SHEARSON H    HO    RATE RISK               85/08/16  HEDGE 3,433,280                  0 3,433,280
      SHEARSON H    HO    RATE RISK               85/08/16  REVAL   423,565                  0   423,565
      SHEARSON H    HO    RATE RISK               85/08/16  REVAL   391,287 87/02/31         0   391,287

                                                       UNIT TOTAL 4,619,729            398,180 5,017,965
```

**Figure 5-9   Aged Trial Balance report.**

PAGE 2    REPORT DATE: 10/01/85
PUBLIC FINANCE DEALS TRACKING SYSTEM              22.42.06
AGED TRIAL BALANCE

| DEAL | ISSUER | UNIT | PRODUCT | ISSUESIZE | CLOSEDATE | TYPE | FEEAMT | DUEDATE | 0 TO 30 DAYS | 31 TO 60 DAYS |
|---|---|---|---|---|---|---|---|---|---|---|
| 62 | TEXAS EAST | HE | AGENT | 60,000,000 | 85/09/12 | COMMI $ | 629,375 | 87/09/01 $ | 629,375 $ | 0 |
| 113 | TEXAS WEST | HE | AGENT | 45,000,000 | 85/09/12 | COMMI | 97,031 | 87/09/01 | 97,031 | 0 |
| 128 | KANSAS | HO | AGENT | 11,500,000 | 85/09/19 | LIQUI | 22,522 | 87/07/15 | 22,522 | 0 |
| 129 | ARKANSAS-1 | HO | AGENT | 175,000,000 | 85/08/21 | TENDE | 465,935 | 87/08/01 | 0 | 465,935 |
| 131 | FLORIDA-PA | HO | LEGAL | 47,300,000 | 85/08/30 | LIQUI | 10,213 | 87/05/30 | 0 | 10,213 |
| 277 | MICHIGAN | HE | LEGAL | 25,000,000 | | COMMI | 89,062 | 86/12/14 | 89,062 | 0 |
| 278 | HARBOR COV | HO | LEGAL | 7,600,000 | 85/10/01 | LIQUI | 7,125 | 87/04/01 | 7,125 | 0 |
| 287 | NEW JERSEY | GM | AGENT | 4,100,000 | 85/09/06 | REVAL | 33,600 | 87/05/01 | 33,600 | 0 |
| | NEW JERSEY | GM | AGENT | 4,100,000 | 85/09/06 | REVAL | 19,465 | 87/05/31 | 19,465 | 0 |
| 364 | SHEARSON H | HO | AGENT | | 85/08/16 | HEDGE | 838,500 | | 0 | 838,500 |
| | SHEARSON H | HO | AGENT | | 85/08/16 | REVAL | 211,782 | 87/05/01 | 0 | 211,782 |
| | SHEARSON H | HO | AGENT | | 85/08/16 | REVAL | 695,643 | | 0 | 695,643 |
| 365 | SHEARSON H | HO | AGENT | | 85/08/16 | HEDGE | 3,433,280 | | 0 | 3,433,280 |
| | SHEARSON H | HO | AGENT | | 85/08/16 | REVAL | 423,565 | | 0 | 423,565 |
| | SHEARSON H | HO | AGENT | | 85/08/16 | REVAL | 391,287 | 87/02/31 | 0 | 391,287 |
| | | | | | UNIT TOTAL | | 5,619,729 | | 898,180 | 5,517,965 |

**Figure 5-9 (continued) Aged Trial Balance report.**

The text '0 TO' is placed over the text '30 DAYS' as a column heading. If no column heading is specified using AS, the heading becomes the name of the field.

This FOCEXEC also shows the use of direct operations on fields in the footing of the report. The total of each column is directly computed and placed in the footing of each page. TOT.DUE30 contains the total of all the fees less than 30 days late. If the report is more than one page, then this total will be placed in the footing of every page. (Instead of using this technique to show column-totals, the command ON TABLE COLUMN-TOTAL could have been placed in the TABLE request to give a column-total on the last line of the report.)

The FOCUS DEFINE command provides the flexibilty to create new fields which may be used in any number of ways to format a report. As another example, we may sort the fees in the DEALS file according to the number of days late, using the field DTYPE as a sort field:

```
TABLE FILE DEALS
PRINT FCODE AS 'TYPE' NEXTFEE AS 'AMOUNT' CDATE AS
'CLOSEDATE'
BY DTYPE NOPRINT
BY DEAL
IF LASTRCVD EQ 0
END
```

## Report 3

This report is a monthly report which is run at the end of each month after all fee payments have been received. It shows the income accrued or taken as cash for each deal. The focexec DEALS is shown in figure 5-10, and the report in figure 5-11.

The FOCEXEC prompts for the month and the year using a -CRTFORM. There is no need to declare the dialogue manager variables as integer format. In a SET statement, the variables may still be used in arithmetic expressions. From these variables &MON and &YY, another dialogue manager variable, &YM, is formed which contains the year and month together. The SET statement is:

```
-SET &YM = 100 * &YY + &MON ;
```

```
-* PROGRAM DEAL3 FOCEXEC - MONTHLY ACCRUALS AND AMORTIZATIONS-
REPORT
-*
-CMS FI OFFLINE DISK DEAL3     LISTING A (RECFM UA LRECL 132
-CMS FI FEECODE DISK FEECODE DATA A (RECFM FB LRECL 80
-CMS FI UCODE   DISK UCODE   DATA A (RECFM FB LRECL 80

OFFLINE
SET MESSAGE = OFF
SET PAGE-NUM = OFF

-RUN
-DEFAULT  &OPT = 'V'
-SET &MSG = ' ';
-SET &MON = '  ';
-SET &PRO = 'DEAL3';
-RUN

-TOP
-CRTFORM
-"    <.W. PUBLIC FINANCE DEALS
- <65 <.Y.D.&DATE "
-"<65 <.Y.D.&TOD "
-"  <.TURQ.  MONTHLY ACCRUALS AND AMORTIZATIONS "
-"   MONTH(MM)    : <.W.T.&MON "
-"   REPORT OPTION: <.W.T.&OPT (P)RINT (V)IEW (E)XIT "
-" "
-"</2 "
-"</1 <.Y.D.&MSG <70 <.Y.D.&PRO"

-IF &OPT EQ 'P' GOTO TBLFILE ;
-IF &OPT EQ 'V' GOTO TBLFILE ;
-IF &OPT EQ 'E' GOTO DONE ;
-GOTO TOP

-TBLFILE
-SET &MSG = '*** ENTER MONTH *** ';
-IF &MON EQ '  ' GOTO TOP ;
-SET &MSG = ' ';
-SET &MON1 = DECODE &MON ('1' 'JAN'
-                         '2' 'FEB'
-                         '3' 'MAR'
-                         '4' 'APR'
-                         '5' 'MAY'
-                         '6' 'JUN'
-                         '7' 'JUL'
-                         '8' 'AUG'
```

Figure 5-10   FOCEXEC for Monthly Accruals and Amortizations report.

```
                          '9'  'SEP'
                          '10' 'OCT'
                          '11' 'NOV'
                          '12' 'DEC'  )  ;

-CRTCLEAR
-RUN

DEFINE FILE DEALS
RECDT/A6  = EDIT(LASTRCVD) ;
RECDT1/A2 = EDIT(RECDT,'$$99');
RECMO/I2  = EDIT (RECDT1) ;
AMOUNTX/D10.2 = IF ACC_CODE EQ 'AC' THEN NEXTFEE * FREQ/12 ELSE
                IF ACC_CODE EQ 'AT' THEN NEXTFEE * FREQ/12 ELSE
                IF RECMO EQ &MON THEN LASTFEE ELSE 0      ;
AMOUNT/D10.2 = IF EXPDATE GE &YMD THEN AMOUNTX ELSE 0;
UNAME/A10    = DECODE UCODE(UCODE ELSE ' ');
ICODE/A15    = EDIT(ISSUER,'999999999999999');
FCD/A20= DECODE FTYPE (FEECODE ELSE ' ' );
END
-RUN

-IF &OPT NE 'V' GOTO PRINT1;
ONLINE
-RUN
-PRINT1
-*
TABLE FILE DEALS
HEADING
"PROG: &PRO    <98 REPORT DATE: <112 &DATE "
"  <112 &TOD    "
"<1 PUBLIC FINANCE DEALS "
"<1 MONTHLY ACCRUALS AND AMORTIZATIONS: &MON1 "
" "
PRINT ICODE   AS 'ISSUER' UCODE AS 'UNIT' IN +1 PNAME AS 'PRODUCT'
IN +1
      SIZE    AS 'ISSUESIZE' IN +1
      FCD     AS 'TYPE' FREQ AS 'TIMES,PER YR' ACC_CODE AS 'ACCNT,CODE'
      LASTRCVD AS 'DATE PAID' AMOUNT AS 'POSTED'

BY ACC_CODE NOPRINT BY DEAL AS 'CODE'
ON ACC_CODE SUBTOTAL POST AS ''
ON ACC_CODE PAGE-BREAK
END
-RUN
```

**Figure 5-10   (continued) FOCEXEC for Monthly Accruals and Amortizations report.**

```
OFFLINE
-IF &OPT EQ 'P' GOTO MSG;
-RUN
-GOTO TOP
-MSG
-SET &MSG = '        THE REPORT HAS BEEN SENT TO PRINTER ';
-GOTO TOP
-DONE
OFFLINE CLOSE
SET MESSAGE = ON
SET LINES = 57
-EXIT
```

**Figure 5-10** (continued) FOCEXEC for Monthly Accruals and Amortizations report.

For example, for &YY=86, &MON=4.

```
&YM = 100*86 + 4
&YM = 8604
```

In the DEFINE, the field AMOUNTX calculates the monthly income taken on each fee. If the fee is accrued (i.e., ACC_CODE is 'AC'), then the income is calculated as

```
NEXTFEE*FREQ/12
```

where FREQ gives how many times per year the fee is paid. If the fee is a cash fee, then the income is the last fee amount received (if received in the present month). For cash fees, if no fee was received in the present month, then no income is taken. The calculation is shown below:

```
AMOUNTX/D12.2=IF ACC_CODE EQ 'AC' THEN
NEXTFEE*FREQ/12 ELSE IF RECMO EQ &YM THEN LASTFEE
ELSE 0;
```

The field RECMO has been defined as the year-month in which the last payment was received — the EDIT is used to mask the year-month from the field LASTRCVD. Notice that the line

```
RECMO/I2 = EDIT (RECDT1) ;
```

```
PROG: DEAL3                                                                                              REPORT DATE: 10/01/87
                                                                                                                      21.03.46
PUBLIC FINANCE DEALS
MONTHLY ACCRUALS AND AMORTIZATIONS:

                                                                              TIMES    ACCNT
CODE  ISSUER             UNIT  PRODUCT      ISSUESIZE    TYPE                 PER YR   CODE   DATE PAID
----  ------             ----  -------      ---------    ----                 ------   -----  ---------
   1  BROWARD             GM                550,000,000  AGENT                   4      AC    86/08/08    20
      BROWARD             GM   CREDIT       550,000,000  COMMITMENT              4      AC    86/11/01    28
  22  BALTIMORE           HO   RATE RISK     50,000,000  LETTER OF CREDIT        2      AC    87/01/02    66
  23  MICHIGAN-HUTTON     HO   RATE RISK    125,000,000  TENDER                  2      AC    87/01/22    12
  25  BENTON              HO   RATE RISK     30,815,000  LETTER OF CREDIT        2      AC    86/11/03     5
  26  LITTLE ROCK, CI     HO   RATE RISK     30,815,000  COMMITMENT              2      AC    86/12/01     3
      LITTLE ROCK, CI     HO   RATE RISK     30,815,000  EVALUATOR               2      AC    86/12/01    96
  35  MISSISSIPPI-1-H     HO   RATE RISK    200,000,000  TENDER                  2      AC    87/03/18    83
  36  NEBRASKA-2-HUTT     HO   RATE RISK    188,000,000  TENDER                  2      AC    87/02/18    95
  40  VIRGINIA-2-HUTT     HO   RATE RISK    201,999,195  TENDER                  2      AC    87/03/09    23
  44  FLORIDA I-HUTTO     HO   RATE RISK     65,460,000  TENDER                  2      AC    86/12/16    79
  45  VIRGINIA-1-HUTT     HO   RATE RISK    160,000,252  TENDER                  2      AC    87/03/09    15
  47  BARTON              HO   RATE RISK     23,205,000  LETTER OF CREDIT        2      AC    87/01/02    17
  49  NEBRASKA-1-HUTT     HO   RATE RISK     58,715,000  TENDER                  2      AC    87/01/14    11
  53  LOUISIANA-2-HUT     HO   RATE RISK     38,672,000  TENDER                  2      AC    87/01/22   104
  73  BREVARD             HO   RATE RISK    146,450,000  LETTER OF CREDIT        2      AC    87/02/02     6
  74  MISSISSIPPI         HO   CREDIT       125,000,000  LETTER OF CREDIT        2      AC    86/12/01     2
  81  DENTON-2            HO   RATE RISK     14,920,000  COLLATERAL              2      AC    86/11/03     1
      DENTON-2            HO   RATE RISK     14,920,000  EVALUATOR               2      AC    86/11/03    15
  82  DENTON-1            HO   RATE RISK     24,655,000  LETTER OF CREDIT        2      AC    86/12/01    11
  83  DENVER-HUTTON       HO   RATE RISK     29,537,352  TENDER                  2      AC    87/03/09    13
  85  DIST OF COLUMBI     HO   RATE RISK     69,999,946  TENDER                  2      AC    86/12/16    14
  86  DIST OF COLUMBI     HO   RATE RISK     29,999,940  TENDER                  2      AC    87/01/22
```

**Figure 5-11  Monthly Accruals and Amortizations report.**

| | | | | | | | |
|---|---|---|---|---|---|---|---|
| 87 | DUVAL-HUTTON | HO | RATE RISK | 20,099,982 | TENDER | 2 | AC | 87/03/09 | 10 |
| 89 | FLORIDA-2-HUTTO | HO | RATE RISK | 134,540,000 | TENDER | 2 | AC | 87/01/22 | 55 |
| 93 | HUTCHINSON | HO | RATE RISK | 18,845,000 | LETTER OF CREDIT | 2 | AC | 87/01/02 | 12 |
| 99 | JOHNSON | HO | RATE RISK | 64,715,000 | LETTER OF CREDIT | 2 | AC | 87/01/02 | 38 |
| 101 | LOUISIANA-1 | HO | RATE RISK | 200,000,000 | LETTER OF CREDIT | 2 | AC | 87/04/03 | 135 |
| 102 | MARYLAND CDA | HO | RATE RISK | 53,070,000 | TENDER | 2 | AC | 86/11/17 | 85 |
| 109 | OKLAHOM-2 | HO | RATE RISK | 63,900,000 | COLLATERAL | 2 | AC | 86/11/03 | 11 |
| | OKLAHOM-2 | HO | RATE RISK | 63,900,000 | EVALUATOR | 2 | AC | 86/11/03 | 7 |
| 114 | ORANGE COUNTY | HO | RATE RISK | 126,770,000 | LETTER OF CREDIT | 2 | AC | 87/02/02 | 84 |
| 115 | PANHANDLE | HO | RATE RISK | 17,005,000 | COLLATERAL | 2 | AC | 87/02/02 | |
| | PANHANDLE | HO | RATE RISK | 17,005,000 | EVALUATOR | 2 | AC | 87/02/02 | |
| 117 | POMONA | HO | RATE RISK | 118,500,000 | LETTER OF CREDIT | 2 | AC | 86/10/01 | 37 |
| 119 | PUEBLO | HO | RATE RISK | 105,000,000 | LETTER OF CREDIT | 2 | AC | 86/12/01 | 65 |
| 120 | PULASKI | HO | RATE RISK | 24,800,000 | LETTER OF CREDIT | 2 | AC | 86/12/01 | 16 |
| 121 | SHAWNEE | HO | RATE RISK | 25,000,000 | LETTER OF CREDIT | 2 | AC | 87/01/02 | 16 |
| 122 | SONYMA | HO | RATE RISK | 104,750,000 | LETTER OF CREDIT | 2 | AC | 86/11/03 | 36 |
| 123 | ST. TAMMANY | HO | RATE RISK | 20,915,000 | COLLATERAL | 2 | AC | 86/11/03 | 3 |
| | ST. TAMMANY | HO | RATE RISK | 20,915,000 | EVALUATOR | 2 | AC | 86/11/03 | 2 |
| 124 | TOM GREEN | HO | RATE RISK | 23,465,000 | LETTER OF CREDIT | 2 | AC | 86/12/01 | 14 |
| 126 | WILLIAMSON | HO | RATE RISK | 24,595,000 | LETTER OF CREDIT | 2 | AC | 86/12/01 | 15 |
| 129 | ARKANSAS-1 | HO | RATE RISK | 175,000,000 | TENDER | 2 | AC | 87/02/03 | 77 |

**Figure 5-11** (continued) Monthly Accruals and Amortizations report.

converts the alphanumeric format to an integer format.

Another calculation is also needed in case the fee payments have expired (EXPDATE is the expiration date):

```
AMOUNT/D12.2=IF EXPDATE GE &YMD THEN AMOUNTX ELSE 0;
```

Since PRINT is used, the TABLE request will list the income taken for every fee and every deal in the system. If the income is zero (e.g., for 'CASH' fees whose fee is received in a different month), then it will also be shown on the report.

The report is sorted by ACC_CODE; page-breaks and subtotals are obtained on ACC_CODE. Note that only the field AMOUNT is subtotaled by using:

```
ON ACC_CODE SUBTOTAL AMOUNT
```

instead of,

```
ON ACC_CODE SUBTOTAL
```

## Report 4

Some reports have more than one part to them and require several TABLE requests run consecutively. FOCUS can easily display or save in a file the output of several TABLE requests. The following report in figure 5-12 has a summary section on the first page followed by a detailed section on the next pages. Since the summary appears only on the first page, using a single TABLE request (with HEADING) will not do.

We will demonstrate two features of FOCUS in this example:

1. How to send more than one report to the same OFFLINE file (or different OFFLINE files).
2. How to format a report using no verbs in the TABLE request.

The command OFFLINE, when placed in a FOCEXEC, tells FOCUS to send any reports created to the offline device (the local printer). However, the reports can be sent to a file, instead, if OFFLINE is assigned using a FILEDEF -

SEPT 1987

FEES SCHEDULE SHOULD BE BROKEN DOWN AS FOLLOWS:

```
HIGHER EDUCATION FEES :        765,981.00
HEALTH CARE FEES      :        650,750.00
GENERAL MARKETS FEES  :        271,257.13
MASTER LENDER         :      1,740,520.00
COLLAT LOAN TO LENDER :        760,750.00
OPTION BONDS          :        111,150.00
                             ---------------
                             3,941,177.00
```

```
                              PUBLIC FINANCE DEALS
                                   SEPT 1987

UNIT: GENERAL MARKETS

                        ISSUE   FEE        ACCOUNTING      AMOUNT
DEAL ISSUER             SIZE    TYPE       CODE
RECEIVED
----  ------            -----   ----       ----------     --------
   1  BROWARD        550,000,000 COMMITMENT     AC        $   20,319.63
  51  NEW ORLEANS U. 250 000,000 COMMITMENT     AC        $   40,000.00
 314  WASHINGTON GO  607,200,000 TENDER 2       AC            210,937.50

TOTAL
                                                          $  271,257.13
```

Figure 5-12  Management report — showing summary and detail.


```
-CMS FILEDEF OFFLINE DISK DEALS LISTING A (RECFM U
LRECL 133
OFFLINE

TABLE FILE DEALS
 . . . .
 . . . .
END
```

The report will not be displayed on the screen, but sent to the offline file DEALS LISTING A. If other TABLE requests are in the same FOCEXEC, their output will also be sent to the same file. If you need to send the reports to separate files, FOCUS allows you to issue OFFLINE CLOSE, which closes any current offline file and allows you to FILEDEF a new one. For example,

```
-CMS FILEDEF OFFLINE DISK DEALS1 LISTING A
OFFLINE
TABLE FILE DEALS
....
....
END

OFFLINE CLOSE
-CMS FILEDEF OFFLINE DISK DEALS2 LISITNG A
TABLE FILE DEALS
....
....
END
```

The first report gets sent to DEALS1 LISTING A, and the second report to DEALS2 LISTING A.

In DEAL5 FOCEXEC (figure 5-13), we use only one OFFLINE file. The first TABLE request totals the income amount for each unit code, and displays a summary for the month. A TABLE request with HEADING only (and no verb) is demonstrated. New fields are defined for each value of UNITCODE. Then, the direct operation (TOT.) can total the amount and display them in the HEADING as shown.

The second part of the report contains the amount of income for each unit code — with details of the fees. In order to order the pages of this report, a FOCUS "trick" is shown. A field USORT has been defined which specifies the order. H1 is first, H2 second, etc. In the TABLE request, this field is the major sort field. A PAGE-BREAK is issued for each value of USORT. On each page, the report lines are sorted by ACCODE, then DEAL number, then FCD. Note, PRINT could have been the verb instead of SUM, since every fee in the file is shown.

## Programming Style: Reusing FOCUS Techniques

While there are many kinds of reports which can be developed from this FOCUS file, you can see that the FOCEXECS are very similar in

```
-* PROGRAM DEAL5 FOCEXEC - PUBLIC FINANCE MANAGEMENT SUMMARY
REPORT.
-*
-CMS FILEDEF OFFLINE CLEAR
-CMS FILEDEF OFFLINE DISK DEALS LISTING A (RECFM UA LRECL 133

-CMS FI FEECODE DISK FEECODE DATA A (RECFM FB LRECL 80
-CMS FI UCODE    DISK UCODE   DATA A (RECFM FB LRECL 80

OFFLINE
SET MESSAGE = OFF
SET PAGE-NUM = OFF
-RUN
-DEFAULT   &OPT = 'V'
-SET &MON = '  ';
-SET &MSG = '  ';
-SET &PRO = 'DEAL5' ;

-SET &YY  = EDIT(&YMD,'99');
-SET &YY1 = '19']&YY ;
-RUN

-TOP
-CRTFORM
-"    <.W. PUBLIC FINANCE DEALS - REPORTS
- <65 <.Y.D.&DATE "
-"<65 <.Y.D.&TOD "
-" <.TURQ. TYPE OF REPORT: MONTHLY FEES BREAKDOWN - MGMT SUMMARY "
-" "
-"   MONTH(MM)     : <.W.T.&MON "
-"   OUTPUT OPTION: <.W.T.&OPT (P)RINT (V)IEW (E)XIT "
-" "
-"</2 "
-"</1 <.Y.D.&MSG <70 <.Y.D.&PRO"

-IF &OPT EQ 'P' GOTO TBLFILE ;
-IF &OPT EQ 'V' GOTO TBLFILE ;
-IF &OPT EQ 'E' GOTO DONE ;
-GOTO TOP

-TBLFILE
-CRTCLEAR
-SET &YM = 100 * &YY + &MON ;
-SET &MON1 = DECODE &MON ('1' 'JAN'
-                         '2' 'FEB'
-                         '3' 'MAR'
-                         '4' 'APR'
```

Figure 5-13   FOCEXEC for Management Summary report.

**148** The Database Experts' Guide to FOCUS

```
      -                    '5'  'MAY'
      -                    '6'  'JUNE'
      -                    '7'  'JULY'
      -                    '8'  'AUG'
      -                    '9'  'SEP'
      -                    '10' 'OCT'
      -                    '11' 'NOV'
      -                    '12' 'DEC'  ) ;

-RUN
-*
DEFINE FILE DEALS
REPMON/I2MT WITH DEAL = &MON ;
RECDT/A6      = EDIT(LASTRCVD);
RECDT1/A4     = EDIT(RECDT,'9999');
RECMO/I4      = EDIT(RECDT1);
POST/D10.2    = IF ACC_CODE EQ 'AC' THEN NEXTFEE * FREQ/12 ELSE
                IF ACC_CODE EQ 'AT' THEN NEXTFEE * FREQ/12 ELSE
IF RECMO EQ &YM   THEN LASTFEE ELSE 0       ;
AMOUNT/D12.2N = POST ;
AMTAT/D12.2N = IF ACC_CODE EQ 'AT' THEN AMOUNT ELSE 0;
AMTAC/D12.2N = IF ACC_CODE EQ 'AC' THEN AMOUNT ELSE 0;
H1/D12.2N= IF UCODE EQ 'H1' THEN AMOUNT ELSE 0 ;
H2/D12.2N= IF UCODE EQ 'H2' THEN AMOUNT ELSE 0 ;
H3/D12.2N= IF UCODE EQ 'H3' THEN AMOUNT ELSE 0 ;
HE/D12.2N= IF UCODE EQ 'HE' THEN AMOUNT ELSE 0 ;
HC/D12.2N= IF UCODE EQ 'HC' THEN AMOUNT ELSE 0 ;
GM/D12.2N= IF UCODE EQ 'GM' THEN AMOUNT ELSE 0 ;
ML/D12.2N= IF UCODE EQ 'ML' THEN AMOUNT ELSE 0 ;
CL/D12.2N= IF UCODE EQ 'CL' THEN AMOUNT ELSE 0 ;
OB/D12.2N= IF UCODE EQ 'OB' THEN AMOUNT ELSE 0 ;
UNAME/A30 = DECODE UCODE (UCODE  ELSE ' ' );
ICODE/A25 = EDIT(ISSUER,'9999999999999999999999999');
USORT/I2  = DECODE UCODE(H1 1           H2 2
                         H3 3           GM 6
                         HE 5           HC 4
                         SL 7           OB 8
                         ML 9           CL 10
                         ELSE 11) ;
FCD/A20 = DECODE FTYPE (FEECODE ELSE ' ' );
END
-RUN

-IF &OPT NE 'V' GOTO PRINT1;
ONLINE
-RUN
-PRINT1
```

Figure 5-13    (continued) FOCEXEC for Management Summary report.

```
TABLE FILE DEALS
HEADING
"PROG: &PRO    <98 REPORT DATE: <112 &DATE "
" <112 &TOD   "
"<40 PUBLIC FINANCE DEALS "
"<40 &MON1 &YY1 "
" "
" "
" FEES SCHEDULE SHOULD BE BROKEN DOWN AS FOLLOWS: "
" "
"<1 HIGHER EDUCATION FEES  :<30 <TOT.HE "
"<1 HEALTH CARE FEES       :<30 <TOT.HC "
"<1 GENERAL MARKETS FEES   :<30 <TOT.GM "
"<1 MASTER LENDER          :<30 <TOT.ML "
"<1 COLLAT LOAN TO LENDER  :<30 <TOT.CL "
"<1 OPTION BONDS           :<30 <TOT.OB "
"<30 ---------------"
"<30 <TOT.AMOUNT   "
END
-RUN

TABLE FILE DEALS
HEADING
"PROG: &PRO    <98 REPORT DATE: <112 &DATE "
" <112 &TOD   "
"<40 PUBLIC FINANCE DEALS "
"<40 &MON1 &YY1 "
" "
"<1 UNIT: <UNAME "
" "
SUM ICODE AS 'ISSUER' SIZE AS 'ISSUE,SIZE' FCD AS 'FEE,TYPE'
  ACC_CODE AS 'ACCOUNTING,CODE' AMOUNT AS 'AMOUNT,RECEIVED' IN +5

BY USORT NOPRINT
BY ACC_CODE NOPRINT
BY DEAL   AS 'DEAL'
BY FCD NOPRINT
IF AMOUNT NE 0
IF UNAME NE ' '
ON USORT SUBTOTAL AMOUNT AS 'TOTAL'
ON USORT PAGE-BREAK

FOOTING
" AC - ACCRUAL "
" AT - AMORTIZATION "
" CA - CASH "
END
```

Figure 5-13  (continued) FOCEXEC for Management Summary report.

```
-RUN

OFFLINE
-IF &OPT EQ 'P' GOTO MSG;
-RUN
-GOTO TOP
-MSG
-*CMS PRINT DEALS LISTING A

-SET &MSG = '          THE REPORT HAS BEEN SENT TO PRINTER ';
-GOTO TOP
-DONE
OFFLINE CLOSE
SET MESSAGE = ON
-EXIT
```

Figure 5-13    (continued) FOCEXEC for Management Summary report.

structure. Usually, a section of code can be copied into another FOCEXEC. In the FOCEXECS in this application, the DEFINE statements which compute the monthly income for each fee are nearly identical from program to program. Even when the code is not identical, the principles of the technique used may be useful in other programs. Examples of this in the last application include:

1. Cross-reference (KU) segments
2. DECODE files
3. ONLINE/OFFLINE options
4. Setting up a menu for selecting reports
5. Defining fields used in sorting pages (or lines)
6. Formatting with ACROSS
7. Short-path segments

Therefore, FOCUS will allow you to design applications with the basic techniques used over and over again. As we all know, repetition reinforces learning. This will not only save time for programmers, but it should also increase the awareness of your organization concerning the availability of techniques to solve information processing problems. Each application should demonstrate to the users that FOCUS contains a variety of techniques which are simple to implement and reusable in other applications.

## Supplying Values as Dialogue Manager Variables

Before continuing to another application, we should discusss further the passing of parameter values (in the form of dialogue manager variables) to FOCEXECS or between FOCEXECS. Many procedures require that the user select values which will be used to determine screening conditions, verb objects, formatting options — almost anything. FOCUS allows values to be selected at run time in a number of simple ways. Dialogue manager variables are prompted for values, or the values are supplied in the execution statement.

The example below illustrates a FOCEXEC used for "inquiry" purposes. The user is prompted twice (with PROMPT) before the TABLE request. The first prompt is for the issuer name (or short abbreviation), the second for date. The FOCEXEC DEAL6 displays all deals for an issuer which were closed after a given date:

```
ONLINE
-TYPE DEAL INQUIRY PROGRAM
-TYPE
-PROMPT &ISSUER. ENTER ISSUER.
-PROMPT &EDATE. ENTER START DATE.
TABLE FILE DEAL
"DEALS FOR ISSUER: &ISSUER"
"AFTER DATE: &EDATE"
" "
PRINT DEAL AS 'DEAL'
UCODE AS 'UNIT'
PCODE AS 'PRODUCT'
SIZE AS 'ISSUE SIZE'
CDATE AS 'CLOSING DATE'
BY DEAL NOPRINT

IF ISSUER CONTAINS &ISSUER
IF CDATE GE &EDATE
END

-RUN
```

When the FOCEXEC is executed, the user will see on the screen:

```
DEAL INQUIRY PROGRAM
ENTER ISSUER
```

(user responds here)

```
ENTER DATE
```

(user responds here)
(The Report is displayed)

Refer to the FOCUS 5.0 manual Chapter 6 Sections 3.8 to 3.13 for a discussion of the various methods of supplying dialogue manager variables. The next example shows how to supply values for variables from the EXEC line.

```
TABLE FILE DEAL
"DEALS FOR ISSUER: &ISSUER"
"AFTER DATE: &EDATE"
" "
PRINT DEAL AS 'DEAL'
 . . . .
 . . . .
IF CDATE GE &EDATE
END
```

When the PROMPT is left out, FOCUS expects the variables &ISSUER and &EDATE to get values from the EXEC line, or it will issue its own prompt statement. The values are supplied on the EXEC line as

```
EXEC DEAL6 ISSUER=issuer name, EDATE=date
```

Another important feature is the DEFAULTS statement, which supplies default values for variable substitutions. This is appropriate when no value is supplied on the EXEC line. For example, if &EDATE is not given a value, a default value may be included in the FOCEXEC.

```
-DEFAULTS &EDATE=860101
```

```
TABLE FILE DEAL
PRINT DEAL ISSUER
 . . . .
 . . . .
IF CDATE GE &EDATE
END
```

You also may provide wild card values through the DEFAULTS statement, which allows any possible value for a field to be accepted in screening conditions.

```
-DEFAULTS &UNIT=$$

TABLE FILE DEAL
PRINT DEAL ISSUER UNITCODE
 . . . .
 . . . .
IF CDATE GE 860101
IF UNIT EQ &UNIT
END
```

## Example 2: Daily Price History for Mortgage Securities

This application demonstrates some of the reporting techniques used when working with large FOCUS files. The FOCUS file is assumed to contain a history of daily security prices covering the period 1980–1986. The MASTER description for the HISTORY file is shown in figure 5-14.

The top segment, SECURITY, contains fields which describe the securities maintained in the file. There are two key fields (e.g., SEGTYPE=S2), LABEL and COUPON, which distinguish each security. Daily prices and yields are in the child segment. For each security, the child segment contains a history of prices and yields — covering each business date between 1980–1986.

It is usually not hard to get an estimate of the number of records in a FOCUS file, by figuring the number of combinations of key field values. If there are 20 labels and 10 coupons for each label, then the number of different securities is 200. If each security has 1500 prices (approximately seven years in business days), then the total number

```
FILENAME = HISTORY, SUFFIX = FOC

SEGNAME = SECURITY,SEGTYPE = S2

        FIELD = LABEL         ,LABEL     ,A04,FIELDTYPE = I,$
        FIELD = COUPON        ,CPN       ,D6.3,$
        FIELD = SECNO         ,SECNO     ,A05,FIELDTYPE = I,$
        FIELD = MATURITY      ,MD        ,A07,$
        FIELD = ISSUE         ,ID        ,A07,$
        FIELD = FACKEY        ,CK        ,A05,FIELDTYPE = I,$
        FIELD = SEC_TYPE      ,SECTYPE   ,I02,$
        FIELD = CALL_DATE     ,C_DATE    ,I07,$
        FIELD = SHORT_NAME    ,SNAME     ,A17,$
        FIELD = ACT_IND       ,IND       ,I1, $
        FIELD = CDATE         ,CDT       ,I6, $
        FIELD = CBID          ,CBD       ,D9.5,$
        FIELD = CASK          ,CAK       ,D9.5,$
        FIELD = CYIELD        ,CSY       ,D6.3,$

SEGNAME = PRICES,PARENT = SECURITY,SEGTYPE = SH1,$

        FIELD = DATE          , DT       ,I6,    FIELDTYPE = I,$ YMD
        FIELD = BID           , BD       ,D9.5,$
        FIELD = ASK           , AK       ,D9.5,$
        FIELD = YIELD         , SY       ,D6.3,$
```

Figure 5-14    History MASTER file.

of records in the file is about 300,000. This a "large" FOCUS file (even for most mainframe systems), because FOCUS will normally not take an insignificant amount of CPU time to retrieve records from the file. Large files may pose some problems for users needing fast online access to data. However, there are several techniques which can improve the retrieval efficiency. We will demonstrate these techniques, such as indexing and alternate views — but keep in mind that these are rarely used for smaller files (less than 10,000 records).

The security prices and yields are used in a number of investment banking applications. Since the securities are traded daily, analysts need ways to compare securities and to spot exceptional price behavior. The types of reports required, daily, range from ad hoc requests for price history to comparisons of price and yield among selected securities. The two reports which use interesting FOCUS techniques are:

1. Calculating Price Spreads between securities with the same label, for selected coupon pairs.
2. Calculating Price Spreads between securities with the same coupon, for selected label pairs.

The FOCEXECS demonstrate the philosophy of writing FOCUS programs using a "piece by piece" or "capsule by capsule" approach. This involves the use of HOLD files which contain the data in a more manageable (and usually aggregated) format. As you will see, HOLD files also make it easier to debug programming and data problems. Other techniques which will be used in this application are:

1. JOINS to files
2. ACROSS WITH HOLD
3. Direct operations
4. Formatting column heading with dialogue manager variables
5. Indexed record retrieval
6. Using -INCLUDE
7. Invoking FOCUS programs through CMS EXECS
8. Identifying FOCUS files with the USE command

The following reports are run daily after the HISTORY file has been updated with the current day's security prices. (This is normally done at the end of the day or at night.) We will assume the data is loaded properly each business day, and that it is available for reporting. We will not discuss the procedures which update the file.

Figure 5-15 lists the labels and coupons which are included in the file. The file may contain additional labels, but the reports only show the six labels representing the six major mortgage security types. The HISTORY file is a single-path file with two segments, SECURITY and PRICES. The top (root) segment contains fields describing other characteristics of each security, such as the issue date, maturity date, etc. These are unimportant to the price reports. Another field, FACKEY, is used to cross-reference information from other files. These other files can contain different kinds of security information — such as mortgage prepayment factors, prepayment forecasts, etc. There is a FACKEY for each LABEL. Figure 5-16 lists the values of FACKEY for each LABEL.

In the following reporting procedures, we will demonstrate using JOINS to access information from other files. For example, we shall access another file, SECFILE, which contains the full description of

```
1 PAGE     1


LABELS   COUPONS
------   -----------
FPCI     7.0, 7.5, 8.0, 8.5, ..., 15.0
FPTI     7.0, 7.5, 8.0, 8.5, ..., 15.0
F15I     7.0, 7.5, 8.0. 8.5, ..., 15.0
PC5I     7.0, 7.5, 8.0. 8.5, ..., 15.0
GNMA     5.5, 6.0, 6.5, 7.0, 7.5, 8.0, ..., 16.0
G15I     5.5, 6.0, 6.5, 7.0, 7.5, 8.0, ..., 16.0
```

**Figure 5-15    Values of Label and Coupon.**

each type of security label. The MASTER description for SECFILE in figure 5-17 contains the field SECKEY which is indexed. See figure 5-18 for a listing of the security descriptions.

### Indexed Fields and Efficiency Considerations

In this example, the number of records in the top segment is not large (several hundred). However, the number of records in the child segment may reach close to 100,000 — since daily prices are maintained for each security. There are several ways to improve the efficiency of retrieving records in the child segment. Consider the request to display the prices of all securities for the time period 1/1/82 to 1/05/82.

```
TABLE FILE HISTORY
PRINT BID ASK
BY LABEL BY COUPON
BY DATE
IF DATE FROM 820101 TO 820105
END
```

FOCUS has to search through a large number of records to obtain the required dates. Since the child records are stored in logical order, based on the key field DATE, the speed of retrieval is improved since records with DATE prior to 820101 will not be searched. (Note the SEGTYPE SH1 indicates that dates are stored in descending order.) However, consider an example with 5000 securities in the top seg-

```
1 PAGE       1


LABEL   FACKEY
-----   ------
FPCG    FM18B
FPCI    FM18B
FPTG    FNCLB
FPTI    FNCLB
F15G    FNCIA
F15I    FNCIA
GNMA    G1SFB
GNMG    G1SFB
GPMG    G1GPG
GPMI    G1GPB
G15G    G1SFA
G15I    G1SFA
PC5G    FM21A
PC5I    FM21A
PG5G    FM20A
PG5I    FM20A
TBCO
TBNC
TBOC
TBOP
TB00
```

Figure 5-16  Listing of FACKEY codes.

ment. The above request would take considerably longer if over a million records must be searched.

You should place fields on which you know screening conditions will be performed in the root segment whenever possible. FOCUS only reads the child records if it cannot accept or reject records based on the information in the root segment. In the HISTORY file, the DATE field cannot be placed in the root segment. However, an ALTERNATE FILE VIEW lets you view the HISTORY file using the child segment as the root. An alternate file view can be requested on any segment in a file, except cross-reference segments. The alternate view is obtained in a TABLE request by naming a field from the new "root" segment. For example,

```
TABLE FILE HISTORY.BID
PRINT BID ASK DATE
```

```
FILE=SECFILE            ,SUFFIX=FOC
SEGNAME=SECFILE
FIELDNAME    =SECKEY       ,          ,A5              ,$
FIELDNAME    =DESCRIP      ,          ,A20             ,$
FIELDNAME    =SEC_LABEL    ,          ,A04    ,A04     ,$
FIELDNAME    =MBSFLAG      ,          ,A01    ,A04     ,$
```

Figure 5-17  SECFILE Master description.

```
BY LABEL BY COUPON
IF DATE FROM 820101 TO 820105
END
```

By viewing the file from the child segment, the IF tests are performed starting with the date segment, not the SECURITY segment.

Another technique to improve retrieval efficiency with alternate views involves taking advantage of INDEXED fields. FOCUS can quickly locate records if a field has FIELDTYPE = I. This is done using an indexed view — by providing equality screening values for the indexed field. For example, since DATE is indexed:

```
TABLE FILE HISTORY.DATE
PRINT BID ASK DATE
BY LABEL BY COUPON
IF DATE EQ 820102 OR 820103 OR 820104 OR 820105
END
```

You may not use "less than" or "greater than" screening conditions, only EQ conditions. If you know the specific values of the indexed field, an indexed view provides very fast retrieval. Indexed retrieval can be performed using any indexed field.

### Report 1: Price Spreads for Securities With the Same Label-Between Pairs of Coupons

Since the HISTORY file contains the daily price (e.g., ASK is the asking price at the end of the day) of each security, we can report the price difference between pairs of securities. The report should do the following:

```
1 PAGE     1

FACKEY  DESCRIPTION
------  -----------
FM18B   FHLMC GUAR (0-30 YEAR) -WAM AT ISSUANCE GT 15 YEARS
FM20A   FHLMC CASH CONVENTIONAL - 15 YEAR
FM21A   FHLMC GUARANTOR - 15 YEAR
FNCIA   FNMA CONV - 15 YEAR
FNCLB   FNMA CONV - 30 YEAR
G1GPB   GNMA I GRADUATED PAYMENT - 5 YEAR
G1SFA   GNMA I SINGLE FAMILY - 15 YEAR
G1SFB   GNMA I SINGLE FAMILY 30 YEAR
```

**Figure 5-18  Security descriptions.**

1. On a separate page for each label, show the price difference between pairs of coupons such as:

   6.5-6.0
   7.0-6.5
   7.5-7.0
   8.0-7.5
   ....
   ....

   The price difference should be shown for:

   - the previous five business days
   - the average difference over the past week
   - the average difference over the past month
   - the average difference over the past year.

Figure 5-19 shows what the report looks like for the label GNMA.

The coupon pairs are listed down the page, while the business, week, month, and year are in columns across the page. The FOCEXEC, HISTREP1, is shown in figure 5-20.

This FOCEXEC can be considered as having several sections, which is typical of many FOCEXECS written for large files:

1. Use dialogue manager variables to describe parameters which may change every time the report is run (e.g., the previous five business dates).

```
                                            MORTGAGE RESEARCH

                                            PRICE SPREADS
                                            GNMA I SINGLE FAMILY 30
                                            09/02/87
                                            --------


-----------------------------------------------------------------------
COUPON        09/02   09/01   08/31   08/28   08/27   AVE.    AVE.    AVE.
RANGE         START   T-1     T-2     T-3     T-4     WEEK    MONTH   YEAR
------        -----   -----   -----   -----   -----   ----    -----   ----
   6.5  5.5 ]  1.28 ]  1.28 ]  1.28 ]  1.28 ]  1.28 ]  1.28 ]  1.28 ]  1.11 ]
-----------------------------------------------------------------------
   7.0  6.5 ] -2.06 ] -2.06 ] -2.06 ] -2.06 ] -2.06 ] -2.06 ] -2.06 ] -1.30 ]
-----------------------------------------------------------------------
   7.5  7.0 ]  3.14 ]  3.14 ]  3.14 ]  3.14 ]  3.22 ]  3.16 ]  3.21 ]  3.20 ]
-----------------------------------------------------------------------
   8.0  7.5 ]  2.17 ]  2.17 ]  2.17 ]  2.17 ]  2.09 ]  2.15 ]  2.11 ]  1.27 ]
-----------------------------------------------------------------------
   8.5  8.0 ]  2.19 ]  2.19 ]  2.17 ]  2.15 ]  2.18 ]  2.18 ]  2.19 ]  1.31 ]
-----------------------------------------------------------------------
   9.0  8.5 ]  3.01 ]  3.01 ]  3.01 ]  3.02 ]  2.30 ]  3.01 ]  2.27 ]  2.09 ]
-----------------------------------------------------------------------
   9.5  9.0 ]  2.30 ]  2.30 ]  2.30 ]  2.31 ]  2.31 ]  2.30 ]  2.28 ]  2.17 ]
-----------------------------------------------------------------------
  10.0  9.5 ]  3.01 ]  3.01 ]  3.01 ]  3.01 ]  3.03 ]  3.01 ]  2.31 ]  2.17 ]
-----------------------------------------------------------------------
  10.5 10.0 ]  3.02 ]  3.02 ]  3.02 ]  3.02 ]  3.03 ]  3.02 ]  2.32 ]  1.32 ]
-----------------------------------------------------------------------
  11.0 10.5 ]  2.25 ]  2.19 ]  2.21 ]  2.22 ]  2.06 ]  2.19 ]  2.10 ]   .24 ]
-----------------------------------------------------------------------
  11.5 11.0 ]  2.05 ]  2.04 ]  2.00 ]  2.01 ]  1.28 ]  2.01 ]  1.17 ]   .17 ]
-----------------------------------------------------------------------
  12.0 11.5 ]  1.21 ]  1.16 ]  1.09 ]  1.14 ]  1.09 ]  1.14 ]  1.08 ]   .25 ]
-----------------------------------------------------------------------
  12.5 12.0 ]  1.08 ]  1.06 ]  1.03 ]   .30 ]   .30 ]  1.03 ]   .30 ]   .19 ]
-----------------------------------------------------------------------
```

Figure 5-19    Price Spread report — between coupons.

```
13.0 12.5 ]  1.18 ]  1.04 ]  1.02 ]  1.02 ]  1.02 ]  1.06 ]  1.03 ]   .27 ]
-------------------------------------------------------------------------------
13.5 13.0 ]  1.00 ]  1.00 ]  1.00 ]   .29 ]   .29 ]   .31 ]   .29 ]   .27 ]
-------------------------------------------------------------------------------
14.0 13.5 ]  1.05 ]   .31 ]   .31 ]   .31 ]   .31 ]  1.00 ]  1.02 ]   .25 ]
-------------------------------------------------------------------------------
14.5 14.0 ]  1.02 ]  1.02 ]  1.02 ]  1.02 ]  1.02 ]  1.02 ]  1.08 ]  1.22 ]
-------------------------------------------------------------------------------
15.0 14.5 ]  1.01 ]  1.01 ]  1.01 ]  1.01 ]  1.01 ]  1.01 ]   .26 ]  1.20 ]
-------------------------------------------------------------------------------
16.0 15.0 ]   .00 ]   .00 ]   .00 ]   .00 ]   .00 ]   .00 ]   .00 ]  -.27 ]
-------------------------------------------------------------------------------
17.0 16.0 ]   .00 ]   .00 ]   .00 ]   .00 ]   .00 ]   .00 ]   .00 ]   .19 ]
-------------------------------------------------------------------------------
```

**Figure 5-19** (continued) Price Spread report — between coupons.

### 162 The Database Experts' Guide to FOCUS

```
-* PROGRAM: HISREP1
-* ROUTINE TO CREATE SECURITY PRICE SPREAD REPORT - BETWEEN COUPONS
-* INCLUDES : HISTSUB1
-*
-*

-DEFAULTS &FM = B

SET TEMP DISK = &FM
SET MSG = OFF, LINES = 66
SET NODATA = ' '

-CMS FILEDEF OFFLINE DISK HISRPT1 LISTING &FM (LRECL 132 RECFM FB
-CMS FILEDEF SAV1       DISK SAV1      FOCTEMP &FM (LRECL 12  RECFM FB

-PROMPT &MMDDYY.A6. ENTER START DATE (MMDDYY) .

-SET &DAY = '     ' ;
-SET &NDAY = '         ' ;
-SET &YMD1 = '         ' ;
-SET &YMD2 = '         ' ;
-SET &YMD3 = '         ' ;
-SET &YMD4 = '         ' ;
-SET &YMD5 = '         ' ;
-SET &YMD6 = '         ' ;
-SET &YMD7 = '         ' ;
-SET &YYMMDD   = EDIT(&MMDDYY,'$$$$99') ] EDIT(&MMDDYY,'9999$$');
-SET &PERIOD  = EDIT(&YYMMDD, '9999$$');
-SET &MSG = ' ';
-SET &OPT = ' ';
-SET &PRO = 'HISTREP1';
-RUN

-GO1
-CRTCLEAR

-* GET ALL DATES FOR REPORT
-INCLUDE HISTSUB1
-RUN

-* &YYMMDD IS THE STARTING DATE, &YMD1 IS THE PREVIOUS BUSINESS
DAY, ...

-SET &YYMMDD = &ZMD1;
```

**Figure 5-20** FOCEXEC for Security Price Spread report — between coupons.

```
-SET &YMD1    = &ZMD2;
-SET &YMD2    = &ZMD3;
-SET &YMD3    = &ZMD4;
-SET &YMD4    = &ZMD5;
-SET &YMD5    = &ZMD6;
-SET &YMD6    = &MAGO;
-SET &YMD7    = &YAGO;

-* USE &AM1, &AM2, ..., AS COLUMN HEADINGS IN THE REPORT.

-SET &AM1    = EDIT(&YMD1 ,'$$99') ] '/' ] EDIT(&YMD1 ,'$$$$99');
-SET &AM2    = EDIT(&YMD2 ,'$$99') ] '/' ] EDIT(&YMD2 ,'$$$$99');
-SET &AM3    = EDIT(&YMD3 ,'$$99') ] '/' ] EDIT(&YMD3 ,'$$$$99');
-SET &AM4    = EDIT(&YMD4 ,'$$99') ] '/' ] EDIT(&YMD4 ,'$$$$99');
-SET &AM5    = EDIT(&YMD5 ,'$$99') ] '/' ] EDIT(&YMD5 ,'$$$$99');
-SET &AM6    = EDIT(&YMD6 ,'$$99') ] '/' ] EDIT(&YMD6 ,'$$$$99');
-SET &AM7    = EDIT(&YMD7 ,'$$99') ] '/' ] EDIT(&YMD7 ,'$$$$99');
-SET &AM0    = EDIT(&YYMMDD,'$$99') ] '/' ] EDIT(&YYMMDD
,'$$$$99');
-SET &DM0    = EDIT(&YYMMDD,'$$99') ] '/' ] EDIT(&YYMMDD ,'$$$$99')
-                                   ] '/' ] EDIT(&YYMMDD,'99');


-RUN

DEFINE FILE HISTORY
  COOP/D4.1       =    COUPON;
  INT_COUP/I3     =    COUPON;
  FRACT_COUP/D7.4=     COUPON - INT_COUP;
  WANT_COUP/I1    =    DECODE FRACT_COUP ( 0.0 1 0.5 1 ELSE 0) ;

END

-RUN

TABLE FILE HISTORY.LABEL
SUM  FACKEY ASK

BY HIGHEST DATE
BY LABEL
BY COOP
BY HIGHEST 1 MATURITY
IF LABEL EQ GNMA OR FPTI OR FPCI OR GPMI OR F15I OR G15I OR PC5I
OR PG5I
IF WANT_COUP EQ 1
IF DATE GE &YMD7
```

Figure 5-20 (continued) FOCEXEC for Security Price Spread report — between coupons.

```
ON TABLE HOLD
END
-RUN

TABLE FILE HOLD
SUM   FACKEY ASK AND COMPUTE
LCOUP/D4.1= IF LABEL EQ LAST LABEL  AND DATE EQ LAST DATE
        THEN LAST COOP ELSE 0;
DIFF/D6.2 = IF LABEL   EQ LAST LABEL AND DATE EQ LAST DATE
        THEN (ASK - LAST ASK) ELSE 0;
SQR/D10.3 =  DIFF * DIFF ;

 BY HIGHEST DATE
 BY LABEL
 BY COOP
 BY MATURITY
ON TABLE HOLD
END
-RUN

DEFINE FILE HOLD
  DSORT/I2       =    IF DATE EQ &YYMMDD THEN 1 ELSE
                      IF DATE EQ &YMD1 THEN 2 ELSE
                      IF DATE EQ &YMD2 THEN 3 ELSE
                      IF DATE EQ &YMD3 THEN 4 ELSE
                      IF DATE EQ &YMD4 THEN 5 ELSE
                      IF DATE LT &YMD4 AND DATE GE &YMD6 THEN 6 ELSE
                      IF DATE LT &YMD6 AND DATE GE &YMD7 THEN 7 ELSE
99;

END

-* THE ONLY FIELDS REQUIRED FOR THE REPORT ARE AVE.DIFF AND FACKEY.
-* THE OTHER FIELDS ARE CARRIED ALONG FOR FUTURE APPLICATIONS.

TABLE FILE HOLD
 SUM   AVE.DIFF FACKEY AVE.ASK CNT.ASK SQR
 BY DSORT
 BY LABEL
 BY COOP
 BY LCOUP
ON TABLE HOLD AS HOLD1
END

-RUN
```

Figure 5-20   (continued) FOCEXEC for Security Price Spread report — between coupons.

```
JOIN CLEAR *
JOIN FACKEY IN HOLD1 TO ALL SECKEY IN SECFILE AS J1
-RUN

DEFINE FILE HOLD1
INT_DIF/I3 =    DIFF;
FRAC/D7.4  =    DIFF - INT_DIF ;
D32/D5.2   =    INT_DIF + .32*FRAC;
END

TABLE FILE HOLD1
WRITE   D32 LABEL

BY FACKEY
BY DESCRIPTION

ACROSS DSORT COLUMNS 1 AND 2 AND 3 AND 4 AND 5 AND 6 AND 7

BY COOP BY LCOUP
ON TABLE HOLD AS HOLD2
END
-RUN

DEFINE FILE HOLD2
BAR/A1     = ']';
SSORT/I1   = DECODE LABEL (FPCI 2
                           FPTI 3
                           F15I 5
                           GNMA 1
                           GPMI 4
                           G15I 6
                           PG5I 8
                           PC5I 7 ELSE 9 ) ;
END
-RUN
-REP1

TABLE FILE HOLD2
HEADING
" <<55  MORTGAGE RESEARCH   <<98 REPORT RUN ON : &DATE "
" <<109 AT : &TOD "
" <<55 PRICE SPREADS "
" <<55 <<FST.DESCRIPTION"
" <<55 &DM0 "
" <<55 -------- "
" "
```

Figure 5-20 (continued) FOCEXEC for Security Price Spread report — between coupons.

166 The Database Experts' Guide to FOCUS

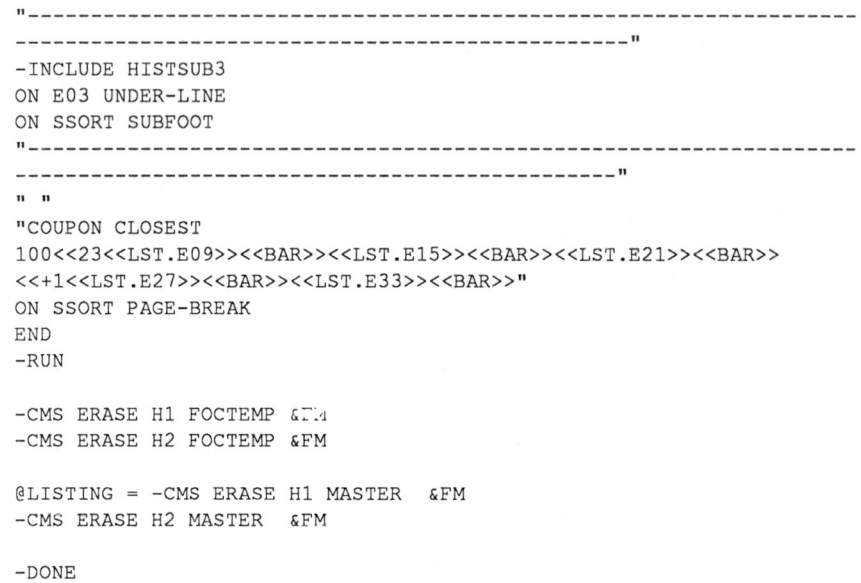

Figure 5-20 (continued) FOCEXEC for Security Price Spread report — between coupons.

2. Extract from the FOCUS file only the data (aggregated and sorted if possible) needed for further calculations. Keep it in a HOLD file.
3. Perform additional calculations on the HOLD file (e.g., DEFINES, more HOLD files, etc.). Format and generate the finished report.

In the first section, the program prompts for today's date (or any other date). Then, the program will determine what the previous five business dates are, as well as the previous month, and previous year (start and end dates). Although we will not discuss the technique used to obtain these dates, several points should be made:

1. The code which generates the previous business dates appears in a separate FOCEXEC (HISTSUB1 shown in figure 5-21). This code is "brought into" the HISTREP1 FOCEXEC via an -INCLUDE statement. This code is executed just as though it

```
-* PROGRAM HISTSUB1 FOCEXEC
-* GIVEN DATE &YYMMDD, RETURNS PREVIOUS BUS. DAY, 2 AGO, 3 AGO, 4 AGO
-*       WEEK AGO, MONTH AGO, YEAR AGO.
-* THE DATES ARE CONTAINED IN THE VARIABLES
 &ZMD1,...,&ZMD6,&MAGO,&YAGO

-START
-* GET DATES OF THE LAST 6 DAYS IN HISTORY FILE
-SET &N = 1 ;

-INIT
-SET &ZMD.&N='         ' ;
-SET &N = &N + 1 ;
-IF &N GT 6 GOTO CONT ELSE GOTO INIT ;
-RUN
-CONT
-SET &N = 1 ;

TABLE FILE HISTORY
PRINT DATE BY HIGHEST DATE
IF LABEL EQ GNMA
IF COUPON EQ 9.0
IF DATE LE &YYMMDD
IF RECORDLIMIT EQ 6
ON TABLE SAVE AS SAV1
END
-RUN

-LOOP1
-READ SAV1 &ZMD.&N
-SET &N = &N + 1 ;
-IF &N GT 6 GOTO CONT1 ELSE GOTO LOOP1;
-RUN
-CONT1
-SET &N = 1;

-* GET MONTH AGO
-SET &ZM = EDIT(&YYMMDD,'$$99');
-SET &ZD = EDIT(&YYMMDD,'$$$$99');
-SET &ZY = EDIT(&YYMMDD,'99$$');
-SET &ZMM = IF &ZM EQ '01' THEN '12' ELSE &ZM - 1;
-SET &ZYY = IF &ZM EQ '01' THEN &ZY - 1 ELSE &ZY ;
-SET &MAGO = 10000*&ZYY + 100*&ZMM + &ZD ;
-SET &DAY = DOWK( &MAGO, A3) ;
-IF &DAY EQ 'SAT' GOTO SAT1;
-IF &DAY EQ 'SUN' GOTO SUN1;
```

Figure 5-21    HISTSUB1 FOCEXEC.

```
-GOTO OKM

-SAT1
-SET &MAGO = AYMD(&MAGO,-1,I6);
-GOTO OKM
-SUN1
-SET &MAGO = AYMD(&MAGO,-2,I6);
-OKM

-* GET YEAR AGO
-SET &ZM = EDIT(&YYMMDD,'$$99');
-SET &ZD = EDIT(&YYMMDD,'$$$$99');
-SET &ZY = EDIT(&YYMMDD,'99$$');
-SET &ZYY = &ZY - 1;
-SET &YAGO = 10000*&ZYY + 100*&ZM + &ZD ;
-SET &DAY = DOWK( &YAGO, A3) ;
-IF &DAY EQ 'SAT' GOTO SAT2;
-IF &DAY EQ 'SUN' GOTO SUN2;
-GOTO OKY

-SAT2
-SET &YAGO = AYMD(&YAGO,-1,I6);
-GOTO OKY
-SUN2
-SET &YAGO = AYMD(&YAGO,-2,I6);
-OKY
-RUN
```

**Figure 5-21  (continued) HISTSUB1 FOCEXEC.**

had originally been placed there. (see FOCUS 5.0 manual chapter 6 section 6.2).

2. There are several ways to generate business dates using techniques which can distinguish between weekdays, weekends, and holidays. HISTSUB1 obtains the dates directly from the HISTORY file — since there are prices in the file for every business day of the year. Notice that one TABLE request extracts the dates:

```
TABLE FILE HISTORY
PRINT DATE BY HIGHEST DATE
IF LABEL EQ GNMA
IF COUPON EQ 9
```

```
IF DATE LE &YYMMDD
IF RECORDLIMIT EQ 6
ON TABLE SAVE AS SAV1
END
```

We arbitrarily selected the GNMA 9.0 security since we know that a price exists for it on every business day. The RECORDLIMIT condition assures that only the prior six dates will be obtained.
3. The dialogue manager variables &YMD1, &YMD2, &YMD3, etc. are assigned values using the -READ command, which reads the values from a SAVE file.
4. Additional variables &AM1, &AM2, etc., are created to convert the dates into MM/DD/YY format (used later as column headings).

The next section of code in HISTREP1 calculates the price of each security for the last five business days, and the average price for the month and year. Note: For each label GNMA, FPTI, etc., we are only interested in every half coupon, such as 7.0, 7.5, 8.0, etc. Therefore, the defined field WANT_COUP is a "flag" whose value is 1 for half-coupons and zero otherwise. It is used as a screening condition in the first TABLE request. Next, a technique is used which is applicable in situations where the same calculation is performed over specified ranges of data. In this case, the average price is to be calculated over the ranges of time specified in the DEFINE. The variable DSORT defines each range of time (note: The first six ranges correspond to a single day, while the last two represent the month, and the year). In the TABLE request, the direct operation AVE.ASK is performed for each range of time, for each label, for each coupon:

```
TABLE FILE HISTORY.LABEL
SUM AVE.ASK ...
BY DSORT
BY LABEL
BY COOP
....
```

The TABLE request (TABLE FILE HISTORY.LABEL) uses an "indexed retrieval" to improve FOCUS's efficiency in searching for records with the required labels. The indexed field LABEL makes this possible — you simply specify an equality screening condition for the indexed field such as:

IF LABEL EQ GNMA OR FPT1 OR . . . . . . .

A HOLD file is created which contains the average price for each time period, for each label and coupon. Then the difference in price is calculated for each set of consecutive half coupons using a COMPUTE expression:

DIFF/D12.2=IF LABEL EQ LAST LABEL THEN (ASK-LAST ASK) ELSE 0;

Note that the field ASK in the HOLD file now represents the average price; the AVE. operation keeps the same name for the field. The result is again extracted into another HOLD file. Additional calculations are required in the next DEFINE for converting decimal prices to prices in 32 NDS.

## Using JOINS to Reference Data in Other Files

The HOLD file is JOINED to SECFILE to get access to the name of each security label (i.e., the field SNAME). The JOIN command is:

JOIN * CLEAR
JOIN FACKEY IN HOLD TO ALL SECKEY IN SECFILE AS J1

(The CLEAR clears out all previous joins initiated in the FOCUS session.)
JOINS are simply another kind of KU or KM cross-reference technique. It is "dynamic" because it can be removed and added to serve the purpose. The "JOINED" segment is accessed as a child segment to the host segment. Unlike a KU segment, however, all segments in the joined file become accessible through the first file. In this example, there is only one segment in each file, creating a joined file structure as shown in figure 5-22.
Whenever possible, JOINS should be originated from HOLD files, which have a single segment. This creates a simple file structure ("single-path"). If JOINS are originated from FOCUS files with more than one segment, the resulting structure could be "multipath" —

```
focus
FOCUS   5.0.2V
>
>
>
>
JOIN FACKEY IN HISTORY TO ALL SECKEY IN SECFILE AS J1
>
>
? join
JOINS CURRENTLY ACTIVE

FACKEY          IN HISTORY   TO ALL SECKEY      IN SECFILE   AS J1
>
>
check file history picture

SECTION 01
            STRUCTURE OF FOCUS      FILE HISTORY   ON 09/04/87 AT
18.04.00

         SECURITY
01       S3
  **************
  *LABEL         **I
  *COUPON        **
  *SECNO         **I
  *FACKEY        **I
  *              **
  **************
  **************
         I
         +----------------+
         I                I
         I PROG           I PRICES
02       I KM         03  I SH1
  ...............      **************
  :SECKEY       ::K    *DATE        **I
  :DESCRIPTION ::      *BID         **
  :            ::      *ASK         **
  :            ::      *YIELD       **
  :            ::      *            **
  :...........::       **************
  ............:        **************
JOINED   SECFILE
```

Figure 5-22   Join of HISTORY file to SECFILE.

```
focus
FOCUS   5.0.2V
>
>
>
>
JOIN FACKEY IN HOLD1 TO ALL SECKEY IN SECFILE AS J1
>
check file hold1 picture

SECTION 01
            STRUCTURE OF FOCJNT    FILE HOLD1    ON 09/04/87 AT
18.42.51

         HOLD1
01       S1
    **************
    *DSORT        **
    *LABEL        **
    *COOP         **
    *LCOUP        **
    *             **
    **************
    **************
         I
         I
         I
         I PROG
02       I KM
    ...............
    :SECKEY      ::K
    :DESCRIPTION ::
    :DELAY       ::
    :IWHMBS      ::
    :            ::
    :............::
    .............:
    JOINED  SECFILE
```

Figure 5-23   Join of HOLD file to SECFILE.

which could make record retrieval more complicated. Figure 5-23 shows the file structure if the top segment of HISTORY is joined with SECFILE. (Note: PC FOCUS does not allow HOLD files to be JOINed to FOCUS files.)

```
FILE=HOLD1            ,SUFFIX=FIX
SEGNAME=HOLD1
FIELDNAME  =DSORT     ,E01       ,I2       ,I04      ,$
FIELDNAME  =LABEL     ,E02       ,A04      ,A04      ,$
FIELDNAME  =COOP      ,E03       ,D4.1     ,D08      ,$
FIELDNAME  =LCOUP     ,E04       ,D4.1     ,D08      ,$
FIELDNAME  =DIFF      ,E05       ,D6.2     ,D08      ,$
FIELDNAME  =FACKEY    ,E06       ,A05      ,A08      ,$
FIELDNAME  =ASK       ,E07       ,D9.5     ,D08      ,$
FIELDNAME  =ASK       ,E08       ,I5       ,I04      ,$
FIELDNAME  =SQR       ,E09       ,D10.3    ,D08      ,$
```

Figure 5-24  HOLD file used in price spread report.

This is a multipath structure, which may require alternate file views to retrieve records from all three segments.

The major advantage of using JOINS over KU or KM segments is that they are used only when needed. The major disadvantage is the "overhead" required by FOCUS to set up the pointers between the two files every time the focexec is executed. These are described in the FOCUS 5.0 manual Chapter 4 section 3.4. Other considerations which are important are:

1. Defined fields should be defined after the JOIN is invoked, since the JOIN will clear all DEFINES on the individual files.
2. Be careful that the same field names (other than the indexed field) are not present in the joined files. If so, use the alias names of the fields in various requests.
3. KU segments are more efficient than JOINS, since pointers are resolved once. However, this makes little difference in situations where the number of values for the indexed field is small; this also makes little difference when the cross-reference file records change quite often.

The MASTER description for the HOLD file is shown in figure 5-24.

In order to format the final report, new fields need to be created representing the price spread for each time period. There are several ways to do this. We've chosen to use the command ACROSS to create a new field for each value of DSORT. The resulting HOLD file has a MASTER description, shown in figure 5-25. Notice that the ACROSS has created eight fields which have the same name D32. However,

```
FILE=HOLD2            ,SUFFIX=FIX
SEGNAME=HOLD2
FIELDNAME   =FACKEY        ,E01      ,A05      ,A08     ,$
FIELDNAME   =DESCRIPTION   ,E02      ,A52      ,A52     ,$
FIELDNAME   =COOP          ,E03      ,D4.1     ,D08     ,$
FIELDNAME   =LCOUP         ,E04      ,D4.1     ,D08     ,$
FIELDNAME   =D32           ,E05      ,D5.2     ,D08     ,$
FIELDNAME   =LABEL         ,E06      ,A04      ,A04     ,$
FIELDNAME   =D32           ,E07      ,D5.2     ,D08     ,$
FIELDNAME   =LABEL         ,E08      ,A04      ,A04     ,$
FIELDNAME   =D32           ,E09      ,D5.2     ,D08     ,$
FIELDNAME   =LABEL         ,E10      ,A04      ,A04     ,$
FIELDNAME   =D32           ,E11      ,D5.2     ,D08     ,$
FIELDNAME   =LABEL         ,E12      ,A04      ,A04     ,$
FIELDNAME   =D32           ,E13      ,D5.2     ,D08     ,$
FIELDNAME   =LABEL         ,E14      ,A04      ,A04     ,$
FIELDNAME   =D32           ,E15      ,D5.2     ,D08     ,$
FIELDNAME   =LABEL         ,E16      ,A04      ,A04     ,$
FIELDNAME   =D32           ,E17      ,D5.2     ,D08     ,$
FIELDNAME   =LABEL         ,E18      ,A04      ,A04     ,$
```

Figure 5-25   HOLD file used for price spread report.

this is no problem since the alias name (E03, E04, etc.) can be used in the next TABLE request. This use of ACROSS is a quick way to create new fields in HOLD files.

The last step is to format the final report using the field names in the previous HOLD file. This is simple, since the alias names of each field can reference each column. The column headings are created from the dialogue manager variables defined earlier. The HISTSUB3 FOCEXEC creates the body of the report. See figure 5-26.

Our approach in generating reports requiring various kinds of calculations, sorting, and data aggregation is to work with HOLD files every step of the way. In this FOCEXEC, certainly less HOLD files could have been used in manipulating the data. You may even save a few seconds in processing time. However, what you lose is:

1. Faster debugging capability in being able to check each HOLD file for specific results.
2. Simplicity in designing the focexec in steps, which may be easier to understand for most FOCUS programmers.

```
SUM E05/D6.2S AS '&AM0,START'         BAR AS ''  IN +1
    E11/D6.2S AS '&AM1,T-1' IN +1 BAR AS ''  IN +1
    E17/D6.2S AS '&AM2,T-2' IN +1 BAR AS ''  IN +1
    E23/D6.2S AS '&AM3,T-3' IN +1 BAR AS ''  IN +1
    E29/D6.2S AS '&AM4,T-4' IN +1 BAR AS ''  IN +1
    WAVE/D6.2S AS 'AVE.,WEEK'  IN +1 BAR AS ''  IN +1
    MAVE/D6.2S AS 'AVE.,MONTH' IN +1 BAR AS ''  IN +1
    YAVE/D6.2S AS 'AVE.,YEAR'  IN +1 BAR AS ''  IN +1

BY SSORT NOPRINT PAGE-BREAK
BY E02 AS 'COUPON,RANGE'
BY E03 AS ''
```

Figure 5-26   HISTSUB3 FOCEXEC

## Report 2: Price Spread Report Between Labels

This report is also a price spread report. Instead of price spreads between consecutive coupons of the same label, price spreads are computed between securities having different labels, same coupon. The report is shown in figure 5-27.

The techniques used in coding this report demonstrate how dialogue manager variables can substitute for verb objects and DEFINED fields, thereby allowing the same code to generate different reports. In this example, a separate page is required for the price spreads between various pairs of labels. The pairs of labels are:

1. GNMA 30 YR and FNMA 30 YR
2. FNMA 30 YR and FHLMC 30 YR
3. GNMA 15 YR and GNMA 30 YR
4. FNMA 15 YR and FHLMC 15 YR

For each pair, the price spread between like coupons is computed on each of the last five business days (as well as the average difference for the month and year). The FOCEXEC, HISTREP2, is shown in figure 5-28. The first part of the program is exactly the same as in HISTREP1 focexec. (The figure also contains a listing of HISTSUB2 FOCEXEC which is included in HISTREP2.) The dates for the previous five business dates, previous month, and previous year are obtained as dialogue manager variables. Then the average price

MORTGAGE RESEARCH

PRICE SPREADS : GNMA - FNMA
09/03/87

| COUPON | 09/03 START | 09/02 T-1 | 09/01 T-2 | 08/31 T-3 | 08/28 T-4 | AVE. WEEK | AVE. MONTH | AVE. YEAR |
|---|---|---|---|---|---|---|---|---|
| 6.5 | 2.22 | 2.30 | 4.00 | 4.02 | 3.27 | 3.16 | 3.25 | 1.28 |
| 7.0 | -.20 | -.12 | .22 | .24 | .17 | .06 | .15 | .04 |
| 7.5 | -1.27 | -1.19 | -.17 | -.15 | -.22 | -1.01 | -.18 | .29 |
| 8.0 | -1.26 | -1.18 | -.16 | -.14 | -.21 | -.32 | -.21 | .18 |
| 8.5 | -1.03 | -.29 | -.27 | -.25 | -.27 | -.29 | -.21 | .09 |
| 9.0 | -1.02 | -.28 | -.26 | -.23 | -.28 | -.28 | -.19 | .09 |
| 9.5 | -1.00 | -.26 | -.22 | -.14 | -.16 | -.22 | -.12 | .17 |
| 10.0 | -.28 | -.20 | -.14 | -.06 | -.08 | -.15 | -.02 | .31 |
| 10.5 | -.11 | .03 | .09 | .17 | .19 | .07 | .23 | 1.27 |
| 11.0 | .24 | .23 | .25 | .31 | .25 | .26 | 1.07 | 1.25 |
| 11.5 | 1.05 | 1.16 | 1.23 | 2.03 | 1.31 | 1.22 | 1.28 | 1.30 |

**Figure 5-27  Price Spread report — between labels.**

| | | | | | | | | |
|---|---|---|---|---|---|---|---|---|
| 12.0 | ] | 1.30 ] | 1.27 ] | 2.05 ] | 2.10 ] | 2.08 ] | 2.03 ] | 2.06 ] | 2.14 ] |
| 12.5 | ] | 2.06 ] | 2.05 ] | 2.15 ] | 2.15 ] | 2.15 ] | 2.11 ] | 2.15 ] | 2.20 ] |
| 13.0 | ] | 2.29 ] | 2.29 ] | 3.06 ] | 3.06 ] | 3.06 ] | 3.02 ] | 3.07 ] | 2.26 ] |
| 13.5 | ] | 3.17 ] | 3.21 ] | 3.30 ] | 4.07 ] | 4.04 ] | 3.29 ] | 3.28 ] | 3.13 ] |
| 14.0 | ] | 4.22 ] | 4.22 ] | 4.25 ] | 4.21 ] | 4.18 ] | 4.22 ] | 4.23 ] | 4.03 ] |
| 14.5 | ] | 5.16 ] | 5.16 ] | 5.19 ] | 5.15 ] | 5.12 ] | 5.16 ] | 5.22 ] | 6.10 ] |
| 15.0 | ] | 6.13 ] | 6.13 ] | 6.16 ] | 6.12 ] | 6.09 ] | 6.13 ] | 6.13 ] | 7.29 ] |
| 16.0 | ] | 6.13 ] | 6.13 ] | 6.16 ] | 6.09 ] | 6.06 ] | 6.11 ] | 6.11 ] | 6.32 ] |

**Figure 5-27** (continued) Price Spread report — between labels.

```
-* PROGRAM: HISREP2
-* ROUTINE TO CREATE SECURITY PRICE SPREAD REPORT - BETWEEN LABELS
-* INCLUDES : HISTSUB1, HISTSUB2
-*
-*

-DEFAULTS &FM = B

SET TEMP DISK = &FM
SET MSG = OFF, LINES = 66
SET NODATA = ' '

-CMS FILEDEF OFFLINE DISK HISRPT1 LISTING &FM (LRECL 132 RECFM FB
-CMS FILEDEF SAV1    DISK SAV1    FOCTEMP &FM (LRECL 12  RECFM FB

-PROMPT &MMDDYY.A6. ENTER START DATE (MMDDYY) .

-SET &DAY  = '     ' ;
-SET &NDAY = '     ' ;
-SET &YMD1 = '     ' ;
-SET &YMD2 = '     ' ;
-SET &YMD3 = '     ' ;
-SET &YMD4 = '     ' ;
-SET &YMD5 = '     ' ;
-SET &YMD6 = '     ' ;
-SET &YMD7 = '     ' ;
-SET &YYMMDD  = EDIT(&MMDDYY,'$$$$99') ] EDIT(&MMDDYY,'9999$$');
-SET &PERIOD  = EDIT(&YYMMDD, '9999$$');
-SET &MSG = ' ';
-SET &OPT = ' ';
-SET &PRO = 'HISTREP1';
-RUN

-GO1
-CRTCLEAR

-* GET ALL DATES FOR REPORT
-INCLUDE HISTSUB1
-RUN

-* &YYMMDD IS THE STARTING DATE, &YMD1 IS THE PREVIOUS BUSINESS
   DAY, ...

-SET &YYMMDD = &ZMD1;
-SET &YMD1   = &ZMD2;
-SET &YMD2   = &ZMD3;
```

Figure 5-28    FOCEXEC for Security Price Spread report — between labels.

```
-SET &YMD3    = &ZMD4;
-SET &YMD4    = &ZMD5;
-SET &YMD5    = &ZMD6;
-SET &YMD6    = &MAGO;
-SET &YMD7    = &YAGO;

-* USE &AM1, &AM2, ..., AS COLUMN HEADINGS IN THE REPORT.

-SET &AM1     = EDIT(&YMD1 ,'$$99')  ] '/' ] EDIT(&YMD1 ,'$$$$99');
-SET &AM2     = EDIT(&YMD2 ,'$$99')  ] '/' ] EDIT(&YMD2 ,'$$$$99');
-SET &AM3     = EDIT(&YMD3 ,'$$99')  ] '/' ] EDIT(&YMD3 ,'$$$$99');
-SET &AM4     = EDIT(&YMD4 ,'$$99')  ] '/' ] EDIT(&YMD4 ,'$$$$99');
-SET &AM5     = EDIT(&YMD5 ,'$$99')  ] '/' ] EDIT(&YMD5 ,'$$$$99');
-SET &AM6     = EDIT(&YMD6 ,'$$99')  ] '/' ] EDIT(&YMD6 ,'$$$$99');
-SET &AM7     = EDIT(&YMD7 ,'$$99')  ] '/' ] EDIT(&YMD7 ,'$$$$99');
-SET &AM0     = EDIT(&YYMMDD,'$$99') ] '/' ] EDIT(&YYMMDD
,'$$$$99');
-SET &DM0     = EDIT(&YYMMDD,'$$99') ] '/' ] EDIT(&YYMMDD ,'$$$$99')
-                                    ] '/' ] EDIT(&YYMMDD,'99');
-RUN

DEFINE FILE HISTORY
  COOP/D4.1       =   COUPON;
  INT_COUP/I3     =   COUPON;
  FRACT_COUP/D7.4=    COUPON - INT_COUP;
  WANT_COUP/I1    =   DECODE FRACT_COUP ( 0.0 1 0.5 1 ELSE 0) ;
END

-RUN

TABLE FILE HISTORY.LABEL
SUM   FACKEY ASK

BY HIGHEST DATE
BY LABEL
BY COOP
BY HIGHEST 1 MATURITY
IF LABEL EQ GNMA OR FPTI OR FPCI OR GPMI OR F15I OR G15I OR PC5I
OR PG5I
IF WANT_COUP EQ 1
IF DATE GE &YMD7
ON TABLE HOLD
END
-RUN
```

**Figure 5-28** (continued) FOCEXEC for Security Price Spread report — between labels.

```
TABLE FILE HOLD
SUM  FACKEY ASK AND COMPUTE
LCOUP/D4.1= IF LABEL EQ LAST LABEL  AND DATE EQ LAST DATE
           THEN LAST COOP ELSE 0;
DIFF/D6.2 = IF LABEL  EQ LAST LABEL AND DATE EQ LAST DATE
           THEN (ASK - LAST ASK) ELSE 0;
SQR/D10.3 = DIFF * DIFF ;

   BY HIGHEST DATE
   BY LABEL
   BY COOP
   BY MATURITY
ON TABLE HOLD
END
-RUN

DEFINE FILE HOLD
  DSORT/I2        =   IF DATE EQ &YYMMDD THEN 1 ELSE
                      IF DATE EQ &YMD1 THEN 2 ELSE
                      IF DATE EQ &YMD2 THEN 3 ELSE
                      IF DATE EQ &YMD3 THEN 4 ELSE
                      IF DATE EQ &YMD4 THEN 5 ELSE
                      IF DATE LT &YMD4 AND DATE GE &YMD6 THEN 6 ELSE
                      IF DATE LT &YMD6 AND DATE GE &YMD7 THEN 7 ELSE
99;

END

-* THE ONLY FIELDS REQUIRED FOR THE REPORT ARE AVE.DIFF AND FACKEY.
-* THE OTHER FIELDS ARE CARRIED ALONG FOR HISTREP2 FOCEXEC.

TABLE FILE HOLD
 SUM   AVE.DIFF FACKEY AVE.ASK CNT.ASK SQR
    BY DSORT
    BY LABEL
    BY COOP
    BY LCOUP
ON TABLE HOLD AS HOLD1
END
-RUN

-* DEFINE FIELDS FOR THE LABELS REQUIRED IN EACH SUMMARY REPORT.
-* DEFINE FIELD SSORT TO REPRESENT EACH LABEL.

DEFINE FILE HOLD1
BAR/A1  = ']';
```

**Figure 5-28 (continued) FOCEXEC for Security Price Spread report — between labels.**

```
SSORT/I1  = DECODE LABEL (FPCI 2
                         FPTI 3
                         F15I 5
                         GNMA 1
                         GPMI 4
                         G15I 6
                         PG5I 8
                         PC5I 7 ELSE 9 ) ;
D1/D6.2 = IF SSORT EQ 1 THEN E07 ELSE 0 ;
D2/D6.2 = IF SSORT EQ 2 THEN E07 ELSE 0 ;
D3/D6.2 = IF SSORT EQ 3 THEN E07 ELSE 0 ;
D4/D6.2 = IF SSORT EQ 4 THEN E07 ELSE 0 ;
D5/D6.2 = IF SSORT EQ 5 THEN E07 ELSE 0 ;
D6/D6.2 = IF SSORT EQ 6 THEN E07 ELSE 0 ;
D7/D6.2 = IF SSORT EQ 7 THEN E07 ELSE 0 ;
D8/D6.2 = IF SSORT EQ 8 THEN E07 ELSE 0 ;
D13/D6.2 = D1 - D3 ;
D32/D6.2 = D3 - D2 ;
D61/D6.2 = D6 - D1 ;
D58/D6.2 = D5 - D8 ;
D57/D6.2 = D5 - D7 ;
END

-* GENERATE THE PRICE SPREAD REPORT FOR PAIRS OF LABELS.
-* REPORT IS FORMATTED IN HISTSUB2.

-SET &D1 = 'D13' ;
-SET &D2 = 'D1' ;
-SET &D3 = 'D3' ;
-INCLUDE HISTSUB2
-RUN

-SET &D1 = 'D32' ;
-SET &D2 = 'D3' ;
-SET &D3 = 'D2' ;
-INCLUDE HISTSUB2
-RUN

-SET &D1 = 'D61' ;
-SET &D2 = 'D6' ;
-SET &D3 = 'D1' ;
-INCLUDE HISTSUB2
-RUN

-SET &D1 = 'D58' ;
-SET &D2 = 'D5' ;
```

**Figure 5-28** (continued) FOCEXEC for Security Price Spread report — between labels.

```
-SET &D3 = 'D8' ;
-INCLUDE HISTSUB2
-RUN

-SET &D1 = 'D57' ;
-SET &D2 = 'D5' ;
-SET &D3 = 'D7' ;
-INCLUDE HISTSUB2
-RUN
-DONE1
```

**Figure 5-28** (continued) FOCEXEC for Security Price Spread report — between labels.

(AVE.ASK) is computed for each label and coupon, and the data extracted into a HOLD file. In HISTREP1, a JOIN was used to get the full name of each label. This report does not show the full name of each label on each page. So, a JOIN is not needed.

In order to compute the price difference between pairs of labels, it is necessary to define additional fields containing the price for each label. Then it is a simple matter to define the difference between any two fields. For example, to compute the price difference between GNMA 30 YR and FNMA 30 YR, two additional fields are defined and the difference between them defined, as follows:

```
DEFINE FILE HOLD
D1/D6.2=IF LABEL EQ 'GNMA' THEN ASK ELSE 0;
D2/D6.2=IF LABEL EQ 'FPTI' THEN ASK ELSE 0;
END
```

Since the field D1 has a value of 0 when the label is not GNMA, it can be summed in a TABLE request (for each coupon and each business day) across all labels to get the GNMA prices. The field D2 can be summed in the same way. As shown below, a new filed D12 can be computed as the difference between D1 and D2.

```
TABLE FILE HOLD
SUM D1 D2 AND COMPUTE
D12/D6.2=D1-D2;
BY DSORT
BY COOP
END
```

The resulting records should contain the difference in price between the pair of labels. Note: The sort fields are DSORT (business days) and COOP (coupon). LABEL is not a sort field. (The difference D12 may be calculated in the DEFINE instead of the COMPUTE.)

The best way to use the same technique over again to calculate and report the spreads between the other pairs of labels is to set up another FOCEXEC which can be executed from HISTREP2. This is done using an INCLUDE which is invoked several times. First, the DEFINE must contain fields which calculate the price difference between each pair of labels. These fields are D12, D13, D32, etc. The field SSORT has values 1 through 8 which represent each label.

Each time the FOCEXEC HISTSUB2 is invoked with a set of dialogue manager variables &D1, &D2, &D3. These variables are set equal to the field names which are used in calculating the price spread between a pair of labels. For example, for labels GNMA 15 and GNMA 30, &D1 is equal to 'D61,' &D2 is equal to 'D6' and &D3 equals 'D1.' These represent the field names in the DEFINE. (DEFINE FILE HOLD). When HISTSUB2 is executed these names will be substituted for the dialogue manager variables in the FOCEXEC. For example, the TABLE request in HISTSUB2 becomes

```
TABLE FILE HOLD
SUM D61 D6 D1
BY DSORT
BY COOP
ON TABLE HOLD AS HOLD1
END
```

For each pair of labels, HISTSUB2 creates the report displaying the price spread between coupons. The report is sent to the offline file HISTREP2 LISTING, and control returns to HISTREP2 FOCEXEC, where the next pair of labels is processed. Using this technique, any number of label pairs can be handled in the reports.

The steps used in HISTSUB2 FOCEXEC to create each report are simple. You may recognize its similarity to HISTREP1.

1. Sum the price spread for each business day, for each coupon.
2. Convert the price spread from decimal to 32nds.
3. Use ACROSS and HOLD to create columns for each business day, month, and year.
4. Format the report.

Notice that additional logic was used to handle the situation where the price spread between two coupons could not be computed due to a missing price (zero price) for one of the labels. In HISTSUB2, the field DIFF is defined as zero if either one of the prices is zero. FOCUS allows you to suppress zeros on the report (as blanks) by using the edit option (S), as in D6.2S. Refer to the FOCUS 5.0 manual chapter 3 section 11 for a description of format edit options.

Chapter

# 6

# Maintaining FOCUS Files

FOCUS files are maintained using the MODIFY command, which contains a number of basic facilities for inputting, updating, and deleting records from a FOCUS file. Like the reporting command TABLE, MODIFY usually operates in a simple, standardized way, but has the capability to handle special processing requirements. File maintenance, which applies only to FOCUS files (not external files), requires that there be an input "stream" of data records generated by the user. The data on an input stream are either input into the FOCUS file, or are used to compute data values which are input.

The purpose of this chapter is to provide a demonstration of how the MODIFY command is used in several situations. If you understand the basic features of MODIFY, you should be able to handle many file maintenance programs. By reading the code used to maintain files familiar to you, you will learn the techniques which others have already developed. You should compile a list of features which are used in various programs. This might help you in writing code for new applications. Although most of the features of file maintenance are simple to understand and use, there may be situations which require sophisticated treatment. This might involve using extensive case logic, updating multiple files with the COMBINE facility, updating multipath files, creating numerous audit trails, etc. The best way to be sure about handling these situations is to study code written by others for handling similar requirements. You will notice that programmers have different styles of writing maintenance programs. There is usually more than one way to write code which accomplishes a particular maintenance task. You may want to enhance the code by adding special features such as logging transactions for audit trails, protecting the file update against CPU crashes, building interactive CRT screens with PF key options. However, one of your goals should be to simplify the code so that other programmers will be able to understand it and maintain it if necessary.

File maintenance is concerned not only with the update of records in a FOCUS file, but sometimes usually with the extraction of data from other FOCUS files. This may involve writing procedures which extract records from several files, format the records as an input stream, and sort the records in a certain order. This also involves checking that the data is extracted at the right time. You may have to build in safeguards that the data is extracted only at the end of each day, or at the end of the month, or after some other event occurs.

The following are the major tasks which can be accomplished using the MODIFY procedure:

1. Update a FOCUS file using records from an input file; the records in the file contain fields either in fixed positions or delimited by commas.
2. Update a FOCUS file using data entered interactively to a fullscreen CRT or prompted one value at a time.
3. Update a FOCUS file using data from more than one transaction file.
4. Validate data on transaction records by testing acceptable ranges and other criteria.
5. Log transactions which are invalid, rejected, etc., onto log files.
6. Write particular data or text from each transaction or computed from each transaction onto other files.
7. Compute transaction values using expressions with other transaction fields.
8. Look up values of fields on cross-reference files.
9. Browse through a file by displaying the children records of a parent segment.
10. Delete records from a file.

Every task can be accomplished using simple MODIFY commands, as we shall demonstrate. These commands do not change much from application to application. The major problem which arises is when one MODIFY procedure is used to do too many tasks. FOCUS may have the capability to handle the tasks, but the amount of effort required by the programmer to design the procedure may be unnecessary. It is usually easier to write two or more MODIFY procedures for such a task, than to handle it with one procedure.

Figure 6-1 presents a FOCEXEC which is used to update a FOCUS file containing the manpower count for an organization's major AREAS. This FOCEXEC illustrates using two MODIFY requests and one transaction file to update the FOCUS file.

The AREASUM FOCUS file is updated on a monthly basis using data extracted from several files. Each file contains a different kind of manpower count — either prior year, plan, or actual. The AREALOAD FOCEXEC extracts the actual counts for each cost center (from the MONSUM file) and loads it into the AREASUM file. In the extraction step, the data for all months up to the present month is obtained from the MONSUM file.

The field AREACD contains the codes of the major organizational AREAS, which consist of a number of COST CENTERS. Notice that the step to extract the data is important since it converts data from one format into records appropriate to the AREASUM file. The AREASUM file has two key fields, AREACD and LINENO. For each AREACD, the LINENO indicates the type of data. For example,

```
LINENO 1: TOTAL ACTUALS
LINENO 2: TOTAL FORECAST
LINENO 3: TOTAL PRIOR YR
LINENO 4: REGULAR ACTUALS
LINENO 5: REGULAR FORECAST
LINENO 6: REGULAR PRIOR YR
```

The MASTERS for AREASUM and MONSUM are shown in figures 6-2 and 6-3. (The AREAG MASTER is found in the previous chapter.)

In this FOCEXEC, the data for TOTAL ACTUALS (LINENO = 1) and REGULAR ACTUALS (LINENO = 4) is loaded into the AREASUM file. (The TOTAL category includes all manpower categories, while the REGULAR category includes only OFF, CFT, and CPT.) Notice that the MONSUM file and AREASUM file are organized differently. In MONSUM, there are six fields which contain the counts of six categories:

```
-* PROGRAM: AREALOAD
-* LOAD MONTHLY SUMMARY STAFF COUNT INTO AREASUM FILE.
-*
SET MSG = OFF

-CMS FILEDEF DATETMP1 DISK DATETMP1 TEMP A ( LRECL 80 RECFM FB
-RUN
-SET &YEAR = '00' ;
-SET &MON  = '000' ;

-* THE CURRENT MONTH AND YEAR ARE READ FROM THE DATETMP1 FILE,
-*    WHICH IS A FLAT FILE CONTAINING 1 RECORD.
-* THE STAFF COUNT IS EXTRACTED FROM THE MONSUM FILE
-*    FOR THE CURRENT MONTH AND YEAR ONLY.

-READ DATETMP1 &YEAR &MON
-IF &IORETURN NE 0 GOTO ERROR ;
-RUN

-SET &LASTYR = &YEAR - 1;
-SET &DEND   = &YEAR ;

-* GET STAFF COUNT FROM MONSUM FILE

JOIN CLEAR *
JOIN CCCD IN AREAG TO ALL CCCD IN  MONSUM AS JOIN1

DEFINE FILE AREAG
  YEAR/I2      =   INT(MMEND/10000);
  MONNO/I2     =   FLDNO ;
  REG/D15.5    =   MOFF + MCFT + MCPT ;
  TOT/D15.5    =   MOFF + MCFT + MCPT + MOVT + MCHP + MCCP ;
END

TABLE FILE AREAG
SUM REG TOT
   BY ACD
   BY FLDNO
IF YEAR EQ &DEND
IF FLDNO LE &MON
IF ACD NE ' '
ON TABLE HOLD
END
-RUN

-* BECAUSE AREASUM STORES THE REG COUNT AND TOTAL COUNT ON DIF-
FERENT
```

**Figure 6-1    AREALOAD FOCEXEC**

```
-*   RECORDS, TWO MODIFY PASSES ARE USED TO LOAD THE DATA.
-*   FIRST POST TOTAL COUNT TO MONSUM FILE. VALUE OF FIELD LINENO IS
1.

SET MSG = ON

MODIFY FILE AREASUM

COMPUTE
MONNO/I2 = ; REG/D15.5 = ; TOT/D15.5 = ;

FIXFORM AREACD/A4 MONNO/I4 REG/D8 TOT/D8

COMPUTE
LINENO/I2 = 1;
JANNEW/D15.5 = IF MONNO EQ 1 THEN TOT ELSE 0 ;
FEBNEW/D15.5 = IF MONNO EQ 2 THEN TOT ELSE 0 ;
MARNEW/D15.5 = IF MONNO EQ 3 THEN TOT ELSE 0 ;
APRNEW/D15.5 = IF MONNO EQ 4 THEN TOT ELSE 0 ;
MAYNEW/D15.5 = IF MONNO EQ 5 THEN TOT ELSE 0 ;
JUNNEW/D15.5 = IF MONNO EQ 6 THEN TOT ELSE 0 ;
JULNEW/D15.5 = IF MONNO EQ 7 THEN TOT ELSE 0 ;
AUGNEW/D15.5 = IF MONNO EQ 8 THEN TOT ELSE 0 ;
SEPNEW/D15.5 = IF MONNO EQ 9 THEN TOT ELSE 0 ;
OCTNEW/D15.5 = IF MONNO EQ 10 THEN TOT ELSE 0 ;
NOVNEW/D15.5 = IF MONNO EQ 11 THEN TOT ELSE 0 ;
DECNEW/D15.5 = IF MONNO EQ 12 THEN TOT ELSE 0 ;

MATCH AREACD LINENO
ON MATCH COMPUTE
JAN = D.JAN + JANNEW ;
FEB = D.FEB + FEBNEW ;
MAR = D.MAR + MARNEW ;
APR = D.APR + APRNEW ;
MAY = D.MAY + MAYNEW ;
JUN = D.JUN + JUNNEW ;
JUL = D.JUL + JULNEW ;
AUG = D.AUG + AUGNEW ;
SEP = D.SEP + SEPNEW ;
OCT = D.OCT + OCTNEW ;
NOV = D.NOV + NOVNEW ;
DEC = D.DEC + DECNEW ;

ON MATCH UPDATE JAN FEB MAR APR MAY JUN JUL AUG SEP OCT NOV DEC
ON MATCH GOTO TOP
ON NOMATCH COMPUTE
JAN = JANNEW ;
```

Figure 6-1   (continued) AREALOAD FOCEXEC

```
FEB = FEBNEW ;
MAR = MARNEW ;
APR = APRNEW ;
MAY = MAYNEW ;
JUN = JUNNEW ;
JUL = JULNEW ;
AUG = AUGNEW ;
SEP = SEPNEW ;
OCT = OCTNEW ;
NOV = NOVNEW ;
DEC = DECNEW ;

ON NOMATCH INCLUDE
ON NOMATCH GOTO TOP
DATA ON HOLD
END
-RUN

-* NEXT  POST REG. COUNT TO MONSUM FILE. VALUE OF FIELD LINENO IS
4.

MODIFY FILE AREASUM

COMPUTE
MONNO/I2 = ; REG/D15.5 = ; TOT/D15.5 = ;

FIXFORM AREACD/A4 MONNO/I4 REG/D8 TOT/D8

COMPUTE
LINENO/I2 = 4;
JANNEW/D15.5 = IF MONNO EQ 1 THEN REG ELSE 0 ;
FEBNEW/D15.5 = IF MONNO EQ 2 THEN REG ELSE 0 ;
MARNEW/D15.5 = IF MONNO EQ 3 THEN REG ELSE 0 ;
APRNEW/D15.5 = IF MONNO EQ 4 THEN REG ELSE 0 ;
MAYNEW/D15.5 = IF MONNO EQ 5 THEN REG ELSE 0 ;
JUNNEW/D15.5 = IF MONNO EQ 6 THEN REG ELSE 0 ;
JULNEW/D15.5 = IF MONNO EQ 7 THEN REG ELSE 0 ;
AUGNEW/D15.5 = IF MONNO EQ 8 THEN REG ELSE 0 ;
SEPNEW/D15.5 = IF MONNO EQ 9 THEN REG ELSE 0 ;
OCTNEW/D15.5 = IF MONNO EQ 10 THEN REG ELSE 0 ;
NOVNEW/D15.5 = IF MONNO EQ 11 THEN REG ELSE 0 ;
DECNEW/D15.5 = IF MONNO EQ 12 THEN REG ELSE 0 ;

MATCH AREACD LINENO
ON MATCH COMPUTE
JAN = D.JAN + JANNEW ;
FEB = D.FEB + FEBNEW ;
```

Figure 6-1    (continued) AREALOAD FOCEXEC

```
MAR = D.MAR + MARNEW ;
APR = D.APR + APRNEW ;
MAY = D.MAY + MAYNEW ;
JUN = D.JUN + JUNNEW ;
JUL = D.JUL + JULNEW ;
AUG = D.AUG + AUGNEW ;
SEP = D.SEP + SEPNEW ;
OCT = D.OCT + OCTNEW ;
NOV = D.NOV + NOVNEW ;
DEC = D.DEC + DECNEW ;

ON MATCH UPDATE JAN FEB MAR APR MAY JUN JUL AUG SEP OCT NOV DEC
ON MATCH GOTO TOP
ON NOMATCH COMPUTE
JAN = JANNEW ;
FEB = FEBNEW ;
MAR = MARNEW ;
APR = APRNEW ;
MAY = MAYNEW ;
JUN = JUNNEW ;
JUL = JULNEW ;
AUG = AUGNEW ;
SEP = SEPNEW ;
OCT = OCTNEW ;
NOV = NOVNEW ;
DEC = DECNEW ;

ON NOMATCH INCLUDE
ON NOMATCH GOTO TOP
DATA ON HOLD
END
-RUN
-ERROR

-EXIT
```

**Figure 6-1    (continued) AREALOAD FOCEXEC**

```
OFF: OFFICIAL
CFT: CLERICAL FULL TIME
CPT: CLERICAL PART TIME
OVT: OVERTIME
CHP: CONTRACT HELP
CCP: CONTRACT COMPUTER PROFESSIONAL
```

```
FILENAME=AREASUM  ,SUFFIX=FOC
SEGNAME=DATA      ,  SEGTYPE=S2
  FIELDNAME=AREACD        ,ALIAS=ACD      ,FORMAT=A4      ,$
  FIELDNAME=LINENO        ,ALIAS=LN       ,FORMAT=I2      ,$
  FIELDNAME=JAN           ,ALIAS=JAN      ,FORMAT=D12.5   ,$
  FIELDNAME=FEB           ,ALIAS=FEB      ,FORMAT=D12.5   ,$
  FIELDNAME=MAR           ,ALIAS=MAR      ,FORMAT=D12.5   ,$
  FIELDNAME=APR           ,ALIAS=APR      ,FORMAT=D12.5   ,$
  FIELDNAME=MAY           ,ALIAS=MAY      ,FORMAT=D12.5   ,$
  FIELDNAME=JUN           ,ALIAS=JUN      ,FORMAT=D12.5   ,$
  FIELDNAME=JUL           ,ALIAS=JUL      ,FORMAT=D12.5   ,$
  FIELDNAME=AUG           ,ALIAS=AUG      ,FORMAT=D12.5   ,$
  FIELDNAME=SEP           ,ALIAS=SEP      ,FORMAT=D12.5   ,$
  FIELDNAME=OCT           ,ALIAS=OCT      ,FORMAT=D12.5   ,$
  FIELDNAME=NOV           ,ALIAS=NOV      ,FORMAT=D12.5   ,$
  FIELDNAME=DEC           ,ALIAS=DEC      ,FORMAT=D12.5   ,$
```

**Figure 6-2    AREASUM MASTER file.**

MONSUM contains two key fields COSTCD and FLDNO; where COSTCD is the cost center code and FLDNO is the month of the year (1–12). The AREALOAD FOCEXEC has four steps:

1. File MONSUM is JOINED to the AREAG file; a DEFINE creates two fields REG and TOT using the above six fields in MONSUM. (These represent the regular and total counts.)
2. A TABLE request is used to extract the regular and total counts for each area code and month. The records are placed in a HOLD file, which will be used as the transaction file for the MODIFY step.
3. The TOTAL count is loaded into the AREASUM file using the first MODIFY procedure.
4. The REGULAR count is loaded into the AREASUM file using the second MODIFY procedure.

## Creating a Transaction File

The records in the transaction file should contain data which has been sorted and aggregated to coincide, as closely as possible, with the structure of the AREASUM file. The extracted data has been summed and sorted by area code, by month. The HOLD file contains records in internal format, not alphanumeric (as in SAVE files). Therefore, the

```
FILENAME=MONSUM   ,SUFFIX=FOC
SEGNAME=COSTC   ,SEGTYPE=S1
  FIELDNAME=COSTCD      ,ALIAS=CCCD    ,FORMAT=I4      ,FIELDTYPE=I, $
SEGNAME=MONTHS   ,SEGTYPE=S1,PARENT=COSTC
  FIELDNAME=FLDNO       ,ALIAS=MONTH   ,FORMAT=I2       ,$
  FIELDNAME=MOFF        ,ALIAS=MOFF    ,FORMAT=D15.5    ,$
  FIELDNAME=MCFT        ,ALIAS=MCFT    ,FORMAT=D15.5    ,$
  FIELDNAME=MCPT        ,ALIAS=MCPT    ,FORMAT=D15.5    ,$
  FIELDNAME=MOVT        ,ALIAS=MOVT    ,FORMAT=D15.5    ,$
  FIELDNAME=MCHP        ,ALIAS=MCHP    ,FORMAT=D15.5    ,$
  FIELDNAME=MCCP        ,ALIAS=MCCP    ,FORMAT=D15.5    ,$
```

Figure 6-3   MONSUM MASTER file

FIXFORM command used to identify the fields on the input record must specify whether a field is alpha, integer, or double precision.

```
FIXFORM AREACD/A4 MONNO/I4 REG/D8 TOT/D8
```

If a SAVE file were used, all fields would have alphanumeric format. The MODIFY uses a COMPUTE to create the fields which are required in the AREASUM file. For example,

```
COMPUTE
JANNEW/D15.5=IF MONNO EQ 1 THEN REG ELSE 0;
```

If an input record contains a value of 1 for the field MONNO, then it represents a JANUARY value, otherwise the value of JANNEW is zero. Similarly, for each of the twelve months. Since each input record contains a different month, the values are set to zero for the remaining eleven months. In this way, it is possible to update each of the twelve fields for each input record. On each MATCH of the key fields, AREACD and LINENO, the fields are recomputed using the command:

```
ON MATCH COMPUTE
JAN=D.JAN+JANNEW;
```

The term D.JAN is the value of the field JAN in the record of the AREASUM FOCUS file. The term JANNEW is the value on the current input record. The term JAN is the new value of the field JAN which will be updated in the database. This may seem to be an unnecessary way to design this procedure. But it is necessary — because all twelve fields JAN through DEC are updated for each input record.

This example is typical of many maintenance procedures — where the input transactions are obtained by extracting records from another FOCUS file. This is usually done to combine data from more than one type of file into a single FOCUS file — which can be more easily used for reporting. (In this example, another procedure might be needed to load the totals for forecast and prior year into the same AREASUM file.)

We will next discuss the basic techniques used in a MODIFY procedure. You should understand, first, that any MODIFY requires some familiarity with the MASTER description file; it is the MASTER which describes the relationship between the segments, the field names, and the formats required for each field. You should review with someone the MASTER files used in several applications with which you are familiar; or review the applications which are presented in this chapter. In particular, check out the fields in each segment, and the key fields, which indicate the relationship between records.

There is much that cannot be covered in one book, and which you will pick up in your applications experience. However, the material and examples used in this chapter should serve as a reference source for many of the standard MODIFY tasks. We shall work with a simple FOCUS file, which uses most of the techniques available in the MODIFY command. Additional examples of MODIFY procedures are presented in Chapter 9.

## Matching Transaction Values to Database Records

File maintenance requires that you know something about the structure of the FOCUS file, and how it is organized. The MASTER description identifies the parent-child relationships, the key fields, and the fields contained in each segment. For each input transaction, FOCUS needs to know the values of the key fields so that it can determine where a database record is to be added or updated. This process is known as "MATCH LOGIC," since the values on an input record are matched with the values of the key fields in the FOCUS file. The matching process can be quite simple for FOCUS files with a single segment, or become more involved when multiple segments are considered. We will demonstrate this process using a simplified FOCUS

```
FILENAME = PRICE , SUFFIX = FOC

SEGNAME = SECINFO ,SEGTYPE = S2

        FIELD = LABEL        ,LABEL     ,A04,FIELDTYPE = I,$
        FIELD = COUPON       ,CPN       ,D6.3,$
        FIELD = MATURITY     ,MD        ,A07,$
        FIELD = ISSUE        ,ID        ,A07,$
        FIELD = MBSFLAG      ,FLAG      ,A1 ,$

SEGNAME = SECPRICE,PARENT = SECINFO ,SEGTYPE = SH1,$

        FIELD = DATE         , DT       ,I6,      FIELDTYPE = I,$ YMD
        FIELD = BID          , BD       ,D9.5,$
        FIELD = ASK          , AK       ,D9.5,$
        FIELD = YIELD        , SY       ,D6.3,$
```

**Figure 6-4   PRICE MASTER file.**

file representing daily prices of mortgage backed securities. The MASTER description is shown in figure 6-4. In this application, we wish to load the daily prices of mortgage securities into the FOCUS file.

From this point on we will use the term "database" to represent any FOCUS file which is being maintained. This term is sometimes helpful in referring to records in the FOCUS file, rather than in the input transaction file. The PRICE FOCUS file contains two segments.

1. SECINFO — the root segment; describes each security by its LABEL and COUPON (key fields); other information contained in the segment is the issue date and maturity date of the security.
2. SECPRICE — the child segment of SECINFO; contains the bid price, ask price, yield, and date. The SECPRICE segment is updated with new prices each business day.

We will consider several MODIFY procedures which may be used to perform file maintenance on the PRICE file. The two major tasks are updating (correcting) data in the SECINFO segment, and inputting daily prices in the child SECPRICE segment. First, we will outline how most MODIFY procedures are set up.

Like any other FOCUS procedure, a MODIFY can be executed interactively from native FOCUS, or using a FOCEXEC. In either case, the MODIFY contains the following parts:

1. MODIFY FILE filename (start procedure)
2. LOG conditions (log records which are rejected, invalid, etc.)
3. Identify, with COMPUTE, new fields (fields not in database must be identified)
4. Specify the source of input transactions (FIXFORM, FREEFORM, PROMPT, or CRTFORM)
5. Validate the input records
6. Perform MATCH logic (determine logic for inputting, updating, and deleting records).
7. COMPUTE new transaction fields from fields on input record (this can be done before or after the MATCH logic).
8. Complete the MODIFY by indicating the source of data.

Some sections, such as the LOG of transactions, or validation of data, are not required.

Consider, as a first example, a procedure which prompts the user for label, coupon, date, and asked price. The following procedure accepts this data interactively, and inputs the ASK price if it's not already there. If the price record for that date already has been entered, the input record is rejected.

```
MODIFY FILE PRICE
PROMPT LABEL COUPON DATE ASK
MATCH LABEL COUPON
ON MATCH CONTINUE
ON NOMATCH REJECT
MATCH DATE
ON NOMATCH INCLUDE
DATA
. . . .
```

After FOCUS sees the DATA statement, it expects the user to start entering data for each prompted field. As shown in figure 6-5, the user enters the data on the screen one field at a time. Any number of records, consisting of label, coupon, date, and ask, can be entered. When there are no more records to enter, the user enters 'END' as an input value. An alternate way to end the procedure is to enter "QUIT."

```
-* PROMPTING FOR TRANSACTION VALUES LINE BY LINE.
MODIFY FILE PRICE
PROMPT LABEL COUPON DATE ASK
MATCH LABEL COUPON
  ON MATCH CONTINUE
  ON NOMATCH REJECT
MATCH DATE
  ON NOMATCH INCLUDE
DATA
DATA FOR TRANS 1
LABEL     =   GNMA
COUPON    =   7.0
DATE      =   870103
ASK       =   99.
DATA FOR TRANS 2
LABEL     =   GNMA
COUPON    =   8.0
DATE      =   870103
ASK       =   99.5
DATA FOR TRANS 3 ...
```

**Figure 6-5    Creating transactions with PROMPT command.**

In this case, the record which is being input will not be processed; the procedure will pass to native FOCUS. (Hitting PF3 will also quit the procedure).

If there is a format error in any data value (e.g., an alpha character is entered for the field DATE — whose format in the MASTER is I6), FOCUS will show an error message and allow you to reenter the value:

```
FORMAT ERROR...FIELD DATE...
```

The PROMPT command is rarely used in "customized" applications, because users prefer entering data interactively onto full screen layouts via FIDEL (CRTFORM). It is useful, however, for making a few updates or corrections to the database. For more examples of using PROMPT, refer to the FOCUS 5.0 manual Chapter 5 section 2.3.

The MATCH LOGIC in this example should be understood before going on to other file maintenance examples. FOCUS performs matching on key fields to determine what to do with the input record. Sometimes all the key fields can be used in a single MATCH, but it is clearer (and better practice) to MATCH fields one segment at a time.

Since the PROMPT requests input values from both the TOP and CHILD segments, FOCUS expects instructions on actions in both segments. If you wish to perform maintenance on only one segment, you should not prompt for values from the other segment.

The KEY FIELDS determine how the records are organized in each segment. LABEL and COUPON are key fields in the top segment, while DATE is the key field in the child segment. The MATCH statement locates specific records in each segment based on the values of the key fields. (Note that file maintenance can sometimes be performed by matching on non-key fields, especially when the values of the non-key fields are unique in the segment. However, FOCUS will issue a warning message if the key fields for a segment are not in the MATCH.)

The MATCH logic on each segment is as follows:

1. The key fields LABEL and COUPON are MATCHED, using the values from the first PROMPTED input record.
2. If there is a match (i.e., a segment is found in the database with those values), nothing happens to the segment (ON MATCH CONTINUE) and the next MATCH is performed. If there is a NOMATCH (i.e. no segment is found with those values), the entire input record is rejected.
3. When matching the child segment — with key field DATE — the segment is included (i.e., is added) if a child segment containing the value for DATE is not found. If the segment already exists, the record is rejected.

Note, the condition to reject the record was not stated explicitly

ON MATCH REJECT

This is the default action when including a segment. The FOCUS 5.0 manual Chapter 5 section 3.1.3 indicates the DEFAULT actions for MATCH logic. The MODIFY processes the input record first for the root segment, then for the child segment — there is a separate MATCH command for each segment. It is usually NOT good practice to use a single MATCH for both segments. For example,

```
MATCH LABEL COUPON DATE
ON NOMATCH INCLUDE
ON MATCH REJECT
```

is almost identical. However, if a label and coupon do not match with a record in the database, it will be included in the database — instead of rejected as is expected.

When a segment is included, as was the PRICE segment, FOCUS assigns a value to every field in the segment, even if a value does not appear on the input transaction. Since only the field ASK has an input value, FOCUS assigns a value of zero to the fields BID and YIELD. (Alphanumeric fields are assigned a value of blank).

In order to update the fields in a segment, the UPDATE command is used. Updates can be performed only on MATCH conditions. (You must specify the fields whose values are to be updated.) For example, to update the field ASK in the PRICE segment if there is a match on DATE,

```
MODIFY FILE PRICE
PROMPT LABEL COUPON DATE ASK
MATCH LABEL COUPON
ON MATCH CONTINUE
ON NOMATCH REJECT
MATCH DATE
ON MATCH UPDATE ASK
ON NOMATCH INCLUDE
DATA
END
```

Any file in a segment, except the key fields, may be updated. Note that the price segment is included if there is no match. To reject it, use

```
MATCH DATE
ON MATCH UPDATE ASK
ON NOMATCH REJECT
```

You can specify other actions in MATCH statements. These actions are:

1. Read additional incoming data.
2. Perform computations and validations.
3. Type messages.

Each action can be assigned on a separate ON MATCH or ON NOMATCH phrase. For example,

```
MATCH LABEL
ON MATCH CONTINUE
ON NOMATCH TYPE
"LABEL CODE IS NOT FOUND"
ON NOMATCH REJECT
```

Note, if include a REJECT action, it must appear last; otherwise, the ON NOMATCH TYPE will be ignored.

The last file maintenance task is DELETE, which removes segment records from a FOCUS file. Any segment can be deleted, the root or child segments. However, when a segment is deleted, all its children segments are also deleted.

For example, if a root segment instance, with key field values

```
LABEL=GNMA and COUPON=10.0
```

contain child segments for DATE=870601, 870602, 870603, etc., all of these records will be deleted when the root segment is deleted. The procedure is:

```
MODIFY FILE PRICE
PROMPT LABEL COUPON
MATCH LABEL COUPON
ON MATCH DELETE
ON NOMATCH REJECT
DATA
END
```

It is important that matching be performed a segment at a time when deleting records. For example, do not use the following when deleting records from the PRICE segment

```
MATCH LABEL COUPON DATE
ON MATCH DELETE
ON NOMATCH REJECT
```

This might delete the root segment as well as the child segment. As a safety measure, FOCUS allows you to specify which segment is to be

```
FILENAME = PRICE2 , SUFFIX = FOC

 SEGNAME = SECINFO ,SEGTYPE = S2

        FIELD = LABEL          ,LABEL        ,A04,FIELDTYPE = I,$
        FIELD = COUPON          ,CPN          ,D6.3,$

 SEGNAME = OTHINFO ,SEGTYPE = U, PARENT = SECINFO

        FIELD = MATURITY       ,MD           ,A07,$
        FIELD = ISSUE          ,ID           ,A07,$

 SEGNAME = SECPRICE,PARENT = SECINFO ,SEGTYPE = SH1,$

        FIELD = DATE           , DT          ,I6,     FIELDTYPE = I,$ YMD
        FIELD = BID            , BD          ,D9.5,$
        FIELD = ASK            , AK          ,D9.5,$
        FIELD = YIELD          , SY          ,D6.3,$
```

Figure 6-6    PRICE MASTER with unique segment.

deleted so that you can be careful not to delete the wrong segment — simply specify the name of any field in the segment to be deleted. For example,

```
MATCH LABEL COUPON DATE
ON MATCH DELETE DATE
```

## Modifying Unique Segments

The above match logic for including, updating, and deleting records applies to all situations and applications. The only exception is maintenance of UNIQUE SEGMENTS. This is described in depth in the FOCUS manual Chapter 5 section 3.4.1. A unique segment can almost be considered as part of its parent segment. Because unique segments are extensions of their parent, they have no key fields. However, in order to include, update, or delete it, an additional step is needed — since you must first locate the parent instance, then proceed to the unique instance. For example, assume the root segment has a unique segment containing the issue date and maturity date of the security. Figure 6-6 shows the MASTER description.

When a parent (TOP) segment is included in the database, the unique segment will also be included using the regular logic (if values for the fields appear in the input transaction). To update a unique segment or include only a unique segment, another match is needed. For example,

```
MATCH LABEL COUPON
ON MATCH CONTINUE TO ISSUE
ON NOMATCH REJECT
MATCH ISSUE
ON MATCH UPDATE ISSUE
ON NOMATCH REJECT
```

OR,

```
MATCH LABEL COUPON
ON MATCH CONTINUE TO ISSUE
ON NOMATCH REJECT
MATCH ISSUE
ON NOMATCH INCLUDE
ON MATCH REJECT
```

The step ON MATCH CONTINUE TO ISSUE is necessary to reach the unique segment. Note that there are no key fields in a unique segment — so any field can be referred to. Also, do not confuse ON MATCH CONTINUE TO field with ON MATCH CONTINUE, which indicates that no action is to be done on a MATCH.

**The FIXFORM Statement — Using an Input Transactions File**

Regular maintenance procedures usually involve processing a large number of input records. When the values occupy the same position on each input record, the FIXFORM (or FORM) command is needed to read the records.

There are two types of FIXFORM commands, which are nearly the same:

1. FIXFORMS for input records in alphanumeric (or text) format.
2. FIXFORMS for input records in internal format.

## Considerations When Using Transaction Files

Before describing the FIXFORM command, there are some preliminary remarks about transaction files which are important. Transaction files are usually generated from some other program; therefore, it is sometimes necessary to check if the file has been created. In a FOCEXEC, this can be done using the CMS STATE command. For example, if the file's name is PLOAD INPUT A, your FOCEXEC might have in it the following dialogue manager statements.

```
-CMS STATE PLOAD INPUT A
-IF &RETCODE NE 0 GOTO DONE;
-*INPUT FILE FOUND. THIS IS A COMMENT.
-*
MODIFY FILE PRICE
FIXFORM LABEL/4 COUPON/6 DATE/6 ASK/7
 . . . .
END
-DONE
-EXIT
```

The system variable &RETCODE will have a value 0 if the file is found. If it is not zero, then skip the MODIFY step. This is not necessary — but is sometimes useful to indicate that no input file was processed.

FOCUS allows you to check the number of transactions which were processed by the MODIFY — using system variables. See FOCUS 5.0 manual Chapter 6 section 3.5 for a list of all the system (statistical) variables. The number of transactions accepted, input, updated, rejected, etc., are automatically displayed on the CRT screen after the MODIFY ends. (See the FOCUS manual Chapter 5 section 1.2.1.) The system variables &ACCEPTS, &INPUT, etc., contain these values and can be used as dialogue manager variables after the MODIFY request. (Note: Be sure to place a -RUN after the end of the MODIFY. Also, the values of these variables get reset when other FOCUS code is executed. So, be sure to save these values as other dialogue manager variables, if needed.)

## Suppressing System Messages

To suppress the display of MODIFY statistics, change the SET parameter before executing the MODIFY — SET MSG=OFF. Note: You can also suppress displays of FOCUS messages, rejected records, etc. using the CMS command HT. To suppress all displays on the CRT, include in the FOCEXEC:

-CMS SET CMSTYPE HT

To resume display, use

-CMS SET CMSTYPE RT

As described in the FOCUS manual Chapter 5 section 5.2, you may use the LOG statement to record transactions into files and to control the display of rejected records. This logging facility enables the programmer to deal with rejected transactions after entering all the data.

## The Sort Order of the Transaction Records

A most important consideration is the sorting of input records on the input transaction file. When segment instances are added to a FOCUS file, FOCUS determines whether the instance goes before or after the "current position" — based on the sort order of the segment. This process is efficient when FOCUS moves through the file in one direction only. Therefore, FOCUS files can be maintained more efficiently when the input transactions are sorted in the same logical order as the key fields in the FOCUS file. (Ascending order for Sn SEGTYPE, descending order for SHn SEGTYPE.) This will result in:

1. Faster MODIFY procedures — since FOCUS can locate quickly where to store the data in each segment.
2. Better organized FOCUS files (with faster reporting), since the records in each segment will be in the right sort order.

With respect to internal sort order, FOCUS files are organized so that

- the ROOT segment's records are sorted in physical order (i.e., determined by the order of the input records).
- the children segments are in logical order (i.e., determined by the key fields).

When creating the input transaction file from another program, it is good practice, therefore, to sort the records. If this can't be done in the extraction program, you can use the system sort or CMS SYNCSORT to do it in any extra step. Syncsort is a software package which has several features useful in special situations. Once available on the mainframe operating system, it is easily invoked by the command:

```
SSORT filename filetype filemode
```

The command, when issued, will prompt you for the fields to be sorted and type of fields. Your response might look like:

```
1, 4, CH, A, 10, 5, CH, A, 20, 6, CH, D
```

In this case, the records in the file will be sorted as follows:

1. Sort first (major sort field) by positions 1 thru 4, in ascending (A) order.
2. Next, sort by positions 10 thru 14 (i.e. start at column 10 for 5 columns), in ascending order.
3. Last, sort by positions 20 thru 25, in descending (D) order.

The parameter 'CH' indicates that a character sort is performed. (Non-character sorts are very rarely needed.) Figure 6-7 shows a CMS EXEC written to syncsort a file created by a FOCEXEC. Because Syncsort is much faster than the FOCUS sort, it is sometimes used to sort large extracted files (note: Records may be first extracted without sorting using the FOCUS TABLEF command), or when rebuilding FOCUS files.

## A Sample Input Transactions File

The MASTER for the PRICE FOCUS file has two keys in the top segment, LABEL and COUPON, and one key field in the bottom segment, DATE. Therefore, an input transaction file should contain

```
&TRACE OFF
****************************************************************PRO00180
*
CLRSCRN
&BEGTYPE 8

    BILLS EXEC


======================================================================

    ENTER THE DATE FOR DATA EXTRACTION (MMDDYY) :
          OR QUIT TO EXIT

&READ VARS &REQ_DATE
&IF .&REQ_DATE  = .      &GOTO -OVER
&IF  &REQ_DATE  = QUIT &GOTO -EXIT

-STARTUP
*
  FILEDEF BILLS    DISK BILLS    &REQ_DATE A   ( LRECL 120 RECFM F
  FILEDEF FUTURES  DISK FUTURES  &REQ_DATE A   ( LRECL 120 RECFM F

  &STACK EX BILLS
  &STACK &REQ_DATE
  EX FOCUS

-SORTMBS
  DESBUF
  &STACK   115,5,CH,A 20,7,CH,A 29,7,CH,A 15,4,CH,A
  SSORT BILLS &REQ_DATE A
*
-WRAPUP
SET CMSTYPE RT
CLRSCRN
&BEGTYPE 7

    BILLS COMPLETE -

        EXTRACTED DATA IS IN THE FOLLOWING FILES :


======================================================================

-EXIT
 &EXIT &RC
```

**Figure 6-7    Example of EXEC using SYNCSORT.**

records sorted by LABEL, then by COUPON, then by DATE. Figure 6-8 shows an input transaction file which has been sorted in this way. The file's name is PR1 DATA A, and contains records which will be used to load into a new PRICE FOCUS file. The PR1 FOCEXEC, below, illustrates the FIXFORM statement which describes the positions of each field on the record:

```
-CMS FILEDEF PR1 DISK PR1 DATA A
MODIFY FILE PRICE
FIXFORM LABEL/4 X1 COUPON/5 X1 MATURITY/6
FIXFORM ISSUE/6 X1 DATE/6 X1 ASK/7
MATCH LABEL COUPON
ON NOMATCH INCLUDE
ON MATCH CONTINUE
MATCH DATE
ON NOMATCH INCLUDE
ON MATCH REJECT
DATA ON PR1
END
```

The FIXFORM statement reads in one logical record at a time — dividing the record into transaction fields. Note: The name of a field doesn't have to be a field in the MASTER. If it is not, you must identify the field to FOCUS using a COMPUTE — such as:

```
COMPUTE
XISSUE/I6 = ;
XMAT/I6 = ;
```

One MODIFY request may contain more than one set of FIX-FORMS for:

1. Reading in the data from another transaction file.
2. Redefining the records from the same file into different sets of fields.

Two, or more, FIXFORM statements act as one statement and reads in one logical record. This is needed when the list of fields is too long to fit on one line. Also, if the FIXFORM reads to the last column on a record, then the next field on the FIXFORM will read from column one of the next record. For example, as in figure 6-9, the input

```
FPCI  7.00  090909  870601  870904  82.062
FPCI  7.00  030909  870601  870904  81.843
FPCI  7.00  090909  870601  870903  82.312
FPCI  7.00  030909  870601  870903  82.093
FPCI  8.00  090909  870601  870902  86.906
FPCI  8.00  090909  870601  870901  87.906
FPCI  8.00  090909  870601  870831  88.343
FPCI  8.00  090909  870601  870828  88.531
FPCI  8.00  090909  870601  870827  89.281
FPCI  8.00  090909  870601  870826  89.906
FPCI  9.00  090909  870601  870904  92.593
FPCI  9.00  090909  870601  870903  92.718
FPTI  7.00  090909  870601  870904  80.656
FPTI  7.00  030909  870601  870904  80.656
FPTI  7.00  090909  870601  870903  80.906
FPTI  7.00  030909  870601  870903  80.906
FPTI  7.00  090909  870601  870902  80.906
FPTI  7.00  030909  870601  870902  80.906
FPTI  7.00  090909  870601  870901  80.906
FPTI  7.00  030909  870601  870901  80.906
FPTI  7.00  090909  870601  870831  81.343
FPTI  7.00  030909  870601  870831  81.343
FPTI  7.00  090909  870601  870828  81.500
FPTI  7.00  030909  870601  870828  81.500
FPTI  7.00  090909  870601  870827  82.250
FPTI  7.00  030909  870601  870827  82.250
FPTI  7.00  090909  870601  870826  82.875
FPTI  7.00  030909  870601  870826  82.875
FPTI  9.00  090909  870601  870904  92.875
FPTI  9.00  090909  870601  870903  93.000
FPTI  9.00  090909  870601  870902  93.000
GNMA  7.00  090909  870601  870904  79.968
GNMA  7.00  090909  870601  870903  80.281
GNMA  7.00  090909  870601  870902  80.531
GNMA  7.00  090909  870601  870901  81.593
GNMA  7.00  090909  870601  870831  82.093
GNMA  7.00  090909  870601  870828  82.031
GNMA  7.00  090909  870601  870827  82.781
GNMA  7.00  090909  870601  870826  83.531
GNMA  8.00  090909  870601  870904  85.843
GNMA  8.00  170131  870601  870904  85.937
GNMA  8.00  090909  870601  870903  86.093
GNMA  8.00  170131  870601  870903  86.250
GNMA  8.00  090909  870601  870902  86.343
GNMA  8.00  170131  870601  870902  86.500
GNMA  8.00  090909  870601  870901  87.406
GNMA  8.00  170131  870601  870901  87.562
```

Figure 6-8   Sorted transactions file.

```
090487 TBNC 050187 99.00
T-NOTE OPTIONS
   COUPON     MATURITY   PRICE    FACTOR    FUTURES      FUTURES
                         (32)               EXPIRATION   PRICE (32)
   -------    --------   -----    ------    ----------   ----------
   8.50000    051597     94.21    1.0320    123187       90.22
```

**Figure 6-9** Transaction file with records extending to next line.

file contains the daily price of a security on one line, then skips several blank lines, and then has another price of the security's option contract. (This type of transaction is unusual, but possible.)

The FIXFORM to read such a logical record is:

```
FIXFORM DATE/6 X1 SECLABEL/4 X1 SECISSUE/6 X62
FIXFORM X10 PRICE/7 X63
FIXFORM X80 X80 X80
FORM X10 OPTION/7 X63
```

In this case, six physical records are considered one logical record. If the record length (LRECL) of the input file is 80, then the FIXFORM should read in (or skip over, eg. X62) to the end of each record.

Most FIXFORMS treat each physical record as a logical record, and there is no need to extend the FIXFORM to the next line. Also, there is usually no need to specify a LRECL for the FILEDEF of the input transaction file. This is only required when one FIXFORM reads beyond one physical record.

### FIXFORM Transaction Field Formats

Getting back to the PR1 focexec, the source of the input transactions is given on the DATA statement, DATA ON ddname. A FILEDEF is required which relates the ddname to a CMS file containing the input records. (CMS commands, such as FILEDEF, should start with -CMS.)

```
-CMS FILEDEF PR1 DISK PR1 DATA A
```

The formats of the fields in the FIXFORM can be alphanumeric, integer, etc. Refer to the FOCUS manual Chapter 5 section 2.1.4 for details. The format will be alphanumeric unless the input file was created as a HOLD or SAVB file (or from some user-written program generating internal formats).

The alphanumeric formats are specified as LABEL/4 or LABEL/A4 (the A is usually dropped). For fields with numeric formats, the width of the field on the input record may be larger or smaller than the width of the field in the MASTER. If the value of the number is too large for the database format, then a format error will appear when extracting that field in a report. However, there will not be an error in the MODIFY procedure. For example, if the database format for the field YIELD is P6.3, the value of 101.16 on the input record will cause a format error. (There is room for only 2 digits before the decimal point.)

For fields with alpha (A) format, the length of the field in the FIX-FORM should usually equal the database format. If not, you will not get a format error, but the resulting stored value may not be as expected. Remember,

1. If the FIXFORM length of a field is too long, leading blanks will be inserted first, then the text, and last the trailing blanks.
2. If the FIXFORM length of a field is too short, the text will be left-justified when stored in the database.

For example, if the value of the field LABEL is TB, it will be stored as 'TB ' (not ' TB') — since its format is A4 in the database.

### Record-by-Record Processing

The MATCH logic is performed on each record in the transaction file. Exceptions to this are when the MATCH statement is bypassed due to:

1. The record fails a VALIDATE condition
2. The record contains a FORMAT error
3. CASE logic or IF conditions are used to skip the MATCH logic or branch to another case.

In PR1 FOCEXEC, MATCH logic is performed first on the LABEL and COUPON, and then on the field DATE. If a new label and coupon appear on a record, a new security is added to the database. If a new date appears, its segment is also added to the database. After performing the MATCH logic, the procedure automatically reads in the next record using the FIXFORM, and the logic repeats.

The fields in a FIXFORM statement can be used in COMPUTES and IF STATEMENTS within the MODIFY request. They also can be used in other statements such as TYPE, VALIDATE, etc. The values of the fields always represent the values on the input records, not the values in the database. When you need to refer to values from the database (when a matched segment is found), use the prefix D. appended to the field name. In the following example, the maturity date of the security is computed from the issue date on the database record. The YMD date function (see FOCUS manual chapter 2 section 6.4.2) is used to increment the issue date by 90 days to get the maturity date.

```
MODIFY FILE PRICE
FIXFORM LABEL/4 X1 COUPON/5
MATCH LABEL COUPON
ON NOMATCH REJECT
ON MATCH COMPUTE
MATURITY/I6=YMD(D.ISSUE, 90, MATURITY);
ON MATCH UPDATE MATURITY
DATA ON PR1
END
```

The COMPUTE statement in a MODIFY procedure provides flexibility, since new fields can be created from values of input fields, database fields, or other computed fields. There are two places in the MODIFY where you can use COMPUTE statements:

1. At the beginning of the request. COMPUTE statements here define temporary fields for every transaction. FOCUS performs these calculations immediately after it reads a transaction record.
2. In MATCH or NEXT statements. Depending whether or not a particular segment instance was located on a MATCH or NEXT statement, the COMPUTE defines temporary fields for each transaction. These COMPUTES may perform calculations using database field values.

Expressions used in a COMPUTE have the same syntax as expressions in a DEFINE. They can contain IF...THEN...ELSE expressions with several IF conditions. For example:

```
COMPUTE
XASK/P7.2=IF LABEL IS 'GNMA' THEN 1.1*ASK ELSE IF
LABEL IS 'FMNA' THEN 1.2*ASK ELSE IF LABEL IS 'FRED'
AND COUPON LE 10 THEN 1.5*ASK ELSE ASK;
```

Several examples follow using the COMPUTE.

1. The bid price is computed from the ask price using an expression which depends on the label.

   ```
   MODIFY FILE PRICE
   FIXFORM LABEL/4 X1 COUPON/5 X1 DATE/6 X1 ASK/7
   MATCH LABEL COUPON
   ON MATCH CONTINUE
   ON NOMATCH REJECT
   MATCH DATE
   ON MATCH COMPUTE
   BID/P7.2=IF LABEL EQ 'GNMA' THEN ASK+.10 ELSE IF
   LABEL EQ 'FNMA' THEN ASK+.15 ELSE ASK +.05;
   ON MATCH UPDATE ASK BID
   ON NOMATCH REJECT
   DATA ON PR1
   END
   ```

   Note that the COMPUTE could have been placed after the FIXFORM. However, it is better to perform the COMPUTE after matching the segment which will contain the computed field. This makes the procedure easier to follow (or document). This is also necessary when using CASE logic, and previously computed fields may have unexpected values.

2. The issue date and maturity date appear on each input record. However, they are recomputed within the MODIFY if the label and coupon are not found in the database. Otherwise, the values on the input record are used.

```
MODIFY FILE PRICE
FIXFORM LABEL/4 X1 COUPON/5 X1 ISSUE/6 X1
MATURITY/6
MATCH LABEL COUPON
ON NOMATCH COMPUTE
ISSUE=870101;
MATURITY=990101;
ON NOMATCH INCLUDE
ON MATCH UPDATE ISSUE MATURITY
DATA ON PR1
END
```

If the field name in the COMPUTE is the same as the field in the FIXFORM, its computed value replaces the value on the input record. Note that the format of the computed field is not needed in this case because the field is a database field (and the format is obtained from the MASTER).

The yield is computed using the bond yield (field BEY) on each input record. Input records which do not match a record in the database are logged to the file NOPE DATA.

```
-CMS FILEDEF PR1 DISK PR1 DATA A
-CMS FILEDEF NOPE DISK NOPE DATA A (LRECL 25
RECFM FB)
MODIFY FILE PRICE
LOG NOMATCH ON NOPE
COMPUTE
BEY/P7.2=;
FIXFORM LABEL/4 COUPON/5 X1 DATE/6 X1 BEY/7
MATCH LABEL COUPON
ON MATCH CONTINUE
ON NOMATCH REJECT
MATCH DATE
ON MATCH COMPUTE
YIELD/P7.2=1.1*BEY;
ON MATCH UPDATE YIELD
DATA ON PR1
END
```

Frequently, it is necessary to compute the values of fields in the database from other fields appearing on the input records. Any field appearing in the FIXFORM which is not a database field must be predefined before the FIXFORM. This is done using a "dummy" COMPUTE statement for the field.

```
COMPUTE
BEY/P7.2=;
```

Only the field name and format are specified. A semicolon ends every COMPUTE. Only fields not in the MASTER description which appear in a FIXFORM, FREEFORM, PROMPT, OR CRTFORM, should be performed in this way. If such a field is not predefined, the MODIFY will not execute. An error message is displayed and execution continues at the next statement after the MODIFY end.

### Logging Transactions

An important feature of the MODIFY is the ability to LOG input records (and other data) which are rejected (or accepted) for various conditions. A complete list of these conditions is in the FOCUS manual Chapter 5 section 5.2. The most common involve records which are:

1. Duplicates
2. Nomatch
3. Invalid

The above conditions apply to records which are rejected for the corresponding reason. For example,

```
LOG DUPL ON DUPE
MATCH LABEL COUPON
ON MATCH CONTINUE
ON NOMATCH REJECT
MATCH DATE
ON MATCH REJECT
ON NOMATCH INCLUDE
```

Only those input records which have a LABEL, COUPON, and DATE matched with a database record are considered duplicates. If only the label and coupon match (and the date doesn't), the record would not be considered a duplicate. More than one LOG condition and LOG file can be used in a MODIFY. The logged records should have exactly the same layout and record length as the input transaction file — they may be used as input to other MODIFY procedures.

When an input record is rejected, it will be displayed on the terminal unless MSG OFF appears in the LOG conditions. E.g., LOG INVALID MSG OFF. If an audit trail is required as a report of the rejected transactions, the log file can be used as a FOCUS external file by creating a MASTER description for it. Example 6 in the last chapter describes creating an audit trail report.

MODIFY procedures can also contain dialogue manager variables. In the following example, the system variable &YMD (which contains today's date in YYMMDD format) is used in a COMPUTE statement. The computed field FLAG is set to one if the maturity date on the input transaction is less than today's date.

```
MODIFY FILE PRICE
FIXFORM LABEL/4 X1 COUPON/5 X1 MATURITY/6
MATCH LABEL COUPON
ON NOMATCH REJECT
ON MATCH COMPUTE
FLAG/I1=IF MATURITY LT &YMD THEN 1 ELSE 0;
 . . . .
 . . . .
DATA ON PR1
END
```

Dialogue manager variables can also be used in a FIXFORM statement, in an UPDATE statement, as numeric or text data in expressions, or for other purposes. For example, the transaction file PR1 DATA may contain the ASK price of a security or it may contain the YIELD of the security. This is determined when the focexec is executed by supplying a value for a dialogue manager variable. The FOCEXEC is:

```
-CMS FILEDEF PR1 DISK PR1 DATA A
-PROMPT &WHICH.A1 ENTER 'P' (PRICE) OR 'Y' (YIELD)
-SET &FLD=IF &WHICH EQ 'P' THEN 'ASK' ELSE 'YIELD';
```

```
-*
MODIFY FILE PRICE
FIXFORM LABEL/4 X1 COUPON/5 X1 DATE/6 X1 &FLD/7
MATCH LABEL COUPON
ON MATCH CONTINUE
ON NOMATCH REJECT
MATCH DATE
ON MATCH UPDATE &FLD
ON NOMATCH INCLUDE
DATA ON PR1
END
```

## Using SAVE Files as Transaction Files

The transaction file containing the input records can come from a number of places. It could have been created earlier by another program and stored on the disk, or it could be created in the same focexec as a SAVE or HOLD file. If the file is a SAVE file, you should know the layout of the records. This is determined by the order of verb objects and sort fields in the TABLE request.

For example, the following FOCEXEC extracts records from the PRICE FOCUS file and puts them in a SAVE file. The request extracts yields for GNMA securities on the day 870501. The MODIFY procedure uses these yields to compute the yields for the day 870502, and to update the file. The FOCEXEC is:

```
TABLE FILE PRICE
PRINT DATE YIELD
BY LABEL
BY COUPON
IF LABEL EQ GNMA
IF DATE EQ 870501
ON TABLE SAVE
END
-RUN
MODIFY FILE PRICE
FIXFORM LABEL/4 COUPON/5 X6 YIELD/7
MATCH LABEL COUPON
```

```
GNMA 8.000870601 9.530
GNMA 8.000870601 9.530
GNMA 8.250870601 9.640
GNMA 8.500870601 9.695
GNMA 8.750870601 9.834
GNMA 9.000870601 9.819
GNMA 9.500870601 9.960
GNMA10.00087060110.076
GNMG 8.000870601 9.130
GNMG 8.000870601 9.510
GNMG 8.250870601 9.610
GNMG 8.500870601 9.295
GNMG 8.750870601 9.334
GNMG 9.000870601 9.419
GNMG 9.500870601 9.360
GNMG10.00087060110.576
```

Figure 6-10  Example of SAVE file.


```
ON NOMATCH REJECT
ON MATCH COMPUTE
DATE=870502;
YIELD=YIELD+.05
ON MATCH CONTINUE
MATCH DATE
ON NOMATCH INCLUDE
ON MATCH UPDATE YIELD

DATA ON SAVE
END
```

When records are extracted to a SAVE file, there are no spaces between the fields on the SAVE file. The above SAVE file contains records as shown in figure 6-10.

You should visually check the records to be sure that the FIXFORM is correct. The DATA statement indicates that the input records come from the SAVE file. No FILEDEF is required since FOCUS will issue one when the SAVE file is created.

Note: Since the DATE is assigned value 870502 in a COMPUTE, the value of DATE on the input record is ignored by skipping over it on the FIXFORM (i.e. X6).

## Transaction Files With Records in Internal Format

The FIXFORM statement is also used when the input records are in internal format. Internal format records are usually created as a HOLD file or SAVB file, although they can be created by other programs. There is little difference in the way the FIXFORM handles these records. (An example at the beginning of this chapter demonstrated other MODIFY techniques used to manipulate input records, as well as handling internal format records.)

Since records in internal format cannot be read as text using the editor, it is necessary to know the formats of the fields as determined by the program which created the file. This is simple to do if the file was created as a HOLD or SAVB file. If the file is created from another type of program, such as FORTRAN or COBOL, it will be necessary to translate several kinds of formats. If you have little familiarity with these formats, it is best to avoid creating internal format records in this way.

The FIXFORM statement specifies the field formats of the transactions file, not the database. A transaction field can modify a database field if the transaction field format is one of the following:

1. The same format type as the database field.
2. Alphanumeric (A) format.
3. Zoned format (if the database format is packed).

The FOCUS MODIFY allows the formats of transaction fields to be redefined using COMPUTES, so that the format type is the same as the database field. There are several kinds of formats, such as alphanumeric integer, packed, etc. The internal format of fields with these formats result in a binary representation of these fields. The important thing to know is how many bytes is required to store each of the formats. The table below lists the various formats and the internal representation in bytes. The last column shows examples of formats which may have been used in the MODIFY which creates the files.

Internal Field Formats:

| | internal format | usage format |
|---|---|---|
| Alphanumeric | An ($1 \leq n \leq 256$) | A4,A5 |
| Integer | I | I1,I6 |
| Floating | F4 | F6.1, F8.3 |

| Packed      | **P8** | **P4.1, P12.2** |
| Double prec.| **D8** | **D5.2, D10.3** |

In effect, the internal format is either four bytes or eight bytes for numeric fields. The packed format also allows an implied decimal point in the value. For example,

```
FIXFORM ... YIELD/P8.2
```

The next eight bytes are a packed number, with the last two digits following an implied decimal point.

The alphanumeric internal format may be any number of bytes (from 1 to 256). However, if the file was created as a HOLD file, the alphanumeric internal format is always a multiple of 4 bytes. For example, a field with a format of A5 has an internal format of A8. Similarly, an A14 field has internal format A16.

Another way to determine the correct internal format is to look at the HOLD file's MASTER description, after it is created by the FOCEXEC. For example,

```
TABLE FILE PRICE
PRINT BID ASK YIELD
BY LABEL
BY COUPON
IF LABEL EQ GNMA
IF DATE EQ 870501
ON TABLE HOLD
END
```

The MASTER description of the HOLD file is in figure 6-11.

A field's internal format is the same as the ACTUAL format given in the MASTER description. (Note: The usage format usually is not the same as the actual format.) When the records in the HOLD file are used as input to a MODIFY procedure, the FIXFORM should use the internal formats of the fields.

Note: it is not necessary to name the fields in the FIXFORM the same as the fields in the MASTER. The names in the FIXFORM should correspond with the names of fields in the FOCUS file which is in the MODIFY. In fact, you may choose any names for the fields in the FIXFORM. If a field is not a database field or if the format of the field is not the same as the field in the database, use a dummy COM-

```
FILE=HOLD1            ,SUFFIX=FIX
SEGNAME=HOLD1
FIELDNAME   =DSORT    ,E01     ,I2      ,I04     ,$
FIELDNAME   =LABEL    ,E02     ,A04     ,A04     ,$
FIELDNAME   =COOP     ,E03     ,D4.1    ,D08     ,$
FIELDNAME   =LCOUP    ,E04     ,D4.1    ,D08     ,$
FIELDNAME   =DIFF     ,E05     ,D6.2    ,D08     ,$
FIELDNAME   =FACKEY   ,E06     ,A05     ,A08     ,$
FIELDNAME   =ASK      ,E07     ,D9.5    ,D08     ,$
FIELDNAME   =ASK      ,E08     ,I5      ,I04     ,$
FIELDNAME   =SQR      ,E09     ,D10.3   ,D08     ,$
```

Figure 6-11    Internal (actual) formats shown in HOLD MASTER.

PUTE to define a temporary field. Refer also to the FOCUS manual Chapter 5 section 2.1.1 for a discussion of the FIXFORM from MASTER feature.

### An Example of Using Internal Format Records

Consider the following example which extracts records from the PRICE file and loads them into a new file REPFILE. The MASTER for REPFILE is in figure 6-12.

The REPFILE MASTER contains one segment with three key fields, LABEL, COUPON, and LINENO. The LABEL and COUPON are self-explanatory (as they describe a security). The field LINENO can have only values 1,2, or 3. The value is 1 if the rest of the record is the average ASK price (for each month). Similarly, the value of LINENO is 2 for the average BID price, and 3 for the average YIELD. The procedure to extract the records from PRICE and load into REPFILE is shown in figure 6-13.

The extract procedure first computes the average bid, ask, and yield in each month for each label and coupon. The records are placed in a HOLD file which will be the input file for the MODIFY procedure. The MASTER for this HOLD file is in figure 6-14.

Notice the actual formats of the fields. The field MONNO takes up 4 bytes, although it was formatted in the DEFINE as I2. The FIXFORM must indicate the actual formats of the fields on the record. The names of the fields in the FIXFORM are arbitrary since they do not coincide with the database fields in REPFILE the field names must be identified using a dummy COMPUTE.

```
FILENAME = REPFILE , SUFFIX = FOC

SEGNAME = SECINFO ,SEGTYPE = S3

        FIELD = LABEL      ,LABEL    ,A04,FIELDTYPE = I,$
        FIELD = COUPON     ,CPN      ,D6.3,$
        FIELD = LINENO     ,LINENO   ,I2    ,$
        FIELD = JAN        ,,        ,D15.5,$
        FIELD = FEB        ,,        ,D15.5,$
        FIELD = MAR        ,,        ,D15.5,$
        FIELD = APR        ,,        ,D15.5,$
        FIELD = MAY        ,,        ,D15.5,$
        FIELD = JUN        ,,        ,D15.5,$
        FIELD = JUL        ,,        ,D15.5,$
        FIELD = AUG        ,,        ,D15.5,$
        FIELD = SEP        ,,        ,D15.5,$
        FIELD = OCT        ,,        ,D15.5,$
        FIELD = NOV        ,,        ,D15.5,$
        FIELD = DEC        ,,        ,D15.5,$
```

Figure 6-12    REPFILE MASTER description.

There are three separate MODIFY procedures used to load the records into REPFILE. Without CASE LOGIC, one MODIFY cannot (easily) load into separate records (i.e., LINENO=1,2,3) the bid, ask, and yield data in each record of the HOLD file. (In the first MODIFY, the BID price will be loaded into REPFILE; Next, the ASK price is loaded; then, the YIELD is loaded.) In each MODIFY, the same FIX-FORM is used to read the input records from the HOLD file. The internal formats of the fields are shown in the FIXFORM. After the FIXFORM, a COMPUTE assigns a value to the key field LINENO. (LINENO equals 1,2, or 3 indicating respectively bid, ask, yield.) The other COMPUTE statements define the month fields in REPFILE — JAN, FEB, ... DEC.

```
COMPUTE
JANNEW/D15.5=IF MONNO EQ 1 THEN BID ELSE 0;
```

These values are accumulated in a MATCH of LABEL, COUPON, and LINENO.

```
ON MATCH COMPUTE
JAN=D.JAN+JANNEW;
```

```
DEFINE FILE PRICE
MON1/A6    = EDIT (DATE) ;
YM/A4      = EDIT (MON1,'9999');
MONNO1/A2  = EDIT (YM, '$$99');
MONNO/I2   = EDIT (MONNO1) ;
END

TABLE FILE PRICE
SUM AVE.BID AVE.ASK AVE.YIELD
BY LABEL BY COUPON BY MONNO
IF YM    FROM 8601 TO 8612
ON TABLE HOLD
END

-* FIRST, UPDATE THE BID PRICE;

MODIFY FILE REPFILE
COMPUTE
BID/D8 = ; ASK/D8 = ; YIELD/D8 = ; MONNO/I2 = ;

FIXFORM LABEL/A4  COUPON/D8  MONNO/I4  BID/D8  ASK/D8  YIELD/D8

COMPUTE
LINENO/I2    = 1 ;
JANNEW/D15.5 = IF MONNO EQ 1 THEN BID ELSE 0;
FEBNEW/D15.5 = IF MONNO EQ 2 THEN BID ELSE 0;
MARNEW/D15.5 = IF MONNO EQ 3 THEN BID ELSE 0;
...
...
MATCH LABEL COUPON LINENO
ON MATCH COMPUTE
JAN = D.JAN + JANNEW ;
FEB = D.FEB + FEBNEW ;
MAR = D.MAR + MARNEW ;
...
ON MATCH UPDATE JAN FEB MAR APR MAY JUN JUL AUG SEP OCT NOV DEC

ON NOMATCH COMPUTE
JAN = JANNEW ;
FEB = FEBNEW ;
MAR = MARNEW ;
...
ON NOMATCH INCLUDE
DATA ON HOLD
END

-* NEXT, UPDATE THE ASK PRICE; THEN THE YIELD.
```

Figure 6-13   Example of updating a FOCUS file with HOLD file records.

```
MODIFY FILE REPFILE
COMPUTE
BID/D8 = ; ASK/D8 = ; YIELD/D8 = ; MONNO/I2 = ;

FIXFORM LABEL/A4  COUPON/D8  MONNO/I4  BID/D8  ASK/D8  YIELD/D8

COMPUTE
LINENO/I2     = 2 ;
JANNEW/D15.5 = IF MONNO EQ 1 THEN ASK ELSE 0;
FEBNEW/D15.5 = IF MONNO EQ 2 THEN ASK ELSE 0;
MARNEW/D15.5 = IF MONNO EQ 3 THEN ASK ELSE 0;
...
...
```

**Figure 6-13** (continued) Example of updating a FOCUS file with HOLD file records.

```
FEB=D.FEB+FEBNEW;
....
....
ON NOMATCH COMPUTE
JAN = JANNEW;
FEB = FEBNEW;
....
....
```

Notice that on the MATCH condition, the value of JANNEW is 0 when MONNO is not 1; when the record is updated, the database value will not change.

The COMPUTED fields have been assigned double-precision (D15.5) formats to coincide with the formats of JAN through DEC in the REPFILE database. However, any double-precision format could have been assigned.

### Conditional Fields

There are situations where values of a field may be present on one input record but absent in another. These fields are called "conditional fields." For example, some input records contain values for both fields ASK and YIELD, while some may contain no value (blank) for one or

```
FILE=HOLD              ,SUFFIX=FIX
SEGNAME=HOLD
FIELDNAME   =LABEL     ,E01    ,A04    ,A04    ,$
FIELDNAME   =COUPON    ,E02    ,D6.3   ,D08    ,$
FIELDNAME   =MONNO     ,E03    ,I2     ,I04    ,$
FIELDNAME   =BID       ,E04    ,D9.5   ,D08    ,$
FIELDNAME   =ASK       ,E05    ,D9.5   ,D08    ,$
FIELDNAME   =YIELD     ,E06    ,D6.3   ,D08    ,$
```

Figure 6-14    HOLD file used as transactions file.

both. By indicating that ASK and YIELD are conditional fields, the MODIFY procedure will not UPDATE the database with a zero value if there is no value on the record for a field.

Conditional fields are not very useful when records are included, since FOCUS sets a field's value to zero or blank if no value appears on the input record. However, if a conditional field is blank, FOCUS will not use the field to modify the database, and the field remains "inactive." This is a good way to avoid updating the database if a value for a KEY FIELD is not present. See the FOCUS manual Chapter 5 section 7.4.

To indicate that a field is conditional, precede the field format with the letter C. For example,

```
FIXFORM LABEL/4 COUPON/5 DATE/6 ASK/C7 YIELD/C7
```

Consider the procedure:

```
MODIFY FILE PRICE
FIXFORM LABEL/4 COUPON/5 DATE/6 ASK/C7 YIELD/C7
MATCH LABEL COUPON
ON MATCH CONTINUE
ON NOMATCH REJECT
MATCH DATE
ON NOMATCH REJECT
ON MATCH UPDATE ASK YIELD
DATA ON PR1
END
```

If you did not describe the ASK and YIELD fields as conditional, the request would change the date's price and yield to zero whenever these fields in the input file were blank. Because they are conditional, there will be no change to the field in the database when the input value is blank. Note: If you know that the field is not to be updated, then simply do not include the field in the list of fields to be updated.

### Validating Transaction Values

In order to check values on input records against certain conditions, a MODIFY request may use the VALIDATE statement. If an input value fails the test, the request rejects the transaction and displays a warning to the user. This is the usual way to check data for errors before it is accepted into the database. However, it is not the only way. FOCUS automatically checks the data for FORMAT errors; i.e., if the format of the input value is not appropriate for the format of the database field. If a FORMAT error occurs, the record is rejected. The other way to test values against certain conditions is to use the MODIFY IF statement (and GOTO statement). The IF statement branches to another case depending on how an expression is evaluated. In effect, it allows you to skip the match logic if a condition is satisfied. It may also be used after a MATCH condition; i.e., ON MATCH IF... Refer to the FOCUS manual Chapter 5 section 6.4 for more about the IF statement.

The VALIDATE statement is used in a similar way as the COMPUTE statement. The only difference is that if the value of the expression is zero, FOCUS rejects the transaction and displays this message:

(FOC421) TRANS n REJECTED INVALID rcode

where n is the transaction number; rcode is the test field assigned in the VALIDATE.

We will present some simple examples using the VALIDATE statement, demonstrating its syntax. Then, we will show how many validates can be performed in one MODIFY request where extensive data checking is required. You can place VALIDATE statements in two places in MODIFY requests:

1. At the beginning of the request, after the FIXFORM statement. VALIDATE statements here test every transaction, rejecting those having invalid values.

2. In MATCH or NEXT statements. The request only performs the validation if the MATCH or NEXT condition is met. These VALIDATE statements may use database fields if these fields are either in the segment instance being modified, or in a parent segment (or parent's parent, etc.).

If a VALIDATE statement invalidates a transaction, the process automatically rejects the whole transaction, and returns to the TOP to read the next transaction record. You can also take different action by branching to another case using CASE LOGIC — discussed later in this chapter. The FOCUS manual Chapter 5 section 4.2 describes other uses of the VALIDATE. As a simple example, consider a MODIFY request which will only accept transactions if the value of the field LABEL is "GNMA." The request might look like:

```
MODIFY FILE PRICE
FIXFORM LABEL/4 X1 COUPON/5 X1 ISSUE/6
LOG INVALID MSG OFF
VALIDATE
V1 = IF LABEL EQ 'GNMA' THEN 1 ELSE 0;
MATCH LABEL COUPON
ON MATCH UPDATE ISSUE
ON NOMATCH REJECT
DATA ON PR1
END
```

In the another MODIFY request, the field DATE is checked for containing valid dates. If a value is not a valid date, e.g., DATE=860022, the record will be rejected as invalid. Every record will be checked for this condition. There are a number of ways to check for a valid date. For example, the year, month, and day can be extracted from the date value using the EDIT command — each can be checked for validity. This involves a number of steps. A quicker way to test for a valid date is to use the YMD function, which calculates the number of days between two dates. It is used when the date is in YYMMDD format. (The functions MDY and DMY can be used with other date formats.) The first argument of the YMD function is any date such as 010101 (other dates might serve the purpose of restricting the date even further). If the second argument is not a valid date, the function will return a value of zero, which indicates an invalid condition. The procedure is:

```
MODIFY FILE PRICE
LOG INVALID MSG OFF
FIXFORM LABEL/4 COUPON/5 DATE/6 ASK/7
VALIDATE
GOODDATE/I9=YMD(010101, DATE);
ON INVALID GOTO TOP
MATCH LABEL COUPON
ON MATCH CONTINUE
ON NOMATCH REJECT
MATCH DATE
ON MATCH UPDATE ASK
ON NOMATCH REJECT
DATA ON PR1
END
```

Any variable can be used as a test variable. In this case, the variable GOODDATE will have a value of zero if the value of DATE on an input record is an incorrect date; otherwise some positive value will be returned. If the value of GOODDATE is non-zero, the transaction is not invalid, and the rest of the procedure continues for that record. Note that invalid warning messages are suppressed by using the statement LOG INVALID MSG OFF. Also, ON INVALID GOTO TOP is the default action taken after rejecting an invalid transaction. Control returns to the TOP case where another record is read. In order to validate that the bid price is less than the asking price, the following can be used:

```
VALIDATE
V1=IF BID LE ASK THEN 1 ELSE 0;
```

The validate variable V1 is used only as a test value. It should always be assigned to zero if an incoming value is unacceptable. This field retains its value after the VALIDATE statement, and can be used in other calculations. An alternate form of the VALIDATE statement is to set the test value equal to a logical expression which can either be true or false. If true the test value is set to 1. Otherwise, the value is 0. For example,

```
V1=BID LE ASK;
```

This is equivalent to the previous VALIDATE statement. Other examples are:

```
V1=ASK LT 120;
V1=LABEL NE 'XXXX'
V1=YMD(860101, DATE) LT 100;
V1=(ASK GT 120) OR (BID GT 120);
V1=DECODE LABEL (GNMA 1 FNMA 1 FPCI 1 ELSE 0);
```

The test expression can span several lines, but it must end with a semicolon. The test variable is usually given a temporary name such as V1, V2, etc. The variable's name can be used again in other test expressions. However, do not use an incoming field name or database field name for this name. The format of the field does not have to be specified, unless you use the field elsewhere in the request.

In the next example, the number of days between today's date and the security's maturity date is computed and used in other calculations. A record is invalid if the maturity date is less than today's date. (The YMD function did not have to be used — since an expression such as IF MATURITY GE &YMD THEN 1 ELSE 0 is ok.)

```
MODIFY FILE PRICE
LOG INVALID MSG OFF
FIXFORM LABEL/4 COUPON/5 MATURITY/6
COMPUTE
DIFF/I5=YMD(&YMD, MATURITY);
VALIDATE
V1=IF DIFF GE 0 THEN 1 ELSE 0;
ON INVALID GOTO TOP;
MATCH LABEL COUPON
. . . .
. . . .
```

## Logging Invalid Transactions

When input records are read from an input transaction file, there is usually no need to see INVALID MESSAGES on the screen. If these are required, messages can be shown using the statement LOG INVALID MSG ON. Also, it is possible to write invalid records to a LOG file by using the statement

LOG INVALID ON ddname MSG OFF

The LOG file should have FILEDEF with the above ddname. Its record length and record format should be the same as the input transaction file. Note: The MODIFY TYPE statement can also be used to display your own message on the terminal or to write out transaction fields and text to a sequential file. The syntax for using TYPE with invalid records is:

ON INVALID TYPE "message"

The FOCUS manual Chapter 5 section 5.1 describes the features of the TYPE statement. The use of TYPE for displaying messages is usually practiced when transactions are input on the CRT screen via the FIDEL screen facility.

As mentioned, the VALIDATE statement can be placed in MATCH (and in NEXT) statements. In this case, the MODIFY only performs the validation if the MATCH condition is met;

ON MATCH VALIDATE
validate condition

or

ON NOMATCH VALIDATE
validate condition

The VALIDATE phrase may use database fields if these fields are retrieved in a previous MATCH statement. To specify database values, affix the D. prefix to the front of the field name.

The VALIDATE statement can contain the same kind of expression as a DEFINE or COMPUTE. When validating alphanumeric fields against literal values be sure to enclose the literals in single quotation marks.

VALIDATE
V1=IF LABEL EQ 'GNMA' THEN 1 ELSE 0;

User-written functions contained in FUSELIB or written yourself can also be also used in VALIDATE statements.

## Other Validate Features

Three additional features are available for performing special validations. They are:

1. DECODE — validating values from a list or table.
2. FIND — testing for the existence of indexed field values.
3. LOOKUP — testing for and using field values on cross-referenced FOCUS files.

The DECODE function is identical to the one used in DEFINE and COMPUTES. It allows you to compare an incoming value against a list of acceptable or unacceptable values. For example, if only labels GNMA, FNMA, and FPTI are acceptable, a DECODE function can be used instead of an IF condition to validate the transactions.

```
VALIDATE
LABTEST=DECODE LABEL (GNMA 1 FNMA 1 FPTI 1 ELSE 0);
```

If you have a long list of values for the DECODE function, you may instead store these values in a separate file, then refer to the file in the DECODE statement. The file must consist of stacked pairs of values, with each value separated by a comma or spaces. For example, if only coupons 7, 7.5, 8, 8.5, 9, 9.5, 10 are valid coupons, the decode file might look like :

```
7.0  1  7.5  1  8.0  1
8.5  1  9.0  1  9.5  1
10.0 1
```

or,

```
7.0  1
7.5  1
8.0  1
8.5  1
9.0  1
9.5  1
10.0 1
```

The DECODE file must have a FILEDEF with ddname, which is referred to in the DECODE statement. For example, if the ddname is CPNFILE, the DECODE statement is:

```
VALIDATE
CPNTEST=DECODE COUPON (CPNFILE ELSE 0);
```

If the incoming COUPON is not in the decode list, the value of CPNTEST is 0 and the record is INVALID.

The second special function is the FIND function. It verifies if an incoming data value is in a FOCUS file. It is similar to the DECODE function. (Instead of the list of values being placed in a DECODE file, they can be placed in a FOCUS file.) The syntax of the FIND function is:

```
testfield=FIND(fieldname [AS dbfield] IN file);
```

where:

testfield is the name of a temporary test field.
fieldname is the full name of the incoming transaction field.
AS dbfield is the full name of the field in the FOCUS file — containing the values. (This is not needed if the incoming field and database field have the same name.) Also, this dbfield must be INDEXED.
file is the name of the FOCUS file containing the values.

NOTE: There is no space between FIND and the left parenthesis.

The FIND function returns a value of 1 if the input value is in the FOCUS file and 0 if it is not. (There is also another function NOT FIND which returns the opposite values as FIND). The only drawback about the FIND function is that too many of them in a MODIFY request increases the processing time somewhat. However, it should be used in most applications because it is an effective, simple way to ensure that a transaction is valid. The only thing needed is another FOCUS file with an INDEXED field whose values represent valid data. For example, the list of all security labels can be placed in FOCUS file LABLIST, whose MASTER is shown in figure 6-15.

The file also contains other fields which describe the label, such as description, coupon payment frequency, etc. — it may also have child

```
FILE = LABLIST, SUF = FOC,$

  SEGNAME = LABELS, SEGTYPE = S1,$

        FIELD = LABEL       , LAB     , A04, FIELDTYPE = I,$
        FIELD = DESCRIPTION, DES      , A24,$
        FIELD = MBSTYPE     , MBS     , A01,$
        FIELD = SORT_RANK  , SRANK    , I03,$
        FIELD = PERIOD      , PER     , I04,$
```

**Figure 6-15    LABLIST MASTER file.**

segments. Since the field LABEL in LABLIST is indexed, the file can be used in a FIND statement to validate incoming transactions. The MODIFY request is:

```
MODIFY FILE PRICE
LOG INVALID MSG OFF
FIXFORM LABEL/4 COUPON/5 MATURITY/6
VALIDATE
TESTLAB=FIND(LABEL IN LABLIST);
MATCH LABEL COUPON
ON MATCH UPDATE MATURITY
ON NOMATCH INCLUDE
DATA ON PR1
END
```

If an incoming label is not in the LABLIST FOCUS file, the FIND function will return a value of 0 and the transaction will be invalid.

The third special function is almost identical to the FIND function. The LOOKUP function retrieves data values from cross-referenced files. A file may be cross-referenced either as a static KU segment or as a dynamic JOINED (or DKU) segment.

Assume that the LABLIST FOCUS file has been joined to the PRICE FOCUS file. Then, an incoming transaction containing the field LABEL can be validated using the LOOKUP function — the technique is almost identical to using the FIND function. Also, if the label is a valid one which exists in the LABLIST file, it will be able to retrieve the data values of other fields in LABLIST. The syntax for the LOOKUP function is:

```
testfield=LOOKUP (fieldname);
```

where fieldname is the field you want to retrieve in the cross-reference file. (Note, this field cannot be the cross-referenced field.) The cross-referenced field is a field in the MODIFIED FOCUS file — its values are obtained from the transaction. The LOOKUP function uses the incoming value of the cross-referenced field, which is indexed, to locate a specific instance in the cross-reference file. If there are no such instances, the function sets the testfield to 0. If there are instances, the value of the testfield is set to 1, and the value of the specified field is retrieved from the first instance it finds.

For example, you need to recompute the yield of a security based on the number of days between coupon payments — for different labels. The field PERIOD in the LABLIST file contains the number of days between coupon payments for each label type. The yield is to be computed as

```
YIELD=(COUPON/12)*PERIOD/30;
```

The LOOKUP function will be used to retrieve the value of PERIOD for each label; also, we can reject invalid transactions for which there is no corresponding instance in LABLIST. The request is:

```
JOIN CLEAR
JOIN LABEL IN PRICE TO ALL LABEL IN LABLIST AS J1
-*
-* THE JOIN IS REQUIRED TO USE LOOKUP
MODIFY FILE PRICE
LOG INVALID MSG OFF
FIXFORM LABEL/4 COUPON/5 MATURITY/6 DATE/6
VALIDATE
TESTFIELD=LOOKUP(PERIOD);
COMPUTE
YIELD=(COUPON/12)*(PERIOD/30);
MATCH LABEL COUPON
ON MATCH UPDATE MATURITY
ON MATCH CONTINUE
ON NOMATCH REJECT
MATCH DATE
ON MATCH UPDATE YIELD
ON NOMATCH REJECT
DATA ON PR1
END
```

This is almost identical to the FIND function, since the input record will be invalid if the label is not found in the LABLIST file.

The LOOKUP function is important since values from other FOCUS files can be returned and used in a MODIFY request. The link to the cross-referenced file is made using the incoming value of the field (LABEL) in making the cross-reference. If there is no incoming value for such a field, you may use the database value of the field, after matching key fields in the MODIFY request.

Caution should be taken when naming fields on cross-referenced segments. Although access to data on cross-reference files is simple using the LOOKUP function, some confusion and errors can arise if the cross-reference file contains fields whose full names are the same as fields in the modified FOCUS file. Although the indexed field can have the same name as the cross-reference field, the other fields should have different names. (The alias names may usually be the same without causing any retrieval problems when the full names are used in a request.) Note that you may change the names of fields in MASTER descriptions at any time if the field is not indexed.

VALIDATES do take up some processing time on each transaction, and should be kept to a minimum when processing a large number of transactions. The next section of FIDEL screen transactions will also illustrate the use of the VALIDATE statement.

Chapter

# 7

# FIDEL: Generating Interactive Data Entry Screens

One of the most powerful features of FOCUS is the FIDEL facility, which permits users to enter data interactively onto custom formatted CRT screens. You can use FIDEL with MODIFY for file maintenance and inquiry purposes, and with Dialogue Manager for applications in which data values are supplied at run time for Dialogue Manager variables.

The simple examples in the next chapters show you how to use the standard FIDEL features for basic data entry needs. Like the TABLE report requests, the basic techniques and operating conventions are easy to describe, and are used repeatedly in even more elaborate screen designs. The FOCUS Users Manual, Chapter 7, is devoted all to FIDEL — and describes other important aspects of FIDEL. These include:

1. Specifying screen attributes and background effects.
2. Dynamically changing screen attributes.
3. Using the Screen Painter from TED to quickly design elaborate screens.
4. Setting PF key fields for branching purposes.

FIDEL is usually used within a MODIFY request to accept data input on the screen before proceeding with MATCH logic, which will determine how the data will be input in the FOCUS file.

With FIDEL, you have access to all the MODIFY commands described in the previous section. Some of the FIDEL features used with CRT data entry are:

1. Entering and changing data fields on the screen
2. Display of text and error messages
3. Validation of data fields
4. Scrolling screen pages upward and downward
5. Clearing a screen or just portions of it
6. Setting fields for display only
7. Adding color and highlighting to screens
8. Handling different screen layouts with case logic.

FIDEL makes it possible to format screens to accept entry of data into fields. Although the screens are very simple to format, many applications use the same (or very similar) screen formats over and over again. This is because the commands used to format a screen can be copied and used in many applications. Screen formatting can be made as sophisticated as you need.

FOCUS provides some shortcuts when the screen format is simple. For example, the AUTOMOD facility, described in a separate users manual, generates FIDEL screens automatically for simple data input and update.

The procedure to create a FIDEL screen within a MODIFY request always starts with the CRTFORM statement. This indicates that the lines following describe the format of a CRT screen.

In MODIFY, you can use up to 20 CRTFORM statements in one procedure. In dialogue manager, there is no limit to the number of CRTFORM statements in a procedure. You may maintain lower-case characters entered from the terminal as lower-case, by using the CRTFORM LOWER option. There are three types of data or dialogue manager variable fields that can be specified on the CRTFORM:

1. Data entry: i.e. — for data entry only.
2. Display: i.e. .field — for display only.
3. Turnaround: i.e. .field — for display and change.

```
        FILENAME = MAIL            ,SUFFIX = FOC
        SEGNAME  = MAILIST         ,SEGTYPE=SH1,$
          FIELDNAME = CUSTNUM         ,SEQ         ,I06,FIELDTYPE=I, $
          FIELDNAME = LAST_NAME       ,LNAME       ,A20              , $
          FIELDNAME = FIRST_NAME      ,FNAME       ,A15              , $
          FIELDNAME = COMPANY_NAME    ,CNAME       ,A45              , $
          FIELDNAME = STREET          ,STR         ,A40              , $
          FIELDNAME = CITY            ,            ,A33              , $
          FIELDNAME = STATE           ,            ,A2               , $
          FIELDNAME = ZIP             ,            ,A5               , $
          FIELDNAME = ACCOUNT_TYPE    ,TYPE        ,A10              , $
          FIELDNAME = CITI_CONTACT    ,CONTACT     ,A35              , $
          FIELDNAME = STATUS          ,            ,A15              , $
          FIELDNAME = EXPENSE_CODE    ,EXP         ,A4               , $
          FIELDNAME = REGCODE         ,RCODE       ,A2               , $
          FIELDNAME = IMDY            ,IMDY        ,I6MDY            , $
INPUT DATE
          FIELDNAME = UMDY            ,UMDY        ,I6MDY            , $
UPDATE DATE
        SEGNAME = REGION , CRFILE = MAILREG, CRKEY = REGCODE,
                 PARENT=MAILIST,SEGTYPE = KU,$
```

**Figure 7-1    MAIL MASTER file.**

Display values are considered "protected" areas on the screen because you cannot alter what is there. (See FOCUS manual chapter 7 section 2.2.)

The following FOCEXEC shows the procedure of setting up a CRTFORM used to input names, addresses, and other data into a MAILING LIST. Only data entry fields are used. The mailing list is stored in a FOCUS file MAIL, whose MASTER is shown in figure 7-1.

```
MODIFY FILE MAIL
LOG DUPL MSG OFF
CRTFORM LINE 1
" CUSTOMER ADDITION SCREEN: "
"/2 "
" CUSTNUM <CUSTNUM "
" LASTNAME <LNAME "
" FIRSTNAME <FNAME "
" COMPANY NAME <CNAME "
" STREET <STREET "
"
```

238  The Database Experts' Guide to FOCUS

```
" CITY <CITY "
. . . .
. . . .
" PRESS PF1 OR PF3 IF YOU WISH TO EXIT "
" PRESS PF2 TO CLEAR SCREEN "
MATCH CUSTNUM
ON MATCH TYPE
" CUSTOMER ALREADY EXISTS "
ON NOMATCH INCLUDE
DATA
END
```

The following screen is displayed:

```
CUSTOMER ADDITION SCREEN

CUSTNUM:
LASTNAME:
FIRSTNAME:
COMPANY NAME:
STREET:
CITY:
STATE:
. . . .
. . . .
PRESS PF1 OR PF3 IF YOU WISH TO EXIT
PRESS PF2 TO CLEAR SCREEN
```

The CRTFORM statement may contain several options. Some of these provide for:

1. Clearing data areas on the screen
2. Indicating which line on the screen to start the CRTFORM
3. Indicating if the screen contains text in upper or lower case.

The CRTFORM can be placed almost anywhere in the MODIFY request. It usually appears before the MATCH logic, at the start of the request. However, a CRTFORM may also be initiated on a MATCH condition (ON MATCH CRTFORM) or on a NOMATCH condition (ON NOMATCH CRTFORM). (Similarly, on NEXT and NONEXT conditions.) The CRTFORM lines, which are enclosed in double quotes, can contain

1. Text and data fields
2. Blank lines for spacing
3. Formats for line skipping and highlighting screens.
4. Line labels used for identifying fields, cursor position, etc.

A CRTFORM can contain up to 1280 lines, although usually 24 lines can fit on the CRT screen at any one time. Scrolling upward and downward with the PF8 and PF7 keys make it possible to see more than 24 lines. The last four lines on a screen are usually reserved for error messages and other messages. This can be changed using the CRTFORM TYPE option. (See the FOCUS manual Chapter 7 section 3.9.3.) If not changed, then only 20 CRTFORM lines can be displayed on the screen at any one time. Note that the physical length and width of the CRT screen may vary with terminal type. See the FOCUS manual Chapter 7 section 3.9.2 on how to specify screen sizes.

## FIDEL CRT Data Entry in Dialogue Manager

Data entry onto full screens can also be accommodated in dialogue manager. This is another variation of using FIDEL. However, this is not a FOCUS file maintenance technique. The CRTFORM screens are set up the same as in a MODIFY request. The major difference is that the input fields are dialogue manager variables. Because they are not data fields and are not part of a MASTER description, they do not have a format. Space is allocated for them using a "dummy" SET statement,

```
-SET &CITY='   ' ;
```

where '' Represents the alphanumeric length of the variable.

Space can also be allocated directly in the -CRTFORM. (See the FOCUS manual Chapter 7 section 4.1.)

The operating conventions for using FIDEL are the same whether in a MODIFY or in dialogue manager. The FOCUS manual Chapter 7 section 1.4 lists these conventions. They are described specifically for the IBM 3270 terminal which supports PF key and cursor control, scrolling, and screen attributes.

### Terminating Data Entry in FIDEL or -CRTFORM

A feature which needs clarification is the convention for exiting from data entry. Regular exiting is done by pressing the ENTER key to transmit the screen. In a MODIFY, you may clear the screen without transmitting it, by pressing the PF2 key. This allows you to start again reentering a transaction.

In order to end data entry, use the PF1, PF3, or PF15 keys. This will end a MODIFY request (but the rest of the FOCEXEC will continue), or terminate the entire FOCEXEC if in dialogue manager. Another way to end data entry is to type END or QUIT in an unprotected area.

The FOCUS manual Chapter 7 section 2.3.2 describes how you may reset the PF key functions.

### Formatting a FIDEL Screen

Although the features described in this section apply to both MODIFY and dialogue manager, our examples will deal with MODIFY applications. Options specific to dialogue manager cn be found in the FOCUS manual Chapter 7 section 4.

In the MODIFY request shown earlier to add a record to the MAIL file, the line containing /2 is used to skip lines after the heading. It can be placed by itself or on any other line containing data fields or text. For example,

"</2 ENTER DATA FOR THE FOLLOWING:"

indicates to skip two lines before displaying the instruction. This formatting statement can be used to skip any number of lines on the screen. Another way to skip lines is to code a blank line (or single blank) between double quote marks.

For example, the line /2 can be replaced by:

```
"      "
"      "
```

This method of skipping lines may sometimes be simpler for the programmer, since the screen will be formatted as it appears while coding.

When coding a FIDEL screen, keep in mind that long lines can be extended onto the next line. This is done by omitting the double quote at the end of the first line and at the start of the second line. For example,

```
"ENTER THE FOLLOWING DATA"
"NAME <NAME    STREET <STREET
  CITY <CITY    STATE <STATE    ZIP <ZIP"
```

The line will appear on the screen as one line when the request is executed. This is similar to the way heading and footing lines in TABLE requests are formatted. By continuing a line onto the next one, it is easy to format long lines. FOCUS will automatically pair off lines if they are coded without double quote marks at the end of a line.

The other formatting technique available in FIDEL controls the spacing between text and/or data on each line. There are two ways to control the spacing:

1. Indicate the column number where the next text or data starts.
2. Indicate the relative number of columns between text or data.

For example,

```
<20 <CITY"
<20 <STATE   <35 <ZIP"
```

You can optionally use the right caret > in the spot marker. This is useful when the next character in the line is a left caret. The marker indicates that the data field CITY starts in column 20, as does the field STATE. The field ZIP starts in column 35. Each field occupies a width on the line equal to its format width. The field STATE has format A2 — so its width on the screen is 2 columns. If a field has format P8.2, its width on the screen is 8 columns — similarly for any numeric format.

In the following example,

```
"CITY: <CITY"
"STATE: <STATE <+10 <ZIP"
```

242   The Database Experts' Guide to FOCUS

The marker 10 indicates that the data field ZIP is to start 10 columns from the field STATE. Another way to interpret 10 is that 10 columns will be skipped from the last non-blank text or data. These space markers are a convenient way to assure precise spacing between text or data. There are several things to note about using space markers. First, any blank space after a spot marker will be considered as text, and gets positioned where the spot marker indicates. For example,

"ENTER NAME:  <20    <NAME"

Since there are several spaces after, the space will show in column 20 and the text will be positioned after the spaces. So, you should not use more than one space after the marker. There is another marker which can be used to assure that no spaces will interrupt the text. The marker assures that no spaces are inserted between it and the next character. It is helpful in positioning data on a screen when a single line is coded as two lines. No spaces are inserted between the spot marker and the start of a continuation line.

A problem with using spot markers can occur when the width of text or a data field interferes with the next spot marker. For example,

"CITY: <CITY <10 STATE: <STATE"

If the data field CITY has a format A8, it will interfere with the text STATE in column 10. This may cause FOCUS to issue a warning message, or truncate part of the text STATE on the screen.

If you need to write over part of another field on the screen, the spot marker <-n will cause the next character to start n columns to the left of the last character. This may be helpful when the values of two fields need to be next to each other on a line. E.g.,

"<PHONE1 <-1 <PHONE2"

Without the <-1, the fields would be separated by one byte, which is the attribute byte at the beginning of a field. With <-1, the attribute byte would be overwritten with the data in field HONE2.

## Display and Turnaround Fields

The following types of data fields can be placed on a line:

1. Data entry: the syntax is <field/length

   The length of the field should be defined only if you want it to be different than the format width that is defined in the MASTER or COMPUTE. The left caret is always used to designate a data field. The right caret is used only to signify a non-conditional field — that is, a field for which data must be entered. If no data is entered for a non-conditional entry field, a value of 0 or blank will replace the value in the database (on an UPDATE). If only the left caret is present, the field is a conditional field. If no data is entered, the database value is not affected. For data entry fields, it is recommended that conditional fields be used. Note: In dialogue manager the right caret is meaningless.

2. Display: The syntax is <D.field/length

   The D. prefix indicates that the data is to be displayed only. The data will appear on the screen in a protected area.

3. Turnaround field: The syntax is <T.field/length

   The current value of the field is displayed on the screen, where it can be changed. In the MODIFY request shown earlier for the MAIL file, there were no turnaround fields. Turnaround fields prefixed with T. could have been used — with no effect (except that integer fields would have a 0 value displayed). In order to display fields (having some data value) for turnaround, a position in the FOCUS file first may be established using a MATCH statement. For example,

ON MATCH CRTFORM

A position is established in the file, and the values of the fields in the matched segment can be displayed. Another way to present data for turnaround is to COMPUTE a field and display the computed value on the screen. Any computed field should have a value based on the values of some other field. By displaying it on the screen, the operator can change the value.

The next example is shown in figure 7-2. In the previous example, the data for each customer in the mailing list was added to the database, using ON MATCH INCLUDE. In this example, the records are updated in the database using the ON MATCH UPDATE.

There are two CRTFORMS in this MODIFY request. The first has only one line, where the operator inputs the customer number; i.e., field SEQ in the database. The record for that customer number is then retrieved after matching to find the position in the database. This data is displayed on the second CRTFORM. However, as soon as the procedure is executed both CRTFORMS are displayed immediately. (See USING MULTIPLE CRTFORMS — in a later section.) However, the turnaround fields will not contain any data until the customer number is entered. If the customer number is not found in the database, a message is shown on the last four lines of the screen.

```
CUSTOMER NUMBER____ DOES NOT EXIST PLEASE PRESS PF1
IF YOU WISH TO EXIT
```

The customer number in the message will flash red since the flash attribute is used as a prefix. (See FOCUS manual Chapter 7 section 2.4 for setting screen attributes.)

The data is retrieved from the FOCUS file on a MATCH condition. The fields are all turnaround fields except for the last two fields — for input date and update date. The input date is when the record was first added. The update date is when the record was last updated. Note: The update date is computed from the system date using the COMPUTE statement.

```
ON MATCH COMPUTE
UMDY=&MDY;
```

Before the values are displayed, some fields were used in COMPUTE statements — for several reasons. The fields for input date and update were reformatted using an I6S format. The edit option S suppresses the display of these dates if their value is 0.

The LOOKUP function was used to retrieve the name of the region from the cross-reference file MAILREG. The value of REGCODE (the cross reference field) provides a link to MAILREG. (The field REGN is a temporary field whose value is equal to REGNAME. It is not neces-

```
****************************************************************
* THIS FOCEXEC IS RESPONSIBLE FOR UPDATING CUSTOMER RECORDS FROM
THE    *
* MAIL DATABASE.
*
****************************************************************

MODIFY FILE MAIL
LOG NOMATCH MSG OFF

CRTFORM
"<.A. PLEASE ENTER THE CUSTOMER NUMBER THAT YOU WANT TO UPDATE"
"        CUSTNUM           <.IBW.SEQ>           "

MATCH   CUSTNUM

ON MATCH COMPUTE
REGCODE = D.REGCODE;
HAVE = LOOKUP(REGNAME);
REGN/A20 = REGNAME ;
INPD/I6S = D.IMDY;
UPDD/I6S = D.UMDY;

    ON MATCH CRTFORM
"       LAST_NAME        <T.LNAME>        "
"       FIRST_NAME       <T.FNAME>        "
"       COMPANY_NAME     <T.CNAME>        "
"       STREET           <T.STR>          "
"       CITY             <T.CITY>         "
"       STATE            <T.STATE>        "
"       ZIP              <T.ZIP>          "
"       ACCOUNT_TYPE     <T.TYPE>         "
"       CITI_CONTACT     <T.CONTACT>      "
"       STATUS           <T.STATUS>       "
"       EXPENSE_CODE     <T.EXP>          "
"       REGION   CODE    <T.REGCODE>      "
"       REGION   NAME    <D.REGN>         "
"       INPUT    DATE    <D.INPD>         "
"       UPDATE   DATE    <D.UPDD>         "
" "
"<.W.    PRESS PF1 IF YOU WISH TO EXIT"
ON MATCH COMPUTE
UMDY = &MDY;

ON MATCH UPDATE * NONKEYS
ON NOMATCH TYPE
" "
```

Figure 7-2    Updating the MAIL FOCUS file.

```
"  <.W. CUSTOMER NUMBER   <.RED.FLAS.CUSTNUM   <.C.W. DOES NOT EXIST
"
ON NOMATCH REJECT
DATA
END
-EXIT
```

**Figure 7-2**   (continued) Updating the MAIL FOCUS file.

sary.) The LOOKUP function may also be used to validate the region code. If the region code does not appear in the MAILREG cross-reference file, it is assumed to be invalid, The following VALIDATE statement may be used:

```
MATCH CUSTNUM
ON MATCH VALIDATE
HAVEIT = LOOKUP(REGNAME);
ON INVALID TYPE
"*** INVALID REGION CODE ***"
```

COMPUTE statements that follow a MATCH may also perform calculations on database field values. The database values of a field, when used in a COMPUTE, are obtained by prefixing the field with D. This is only to distinguish it from the value of the transaction field with the same name. Do not confuse this with the prefix D. used on a CRTFORM for display-only fields.

### Clearing the Screen

#### CLEAR/NOCLEAR Option

After each screen of data is successfully processed, the data areas are automaticlly cleared. You can override this default by using the NOCLEAR option. Then, the screen will remain unchanged after processing the data on a screen. This is useful when there is a large amount of data which carries over from one screen to the next. It is also useful after validating data on the screen — if an invalid field value is found, the screen will not be cleared (although an error message will appear at the bottom of the screen). The syntax is:

```
CRTFORM blank
        NOCLEAR
        CLEAR
```

The default option is blank — it causes the screen to clear after the data is transmitted. After an invalid condition, the screen will not be cleared. Note: The CRTFORM options may be different from one CRTFORM to the next.

## Using Multiple CRTFORMS

### The LINE Option

FIDEL allows a great deal of flexibility in designing CRTFORMS. Using the LINE option, you can choose what screen line the CRTFORM will begin on. CRTFORM screens may overlap each other — as you may control the placement of CRTFORMS. In the procedure to update the MAIL file, there were two CRTFORMS: input the CUSTNUM and update the CUSTOMER DATA. The default condition is to display both CRTFORMS at the same time — when the program is executed. Each CRTFORM is displayed one after the other on the screen — into one visual form.

There may be times when you do not need to display the second CRTFORM at the same time as the first. In the MAIL example, it may be necessary to first display only the field CUSTNUM, followed by the rest of the data on a MATCH condition. In order to display the CRTFORMS separately, the CRTFORM LINE option should be used. The syntax is:

```
CRTFORM LINE n
```

where n indicates the starting line number for the CRTFORM.

Using the LINE option gives the following options:

1. Several CRTFORMS may be used in one case of the MODIFY procedure. You can build mixed screens by saving lines from the previous CRTFORM, or by overwriting lines.
2. One CRTFORM may replace another CRTFORM after entering data, by having the CRTFORMS begin on the same line.

When the LINE option is used, subsequent CRTFORMS will not be displayed at the same time as one visual form.

A combination of two or more CRTFORMS can occupy specific lines on one screen. To obtain a mixed screen, indicate the starting line number on the subsequent CRTFORM. To completely replace one screen with the next, both CRTFORMS must start on the same line.

Chapter

# 8

# Using Case Logic in Modify Procedures

This chapter demonstrates how more sophisticated maintenance procedures may be designed using the CASE LOGIC technique in MODIFY procedures. As we have suggested in the previous chapter, MODIFY techniques should be simplified wherever possible — by creating input transaction files which are simple to work with, or by using additional MODIFY procedures to handle different sets of input records. When maintaining small FOCUS files, you sacrifice very little processing time by adding steps, because the size of the FOCUS file is small. What you gain is a simplified file maintenance procedure, which can be easily changed if the data requirements change. However, if the size of the FOCUS file is large, you may not have the flexibility to process large transaction files using separate MODIFY procedures. CASE LOGIC provides the flexibility to enhance one MODIFY procedure with alternate ways of processing the input transactions. We shall present several examples of CASE LOGIC, and discuss some basic situations when CASE LOGIC should be used.

CASE LOGIC can be used in various kinds of MODIFY situations — where the programmer needs added capabilities when processing transactions. Typical situations where CASE LOGIC is helpful are for:

1. FIXFORM files containing more than one type of input record.
2. Updating multiple child segments with the same input record.
3. Providing the operator with choices to process the input record in different ways, or to enter different kinds of data.
4. Using a special case to validate transactions, and to process errors.
5. Allowing the operator to verify data entry with FIDEL.
6. Browsing through the child records in a particular segment.
7. Performing additional processing depending on the value of a field in each record.
8. Permitting the operator to check (LOOKUP) data on cross-reference files or JOINED files.
9. Modifying several unique segments descended from one parent.

FOCUS programmers also use CASE LOGIC for separating out additional steps — such as COMPUTES, VALIDATES, etc. This makes the code more legible, and helps to organize each step in the procedure. The FOCUS manual Chapter 5 section 6.2 identifies the rules applicable to CASE LOGIC. These rules are easily understood — and we can summarize them as follows:

1. The first case in the MODIFY is the TOP case — although it is not named explicitly. There is also an EXIT case in all MODIFY procedures — included by FOCUS automatically. This case may be branched to if you want to exit the modify procedure before processing all the input transactions (useful with FIXFORM transactions).
2. After performing instructions in any case, control returns to the TOP case (usually where another input record is read) unless directed to go to another case. In any case, if an ON NOMATCH INCLUDE is processed (after a MATCH statement), control returns to the TOP case unless directed to go to another case.
3. A case must contain complete MODIFY statements — with no partial MATCH process. If MATCH logic is started in a case, it cannot be continued in another case unless another MATCH command is issued in the case. Also, a case need not contain any MATCH process — since it may be used solely for CRTFORMS, COMPUTES, VALIDATES, TYPES, etc.
4. A MODIFY procedure may contain two special cases — called CASE AT START and CASE AT END — which may be used for

special processing before the input records are processed, or after the last record has been processed.
5. After a field has been updated or included, the field becomes "inactive" — and may not be used in other MATCH processes unless the field is activated. One simple way to activate fields at the start of a case is to use a COMPUTE, E.g.,

```
COMPUTE
field1 = field1 ;
field2 = field2 ;
field3 = field3 ;
```

The above activates fields — field1, field2, field3 — if they were inactive. Also, see examples and discussion in this chapter, and the FOCUS manual Chapter 5 section 7.4 and Chapter 7 section 3.1.

The following example shows a legal way of continuing MATCH logic in another case:

```
MATCH LABEL
ON NOMATCH INCLUDE
ON MATCH GOTO CHECK
CASE CHECK
COMPUTE
ISSUE = 870101;
MATCH LABEL
ON MATCH UPDATE ISSUE
ON NOMATCH REJECT
ENDCASE
```

However, the following is illegal:

```
MATCH LABEL
ON NOMATCH INCLUDE
ON MATCH GOTO CHECK
CASE CHECK
COMPUTE
ISSUE = 870101;
ON MATCH UPDATE ISSUE
ENDCASE
```

There are only two additional commands, which distinguish CASE LOGIC from a regular MODIFY request (See the FOCUS manual Chapter 5 section 6.4 for details):

1. The unconditional branch statement — GOTO.
2. The conditional branch statement — IF ..THEN..GOTO.

FOCUS provides several facilities for making it easy to debug procedures containing CASE LOGIC. The TRACE facility displays the name of each case that is processed during the execution of a MODIFY procedure. With TRACE on, FOCUS will list on the CRT (or in a file) the name of the case processed. By seeing cases executed during processing, one can determine if the logic is working properly. To turn on the TRACE, a FILEDEF must be issued for the ddname HLIPRINT (or assigned to the CRT terminal). Other facililites which are useful in debugging CASE LOGIC are:

1. TYPE statements — which display values of data fields and text at various points in the procedure.
2. dialogue manager ECHO command — which displays FOCUS commands when they are executed, and values of dialogue manager variables.
3. MODIFY ECHO facility — which displays the cases processed, as well as the match-actions, the name of the segment which is updated, and the statements used in each case (such as COMPUTE, GOTO, TYPE). This facility does not update the FOCUS file; rather, it only displays the ECHO listing at the terminal. Using a FILEDEF for ddname HLIPRINT, the listing may also be stored in a file.

### Considerations When Using Case Logic With CRTFORMs

There is a great deal of flexibility which can be designed into FIDEL CRTFORMS when CASE LOGIC is used. It is simple to show data fields for data entry or display, then update a segment in the FOCUS file. The request may then branch to another case, where new fields in a new segment may be displayed on another CRTFORM. Even after a field is updated in the database, its value may be later displayed on another CRTFORM.

When there are more than one CRTFORM in one MODIFY request, it is recommended that you use the CRTFORM LINE 1 option to replace one screen with another — especially if each CRTFORM is in a different case. If a different screen pattern is needed, where lines from the prior screen are to be combined with new lines, then use the option CRTFORM LINE n — where n is the desired line number for the new lines. Several examples in this chapter and in the last chapter demonstrate using FIDEL screens with CASE LOGIC.

When using COMPUTED fields with CASE LOGIC, keep in mind that a computed field will not be visible on a CRTFORM in another case, unless it is reactivated in the case. That is,

```
COMPUTE
field1 = field1 ;
```

Another way to activate fields is to use the ACTIVATE statement:

```
ACTIVATE field1
```

See the FOCUS manual Chapter 5 section 7.4 on ACTIVATE and DEACTIVATE.

## Branching to Cases Using the IF and GOTO Statements

The IF statement branches to another case depending on how an expression is evaluated. It may extend over several lines — ending with a semicolon (;). The IF statements can be nested in several ways. For example:

```
IF expression1 THEN GOTO case1
ELSE IF expression2 THEN GOTO case2
ELSE IF expression3 THEN GOTO case3
ELSE ...;
```

The expressions may use fields in the transaction, fields from the database (after matching), dialogue manager variables, or text. The IF statement allows the procedure to branch to any other case (even to the same case). The IF condition may also positioned after a MATCH statement — so that branching may take place only after a match or nomatch.

The expression contained in the IF condition may be any logical expression legal in a DEFINE or COMPUTE IF statement. Literals must be enclosed in single quotation marks; parentheses are necessary around the parts of a compound expression.

The unconditional GOTO statement is similar in function to the conditional IF statement. When executed, it causes the request to branch to a case. For example, the following request prompts for employee information in the TOP case, and performs MATCH logic in another case.

```
MODIFY FILE EMPLOYEE
PROMPT CUSTNUM SALARY LEVEL
GOTO INPUT
CASE INPUT
MATCH CUSTNUM
ON MATCH UPDATE SALARY LEVEL
ON NOMATCH INCLUDE
ON NOMATCH GOTO MESSAGE
ENDCASE
CASE MESSAGE
TYPE
" NEW EMPLOYEE ADDED "
ENDCASE
DATA
END
```

The GOTO directs the process to the INPUT CASE — after prompting the user for input values in the TOP CASE.

The following example demonstrates how to use the special case — CASE AT START — to obtain initial values for some field.

```
-READ SECNUM &SECNO
-RUN
MODIFY FILE PRICE
FIXFORM LABEL/4 COUPON/6 DATE/6 ASK/6
MATCH LABEL COUPON
ON NOMATCH COMPUTE
SECNO = SECNO + 1;
ON NOMATCH INCLUDE
ON MATCH CONTINUE
```

## Using Case Logic in Modify Procedures

```
MATCH DATE
ON MATCH REJECT
ON NOMATCH INCLUDE

CASE AT START
SECNO/I6 = &SECNO ;
ENDCASE

DATA ON INPUT
END
```

The START CASE initializes the security number SECNO to a value determined of the dialogue manager variable &SECNO. The value of &SECNO is read from a flat file, whose ddname is SECNUM. The CASE AT START is executed before the first input record is processed. Then, for each new security (label and coupon), the field SECNO is incremented by one.

If a request performs match logic on multiple segments, you may need to match on one segment at a time when using case logic. For example, the following request adds instances to the SECINFO and DATESEG segments of the PRICE FOCUS file:

```
MODIFY FILE PRICE

PROMPT LABEL COUPON ISSUE DATE YIELD
GOTO ADD
CASE ADD
MATCH LABEL COUPON DATE
ON MATCH REJECT
ON NOMATCH INCLUDE
ON NOMATCH GOTO MESSAGE
ENDCASE
CASE MESSAGE
TYPE
"NEW RECORD ADDED "
ENDCASE
DATA
END
```

As discussed in Chapter 4, match logic can be performed one segment at a time, or on just the lower segment. In this example, the

ADD case branches to the MESSAGE case only when a new record is included in the lower segment (DATESEG, which contains the field DATE). If you want to branch to the MESSAGE case when it includes a new instance in any of the segments, then a separate MATCH statement for each segment should be used:

```
CASE ADD
MATCH LABEL COUPON
ON MATCH CONTINUE
ON NOMATCH INCLUDE
ON NOMATCH GOTO MESSAGE
MATCH DATE
ON MATCH REJECT
ON NOMATCH INCLUDE
ON NOMATCH GOTO MESSAGE
ENDCASE
```

## Examples of Case Logic

There are several important topics related to CASE LOGIC for which we refer you to the FOCUS manual. These include:

1. Modifying multiple unique children segments — Chapter 5 section 6.5.2.
2. Specifying groups of fields — Chapter 7 section 3.6.
3. The NEXT statement — Chapter 5 section 3.5.
4. The repeat and hold technique for processing multiple records at a time — Chapter 5 section 7.1.
5. Modifying muliple FOCUS files in one MODIFY request, using the COMBINE command.

In this section we will present additional examples of applications for CASE LOGIC.

## Example 1: Allowing the Operator to Confirm Data Entry

Normally, when using FIDEL data entry, the data will be processed and used to update the database — after the operator presses 'enter.'

If it is required for the operator to check the data again before it is processed, then the following technique is applicable:

```
MODIFY FILE EMPLOYEE
CRTFORM
"EMPLOYEE:    <CUSTNUM "
"CURRENT LEVEL:   <LEVEL "
"CURRENT TITLE:   <TITLE "
"CURRENT DEPT :   UPDATE THE RECORD(Y,N): <AOK "
MATCH CUSTNUM
ON MATCH IF AOK NE 'Y' GOTO NOGO;
ON MATCH UPDATE LEVEL TITLE DEPT
ON NOMATCH REJECT

CASE NOGO
COMPUTE
CUSTNUM = CUSTNUM ;
TYPE
" CUSTNUM FOUND, BUT DATA NOT UPDATED "
GOTO TOP
ENDCASE
DATA
END
```

The IF condition can be placed after the MATCH, so that a warning message can be issued if the operator chooses not to update the data. Note: If the value of AOK is "y," then the data will be updated as usual.

## Example 2: Processing FIXFORM Transactions Based on Values of a Field

Another common application of CASE LOGIC is to process transactions according to the value of a particular field. The purpose of the field may be to indicate the type of record. The field may indicate that the record contains information of a particular kind, or it might indicate that the transaction has a new segment instance, or it might indicate the type of action to perform on the segment.

For example, a FOCUS file may store information on the inspection results of assembled parts. In a quality control system, parts enter an inspection station daily. The part's history, including inspection results, is maintained in FOCUS files. Before a part is inspected, the historical quality record for the part is obtained from the historical database. The part can be inspected based on past performance.

When the part enters the inspection station, the following occurs:

1. The part number, lot quantity, work order number, etc. are entered into a transaction file.
2. The inspection characteristics of the part and rejection history are obtained from an historical file.
3. An inspection form is generated, which will be used to record the results of the inspection.
4. The inspection results are entered into a transaction file, and later loaded into the historical file. Accepted parts pass to the next work center; rejected parts get sent back for rework or more detailed inspection.

This is a complicated scenario, which involves several procedures, and several databases. We shall discuss how inspection records may be handled. Assume the transaction file contains two types of records:

1. Part numbers, part characteristics, and other part details — for new parts entering the inspection station.
2. Part numbers, and inspection results for each characteristic — after inspection.

Assume that the new parts and data are contained on a transaction record — with a code of "RC10;" inspected parts and results are described in the same transaction file with a code of "RC20." The following MODIFY procedure is used to maintain a FOCUS file. Depending on the record code, which is contained in the first four columns of the record, the procedure will branch to the appropriate case.

```
MODIFY FILE INSPECT
COMPUTE
CODE/A4 = ;
FIXFORM CODE/4 X76
IF CODE IS 'RC10' THEN GOTO TYPE10 ELSE
IF CODE IS 'RC20' THEN GOTO TYPE20 ELSE;
TYPE
```

## Using Case Logic in Modify Procedures 259

```
"INVALID RECORD CODE   "
GOTO TOP

CASE TYPE10
FIXFORM X-76 PARTNO/10 WORKCEN/5 PTYPE/2 LOTSIZE/6
PLANT/2 FIXFORM X51
MATCH PARTNO
ON MATCH UPDATE WORKCEN PTYPE LOTSIZE PLANT
ON NOMATCH COMPUTE
IND/A1 = 'N';
ON NOMATCH INCLUDE
ENDCASE

CASE TYPE20
FIXFORM X-76 PARTNO/10 CHAR/4 QI/6 QR/6 ICODE/1
BADGE/7
FIXFORM COMMENT/30 X12
MATCH PARTNO
ON MATCH COMPUTE
IND/A1 = 'I' ;
ON MATCH UPDATE IND BADGE
ON NOMATCH TYPE ON PARTLOG
"PART NO. ARTNO NOT FOUND "
ON NOMATCH REJECT
ON MATCH CONTINUE
MATCH CHAR
ON NOMATCH INCLUDE
ON MATCH UPDTE QI QR ICODE COMMENT
ENDCASE
DATA ON INPUT
END
```

In this example, the field CODE is first read from each record. After branching to the relevant case, the rest of the record is read using another FIXFORM statement. These FIXFORMS begin with X-76, which allows the case to redefine the 80-byte record from column 5. This demonstrates a convenient way to read part of the record in the TOP case, and the rest of the record in another case. See the FOCUS manual Chapter 5 section 6.5.4 — for a discussion of when the FIXFORM reads the next record. One of the conditions when the FIXFORM reads the next record is when the FIXFORM is the first one in a request. Since the FIXFORMS in CASE TYPE10 and CASE TYPE20 are not the first ones in the request, the FIXFORM stays with the same record.

### Example 3: Multiple Record Processing (Repeating Groups)

Users sometimes require capabilities to process more than one segment instance at one time. This can be handled in a number of ways — whether the data is entered using FIDEL or as FIXFORM transactions. The techniques are:

1. Repeating groups — where the same field is repeated on a single transactions, and FOCUS automatically updates multiple instances in a segment.
2. CASE LOGIC — where multiple instances are updated on each record, by looping back to a common case to process each value of the same field.
3. Repeat and Hold technique — where multiple segment instances can be processed, or retrieved from the database, using the REPEAT and HOLD technique described in the FOCUS manual Chapter 5 section 7.1.

Typical applications requiring multiple record processing include:

1. Browsing through the child segments for a given parent.
2. Adding, deleting, or updating several child segment instances at a time — from a single transaction.

The above techniques, except for repeating groups, use CASE LOGIC. The repeating group technique is described in the FOCUS manual Chapter 5 section 2.1.5 and Chapter 7 section 3.7.2. It is applicable to FIDEL data entry or FIXFORM transactions. In short, the set of transaction fields in one record is called a "repeating group" because one or more fields repeat on the records. An example of such a FIXFORM transaction is:

```
FIXFORM REGION/4 X1 5 (PRODUCT/2 SALES/8)
```

Each transaction contains a region code and five pairs of fields for product and sales amount. FOCUS will process each repeating group separately, performing an include, update, etc. This can also be done with FIDEL by specifying the same name of one or more fields repeatedly on the screen. For example:

```
CRTFORM
"         "
" REGION: <REGION "
" "
" PRODUCT     SALES "
" -------     ----- "
"1. <PRODUCT <SALES "
"2. <PRODUCT <SALES "
"3. <PRODUCT <SALES "
```

Repeating groups is appropriate for simple MODIFY requests; however, it does not easily handle other MODIFY features — such as error handling, validates, etc. Using ordinary MATCH logic, FOCUS automatically updates the database with each group. In the following MODIFY request, three segment instances are updated after specifying three groups of fields in the CRTFORM:

```
CRTFORM
"         "
" REGION: <REGION "
" "
" PRODUCT     SALES "
" -------     ----- "
"1. <PRODUCT <SALES "
"2. <PRODUCT <SALES "
"3. <PRODUCT <SALES "

MATCH REGION
ON MATCH CONTINUE
ON NOMATCH REJECT
MATCH PRODUCT
ON MATCH UPDATE SALES
ON NOMATCH INCLUDE
DATA
END
```

An important technique for processing multiple segment instances at a time involves CASE logic. Sometimes, when processing multiple records at a time, it is required to perform additional processing which depends on the record in the group. This involves counting the records in the group by branching to the same case several times. Figure 8-1 describes a FOCEXEC which updates three child segment instances at one time. The procedure can be easily adapted to similar applications — such as browsing the child records for a given parent. Assume the SALEREG FOCUS file contains a root segment — with key field REGION, and a child segment — with key field PRODUCT.

In the CASE ENTRY, the user enters a region code and the sales amount for three products sold in the region. The procedure then uses CASE logic to process each of the three child records. After the user presses "enter," the procedure performs a validation on each of the three groups. If all the groups are valid, the records are then updated in the database; if not, an INVALID message is displayed, and operator may reenter the data. In CASE GETNEXT, dummy fields XPROD and XSALE are computed from each separate group. The technique uses a field for counting (CTR) to determine which record is to be processed next. After each three groups are validated, the process branches to CASE PUTBACK, where they are updated in the database.

Note that in both cases, GETNEXT and PUTBACK, there is a test for blank data values,

```
IF XPROD EQ ' ' GOTO PUTBACK
```

This statement is required since the operator may not fill in all three groups on the screen. When a blank value is found, no more processing is required in that case.

The next example again demonstrates using CASE logic to create a pattern of many CRTFORMS. A maintenance procedure is to maintain an inventory file — for supplies used in the office. The quantity on hand of each item is maintained, as well as other data, such as the purchase order numbers used to stock the item, the date the purchase order was filled, the unit cost of the item, the minimum on hand, etc. When an item's inventory on hand drops below the minimum required, another purchase order is issued for the item. After the quantity is received from the vendor, the quantity on hand becomes the quantity received. In this example, the procedure will allow the user

```
-* FOCEXEC TO ENTER AND VALIDATE MULTIPLE INSTANCES - USING CASE
LOGIC
-*
MODIFY FILE SALEREG
COMPUTE
XPROD1/A10 = ;
XPROD2/A10 = ;
XPROD3/A10 = ;
XSALE1/F7.2 = ;
XSALE2/F7.2 = ;
XSALE3/F7.2 = ;
CTR/I9   = 0 ;
CTR2/I9 = 0 ;
GOTO ENTRY

CASE ENTRY
CRTFORM LINE 1
" "
" REGION IS <REG "
"</5 "
" PRODUCT IS <XPROD1>   SALES ARE <XSALE1> "
" PRODUCT IS <XPROD2>   SALES ARE <XSALE2> "
" PRODUCT IS <XPROD3>   SALES ARE <XSALE3> "
GOTO GETNEXT
ENDCASE

CASE GETNEXT
COMPUTE
CTR/I4 = CTR + 1;
IF CTR GT 3 GOTO PUTBACK;
COMPUTE
REG = REG ;
XPROD/A10 =  IF (CTR EQ 1) THEN XPROD1 ELSE
             IF (CTR EQ 2) THEN XPROD2 ELSE
             IF (CTR EQ 3) THEN XPROD3 ;
XSALE/F7.2=  IF (CTR EQ 1) THEN XSALE1 ELSE
             IF (CTR EQ 2) THEN XSALE2 ELSE
             IF (CTR EQ 3) THEN XSALE3 ;
IF XPROD EQ ' ' GOTO PUTBACK
GOTO VAL1
ENDCASE

CASE VAL1
VALIDATE
V1 = IF XPROD EQ 'X101' OR 'X102' OR 'X103'
     THEN 1 ELSE 0 ;
V2 = IF XSALE GT 10000 THEN 0 ELSE
```

**Figure 8-1  Using repeating groups.**

```
   IF XSALE LT 1000   THEN 0 ELSE 1 ;
ON INVALID TYPE
" *** INVALID DATA - REENTER "
ON INVALID GOTO ENTRY
GOTO GETNEXT
ENDCASE

CASE PUTBACK
COMPUTE
REG  = REG ;
CTR2= CTR2+ 1;
MATCH REG
ON NOMATCH GOTO TOP
ON MATCH IF CTR2 GT 3 THEN GOTO TOP   ;
ON MATCH COMPUTE
 PROD/A10 =  IF (CTR2 EQ 1) THEN XPROD1 ELSE
             IF (CTR2 EQ 2) THEN XPROD2 ELSE
             IF (CTR2 EQ 3) THEN XPROD3 ;
 SALE/F7.2=  IF (CTR2 EQ 1) THEN XSALE1 ELSE
             IF (CTR2 EQ 2) THEN XSALE2 ELSE
             IF (CTR2 EQ 3) THEN XSALE3 ;
ON MATCH IF PROD EQ ' ' THEN GOTO TOP ;

MATCH PROD
ON MATCH UPDATE SALE
ON MATCH GOTO PUTBACK
ON NOMATCH REJECT
ON NOMATCH GOTO PUTBACK
GOTO PUTBACK
ENDCASE
DATA
END
```

Figure 8-1    (continued) Using repeating groups.


to adjust the quantity on hand whenever a request is made for the item.

The MASTER file description for this INVENT FOCUS file is in figure 8-2. There are two segments in the file. The top segment contains the item number, unit of measurement (e.g., cartons, cases, etc.), unit cost, minimum on hand, vendor number, most recent purchase order number, and the type of item. The child segment contains the purchase order number (key field), the quantity remaining from the purchase order, etc. Notice that the quantity remaining should be zero

```
FILENAME=INVENT  ,SUFFIX=FOC,$
SEGNAME=ITEMSEG ,SEGTYPE=S1,$
  FIELDNAME=ITEM_NO    ,ITEM,A5  ,FIELDTYPE = I , $
  FIELDNAME=UNIT       ,UNIT ,A4    ,$
  FIELDNAME=VNUM       ,VNUM ,A10   ,$
  FIELDNAME=VNAME      ,VNAM ,I6    ,$
  FIELDNAME=PPPK       ,PPPK ,I5    ,$
  FIELDNAME=MINQ       ,MINQ ,I5    ,$
  FIELDNAME=ITMTYPE    ,ITYP ,I1    ,$
SEGNAME=INVSEG  ,SEGTYPE=S1,PARENT=ITEMSEG, $
  FIELDNAME=PNUM       ,PNUM,I5  ,FIELDTYPE = I , $
  FIELDNAME=OQNTY      ,OQTY ,I5    ,$
  FIELDNAME=QNTY       ,QTY  ,I5    ,$
  FIELDNAME=RDATE      ,RDATE,I6YMD,$
  FIELDNAME=PPKTN      ,PPKTN,I5    ,$
  FIELDNAME=PSTAT      ,STAT ,I1    ,$
```

Figure 8-2    MASTER file for Inventory file.


(or close to zero) for all purchase orders except the most recent purchase order.

There are several cases in this request:

1. CASE TOP: The operator enters the item number; the process branches to CASE1.
2. CASE CASE1: After matching to determine if the item number exists, the CRT displays the fields in the top segment. If the item exists in the FOCUS file, the values of the fields are displayed. The operator selects an action: delete the item, input a new item, or update the values in the top segment.
3. CASE INPUPD: The match logic is repeated. The values are updated or input in the top segment. For new items, the process branches to CASE INPPO; For existing items, the process branches to CASE UPDATE.
4. CASE UPDATE: The operator enters the purchase order number, whose inventory is to be updated. The inventory data is displayed on the CRT, and updated in the child segment.
5. CASE INPPO: For new purchase orders or new items, the inventory is input to the child segment.
6. CASE INVALID: If the operator selects an invalid action, the process branches to this case — where a message is displayed.

7. CASE DELETE: This case is for deleting items from the FOCUS file.

This procedure demonstrates a number of techniques such as IF logic to determine the action to be performed; inputting or updating multiple child segment instances; using ON MATCH/NOMATCH CRTFORM. Using turnaround (T.) fields, the operator may change any of the displayed data. The FOCEXEC is shown in figure 8-3

Notice that the cases INPPO and UPDATE, appear to be very similar. One performs an include if new purchase order data, while the other updates existing inventory data for a purchase order. Although a single case could have been designed, the logic is simpler to understand if two cases are used. After inputting or updating the purchase order inventory — including the quantity on hand, pieces per carton, date received, etc., control branches back to the same case (where another purchase order number may be updated or input). At any time, the operator may press 'PF1' to exit the MODIFY procedure, or 'PF2' to clear the screen and start again with a new item.

The previous example demonstrated how to maintain the parent and child segments — such that the operator can select the action to be performed. In the following example, a similar procedure will be used to update a three-segment file. The SALES FOCUS file, whose MASTER is shown in figure 8-4, contains monthly sales data for each brand and product. The sales are also reported in the file by district. The SALES MASTER file is linked with another FOCUS file, PRDDESC, which contains the brand code for each product, as well as other information. The PRDDESC MASTER is shown in figure 8-5.

The file is again to be updated using FIDEL screens; however, the screens will allow the operator to enter the product code, district code, and date on one screen — without branching from one case to the next. The FOCEXEC shown in figure 8-6 is simple to follow:

1. In the TOP case, the operator selects the action to be performed.
2. In CASE UPDATE, the operator enters the key field values via a FIDEL screen. The product code is validated using the FIND function — described in the previous chapter. If the codes are valid, the match logic locates the child segment containing the DATE, and displays the database values on the screen, where they may be changed by the operator.

```
FILE: INVENT    FOCEXEC   A           VM/SP CMS
PAGE 001

-*
-* OFFICE SERVICES DEPARTMENT
-*
-* SYSTEM       - INVENTORY SYSTEM
-* DATABASE     - INVENT    DATABASE
-* FUNCTION     - CENTRAL   FOCEXEC
-* FILENAME     - INVENT    FOCEXEC
-* DESCRIPTION  - SYSTEM FILE MAINTENANCE
-*              - DELETE, INPUT, UPDATE INFORMATION
-*
-* AUTHOR       - J. DEVITA
-* WRITTEN      - SEPT. 26, 1984
-*

CMS CP SET MSG OFF
-RUN
MODIFY FILE INVENT
CHECK 1

CRTFORM NOCLEAR LINE 1
"*****************************************************************"
"(INVENT)            INVENTORY FILE MAINTENANCE           &DATE"
"*****************************************************************"
" "
"ITEM NUMBER       : <ITEM>"
" "
"*****************************************************************"
"     INPUT THE APPROPRIATE INFORMATION AND PRESS ENTER           "
"     PRESS: PF1 TO EXIT            PF2 TO START NEXT ITEM        "
"*****************************************************************"
GOTO CASE1
CASE CASE1
COMPUTE
A/A1 = ' ' ;
MATCH ITEM
ON MATCH COMPUTE
ACTION/A6 = 'UPDATE' ;
DUMMY/A5 = ITEM ;
ON NOMATCH COMPUTE
ACTION/A6 = 'INPUT' ;
DUMMY/A5 = ITEM ;
ON MATCH/NOMATCH CRTFORM LINE 1
```

Figure 8-3  Updating the Inventory file.

```
"********************************************************************"
"(INVENT)             INVENTORY FILE MAINTENANCE              &DATE"
"********************************************************************"
" "
"ITEM NUMBER      : <D.DUMMY><41>( <T.ACTION>)<54>THIS RECORD"
"                              <38>OVERWRITE COLORED AREA WITH :"
"                              <35>(DELETE, INPUT, UPDATE) AS NECESSARY "
"********************************************************************"
"DESCRIPTION      : <T.DESC>"
"UNIT             : <T.UNIT>"
"UNIT_COST        : <T.UCOST>"
"PIECES PER KTN.  : <T.PPPK>"
"MINIMUM ON HAND  : <T.MINQ>"
"VENDOR NUMBER    : <T.VNUM>    <50 PF1 TO EXIT                "
"VENDOR NAME      : <T.VNAME>   <50 PF2 TO START NEXT ITEM "
"CURRENT PO NO.   : <T.PNUMB>"
"LAST ORDER DATE  : <T.LORD>"
"PREVIOUS PO NO.  : <T.PNUMA>"
"ITEM-TYPE (1-5)  : <T.ITMTYPE>"
"********************************************************************"
IF ACTION NE 'DELETE' OR 'INPUT' OR 'UPDATE' GOTO INVALID ;
IF ACTION EQ 'DELETE' GOTO DELETE ;
IF ACTION EQ 'INPUT' OR 'UPDATE' GOTO INPUPD ;
ENDCASE
CASE DELETE
MATCH ITEM
ON NOMATCH REJECT
ON NOMATCH GOTO TOP
ON MATCH DELETE
ON MATCH TYPE
"=================================================================="
"            ITEM NUMBER <ITEM> HAS BEEN DELETED"
"=================================================================="
" "
ON MATCH GOTO TOP
ENDCASE
CASE INPUPD
MATCH ITEM
ON NOMATCH INCLUDE
ON NOMATCH TYPE
"=================================================================="
"            ITEM NUMBER <ITEM>HAS BEEN INPUT"
"=================================================================="
" "
ON NOMATCH GOTO INPPO
```

Figure 8-3   (continued) Updating the Inventory file.

## Using Case Logic in Modify Procedures 269

```
ON MATCH UPDATE DESC MINQ MAXQ UNIT UCOST VNUM PNUMA PNUMB LORD
LRCV PPPK
ON MATCH TYPE
"===================================================================="
"              ITEM NUMBER <ITEM> HAS BEEN UPDATED"
"===================================================================="
" "
ON MATCH GOTO UPDATE
ENDCASE
CASE UPDATE
COMPUTE
NXT/A1=;
CRTFORM CLEAR LINE 1
"********************************************************************"
"(INVENT)           INVENTORY QUANTITIES FOR PO          &DATE"
"********************************************************************"
" "
"PO NUMBER       : <PNUM>"
" "
"********************************************************************"
"     INPUT THE APPROPRIATE INFORMATION AND PRESS ENTER            "
"     PRESS: PF1 TO EXIT              PF2 TO START NEXT ITEM       "
"********************************************************************"
MATCH PNUM
ON NOMATCH TYPE
"===================================================================="
"            PO NOT FOUND; INPUT <PNUM> ABOVE"
"===================================================================="
" "
ON NOMATCH GOTO INPPO
ON MATCH COMPUTE
DUMPO/I5 = PNUM ;
ON MATCH CRTFORM LINE 1
"********************************************************************"
"(INVENT)
&DATE"
"********************************************************************"
" "
PO NUMBER       : <D.DUMPO><41>(    UPDATE)<54>THIS RECORD"
"********************************************************************"
"PO STAT (0 FILL): <T.PSTAT>"
"QUANTITY RCVD.  : <T.OQNTY>"
"QUANTITY ON HAND: <T.QNTY>"
"PCS. PER CARTON : <T.PPKTN>"
"DATE RECEIVED   : <T.RDATE>"
```

**Figure 8-3** (continued) Updating the Inventory file.

```
"*********************************************************************"
"         INPUT THE APPROPRIATE INFORMATION AND PRESS ENTER            "
"       PRESS: PF1 TO EXIT      <T.A>   PF2 TO START NEXT ITEM         "
"*********************************************************************"
ON MATCH UPDATE OQNTY QNTY PPKTN RDATE PSTAT
ON MATCH TYPE
"====================================================================="
"         INVENTORY SEGMENT FOR PO <DUMPO> HAS BEEN UPDATED"
"====================================================================="
" "
ON MATCH GOTO UPDATE
ENDCASE
CASE INPPO
CRTFORM CLEAR LINE 1
"*********************************************************************"
"(INVENT)            INVENTORY QUANTITIES FOR PO           &DATE"
"*********************************************************************"
" "
PO NUMBER          : <T.PNUM>     (INPUT) "
" "
"*********************************************************************"
"         INPUT THE APPROPRIATE INFORMATION AND PRESS ENTER            "
"       PRESS: PF1 TO EXIT              PF2 TO START NEXT ITEM         "
"*********************************************************************"
MATCH PNUM
ON NOMATCH COMPUTE
DUMPO/I5 = PNUM ;
ON NOMATCH CRTFORM LINE 1
"*********************************************************************"
"(INVENT)            INVENTORY QUANTITIES FOR PO           &DATE"
"*********************************************************************"
" "
"PO NUMBER          : <D.DUMPO><41>(        INPUT)<54>THIS RECORD"
"*********************************************************************"
"PO STAT (0 FILL):  <T.PSTAT>"
"QUANTITY RCVD.   : <T.OQNTY>"
"QUNATITY ON HAND: <T.QNTY>"
"PCS. PER CARTON  : <T.PPKTN>"
"DATE ORDERED     : <T.ODATE>"
"DATE RECEIVED    : <T.RDATE>"
"*********************************************************************"
"         INPUT THE APPROPRIATE INFORMATION AND PRESS ENTER            "
"       PRESS: PF1 TO EXIT      <T.A>   PF2 TO START NEXT ITEM         "
"*********************************************************************"
ON NOMATCH INCLUDE
```

Figure 8-3   (continued) Updating the Inventory file.

```
ON NOMATCH TYPE
"================================================================="
"           INVENTORY SEGMENT FOR PO <DUMPO> HAS BEEN INPUT"
"================================================================="
" "
ON MATCH GOTO INPPO
ON MATCH TYPE
"================================================================="
"      PO ALREADY EXISTS"
"================================================================="
" "
ON MATCH GOTO INPPO
ENDCASE
-************************ INVALID CASE ************************
CASE INVALID
TYPE
"================================================================="
"                    THAT IS AN INVLAID ACTION CHOICE"
"                    PLEASE RE-ENTER A NEW ACTION CHOICE"
"================================================================="
GOTO CASE1
ENDCASE
DATA
END
-RUN
SET MSG = ON
-RUN
CMS CP SET MSG ON
```

**Figure 8-3** (continued) Updating the Inventory file.

3. In CASE DELETE, the operator enters the key field values, and match logic retrieves the DATE record which is to be deleted. The operator selects an 'X' on the screen to delete the record. If 'X' was not selected, the process branches to CASE ERROR1 — where a message is displayed.
4. In CASE INCLUDE, the operator enters all the data values on one screen. The product code is validated, and match logic includes the DATE record.

At any time, the operator may press 'PF2' to clear the screen, and return to the TOP case to select a new action. Using CASE LOGIC, the procedure enables the operator to perform several maintenance processes in one procedure.

```
FILENAME=SALES,SUFFIX=FOC,$
SEGNAME=PRODUCT,SEGTYPE=S1,$
   FIELDNAME=PRODKEY,PKEY,A10,$
SEGNAME=PRDTWO,PARENT=PRODUCT,SEGTYPE=KU,CRFILE=PRDDESC,CRKEY=PROD-
KEY,$
SEGNAME=PRDONE,PARENT=PRDTWO,SEGTYPE=KLU,$
SEGNAME=SALESEG,SEGTYPE=S1,PARENT=PRODUCT,$
   FIELDNAME=DISTKEY,DKEY,A4,$
SEGNAME=DATASEG,PARENT=SALESEG,SEGTYPE=S1,$
   FIELDNAME=DATE,MONTH,A4YM,$
   FIELDNAME=CASES,CS,D8,$
   FIELDNAME=PRICECASE,PC,D8.2M,$
```

**Figure 8-4   Sales MASTER file.**

```
FILENAME=PRDDESC,SUFFIX=FOC,$
SEGNAME=PRDONE,SEGTYPE=SH1,$
   FIELDNAME=BRANDKEY,BKEY,A10,$
   FIELDNAME=BRAND,BND,A20,$
SEGNAME=PRDTWO,SEGTYPE=SH1,PARENT=PRDONE,$
   FIELDNAME=PRODKEY,PKEY,A10,FIELDTYPE=I,$
   FIELDNAME=PRODUCT,PRD,A20,$
```

**Figure 8-5   PRDDESC MASTER file.**

## Using Case Logic in Modify Procedures 273

```
SET MSG=OFF
MODIFY FILE SALES
LOG NOMATCH MSG OFF
LOG INVALID MSG OFF
LOG DUPL MSG OFF

COMPUTE
UPD/A1= ;
INC/A1= ;
DEL/A1= ;
EXT/A1= ;
PRODTEST/I1= ;
DISTEST/I1= ;
XTEST/A4= ;
DTEST/A1= ;
CRTFORM LINE 1
"                                                                    "
"                                                                    "
"           SALES DATA BASE MAINTAINCE PROCEDURE                     "
"                                                                    "
"                                                                    "
"                                                                    "
"   PLACE AN X NEXT TO THE DESIRED ACTIVITY AND PRESS 'ENTER'        "
"                                                                    "
"                          UPDATE  : <UPD>                           "
"                          DELETE  : <DEL>                           "
"                          INCLUDE : <INC>                           "
"                          EXIT    : <EXT>                           "
"                                                                    "
"                                                                    "
IF UPD IS 'X' THEN GOTO UPDATE ELSE
IF DEL IS 'X' THEN GOTO DELETE ELSE
IF INC IS 'X' THEN GOTO INCLUDE ELSE
IF EXT IS 'X' THEN GOTO EXIT ELSE
GOTO TOP ;

CASE UPDATE
CRTFORM LINE 1
"                                                                    "
"                                                                    "
"           SALES DATA BASE MAINTAINCE PROCEDURE                     "
"                        UPDATE SCREEN                               "
"                                                                    "
"                  ENTER THE FOLLOWING VALUES                        "
"              (PRESS PF2 TO RETURN TO MAIN MENU)                    "
```

**Figure 8-6** Using CASE logic to maintain the Sales file.

```
"                                                                "
"              PRODKEY          :<PRODKEY>                       "
"              DISTKEY          :<DISTKEY>                       "
"              DATE (YYMM)      :<DATE>                          "
VALIDATE
   PRODTEST=FIND(PRODKEY IN PRDDESC);
     ON INVALID TYPE
"*******A PRODUCT KEY OF <PRODKEY> IS NOT IN PRODUCT FILE*******"
     ON INVALID GOTO UPDATE
MATCH PRODKEY
ON MATCH CONTINUE
ON NOMATCH REJECT
MATCH DISTKEY
ON MATCH CONTINUE
ON NOMATCH REJECT
MATCH DATE
ON MATCH CRTFORM LINE 15
"****************************************************************"
"                    CURRENT VALUES ARE                          "
"                    TYPE IN NEW VALUES                          "
"              CASES            : <T.CASES>                      "
"              PRICE PER CASE : <T.PRICECASE>                    "
"****************************************************************"
ON MATCH TYPE
"************UPDATE PROCEDURE HAS BEEN COMPLETE******************"
ON MATCH UPDATE CASES PRICECASE
ON NOMATCH TYPE
"***DATE OF <DATE NOT FOUND IN FILE TRANSACTION BEING REJECTED***"
ON NOMATCH REJECT
ON NOMATCH GOTO UPDATE
ENDCASE
CASE DELETE
CRTFORM LINE 1
"              SALES DATA BASE MAINTAINCE PROCEDURE              "
"                         DELETE SCREEN                          "
"                                                                "
"                                                                "
"              ENTER THE FOLLOWING VALUES                        "
"              (PRESS PF2 TO RETURN TO MAIN MENU)                "
"                                                                "
"              PRODKEY          :<PRODKEY>                       "
"              DISTKEY          :<DISTKEY>                       "
"              DATE (YYMM)      :<DATE>                          "
"                                                                "
"                                                                "
VALIDATE
   PRODTEST=FIND(PRODKEY IN PRDDESC);
```

Figure 8-6   (continued) Using CASE logic to maintain the Sales file.

```
         ON INVALID TYPE
"*******A PRODUCT KEY OF <PRODKEY> IS NOT IN PRODUCT FILE*******"
         ON INVALID GOTO DELETE
MATCH PRODKEY
ON MATCH CONTINUE
ON NOMATCH TYPE
"***DATE OF <DATE NOT FOUND IN FILE TRANSACTION BEING REJECTED***"
ON NOMATCH REJECT
MATCH DISTKEY
ON MATCH CONTINUE
ON NOMATCH REJECT
MATCH DATE
ON MATCH CRTFORM LINE 14
"****************************************************************"
"                    CURRENT VALUES ARE                          "
"                                                                "
"                    CASES         : <D.CASES>                   "
"                    PRICE PER CASE : <D.PRICECASE>              "
"   IF YOU WANT TO DELETE THESE VALUES TYPE AN X HERE: <DTEST "
"****************************************************************"
ON MATCH IF DTEST NE 'X' THEN GOTO ERROR1;
ON MATCH TYPE
"***************DELETE PROCEDURE HAS BEEN COMPLETED***************"
ON MATCH DELETE
ON NOMATCH TYPE
"***************DATE OF <DATE NOTE FOUND**************************"
ON NOMATCH REJECT
ON NOMATCH GOTO DELETE
ENDCASE
CASE INCLUDE
CRTFORM LINE 1
"              SALES DATA BASE MAINTAINCE PROCEDURE             "
"                         INCLUDE SCREEN                        "
"                                                               "
"                                                               "
"                 ENTER THE FOLLOWING VALUES                    "
"                (PRESS PF2 TO RETURN TO MAIN MENU)             "
"                                                               "
"                                                               "
"              PRODKEY         :<PRODKEY>                       "
"              DISTKEY         :<DISTKEY>                       "
"              DATE (YYMM)     :<DATE>                          "
"              CASES           :<CASES>                         "
"              PRICE PER CASE  :<PRICECASE>                     "
VALIDATE
   PRODTEST=FIND(PRODKEY IN PRDDESC);
      ON INVALID TYPE
```

Figure 8-6  (continued) Using CASE logic to maintain the Sales file.

```
"*******A PRODUCT KEY OF <PRODKEY> IS NOT IN PRODUCT FILE*******"
      ON INVALID GOTO INCLUDE
MATCH PRODKEY
ON MATCH CONTINUE
ON NOMATCH REJECT
MATCH DISTKEY
ON MATCH CONTINUE
ON NOMATCH REJECT
MATCH DATE
ON MATCH TYPE
"****DATE OF <DATE IS ALREADY IN FILE REJECTING TRANSACTION*******"
ON MATCH REJECT
ON MATCH GOTO INCLUDE
ON NOMATCH TYPE
"***************NEW SEGMENT HAS BEEN INCLUDED********************"
ON NOMATCH INCLUDE
ENDCASE

CASE ERROR1
MATCH DATE
ON MATCH TYPE
" "
"*******************DELETION CANCELLED***************************"
ON MATCH REJECT
ON MATCH GOTO DELETE
ENDCASE
DATA
END
SET MSG=ON
```

Figure 8-6   (continued) Using CASE logic to maintain the Sales file.

Chapter

# 9

# Designing FOCUS Applications: Case Studies

This chapter further demonstrates the use of the basic features of FOCUS in common applications. By presenting more examples of real FOCUS systems, I hope the programmer will gather further insight on how the features fit together and are organized. I make no attempt to be exhaustive in the treatment of FOCUS features, since these features can usually be used in different ways in different applications. Some of these features will appear in more than one example. This will assist you in learning it, as you use it repetitively. I leave to the reader who needs clarification to find it by asking friends, experimenting himself, or using my hot-line consulting service if I ever figure out how to set it up.

## Working With the End User

The process of implementing FOCUS applications requires that you understand what the user expects from the application. Many users may need your help in clarifying what are the important requirements. Since most applications evolve over time to include new features, it is essential to build a comfortable rapport with the user. Let the user know from the start that building the application will be a cooperative effort.

While the user is trying to clarify the requirements, you can begin to demonstrate the capabilities of a tool like FOCUS in various ways:

1. Present a brief description of how FOCUS files are used, how they are accessed to create reports, and how they can be maintained.
2. Discuss the features of his application by relating it possibly to other FOCUS applications with which the user has been involved. You might consider giving a demonstration of similar applications which you have developed — so that some of the features of data entry, reporting, etc., may become clear.
3. If the FOCUS files are likely to have a simple design, you can create a sample database using real or test data, and develop some reporting procedures which the user may ask for. The goal is to demonstrate that FOCUS is already effective, and can provide results quickly. As the user understands the tool better, the results will help guide what he needs to have next.

As a programmer, you should try to clarify the following as soon as possible:

1. Where the data will come from, and how it will be entered into the FOCUS files.
2. What the time frame is for developing the system; what procedures and programs are the highest priority; what should be done first.
3. How the data should be organized so that the natural relationships between the data can be kept in order; how the data can be organized so that it can be accessed efficiently and simply in most of the expected reports.
4. How large the FOCUS files are likely to get; are they likely to be used in other applications; who will need to have access to the files.

## Basic Utilities for Implementing FOCUS Procedures

FOCUS contains aids to assist the programmer in the actual work of coding, testing and implementing various procedures. However, much of the programmer's time and effort can be reduced by simply being aware of what FOCUS does best, and when to use the features that are offered in the various FOCUS commands. Most FOCUS applications are built around a small number of commands or procedures, such as DEFINE, TABLE, MODIFY, COMPUTE, etc. Each of these commands can be designed and tested for a particular application, and then combined in a piecemeal fashion into FOCEXECS — perhaps using dialogue manager to control various options.

The programmer has the luxury of testing procedures one section at a time. This can be done a number of ways — by taking advantage of such features as:

1. Creating HOLD files which contain a smaller or more manageable number of records extracted from FOCUS files.
2. Experimenting with formatting or computational logic using a small number of fields, defines, etc.
3. Inserting dialogue manager features such as EXIT statements to test and display the results of each section of code, or ECHO to trace the substitution of values into dialogue manager variables.
4. Displaying system statistics and messages at various points in the execution of a procedure by using the SET command (SET MSG ON) or the ? query commands.

There are a number of utility commands which assist the programmer in accomplishing special tasks such as transferring data to a PC, or recording what happened in a FOCUS session. Some of these are used infrequently, but you should be aware that they exist by referring to Chapter 12 of the FOCUS manual. We shall present a checklist of features which are basic to developing all applications, since they were designed to help you organize and debug programs. You should also refer to the Appendix for using these features under different operating systems.

## The USE Command

In any FOCUS request such as TABLE, MODIFY, DEFINE, JOIN, etc., FOCUS searches for CMS files having the filetype of FOCUS and the filemode of A.

For example, the command TABLE FILE SALES causes FOCUS to search for the CMS file SALES FOCUS A. The USE command allows greater flexibility in the selection of filename, filetype, and filemode as FOCUS files. It permits more than one physical file to be used with a particular MASTER description. It also has other functions such as protecting databases from changes, identifying new databases to FOCUS, etc. The USE statement may be placed in any FOCEXEC, or executed from native FOCUS. Consider the following USE request:

```
USE
NEWYORK FOCUS E AS SALES
PRODUCTS FOCUS E
BONUS1 FOCUS A AS BONUS
END
```

The first two files are on the E disk and the third is on the A disk. FOCUS will use these physical files in any request which refers to them. If another application requires, say, a different SALES file, then you only need to change the statement in the USE request. E.g.,

```
USE DETROIT FOCUS E AS SALES
```

The USE request can be placed in a separate FOCEXEC, which can be executed at any time (even from within another FOCEXEC). However, it is usually placed in the PROFILE FOCEXEC, which is executed automatically when entering FOCUS. It can be cleared in other FOCEXECS or in native FOCUS with the command USE CLEAR, or you can add to it with USE ADD. You can identify new files to FOCUS which are to be described by its MASTER file with the request:

```
USE
filename filetype filemod NEW
END
```

If your application uses a number of FOCUS files for various purposes, the USE request can identify where the physical files are located. Without any USE request, the default filemode of a FOCUS file is the A disk. However, if a USE request exists, then the filemode of the first file identified determines the default filemode of other FOCUS files. For example,

```
USE
CHICAGO FOCUS B AS SALES
END
```

The B disk is the default filemode for any other FOCUS file which may be used in a FOCUS command. This is fine if the other FOCUS files to be used are on the B disk. Note that in CMS, your id must be linked to the disks which contain the FOCUS files in your application. (The exception to this are files in the SIMULTANEOUS USAGE mode.) At any time during a FOCUS session, the files in the USE request can be displayed by issuing the query command ? USE.

Some of the more sophisticated functions of the USE command are:

1. Indicating which FOCUS file will be used as databases for different users and in different situations.
2. Allowing files to be used interchangeably as cross-reference files.
3. Concatenating several physical files as one FOCUS file.
4. Protecting FOCUS files from changes while testing a MODIFY procedure.
5. Allowing more than one user to change a FOCUS file from different ids (SIMULTANEOUS USERS).

## Debugging Features and Checking for Errors

FOCUS issues error messages during the execution of various requests usually because the syntax of a statement is incorrect, or because a field or keyword is undefined. There are other errors which are common to expressions — such as the result of an expression is incompatible with the format of a field, or an operation or relation is unrecognized. There may also be errors in dialogue manager statements such as an illegal expression or a missing label. In most cases, the execution passes to the end of the command, and the rest of the FOCEXEC is executed. If the rest of the FOCEXEC depends on a previous step in error — such as the creation of a HOLD file, transaction file, DEFINED fields, etc., then there will be further error messages. The best way to exit from the procedure entirely is to enter the command FX — which will halt execution and return to native FOCUS. Sometimes, FOCUS will give the operator the opportunity to reenter a correct fieldname or some keyword. In this case, the command QUIT can be entered to quit the FOCEXEC.

After a program has been debugged, and tests out to run correctly, there are only a few situations which may cause a problem for the operator. These are usually identified quickly, since they are due to external problems unrelated to the programming logic. Some of these are:

1. A TABLE request cannot be issued for a FOCUS file which has been changed on a linked disk. If the change occurs after the operator has already linked to the disk, then the operator must reaccess the disk — establishing a new link. If not, an address exception error will occur. Note: If the FOCUS file is available on a "sink id" through simultaneous users, then a report request may be issued while another user is updating the file.
2. An operator's id does not have to contain any FOCEXECS, MASTER files, etc. — since he may be linked to a disk where these reside. However, if the operator tries to execute any procedure which has changed on a disk after he has linked to it, there will be an address or specification error. He must first reaccess the disk.
3. FOCUS requires work space to perform sorting, extract HOLD files, etc. This will usually be found on the operator's A disk. If there is not enough space there, TEMP space should be allocated. If you run out of space during a FOCUS session, an error will occur and the session will be returned to CMS.
4. As FOCUS files undergo maintenance such as adding or deleting records, the file's organization of internal pointer's may eventually be degraded. This would cause performance in MODIFY and TABLE commands to slow down — since locating internal FOCUS pages would take longer. When this happens, the FOCUS REBUILD command (see FOCUS manual pages 12–43 to 12–50) can reestablish the structure of the file.
5. Sometimes during a FOCUS session, the operating system may fail or crash, resulting in an end to the FOCUS session. Although there is little which can be done to prevent this, FOCUS does provide file integrity features automatically in CMS so that the database pages or pointer are not lost during a MODIFY procedure.

### Designing FOCUS Applications: Case Studies

There are a number of features which can assist the programmer in testing for conditions which may require special action. After a TABLE or MODIFY command is run, you may issue the command ?STAT to determine how many lines were generated or how many records were input, updated, etc. This is useful if you forget which command has just been processed, or if the FOCUS informational messages have been turned off. In addition, these statistics can be obtained as system variables after a command is processed and used in dialogue manager statements within a FOCEXEC.

Dialogue manager has several techniques assisting the user in a check for programming errors. Most important is the use of the EXIT statement, which can be placed anywhere in a FOCEXEC in order to test various sections of code without processing the rest of the code. As an alternative to using an EXIT statement, a program can set return codes using dialogue manager variables. These variable may be displayed at the terminal using the TYPE statement, or even passed to other FOCEXECS as GLOBAL variables. If a FOCUS procedure is called from a CMS EXEC, a special return code can be returned to the EXEC to control the remaining parts of the exec. We shall present this technique in one of the examples.

### Setting Up TEMP Space

On CMS, there are occasions when there is not enough space on the user's A-disk to execute various FOCUS procedures which create temporary HOLD files, perform sorting, etc. You may need to attach a temporary disk or another DASD unit as another writeable disk.

As a rule, FOCUS will use as workspace the disk with the largest amount of available space. This feature is quite nice to have most of the time. But, there are times when the program has been designed to expect HOLD or SAVE files on a particular disk. There are two ways to specify the disk to be used in a FOCUS session or FOCUS program.

1. SET TEMP parameter.
2. FILEDEFS for individual files.

The command SET TEMP = filemode indicates which writeable disk FOCUS should use, regardless of how much space is available. Any HOLD or SAVE files are created on the disk specified. However, this may be overriden with the use of FILEDEFS for particular files. For example, if a FOCEXEC is to create a file HOLD1 on the A-disk, a FILEDEF can accomplish this even if the the TEMP parameter has been set to B.

```
-CMS FILEDEF HOLD1 DISK HOLD1 FOCTEMP A
```

You should test out this feature before using it in an application.

In the earlier chapters of the book, I have presented the basic capabilities of FOCUS for writing reports, creating and maintaining FOCUS files, performing data entry with FIDEL, and adding control with dialogue manager. The examples already presented are of simple to moderate complexity, allowing you, as a novice or training programmer, to obtain insight on a number of basic features. By using this information as a starting point, you should have the ability to build some simple databases or obtain reports from existing databases. To supplement this, every FOCUS user should have a familiarity with the subjects covered in the FOCUS 5.0 manual, so that you can refer back to details on a subject when the need arises. Most of the time, you will only be using a few FOCUS features, so you should know where these are described in the FOCUS users manual. (In my opinion, either the FOCUS 4.5 or 5.0 manual can be used as a reference.)

### Example 1: Member Enrollment Application

The example describes a simple database which includes basic information on individuals who may enroll in a special life insurance program. The program is open to individuals who have been identified as holders of various credit cards — such as VISA, DINERS CLUB, etc. The purpose of the application is:

1. To store data on potential clients.
2. To generate enrollment forms which will be sent to the individuals.
3. To record whether the individual has accepted or declined the invitation to join the insurance program.

We will describe the procedures used to maintain the FOCUS database with client information, as well as the procedure used for generating the enrollments forms.

There are 2 FOCUS files — the ULIFE file contains data on the potential clients; the ULIFEREG file is used in data entry to lookup the values of insurance amount and premium according to the age of each individual. Their MASTER descriptions are shown in figures 9-1 and 9-2.

The key field in the ULIFE file is a control number (CONTROL_NUM) which is assigned to each individual. Each record in the file contains the name, address, birthdate — as well as information on the individual's association, credit card account number, etc. The procedure to input this data into the ULIFE file is contained in figure 9-3. The procedure to update (correct) this data is contained in figure 9-4.

The ULIFEINP FOCEXEC was designed with CASE LOGIC. It allows the operator to enter the data onto a FIDEL screen for any number of individuals. The major steps are:

1. The date of data entry is obtained from today's date. The starting control number is 1.
2. The BEGIN case will automatically generate the next control number by incrementing the last control number by 1. The NEXT command is used to locate the next segment instance after the current position. (See the FOCUS manual chapter 5 section 3.5 for details on the NEXT command.) The control numbers are entered into the file in ascending order. Therefore, the latest record in the root segment will be the highest control number. When found by the NEXT command, it is incremented by 1 — to obtain the next control number which is displayed to the operator.
3. The operator enters the relevant data onto the FIDEL screen for that control number. In the last case, the age of the individual is compute in order to LOOKUP the premium amount and face value from the ULIFEREG file. (Notice that the ULIFE file must first be JOINED to the ULIFEREG file in order to use LOOKUP.) The record is included in the file — and the procedure branches to CASE ENTRIES where the next control number is displayed and the operator enters new data.

```
FILENAME  = ULIFE             ,SUFFIX = FOC
SEGNAME   = CLIENT            ,SEGTYPE=SH1,$
FIELDNAME = CONTROL_NUM       ,CNUM       ,I04,FIELDTYPE=I, $
FIELDNAME = FULL_NAME         ,NAME       ,A30             , $
FIELDNAME = ADDRESS           ,ADRME      ,A30             , $
FIELDNAME = CITY              ,CITY       ,A30             , $
FIELDNAME = STATE_CODE        ,STATE      ,A2              , $
FIELDNAME = ZIP_CODE          ,ZIP        ,A9              , $
FIELDNAME = MARKET_CODE       ,MARKET     ,A20             , $
FIELDNAME = ACCOUNT_CODE      ,ACCOUNT    ,A20             , $
FIELDNAME = CLIENT_CODE       ,CLIENT     ,A14             , $
FIELDNAME = ASSOC_NUM         ,ASSN       ,A10             , $
FIELDNAME = BIRTH_DATEM       ,BDATEM     ,I2              , $
FIELDNAME = BIRTH_DATED       ,BDATED     ,I2              , $
FIELDNAME = BIRTH_DATEY       ,BDATEY     ,I2              , $
FIELDNAME = AGE               ,AGE        ,I2              , $
FIELDNAME = FACE_AMOUNT       ,FACE       ,I6CM            , $
FIELDNAME = PREMIUM_AMT       ,PREMIUM    ,F5.2M           , $
FIELDNAME = BOUGHT_YN         ,BYN        ,A1              , $
FIELDNAME = DATE_ENTRY        ,EDATE      ,I6              , $
FIELDNAME = DATE_SENY         ,SDATE      ,I6              , $
```

Figure 9-1  ULIFE Master description.

We have used CASE LOGIC here primarily to better identify the steps in the procedure. The ULIFEUPD FOCEXEC is relatively simple — since it only performs corrections on the data already entered. The control number is first entered by the operator. If the control number is found, the data for the individual is displayed on the screen — where it may be changed. The last procedure is the ULIFEFRM FOCEXEC, in figure 9-5. Its purpose is to generate the enrollment forms for a number of individuals. The data is to be printed on special forms — instead of as a regular report.

This FOCEXEC demonstrates how a report can be formatted using only HEADING in a TABLE request. The reports are generated as an enrollment form, with the data on individuals displayed on separate pages. The reports are printed onto preprinted forms which already look like enrollment forms. By displaying the values of the fields in the HEADING, the fields may be positioned anywhere on the form — with one page per record. Also, note the following:

1. The START and END control numbers are prompted for as dialogue manager variables.

```
FILENAME = ULIFEREG        ,SUFFIX = FOC
SEGNAME  = REGMKT          ,SEGTYPE=S1,$
FIELDNAME = ISSUE_AGE       ,AGE     ,I2  ,FIELDTYPE=I, $
FIELDNAME = FACE_AMT        ,FACE    ,I6              , $
FIELDNAME = PREM_AMT        ,PREMIUM ,F5.2            , $
```

**Figure 9-2 ULIFEREG Master description.**

2. Setting SET PAGE = OFF is necessary to prevent page numbers from appearing at the top of each form.3. The procedure uses a - INCLUDE for the UWAIT FOCEXEC — which simply displays a 'WAIT' message to the operator.

## Example 2: Sales Tracking and Analysis System

One of the best features of FOCUS is the capability it gives the user to understand the relationships between the data simply by looking at the MASTER description file. The student of the application, of course, must first have some knowledge of the following:

1. Parent-child relationships between FOCUS segments or records.
2. The notion of a key field, which describes how the records in a segment are organized, what makes them unique, etc.
3. The concept of virtual segments on cross-reference files, which relate records and fields in another file to the "main" FOCUS file.

The following application describes a sales tracking system, not unlike those used in the sales departments or regional offices of major companies. Each month a clerk posts the cases sold (shipped) and unit prices of various products contained in the company's product line. These amounts are summarized for each sales district.

There are several ways to design the MASTER description for this file. The point we wish to make is that it makes little difference which method we choose — as long as the relationships between the data are valid, and can be understood easily by someone else.

In the MASTER shown in figure 9-6, the root segment contains the product code or PRODKEY. There are no other fields in the segment, although others could have been added. For example, if each product

## 288 The Database Experts' Guide to FOCUS

```
-*****************************************************************
-* ULIFENP.FEX - ACCEPTS NEW RECORD INPUT, AUTOMATICALLY ASSIGNS
-*               NEXT HIGHEST CONTROL NUMMBER, CALCULATES AGE AND
-*               LOOKS UP IN A TABLE THAT IS SPECIFIED IN
-*               ENSUING "JOIN" COMMAND (E.G. ULIFEREG)
-*               AND UPDATES RECORD FOR FACE, PREMIUM AND ENTRY
-*               DATE
-*
-*      CALLED BY MAIN MENU ONLY - ULIFEMEN.FEX
-*****************************************************************
JOIN CLEAR
JOIN AGE IN ULIFE TO ISSUE_AGE IN ULIFEREG AS ISSUEAGE
-SET &QUIT=OFF ;
-SET &MSG=OFF ;
-SET &PAUSE=OFF ;
-TOP
EX UWAIT
-RUN
MODIFY FILE ULIFE
COMPUTE
    WORK_CTL/I5L = 1 ;
    DENTRY = &MDY ;
    TODAY/I6MDY  = &MDY ;
    TDM/A2       = EDIT(TODAY,'99$$$$') ;
    TDD/A2       = EDIT(TODAY,'$$99$$') ;
    TDY/A2       = EDIT(TODAY,'$$$$99') ;
    TTDM/I2      = EDIT(TDM) ;
    TTDD/I2      = EDIT(TDD) ;
    TTDY/I2      = EDIT(TDY) ;
GOTO BEGIN

CASE BEGIN
NEXT CONTROL_NUM
ON NONEXT GOTO ENTRIES
ON NEXT COMPUTE
WORK_CTL=D,CONTROL_NUM + 1 ;
ON NEXT GOTO ENTRIES
ENDCASE

CASE ENTRIES
CRTFORM LOWER LINE 1
"                  ***   REPLY CARD DATA INPUT    ***
" "
"CONTROL          <16 <D.WORK_CTL> "
"FULLNAME         <16 <NAME> "
"ADDRESS          <16 <ADR> "
```

Figure 9-3    Inputting transactions to ULIFE file.

```
"CITY            <16 <CITY"
"STATE           <16 <STATE    <40 ZIP CODE   <53 <ZIP
" "
"MARKET CODE     <16 <MARKET  "
"ACCOUNT CODE    <16 <ACCOUNT "
"CLIENT CODE     <16 <CLIENT  "
"ASSN. NO.       <16 <ASSN    "
"
"
"BIRTHDAY        <16 <BDATEM / <BDATED / <BDATEY  <MM DD YY> "
" "
" "
"***   USE TAB KEY TO POSITION CURSOR   *****   WHEN FINISHED HIT
ENTER    ***"
" "
"***   WHEN DONE ENTERING DATA, HIT PF3 TO RETURN TO MAIN MENU
***"
"-----------------------------------------------------------------"
GOTO UPDATE
ENDCASE

CASE UPDATE
COMPUTE
  CONTROL_NUM = WORK_CTL ;
  WORK_CTL    = WORK_CTL + 1 ;
  DATE_ENTRY  = DENTRY ;
AGELESS1/I2=(TTDY-1)-BDATEY ;
AGE/I2=IF BDATEM LT TTDM THEN AGELESS1 + 1 ELSE
    IF BDATEM GT TTDM THEN AGELESS1 ELSE
    IF BDATEM EQ TTDM AND BDATED LE TTDD THEN AGELESS + 1 ELSE
    IF BDATEM EQ TTDM AND BDATED GT TTDD THEN AGELESS ELSE 0 ;
VALIDATE
RC=LOOKUP(FACE_AMT) ;
RC=LOOKUP(PREM_AMT) ;
ON INVALID TYPE "AGE <AGE NOT IN TABLE, CHECK AND RE-ENTER LATER"
ON INVALID GOTO ENTRIES
ON VALID TYPE "AGE; <AGE FACE: <FACE_AMT PREMIUM: <PREM_AMT"
COMPUTE
FACE_AMOUNT=FACE_AMT ;
PREMIUM_AMT=PREM_AMT ;
MATCH CONTROL_NUM
ON NOMATCH INCLUDE
ON NOMATCH TYPE
    "ADD SUCCESSFUL FOR CONTROL <CONTROL_NUM> - <NAME>"
ON NOMATCH GOTO ENTRIES
ON MATCH    GOTO UPDATE
```

Figure 9-3   (continued) Inputting transactions to ULIFE file.

```
ENDCASE
DATA VIA FIDEL
LOG INVLAID MSG OFF
END
-EXIT
```

**Figure 9-3**  (continued) Inputting transactions to ULIFE file.

is contained in a product group or brand category, this information could have been placed in this segment. Notice the other MASTER file in the figure, PRDDESC, contains fields describing the product — such as its name, brand category, etc. The PRDDESC file is used as cross-reference file (SEGTYPE KU) — so that this brand information may be obtained.

There are two child segments for this root segment:

1. SALESEG — containing the district code or DISTKEY — where the product was sold.
2. DATASEG — containing the cases sold and price for each month of the year.

The MASTER describes a single-path file, since all segments have at most one child segment. Notice that the cross-reference segment has SEGTYPE of KU. For each product code in the PRODUCT segment, there is only one record in the cross-reference segment. This makes sense, since you would expect each product code to have one name, one brand-category, etc. If the cross-reference file may contain more than one record for each cross-reference key (ie. PRODKEY), you would need a SEGTYPE of KM. The FOCUS manual, Chapter 4 section 3.1.2 describes a simple design using a KM SEGTYPE. (In practice, a KM segtype is usually not anticipated by the programmer, in which case a JOIN may used used to link the segments if the need arises.)

Once the data is loaded into the FOCUS files, there are a number of reports which can be developed. We shall present several reports which use some of the basic features of TABLE. In addition, the FOCUS MATCH FILE command will also be discussed. As you go through the FOCEXECS, keep in mind that the MASTER description could have been designed differently — for example, with DISTKEY in the root segment — with no change in the way the reporting programs are developed.

```
************************************************************************
-* ULIFEUPD.FEX - ALLOWS UPDATE OF CERTAIN NON-CALCULABLE FIELDS
-*                                         COMPUTER CONSULTANTS, INC.
-*
-*
-* CALLED BY MAIN MENU ONLY - ULIFEMEN.FEX
-
************************************************************************
-SET MSG=OFF ;
-TOP

-START
MODIFY FILE ULIFE
CASE BEGIN
CRTFORM LINE 1 CLEAR
" "
" "
" "
" "
" "
"                    ***    REPLY CARD DATA UPDATE    ***"
" "
"        RESPONDENT CONTROL NUMBER TO BE UPDATED: <CNUM> "
" "
" "
"*** ENTER CONTROL NUMBER, HIT RETURN *** HIT F3 WHEN DONE UPDAT-
ING ***"
" "
MATCH CONTROL_NUM
ON NOMATCH TYPE
"THIS CONTROL NUMBER <CNUM> DOES NOT EXIST. CHECK AND RE-ENTER"
ON MATCH REJECT
ON MATCH GOTO ENTRIES
ENDCASE
CASE ENTRIES
CRTFORM LOWER LINE 1
"CONTROL NUM      <16 <D.CONTROL_NUM"
" "
"FULL NAME        <16 <T.NAME> "
"ADDRESS          <16 <T.ADDR"
"CITY             <16 <T.CITY"
"STATE            <16 <T.STATE   <40 ZIP CODE    <53 <T.ZIP"
" "
"MARKET CODE      <16 <T.MARKET  "
"ACCOUNT CODE     <16 <T.ACCOUNT "
"CLIENT CODE      <16 <T.CLIENT  "
"ASSN. NO.        <16 <T.ASSN    "
```

Figure 9-4    Updating the ULIFE file.

292   The Database Experts' Guide to FOCUS

```
"


" "
" "
"***   USE TAB KEY TO POSTION CURSOR    *****   WHEN FINISHED HIT
ENTER    ***"
" "
"-----------------------------------------------------------------"
MATCH CONTROL_NUM
  ON MATCH UPDATE NAME ADDR CITY STATE ZIP MARKET ACCOUNT CLIENT
ASSN

  ON MATCH TYPE
     "UPDATE SUCCESSFUL FOR CONTROL <CONTROL_NUM> - <NAME>"
  ON NOMATCH TYPE
  " CONTROL NUMBER NOT IN FILE, CHECK AND RE-ENTER"
  ON NOMATCH GOTO BEGIN
ENDCASE
```

**Figure 9-4   (continued) Updating the ULIFE file.**


**Report 1**

This report displays the number of cases shipped each month by district, by brand. The months are displayed across the top of the page, as shown in the sample report in figure 9-7. The focexec is in figure 9-8.

In order to compute the average cases sold per month, and display it in the last column, several techniques are used which deserve explanations.

1. In the first request, cases are summed by product by district code, by month and the result is placed into a HOLD file. Also, the number of months (records) is counted for each product and district code — so that the average per month can be computed for the report. The resulting HOLD file MASTER looks like figure 9-9. Each field has an ALIAS given by E01, E02, E03,..., which should be used when more than one fieldname is the

## Designing FOCUS Applications: Case Studies

```
************************************************************
-* ULIFEFRM.FEX - PRINTS ENROLLMENT FORM
-*
-*
-*  CALLED BY MAIN MENU ONLY - ULIFEMEN.FEX
-
************************************************************
-START
-PROMPT &START_CNUM.I4.ENTER STARTING CONTROL NUMBER:
-PROMPT &END_CNUM.I4.ENTER ENDING CONTROL NUMBER (OR 9999).
-PROMPT &CR.A2.TYPE 'GO' PREPARE PRINTER, TYPE 'GO' WHEN READY .
-IF &CR NE 'GO' GOTO START ;
-INCLUDE UWAIT
DEFINE FILE ULIFE
TYPE_ACT4/A4=EDIT (MARKET_CODE, '9999$') ;
TYPE_ACT1/A1=EDIT(MARKET_CODE,'9$') ;
TYPE_NAME/A40=IF TYPE_ACT1 EQ '3' THEN 'DINERS CLUB Account
Number' ELSE
 IF TYPE_ACT4 EQ '4128' THEN 'CITIBANK VISA Account Number' ELSE
 IF TYPE_ACT4 EQ '4271' THEN 'CITIBANK Preferred VISA Account
Number' ELSE
 IF TYPE_ACT4 EQ '5424' THEN 'CITIBANK MASTERCARD Account Number'
ELSE
 IF TYPE_ACT1 EQ '4' AND TYPE_ACT4 NE '4128' OR '4271' THEN
'VISA Account Number' ELSE
 IF TYPE_ACT1 EQ '5' AND TYPE_ACT4 NE 5424 THEN
'MASTERCARD Account Number' ELSE ' ' ;
END
SET PAGE=OFF
SET PRINT=OFFLINE
SET MSG=OFF
SET PAUSE=ON
TABLE FILE ULIFE
HEADING
"</3"
"<55 <FACE"
"</1"
"<5 <MARCKET_CODE <ASSOC_NUM <CONTROL_NUM"
"</2 <55 <BDATEM - <BDATED - <BDATEY "
"</1 "
"<10 <FULL_NAME       "
"<10 <ADDR       "
"<10 <CITY <STATE <ZIP"
"</22 <30 <PREMIUM    "
"</2"
"<10 <TYPE_NAME : <+2 <ACCOUNT "
```

**Figure 9-5** Generating the ULIFE enrollment form.

```
" "
PRINT CONTROL_NUM NOPRINT
BY CONTROL_NUM NOPRINT
IF CONTROL_NUM GE &START_CNUM
IF CONTROL_NUM LE &END_CNUM
END
```

**Figure 9-5** (continued) Generating the ULIFE enrollment form.

same. Note, the number of months (counted) is in field E04, and has the same name DATE as the field E05.

2. The second TABLE request creates the report by summing across the months. The sort (BY) fields are BRAND and DISTKEY. The field FST.E04 indicates that the field E04 (number of months) will not be summed in each record — it represents the number of months.
3. The ACROSS is used to spread the months across the page. Then, column notation can be used to refer to each column on the report. First, the 5 columns are summed as TOTSHP, and the average per month is computed as AVESHP. This technique is not recommended when you do not know the number of columns on the page.
4. On each break for district code, the report summarizes the cases in each month, as well as the total and average shipments.

The FOCEXEC is shown in figure 9-8. An alternative way to compute the average cases per month is to use the direct operation AVE. in the first TABLE request. (Then there is no need to use CNT.)

Almost transparent to the programmer is the use of the PRDDESC file as a cross-reference file. From the SALES file, the brand-category and the product name can be accessed through any TABLE request. Note, the brand segment is indicated in the SALES MASTER as a KLU segment — since it is the parent of the cross-reference segment. (See the FOCUS manual chapter 4 section 3.2.)

### Report 2

This report demonstrates further how to use direct operations to compute various statistics on cases shipped. For each district and brand,

```
FILENAME=SALES,SUFFIX=FOC,$
SEGNAME=PRODUCT,SEGTYPE=S1,$
    FIELDNAME=PRODKEY,PKEY,A10,$
SEGNAME=PRDTWO,PARENT=PRODUCT,SEGTYPE=KU,CRFILE=PRDDESC,
CRKEY=PRODKEY,$
SEGNAME=PRDONE,PARENT=PRDTWO,SEGTYPE=KLU,$
SEGNAME=SALESEG,SEGTYPE=S1,PARENT=PRODUCT,$
    FIELDNAME=DISTKEY,DKEY,A4,$
SEGNAME=DATASEG,PARENT=SALESEG,SEGTYPE=S1,$
    FIELDNAME=DATE,MONTH,A4YM,$
    FIELDNAME=CASES,CS,D8,$
    FIELDNAME=PRICECASE,PC,D8.2M,$

========================================================================

FIELDNAME=PRDDESC,SUFFIX=FOC,$
SEGNAME=PRDONE,SEGTYPE=SH1,$
    FIELDNAME=BRANDKEY,BKEY,A10,$
    FIELDNAME=BRAND,BND,A20,$
SEGNAME=PRDTWO,SEGTYPE=SH1,PARENT=PRDONE,$
    FIELDNAME=PRODKEY,PKEY,A10,FIELDTYPE=I,$
    FIELDNAME=PRODUCT,PRD,A20,$
```

**Figure 9-6  MASTER files for sales tracking example.**

the percentage of cases shipped can be computed relative to the total cases shipped. The TABLE request for this is:

```
TABLE FILE SALES
SUM PCT.CASES
BY DISTKEY BY BRAND
IF DATE FROM &BMONTH TO &EMONTH.
END
```

However, the SALEREP2 FOCEXEC (figure 9-10) shows the added feature WITHIN, which indicates within which sortfield to perform the percentage operation. The direct operation is performed within the section specified rather than over the entire report. The percentage cases are computed relative to the total cases in each district, while the average cases are computed relative to the total cases shipped in each brand. The TABLE request does not sort by month; so the computations are performed across all months. See the report out-

PAGE 1
                    BRAND SIZE INFORMATION SYSTEM
                              REPORT 1
                    REPORT ON 11/30/87 AT 22.22.31

```
              DATE
              87/01         87/02         87/03         TOTSHP        AVESHP
DISTKEY       CASES         CASES         CASES
-------------------------------------------------------------------------------
GENERIC REPORT
1011            714           697             .          1,411         705.50

MOPGLO PRODUCT REPORT
1011            323           319             .            642         321.00

PINESOL BRAND REPORT
1011          6,884         4,769         6,951         18,604       6,201.33
1012          7,020         7,141         6,930         21,091       7,030.33
1013          4,820         4,471         4,764         14,055       4,685.00
1014          4,800         4,660         4,943         14,403       4,801.00
1015          6,910         6,903         7,177         20,990       6,996.67

*TOTAL PINESOL BRAND
             30,434        27,944        30,765         89,143       5,942.87

TOTAL        31,471        28,960        30,765         91,196       4,799.79
```

Figure 9-7   Sales Report 1 output.

put in figure 9-11. The FOCUS manual chapter 2 section 5.2, presents another example to help clarify the use of WITHIN.

### Report 3 (The MATCH FILE Command)

In this example, the percentage of cases shipped in each district is computed for each product in the district. The result is MATCHED against the total budget available in each district so that dollars can be allocated to product managers based on the percentage to district sales.

# Designing FOCUS Applications: Case Studies

```
SET JOE=OFF OR ON, WHO'LL KNOW THE DIFFERENCE

TABLE FILE SALES
WRITE CNT.DATE BY BRAND BY PRODUCT BY DISTKEY
SUM CASES BY BRAND BY PRODUCT BY DISTKEY BY DATE
IF BRAND NE 'POPULATION'
ON TABLE HOLD AS HOLD1
END
SET MSG=ON
TABLE FILE HOLD1
HEADING CENTER
"BRAND SIZE INFORMATION SYSTEM"
"REPORT 1"
"REPORT ON &DATE AT &TOD"
"</2>"
SUM CASES AND FST.E04 NOPRINT ACROSS E05 AND COMPUTE
TOTSHP/D8=(C1+C3+C5+C9+C11);
AVESHP/D10.2=TOTSHP/FST.E04;
BY BRAND NOPRINT BY DISTKEY
ON DISTKEY   SUMMARIZE MULTILINES
ON BRAND SUBHEAD
"<BRAND REPORT"
" "
END
```

**Figure 9-8   FOCEXEC for Sales Report 1.**

### Using the MATCH Command

The FOCUS MATCH command is a very useful way to combine two or more files. We shall discuss the technique here. The MATCH command can merge records from several files, and can also merge data from the save file more than once. The syntax of the MATCH command is similar to the TABLE command.

```
MATCH FILE filename
....
....
RUNFILE filename
....
....
AFTER MATCH relational operator
RUN
FILE filename
```

```
FILE=HOLD1            ,SUFFIX=FIX
SEGNAME=HOLD1
FIELDNAME  =BRAND     ,E01      ,A20    ,A20   ,$
FIELDNAME  =PRODUCT   ,E02      ,A20    ,A20   ,$
FIELDNAME  =DISTKEY   ,E03      ,A4     ,A04   ,$
FIELDNAME  =DATE      ,E04      ,I5     ,I04   ,$
FIELDNAME  =DATE      ,E05      ,A4YM   ,A04   ,$
FIELDNAME  =CASES     ,E06      ,D8     ,D08   ,$
```

Figure 9-9   HOLD file MASTER.

```
. . . .
. . . .
AFTER MATCH relational operator
END
```

The actual way MATCH merges the records depends on several things:

1. The order in which you name the files in the request.
2. The BY fields used with each file.
3. The verb (SUM or PRINT) used with each file.
4. The relational operator.

In general, the MATCH command compares the retrieved records from each step based on the values of the BY fields. The merged records are saved in a HOLD file. A MATCH request can compare values based on any number of BY fields. The first BY field in each MATCH is called the "high-order" sort field. FOCUS performs the match by first comparing the values of the common high-order sort fields. The next BY fields are called "low-order" sort fields — these are matched if they are common, and if there was a common high-order sort field. The BY fields need not have the same name — but they must have the same format. If the names are different, you may refer to a common name by placing — AS fieldname — after the BY field. As will be demonstrated in this example, the way in which the records are matched also depends on the verbs used — SUM or PRINT.

In this example, we wish to merge records in the SALES file with records in the DISTRICT file. The DISTRICT file contains the name of each district, and the total budget dollars available to each district — for the categories PROMOTION, ADVERTISING, SALARIES, etc.

```
SET MSG=ON
TABLE FILE SALES
HEADING CENTER
"BRAND SHARES BY DISTRICT "
"REPORT ON &DATE AT &TOD"
"</2>"
SUM PCT.CASES WITHIN DISTKEY AVE.CASES WITHIN BRAND
BY DISTKEY NOPRINT BY BRAND
ON DISTKEY  SUBTOTAL CASES
ON DISTKEY SUBHEAD
"<DISTKEY REPORT"
" "
IF DATE FROM &BMONTH TO &EMONTH
END
```

Figure 9-10    FOCEXEC for Sales report 2.

See the MASTER description in figure 9-12. The final report will show the budget dollars allocated to each PRODUCT based on the PERCENTAGE of sales of the PRODUCT in the DISTRICT.

The FOCEXEC is shown in figure 9-13. The first TABLE request sums cases by district code and product, and computes the percentage of total cases sold in the district for each product. The resulting records in the HOLD file look like those in figure 9-14. In order to compute the budget dollars allocated to each product, the total budget must be multiplied by the percentage of district sales for each product. The two files (HOLD1 and DISTRICT) can be MATCHED BY DISTRICT CODE to create another file which contains budget data as well as sales percentages on records for each product in the district. MATCHING requires at least one common sort key (DISTKEY). When two files are matched, the records are aggregated, summed, or listed, in each section of the MATCH, based on the verb phrase and sort fields. Screening conditions can be placed within the MATCH request, but no COMPUTE phrases. FOCUS tries to perform the matching by first comparing the values of the common high-order sort fields. In the above example, the budget records for each district code are matched with records in the HOLD1 file containing the same district codes. (Note: the fields E03 and E04 represent the cases and percentage of district totals — for each product.) The MATCH logic also depends on the concept of "OLD" and "NEW" files. The result of the match may contain records from both the first file (OLD) and the second file (NEW) in the request. You have the option of selecting

1 PAGE     1

```
              BRAND SHARES BY DISTRICT
              REPORT ON 12/01/87 AT 00.39.24

                             PCT           AVE
BRAND                        CASES         CASES
-----                        -----         -----
1011 REPORT

GENERIC                         0            353
MOPGLO PRODUCT                  0            321
PINESOL BRAND                   3          1,550
POPULATION                     96        180,000

*TOTAL 1011                   100

1012 REPORT

PINESOL BRAND                   2          1,758
POPULATION                     98        341,333

*TOTAL 1012                   100

1013 REPORT

PINESOL BRAND                   3          1,171
POPULATION                     97        150,667

*TOTAL 1013                   100

1014 REPORT

PINESOL BRAND                   1          1,200
POPULATION                     99        331,000

*TOTAL 1014                   100

1015 REPORT

PINESOL BRAND                   3          1,749
POPULATION                     97        248,667

*TOTAL 1015                   100

TOTAL                         500
```

**Figure 9-11    Sales Report 2 output.**

```
FILENAME=DISTRICT,SUFFIX=FOC,$
SEGNAME=DIST    ,SEGTYPE=SH1,$
   FIELDNAME=DISTKEY,DKEY,A4,FIELDTYPE=I,$
   FIELDNAME=DISTNAME,DST,A18,$
   FIELDNAME=BUD_ADV,ADV,P10.2,$
   FIELDNAME=BUD_PRO,PRO,P10.2,$
   FIELDNAME=BUD_SAL,SAL,P10.2,$
   FIELDNAME=BUD_OTH,OTH,P10.2,$
```

**Figure 9-12    District MASTER file.**

which set of values of the BY fields will be included in the matched file. This is specified in the statement:

```
AFTER MATCH HOLD [AS name] relational operator
```

where the possible choices for the relational operator are:

   OLD-OR-NEW: All records from both the old and new file.
   OLD-AND-NEW: Records that appear in both the old and new file. (The intersection of BY field values.)
   OLD-NOT-NEW: Records in the old file which are not in the new file.
   NEW-NOT-OLD: Records in the new file which are not in the old file.
   OLD-NOR-NEW: Only records which are in the old file and not in the new file; or in the new file and not in the old file.
   OLD: Only records in the old file.
   NEW: Only records in the new file.

In this example, we wish to retain records only from the SALES file (HOLD1 file), since there may be districts in the DISTRICT file for which there is no shipments data. To do this, we use the operation,

```
AFTER MATCH HOLD OLD.
```

MATCHING does not match one record in one file with one record in another file. The first HOLD1 file is sorted by product code, as well as district code — containing more records than the DISTRICT file. The process will attempt to match the records in the district file with each record in the HOLD1 file which has a common district code. The

```
SET MSG=OFF

TABLE FILE SALES
SUM   CASES PCT.CASES WITHIN DISTKEY BY DISTKEY BY PRODUCT
IF PRODKEY OMITS '999'
ON TABLE HOLD AS HOLD1
END
-RUN

MATCH FILE HOLD1
SUM E03 E04
BY DISTKEY BY PRODUCT
RUN
FILE DISTRICT
SUM ADV PRO SAL OTH
BY DISTKEY
ON MATCH HOLD OLD
END
-RUN

SET MSG=ON
TABLE FILE HOLD
HEADING CENTER
"BUDGET ESTIMATE BY DISTRICT (BASED ON PERCENTAGE SALES) "
"REPORT ON &DATE AT &TOD"
"</2>"
SUM E03 E04 AS 'PCT.' AND COMPUTE
ADV/P10.2 = E04 * E05 * .01 ;
PRO/P10.2 = E04 * E06 * .01 ;
SAL/P10.2 = E04 * E07 * .01 ;
OTH/P10.2 = E04 * E08 * .01 ;

BY DISTKEY NOPRINT BY PRODUCT
ON DISTKEY   SUMMARIZE
ON DISTKEY SUBHEAD
"<DISTKEY REPORT"
" "
END
```

**Figure 9-13    FOCEXEC for Sales Report 3.**

way in which the records are matched also depends on the verb. The FOCUS manual chapter 2 section 11.2.1 describes the effect of using SUM or PRINT in different situations. In this FOCEXEC, we have used the verb SUM for both files. This will assure us that records from the DISTRICT file will be matched with all records in the HOLD1 file which have the same district code. The MATCH request

```
FILE=HOLD              ,SUFFIX=FIX
SEGNAME=HOLD
FIELDNAME   =DISTKEY    ,E01     ,A4       ,A04     ,$
FIELDNAME   =PRODUCT    ,E02     ,A20      ,A20     ,$
FIELDNAME   =CASES      ,E03     ,D8       ,D08     ,$
FIELDNAME   =CASES      ,E04     ,D8       ,D08     ,$
FIELDNAME   =BUD_ADV    ,E05     ,P10.2    ,P08     ,$
FIELDNAME   =BUD_PRO    ,E06     ,P10.2    ,P08     ,$
FIELDNAME   =BUD_SAL    ,E07     ,P10.2    ,P08     ,$
FIELDNAME   =BUD_OTH    ,E08     ,P10.2    ,P08     ,$
```

Figure 9-14    HOLD file MASTER.

results in a single-segment HOLD file. If the contents of the HOLD file are printed, the records look like those in figure 9-15.

Notice, that the same DISTRICT file records are used in all HOLD1 file records that have the same district code. We would have obtained a different result if the verb PRINT had been used in the second MATCH.

```
MATCH FILE HOLD1
SUM E03 E04
BY DISTKEY BY PRODUCT
RUN
FILE DISTRICT
PRINT ADV PRO SAL OTH
BY DISTKEY
ON MATCH HOLD OLD
END
```

In this case, the records for each district code would not be duplicated in each HOLD1 record having the same district code — they would only be matched with the first record in HOLD1 which has the same district code. As shown in figure 9-16, the other HOLD1 records will contain zeros or blanks for the fields in the DISTRICT file. This is an important distinction between the verbs SUM and PRINT in a MATCH command.

The final step is to format the report which shows the budget dollars allocated to each product according to the percent of sales in the district. Since percents and budget amounts are contained in the same record of the HOLD file, it is a simple matter to COMPUTE the allocations. The report output is shown in figure 9-17.

MATCH0.LIS

1 PAGE    1

| DISTKEY | PRODUCT | CASES | CASES | BUD_ADV | BUD_PRO | BUD_SAL | BUD_OTH |
|---|---|---|---|---|---|---|---|
| 1011 | GENERIC LRG   | 684    | 3  | 550.00 | 550.00 | 500.00 | 100.00 |
| 1011 | GENERIC SML   | 727    | 4  | 550.00 | 550.00 | 500.00 | 100.00 |
| 1011 | MOPGLO SML    | 642    | 3  | 550.00 | 550.00 | 500.00 | 100.00 |
| 1011 | PINESOL 10LB  | 6,905  | 33 | 550.00 | 550.00 | 500.00 | 100.00 |
| 1011 | PINESOL 25 LB | 220    | 1  | 550.00 | 550.00 | 500.00 | 100.00 |
| 1011 | PINESOL 5 LB  | 915    | 4  | 550.00 | 550.00 | 500.00 | 100.00 |
| 1011 | PINESOL 50 LB | 10,564 | 51 | 550.00 | 550.00 | 500.00 | 100.00 |
| 1012 | PINESOL 10LB  | 9,540  | 45 | 550.00 | 550.00 | 400.00 | 100.00 |
| 1012 | PINESOL 25 LB | 919    | 4  | 550.00 | 550.00 | 400.00 | 100.00 |
| 1012 | PINESOL 5 LB  | 955    | 5  | 550.00 | 550.00 | 400.00 | 100.00 |
| 1012 | PINESOL 50 LB | 9,677  | 46 | 550.00 | 550.00 | 400.00 | 100.00 |
| 1013 | PINESOL 10LB  | 9,996  | 71 | 350.00 | 650.00 | 400.00 | 100.00 |
| 1013 | PINESOL 25 LB | 940    | 7  | 350.00 | 650.00 | 400.00 | 100.00 |
| 1013 | PINESOL 5 LB  | 994    | 7  | 350.00 | 650.00 | 400.00 | 100.00 |
| 1013 | PINESOL 50 LB | 2,125  | 15 | 350.00 | 650.00 | 400.00 | 100.00 |
| 1014 | PINESOL 10LB  | 2,693  | 19 | 350.00 | 250.00 | 100.00 | 100.00 |
| 1014 | PINESOL 25 LB | 698    | 5  | 350.00 | 250.00 | 100.00 | 100.00 |
| 1014 | PINESOL 5 LB  | 696    | 5  | 350.00 | 250.00 | 100.00 | 100.00 |
| 1014 | PINESOL 50 LB | 10,316 | 72 | 350.00 | 250.00 | 100.00 | 100.00 |
| 1015 | PINESOL 10LB  | 10,575 | 50 | 250.00 | 250.00 | 100.00 | 100.00 |
| 1015 | PINESOL 25 LB | 972    | 5  | 250.00 | 250.00 | 100.00 | 100.00 |
| 1015 | PINESOL 5 LB  | 273    | 1  | 250.00 | 250.00 | 100.00 | 100.00 |
| 1015 | PINESOL 50 LB | 9,170  | 44 | 250.00 | 250.00 | 100.00 | 100.00 |

**Figure 9-15    HOLD file from MATCH procedure.**

| DISTKEY | PRODUCT | CASES | CASES | BUD_ADV | BUD_PRO | BUD_SAL | BUD_OTH |
|---|---|---|---|---|---|---|---|
| 1011 | GENERIC LRG | 684 | 3 | 550.00 | 550.00 | 500.00 | 100.00 |
| 1011 | GENERIC SML | 727 | 4 | .00 | .00 | .00 | .00 |
| 1011 | MOPGLO SML | 642 | 3 | .00 | .00 | .00 | .00 |
| 1011 | PINESOL 10LB | 6,905 | 33 | .00 | .00 | .00 | .00 |
| 1011 | PINESOL 25 LB | 220 | 1 | .00 | .00 | .00 | .00 |
| 1011 | PINESOL 5 LB | 915 | 4 | .00 | .00 | .00 | .00 |
| 1011 | PINESOL 50 LB | 10,564 | 51 | .00 | .00 | .00 | .00 |
| 1012 | PINESOL 10LB | 9,540 | 45 | 550.00 | 550.00 | 400.00 | 100.00 |
| 1012 | PINESOL 25 LB | 919 | 4 | .00 | .00 | .00 | .00 |
| 1012 | PINESOL 5 LB | 955 | 5 | .00 | .00 | .00 | .00 |
| 1012 | PINESOL 50 LB | 9,677 | 46 | .00 | .00 | .00 | .00 |
| 1013 | PINESOL 10LB | 9,996 | 71 | 350.00 | 650.00 | 400.00 | 100.00 |
| 1013 | PINESOL 25 LB | 940 | 7 | .00 | .00 | .00 | .00 |
| 1013 | PINESOL 5 LB | 994 | 7 | .00 | .00 | .00 | .00 |
| 1013 | PINESOL 50 LB | 2,125 | 15 | .00 | .00 | .00 | .00 |
| 1014 | PINESOL 10LB | 2,693 | 19 | 350.00 | 250.00 | 100.00 | 100.00 |
| 1014 | PINESOL 25 LB | 698 | 5 | .00 | .00 | .00 | .00 |
| 1014 | PINESOL 5 LB | 696 | 5 | .00 | .00 | .00 | .00 |
| 1014 | PINESOL 50 LB | 10,316 | 72 | .00 | .00 | .00 | .00 |
| 1015 | PINESOL 10LB | 10,575 | 50 | 250.00 | 250.00 | 100.00 | 100.00 |
| 1015 | PINESOL 25 LB | 972 | 5 | .00 | .00 | .00 | .00 |
| 1015 | PINESOL 5 LB | 273 | 1 | .00 | .00 | .00 | .00 |
| 1015 | PINESOL 50 LB | 9,170 | 44 | .00 | .00 | .00 | .00 |

**Figure 9-16** HOLD from MATCH procedure. (Using PRINT verb.)

BUDGET ESTIMATE BY DISTRICT (BASED ON PERCENTAGE SALES)
REPORT ON 11/30/87 AT 22.06.05

| PRODUCT | CASES | PCT. | ADV | PRO | SAL | OTH |
|---|---|---|---|---|---|---|
| ------- | ----- | ---- | --- | --- | --- | --- |
| 1011 REPORT | | | | | | |
| GENERIC LRG | 684 | 3 | 18.21 | 18.21 | 16.56 | 3.31 |
| GENERIC SML | 727 | 4 | 19.36 | 19.36 | 17.60 | 3.52 |
| MOPGLO SML | 642 | 3 | 17.09 | 17.09 | 15.54 | 3.11 |
| PINESOL 10LB | 6,905 | 33 | 183.85 | 183.85 | 167.13 | 33.43 |
| PINESOL 25 LB | 220 | 1 | 5.86 | 5.86 | 5.33 | 1.07 |
| PINESOL 5 LB | 915 | 4 | 24.36 | 24.36 | 22.15 | 4.43 |
| PINESOL 50 LB | 10,564 | 51 | 281.27 | 281.27 | 255.70 | 51.14 |
| *TOTAL 1011 | 20,657 | 100 | 3850.00 | 3850.00 | 3500.00 | 700.00 |
| 1012 REPORT | | | | | | |
| PINESOL 10LB | 9,540 | 45 | 248.78 | 248.78 | 180.93 | 45.23 |
| PINESOL 25 LB | 919 | 4 | 23.97 | 23.97 | 17.43 | 4.36 |
| PINESOL 5 LB | 955 | 5 | 24.90 | 24.90 | 18.11 | 4.53 |
| PINESOL 50 LB | 9,677 | 46 | 252.35 | 252.35 | 183.53 | 45.88 |
| *TOTAL 1012 | 21,091 | 100 | 2200.00 | 2200.00 | 1600.00 | 400.00 |

**Figure 9-17    Sales Report 3 output.**

```
1014 REPORT

PINESOL 10LB        2,693    19    65.44    46.74    18.70    18.70
PINESOL 25 LB         698     5    16.96    12.12     4.85     4.85
PINESOL 5 LB          696     5    16.91    12.08     4.83     4.83
PINESOL 50 LB      10,316    72   250.68   179.06    71.62    71.62

*TOTAL 1014        14,403   100  1400.00  1000.00   400.00   400.00

1015 REPORT

PINESOL 10LB       10,575    50   125.95   125.95    50.38    50.38
PINESOL 25 LB         972     5    11.58    11.58     4.63     4.63
PINESOL 5 LB          273     1     3.25     3.25     1.30     1.30
PINESOL 50 LB       9,170    44   109.22   109.22    43.69    43.69

1 PAGE    2
```

BUDGET ESTIMATE BY DISTRICT (BASED ON PERCENTAGE SALES)
REPORT ON 11/30/87 AT 22.06.05

```
PRODUCT        CASES    PCT.     ADV       PRO       SAL       OTH
-------        -----    ----     ---       ---       ---       ---
*TOTAL 1015   20,990    100   1000.00   1000.00    400.00    400.00

TOTAL         91,196    500  49250.00  53250.00  37500.00  11500.00
```

**Figure 9-17** (continued) Sales Report 3 output.

```
    FILENAME = MAIL                ,SUFFIX = FOC
    SEGNAME  = MAILIST             ,SEGTYPE=SH1,$
      FIELDNAME = CUSTNUM             ,SEQ       ,I06,FIELDTYPE=I, $
      FIELDNAME = LAST_NAME           ,LNAME     ,A20              , $
      FIELDNAME = FIRST_NAME          ,FNAME     ,A15              , $
      FIELDNAME = COMPANY_NAME        ,CNAME     ,A45              , $
      FIELDNAME = STREET              ,STR       ,A40              , $
      FIELDNAME = CITY                ,          ,A33              , $
      FIELDNAME = STATE               ,          ,A2               , $
      FIELDNAME = ZIP                 ,          ,A5               , $
      FIELDNAME = ACCOUNT_TYPE        ,TYPE      ,A10              , $
      FIELDNAME = CITI_CONTACT        ,CONTACT   ,A35              , $
      FIELDNAME = STATUS              ,          ,A15              , $
      FIELDNAME = EXPENSE_CODE        ,EXP       ,A4               , $
      FIELDNAME = REGCODE             ,RCODE     ,A2               , $
      FIELDNAME = IMDY                ,IMDY      ,I6MDY            , $
INPUT DATE
      FIELDNAME = UMDY                ,UMDY      ,I6MDY            , $
UPDATE DATE
    SEGNAME = REGION , CRFILE = MAILREG, CRKEY = REGCODE,
            PARENT=MAILIST,SEGTYPE = KU,$
```

**Figure 9-18   MAIL MASTER file.**

## Example 3: Client Mailing List System

This is a relatively common clerical application for FOCUS. An organization has a list of clients which receive its newsletter each month. The client data is entered into a single segment MAIL FOCUS file. The data on clients is usually made available through sales persons in various sales regions. The list of region codes and region names are contained in a cross-reference file MAILREG. The MAIL MASTER is in figure 9-18.

The data entry procedure is described first for adding and updating client data. We also present FOCEXECS which allow the user to print the records in the form of address labels. The labels may be printed as a regular report for viewing, or they may be printed onto special mailing label forms.

This example also discusses the use of dialogue manager to set up a menu for the MAIL system. The purpose of the menu is to allow the user to select an option from a list. The MAIL FOCEXEC is shown in figure 9-19.

There are several ways to use dialogue manager to "drive" the user's selections. One way is to branch to a label depending on the

```
-SET &OPT = ' ' ;
-SET &PRO = 'MAIL' ;
-SET &MSG = ' ' ;
-SET &QUIT = OFF ;
-START
-CRTCLEAR
-CRTFORM
_" "
-"<.W.                   MAIL GENERATION FACILITY "
_" "
-"    SELECT: <T.&OPT <.TURQ. "
_" "
-"                        1.   ADD CUSTOMER RECORDS "
-"                        2.   DELETE CUSTOMER RECORDS "
-"                        3.   UPDATE CUSTOMER RECORDS "
-"                        4.   VIEW CUSTOMER RECORDS "
-"                        5.   PRINT CUSTOMER LABELS "
-"                        6.   PRINT CUSTOMER REPORT "
-"                        7.   COUNT CUSTOMERS "
-"                        8.   REGION CODES "
-"                        9.   SEND REPORT TO PRINTER "
_" "
-"                        X.   EXIT "
-" </2  <.Y.D.&MSG "

-RUN
-SET &&RECS = 1 ;
-SET &MSG = ' ';
-TOP
-IF &OPT EQ 'X' GOTO DONE ;
-IF &OPT EQ '9' GOTO PRTIT;
-IF &OPT GT '9' GOTO ERROR ;
-IF &OPT LT '1' GOTO ERROR ;

EX FMAIL&OPT
-RUN
-IF &&RECS EQ 0 GOTO NORECS ;
-SET &MSG = 'REQUEST COMPLETED' ;
-GOTO START

-PRTIT
-SET &MSG = '**** NOT AVAILABLE ****' ;
-GOTO START

-ERROR
-SET &MSG = '**** INVALID INPUT - PLEASE TRY AGAIN ****';
-RUN
```

Figure 9-19  Driver program for MAIL system.

```
-GOTO   START

-NORECS
-SET &MSG = '**** NO REPORT CREATED **** ';
-RUN
-GOTO   START

-DONE
FIN
```

**Figure 9-19** (continued) Driver program for MAIL system.

selection made. There are several labels, which are starting points for executing the various FOCEXECS. Another way is to assign simple names to each FOCEXEC, so that they all differ by a number — e.g., FMAIL1, FMAIL2, FMAIL3, ... In this way, a single statement for executing the intended FOCEXEC can be set up. I.e.,

```
EX FMAIL&OPT
```

The value of &OPT is assigned after the selection is made. So, if option 5 is selected, the statement which is executed is EX FMAIL5. A dialogue manager variable can be used in this way to alter a FOCUS command or statement. Note that in the above statement, the variable is placed to the right of FMAIL. If the user makes an incorrect selection, then the procedure immediately branches back to the start of the CRTFORM, where a message is displayed.

The FMAIL1 FOCEXEC in figure 9-20 provides for data entry of client records using FIDEL. The procedure automatically generates the next client number to be assigned. Using the NEXT command, the process positions itself at the last record in the root segment. The statement

```
ON NEXT COMPUTE
SEQ = D.CUSTNUM + 1 ;
```

increments the last number by 1, and then branches to CASE CASEONE, where the operator may enter the data. The FIDEL SCREEN uses highlighting prefixes for each field. as well as for the ON MATCH TYPE message. In this procedure, the field IMDY contains the date in which a record was added. Similarly, the update pro-

```
*******************************************************************
* THIS FOCEXEC IS RESPONSIBLE FOR ADDING CUSTOMER RECORDS TO THE
MAIL   *
* DATABASE.
*
*******************************************************************

MODIFY FILE MAIL
LOG DUPL MSG OFF
CRTFORM
"<.B.                   --= CUSTOMER ADDITION SCREEN =--"
"</2 ENTER DATA FOR THE FOLLOWING : "                            "
" "
"      CUSTNUM             <CUSTNUM>     "
"      LAST_NAME           <LNAME>       "
"      FIRST_NAME          <FNAME>       "
"      COMPANY_NAME        <CNAME>       "
"      STREET              <STR>         "
"      CITY                <CITY>        "
"      STATE               <STATE>       "
"      ZIP                 <ZIP>         "
"      ACCOUNT_TYPE        <TYPE>        "
"      CITI_CONTACT        <CONTACT>     "
"      STATUS              <STATUS>      "
"      EXPENSE_CODE        <EXP>         "
"      REGION  CODE        <REGCODE>     "
"                                "
COMPUTE
IMDY = &MDY ;

MATCH CUSTNUM
 ON NOMATCH INCLUDE
 ON NOMATCH TYPE
 " "
 "<.W. PRESS PF1 IF YOU WISH TO EXIT"
 ON MATCH TYPE
 " "
 "<.W. CUSTOMER NUMBER <.R.FLAS.CUSTNUM <.W. ALREADY EXISTS"
 "<.W. PRESS PF1 IF YOU WISH TO EXIT"
 ON MATCH REJECT
DATA
END
FIN
```

Figure 9-20   FOCEXEC for adding customers to MAIL file.

312 The Database Experts' Guide to FOCUS

cedure FMAIL2 (figure 9-21) computes the date in which a record is updated.

We next describe the procedure which prints customer labels as a report (option 6). We shall not discuss the procedures for viewing records, or maintaining the region code (MAILREG) file — although these are very simple.

The FMAIL6 FOCEXEC is shown in figure 9-22. It allows the user to display as a report the name, address, etc., of clients. The user can also select how the report will be sorted, e.g., by region, by state, by contact, etc. Since there may be several thousand names in the MAIL file, the user may also choose to see only clients with a particular value for city, state, contact, etc. To do this, the program prompts for the sort field, which can be chosen from the list displayed (using a dialogue manager TYPE statement). Another prompt is issued to select a particular value of the sort field, or "ALL."

The rest of the FOCEXEC contains several useful techniques:

1. The variables &SRT and &CMD can have values of any length; so, there is no need to try to specify their length with a SET statement.
2. If a particular value of the sort field is requested, a screening condition is composed using the SET statement:

    -SET &CMD = 'IF' | &SRT | ' CONTAINS ' | &CMD ;

    The concatenation bars create one character string out of each portion. If 'All' values are requested, then no screening condition is needed.

    -SET &CMD = ' ' ;

    Note, the screening operator CONTAINS is used instead of 'IS' since the operator may wish to supply an abbreviated value for name, city, etc.
3. After the user makes a selection, it may take several seconds to retrieve the report. A 'waiting' message on the screen.
4. Before concatenating together the city, state, and zip as a single field, the field CITY must be "cleaned up" by removing any ',' which may have been inadvertently entered. This is accomplished using the user-written routine GETTOK. (See the table of user-written routines on page 2-90 of the FOCUS

```
**************************************************************
* THIS FOCEXEC IS RESPONSIBLE FOR UPDATING CUSTOMER RECORDS FROM
THE    *
* MAIL DATABASE.
*
**************************************************************

MODIFY FILE MAIL
LOG NOMATCH MSG OFF

CRTFORM
"<.A. PLEASE ENTER THE CUSTOMER NUMBER THAT YOU WANT TO UPDATE"
"      CUSTNUM           <.IBW.SEQ>        "

MATCH CUSTNUM

ON MATCH COMPUTE
REGCODE = D.REGCODE;
HAVE = LOOKUP(REGNAME);
REGN/A20 = REGNAME ;
INPD/I6S = D.IMDY;
UPDD/I6S = D.UMDY;

   ON MATCH CRTFORM
 "       LAST_NAME          <T.LNAME>      "
 "       FIRST_NAME         <T.FNAME>      "
 "       COMPANY_NAME       <T.CNAME>      "
 "       STREET             <T.STR>        "
 "       CITY               <T.CITY>       "
 "       STATE              <T.STATE>      "
 "       ZIP                <T.ZIP>        "
 "       ACCOUNT_TYPE       <T.TYPE>       "
 "       CITI_CONTACT       <T.CONTACT>    "
 "       STATUS             <T.STATUS>     "
 "       EXPENSE_CODE       <T.EXP>        "
 "       REGION  CODE       <T.REGCODE>    "
 "       REGION  NAME       <D.REGN>       "
 "       INPUT   DATE       <D.INPD>       "
 "       UPDATE  DATE       <D.UPDD>       "
" "
"<.W.   PRESS PF1 IF YOU WISH TO EXIT"
ON MATCH COMPUTE
UMDY = &MDY;

ON MATCH UPDATE * NONKEYS
ON NOMATCH TYPE
" "
```

Figure 9-21    FOCEXEC for updating customers in MAIL file.

```
"   <.W. CUSTOMER NUMBER    <.RED.FLAS.CUSTNUM    <.C.W. DOES NOT EXIST
"
ON NOMATCH REJECT
DATA
END
-EXIT
```

**Figure 9-21** (continued) FOCEXEC for updating customers in MAIL file.

manual.) GETTOK extracts a character string from a larger data string, searching for a delimiter in the string. The delimiter in this case is a comma.

5. The TABLE request formats the lines by placing several fields over others. Blank lines are inserted wherever needed using the field BLANK in the DEFINE. The output is shown in figure _.
6. After the report is created, the procedure exits back to the MAIL FOCEXEC, where the menu is displayed. The report, if successfully created, is in an OFFLINE file MAIL LISTING. In case a report was not created due to an error in the user's selection, the procedure will display a message on the menu CRTFORM. This is easily tested for by testing the system variable &RECORDS, which indicates how many records were retrieved in the TABLE request. This value is passed back to the MAIL FOCEXEC as a dialogue manager global variable &&RECS. Global variables (&&) retain their values throughout the FOCUS session, once set. Otherwise, they have the same features as a regular (&) dialogue manager variable.

## Example 4: Project Tracking System

FOCUS is used extensively in assisting managers to track ongoing projects within large departments. Managers can use the FOCUS database to store the details and status of various projects, while using FOCUS reporting to obtain periodic evaluations of these projects. Because of the flexibilty in FOCUS, there are many reports which may be developed to assist managers.

This example demonstrates how a project tracking system might get started using a simple single-segment FOCUS file. The file contains a few data elements which are relevant to tracking such things as:

```
*******************************************************************
* FMAIL6 FOCEXEX PRINTS CUSTOMER RECORDS FROM THE
*
* MAIL DATABASE.
*
*******************************************************************

SET PAGE = OFF
SET MSG = OFF
SET NODATA = ' '
SET LINES=57,PAPER=66

-CMS FI OFFLINE DISK MAILL LISTING A
OFFLINE

-CRTCLEAR
-TYPE
-TYPE ----------------------------------------------------------------
-TYPE -      CHOOSE FROM AMONG THE FOLLOWING FIELD NAMES
-
-TYPE ----------------------------------------------------------------
-TYPE -      CUSTNUM            LAST_NAME            FIRST_NAME
-
-TYPE -      COMPANY_NAME       STREET               CITY
-
-TYPE -      ACCOUNT_TYPE       CITI_CONTACT         STATUS
-
-TYPE -      EXPENSE_CODE       STATE                ZIP
-
-TYPE -      REGCODE
-
-TYPE ----------------------------------------------------------------
-TYPE

-PROMPT &SRT.ENTER ONE OF THE ABOVE AS A SORT FIELD ( 'EXIT' TO
QUIT ).
-IF &SRT EQ 'EXIT' GOTO LEAVE5;
-TYPE WHAT VALUE OF THE SORT FIELD DO YOU WANT IN THE OUTPUT?
-PROMPT &CMD.PLEASE TYPE ONE VALUE, OR 'ALL', OR 'EXIT' TO QUIT.
-IF &CMD EQ 'EXIT' GOTO LEAVE5;
-CRTCLEAR

DEFINE FILE MAIL
NAME/A40    = FIRST_NAME || (' ' | LAST_NAME);
MOD1/A32    = GETTOK (CITY,33,1,',',32,MOD1);
MOD2/A32    = GETTOK (CITY,33,2,',',32,MOD2);
CITYA/A33   = IF MOD1 EQ ' ' THEN CITY ELSE MOD1 || MOD2 ;
```

Figure 9-22  FOCEXEC for printing customer mailing list.

```
ADDRESS/A50 =CITYA || (', ' | STATE) || (' ' | ZIP);
BLANK/A1    = ' ';
END
-RUN
-IF &CMD EQ 'ALL'  GOTO START1;
-SET &CMD          = 'IF ' | &SRT | ' CONTAINS ' | &CMD;
-GOTO START2
-START1
-SET &CMD = '       ';
-START2

TABLE FILE MAIL
PRINT BLANK AS ''
NAME AS '' AND CONTACT AS '' AND RCODE   AS ''
AND EXP AS '' AND SEQ AS ''
OVER COMPANY_NAME AS '' OVER STREET AS ''
OVER ADDRESS AS ' ' OVER BLANK AS ''
BY &SRT AS '' NOPRINT ON CUSTNUM SKIP-LINE
&CMD
END
-RUN
-SET &&RECS = &RECORDS;
-EXIT
```

**Figure 9-22** (continued) FOCEXEC for printing customer mailing list.

1. Project status
2. Project costs and estimates
3. Start and end dates
4. Priorities and actions required
5. Comments and remarks

The example will present several FOCEXECS that can generate several reports which track the status of project costs. First, the FOCUS file will be discussed with respect to the fields used. The TASK MASTER is shown in figure 9-23. When a new project is requested, the manager should know the type of system, the priority code, the nature or type of request, the requesting department, and a description of the project. This data can be entered into the FOCUS file from the start. As the scope of the project becomes clear, other data can be entered — such as estimated hours, date assigned, next action, employee assigned, etc.

There is nothing special about the formats of the data fields — although they are coded in a simple way using single digit or single

```
FILE=TASK, SUFFIX=FOC

SEGNAME=ONE, SEGTYPE = S1,$
       FIELD= REQUEST_NO   ,RNO           ,I5      ,$
       FIELD= PROJECT      ,              ,A10     ,$
       FIELD= PROJ_SUB     ,              ,I2      ,$
       FIELD= SYSTEM       ,              ,A1      ,$
       FIELD= RECEIVED     ,RDATE         ,I6YMD   ,$
       FIELD= DEPT         ,              ,A1      ,$
       FIELD= REQUESTOR    ,RQR           ,A15     ,$
       FIELD= REQUEST_TYPE,RTYPE          ,A1      ,$
       FIELD= PRIORITY     ,              ,A1      ,$
       FIELD= STATUS       ,              ,A1      ,$
       FIELD= DESCRIPTION  ,              ,A75     ,$
       FIELD= DETAIL1      ,D1            ,A75     ,$
       FIELD= DETAIL2      ,D2            ,A75     ,$
       FIELD= DETAIL3      ,D3            ,A75     ,$
       FIELD= DETAIL4      ,D4            ,A75     ,$
       FIELD= DETAIL5      ,D5            ,A75     ,$
       FIELD= DETAIL6      ,D6            ,A75     ,$
       FIELD= DETAIL7      ,D7            ,A75     ,$
       FIELD= COMMENTS     ,              ,A75     ,$
       FIELD= EST_HOURS    ,EH            ,D7.1    ,$
       FIELD= ASSIGNED_TO  ,ATO           ,A15     ,$
       FIELD= ASSIGN_DATE  ,ADATE         ,I6YMD   ,$
       FIELD= EST_DATE     ,EDATE         ,I6YMD   ,$
       FIELD= EST_REVISION,EREV           ,I6YMD   ,$
       FIELD= COMP_DATE    ,CDATE         ,I6YMD   ,$
       FIELD= ACT_HOURS    ,AH            ,D7.1    ,$
       FIELD= TEST_START   ,TDATE         ,I6YMD   ,$
       FIELD= TEST_EST     ,T_EST         ,I6YMD   ,$
       FIELD= NEXT_ACTION  ,NDATE         ,I6YMD   ,$
       FIELD= TEST_COMPLET,TCDATE         ,I6YMD   ,$
       FIELD= INSTALL_DATE,IDATE          ,I6YMD   ,$
       FIELD= CHG_REASON   ,CREASON       ,A75     ,$
```

Figure 9-23    TASK MASTER file.

alpha code to represent the status, priority, etc. The cost of the project is to be determined based on the man-hours required to complete the project. All important dates, such as assigned date, test date, etc. should have a consistent format — such as **YYMMDD** or **MMDDYY**. This will make easier calculations of the elapsed days between various dates. Also, dates appearing on reports should have a consistent format.

Although the MASTER has been designed as a single segment file, there could have been other designs containing parent-child relationships. For example, the root segment might contain an employee code and employee data, with the project numbers and project data as a child segment. Or, the root segment may be the department code requesting the project.

Since the size of the file is expected to be small, there are few efficiency considerations to discuss. Retrieval of simple status reports or cost summaries should be affected little by the design of this file. However, you may want to use multiple segments if there is a one-to-many relationship between the data. For example, if more than one employee may be assigned to a project, then a single segment file with one key field may not do.

Another consideration is the capability to perform simple data entry. A single segment file is usually a simple design for data entry. Each requested project is easily represented as a single record in the FOCUS file. Also, by making the REQUEST_NO the key field, new request numbers can be automatically assigned by incrementing the last request number by one. (See EXAMPLE 3, the MAIL1 FOCEXEC, for a similar example.)

The TASK file can be used in a number of ways to assist in tracking projects. The reports presented here display projects in a particular order. The projects are sorted by the SYSTEM NAME, TYPE OF TASK, PRIORITY CODE, AND DATE THE PROJECT WAS RECEIVED.

The STATCOST FOCEXEC is in figure 9-24. It summarizes the costs incurred by each project, using calculations based on a dollar rate per man-hour. Since the report must show the full names of projects, employees, etc., it is also necessary to perform a DECODE on various fields. As shown in figure 9-25, one DEFINE can be placed into a separate FOCEXEC and invoked whenever needed by executing it. I.e.,

```
EX STATDEF
```

The DEFINE contains statements for decoding the system codes, decoding the status code, decoding the employee codes, and other codes. Remember that defined field are like database fields, since they can be used as verb objects, sort fields, screening conditions, COMPUTES, etc.

```
-*CMS FI OFFLINE DISK REPPY LISTING A
OFFLINE
EX TASKDEF
-RUN
TABLE FILE TASK
HEADING CENTER
"PROJECT STATUS COST REPORT AS OF: &DATE &TOD"
" "
"SYSTEM : <SYS_NAME"
" "
PRINT RNO IN 1 AS ' REQ ' PRI_NAME IN +1 AS 'PRI '
DESC
MANDAYS AS 'MAN,DAYS'
REQUESTOR AS '   REQ BY  '
ESTCOST AS 'ESTIMATED,COST'
ACTCOST AS ' ACTUAL,COST'
BY SYS_NAME NOPRINT
BY STATORDER NOPRINT
BY STATUS_NAME NOPRINT
BY PRI_ORDER NOPRINT
BY RECEIVED NOPRINT
ON SYS_NAME PAGE-BREAK

ON SYS_NAME       SUBTOTAL MANDAYS ESTCOST ACTCOST AS 'TOTAL'
ON STATUS_NAME SUBTOTAL MANDAYS ESTCOST ACTCOST AS 'TOTAL'
ON STATUS_NAME SUBHEAD
"<50<STATUS_NAME"
"----------------------------------------------------------------
----------------------------------------------------------------"
END

FIN
```

Figure 9-24   FOCEXEC for Status Cost report.

Additional fields are also defined to calculate the man days, estimated costs, and actual costs for each project.

Using the defined fields, it is a simple matter to format various kinds of reports. Notice the following features:

1. There is a PAGE-BREAK at the end of each system, so that the projects of the next system can start on a separate page.
2. There is another break containing subtotals after each STATUS NAME (e.g., INITIAL ANALYSIS, TESTING, PROGRAMMING, etc.). Subtotals are also displayed for each system.
3. The sort fields are not printed as columns on the report.

**320** The Database Experts' Guide to FOCUS

```
DEFINE FILE TASK
SYS_NAME/A15    = DECODE SYSTEM(A 'ADMIN'
                                C 'CONDUIT'
                                E 'COMMERCIAL R.E.'
                                L 'CLASS'
                                M 'MARK-TO-MARKET'
                                N 'NEW YORK'
                                O 'CMO'
                                P 'POOL ALLOCATION'
                                R 'RISK MANAGEMENT'
                                S 'RESEARCH'
                                V 'SERVICING'
                                T 'TAPE CRACKING');
DIVISION/I1= DECODE SYSTEM(A 1 C 1 E 1 L 1 M 1 N 1 T 1 V 2 ELSE 3);

STATUS_NAME/A20 = DECODE STATUS(R 'INITIAL ANALYSIS'
                                P 'PROGRAMMING'
                                C 'PROGRAMMING COMPLETE'
                                T 'USER TESTING'
                                I 'INSTALLED'
                                H 'ON HOLD'
                                F 'NEEDS CLARIFICATION'
                                Z 'CANCELLED'
                                S 'FUTURE PROJECTS'
                                A 'AWAITING PROGRAMMING');

MANDAYS/D5.1=IF STATUS EQ 'I' OR 'C' OR 'T' THEN ACT_HOURS/7
                                            ELSE EST_HOURS/7;
STATORDER/I1=DECODE STATUS(S 0 R 1 F 2 H 3 A 4 P 5 C 6 T 7 I 8 Z
9);
PRI_NAME/A4     = DECODE PRIORITY(H 'HIGH'
                                  M 'MED'
                                  L 'LOW');

TYPE_NAME/A11   = DECODE REQUEST_TYPE(E 'ENHANCEMENT'
                                      B 'BUG'
                                      S 'SPEC CHANGE');

DEP_NAME/A15    = DECODE DEPT(F 'FRONT OFFICE'
                              O 'OPERATIONS');
RECEIVED/I6=RECEIVED;
PRI_ORDER/I1    = DECODE PRIORITY(H 1 M 2 L 3);
REQUESTOR/A10=EDIT(REQUESTOR,'9999999999');
ATO/A10=EDIT(ATO,'9999999999');
EMPTYPE/A1=DECODE ASSIGNED_TO(NAHOUM     E
                              GRIST      E
```

**Figure 9-25** Define statements — executed from TASK1 FOCEXEC.

```
                        METZNER     E
                        EASER       E
                        RAAB        E
                        KOWAL       E
                        RAJ         E
                        FISHER      C
                        CHERNICK    C
                        KLAHR       C
                        LUCAS       C);
ESTCOST/P8S = IF EST_HOURS EQ 0 THEN 0 ELSE
              IF EMPTYPE EQ 'C' THEN (EST_H/7) * 500 ELSE
                         IF EMPTYPE EQ 'E' THEN (EST_H/7) * 300
                         ELSE (EST_H/7) * 400;
ESTCOST = IF ACT_HOURS NE 0 THEN 0 ELSE ESTCOST;
ACTCOST/P8S= IF ACT_HOURS EQ 0 THEN 0 ELSE
             IF EMPTYPE EQ 'C' THEN (ACT_H/7) * 500 ELSE
                        IF EMPTYPE EQ 'E' THEN (ACT_H/7) * 300;
END
```

**Figure 9-25**  (continued) Define statements — executed from TASK1 FOCEXEC.

A similar report is generated by STATREP1 FOCEXEC (see figure 9-26). The purpose of the report is to group the projects according to the requesting division, the status, and priority code. The number of estimated man days is also displayed for each project. Notice that the STATDEF FOCEXEC is also invoked from the FOCEXEC.

## Example 5: Security Trading System

NOTE: The focexecs, report menu, and sample databases are available for this application. For further information on how to obtain this, please see chapter 1.

You have seen several examples of how relatively simple FOCUS files have been designed to handle a variety of requirements for reporting and data maintenance. We have not tried to give rules to follow in designing databases. Instead, we have taken an approach which recognizes that FOCUS programmers need to know the relationships between the data, and how the data is to be used in reporting. Even if the FOCUS files are incorrectly designed, they may serve the purpose of opening the lines of communication between the user and programmer. Usually, the FOCUS files can be redesigned

```
OFFLINE
SET MSG=OFF
EX STATDEF
-RUN
TABLE FILE TASK
HEADING CENTER
"PROJECT STATUS SUMMARY REPORT AS OF: &DATE &TOD"
"</2"
PRINT RNO IN 1 AS ' REQ ' PRI_NAME IN +1 AS 'PRI '
DESC
MANDAYS AS 'MAN,DAYS'
RECEIVED AS 'RECVD'
COMPDATE   AS 'EST/,ACT,COMP';
REQUESTOR AS '   REQ BY  '
ATO AS ' ASSIGNED '
BY DIVISION NOPRINT
BY STATORDER NOPRINT
BY STATUS_NAME NOPRINT
BY PRI_ORDER NOPRINT
BY RECEIVED NOPRINT
ON STATUS_NAME SUBTOTAL MANDAYS AS 'TOTAL'
ON STATUS_NAME SUBHEAD
"</2"
"<50<STATUS_NAME"
"----------------------------------------------------------------
-----------------------------------------------------------------"
END

FIN
```

Figure 9-26    FOCEXEC for Status Summary report.

using the REBUILD feature, with minor effects on existing reports and procedures.

As a novice FOCUS programmer, you may feel that you will run into situations which are difficult to handle, or you may not have any luck in understanding what the user requires. This may be quite true not only for the novice programmer, but for the experienced programmer as well. If the programmer is to contribute to the user, there should be a willingness to experiment with new tools. FOCUS is a new tool, which has only been around for about ten years. There are very few programmers who use it perfectly, and probably very few programmers who wish to use it perfectly.

You may well be saying something like, "I understand how you designed an application, but that doesn't mean that I could do it myself!" This may be a problem if you always insist on working by yourself. However, as you make friends with other programmers, you should be able to obtain support when you need it, because FOCUS techniques are usually easy to copy from others. It is one of the Fourth-generation programming languages where you can "get a little help from your friends."

This example will bring up several new issues related to implementing FOCUS systems. These issues deal with not only technical areas, but also with the capabilities of an organization to provide access to various resources and technologies. With respect to the latter, the best thing that an organization can do is to encourage communication between managers, users, and support staff. Without a great deal of communication, there are bound to be lost opportunities, duplication of effort, and a lack of common understanding.

This application involves developing a database for tracking daily trades of mortgage securities. The type of securities is not relevant to this discussion, but the type of data required is important. Because many traders and analysts may be uncomfortable with new computer tools, it is necessary to demonstrate the ease of use of the tool, as well as how the tool can help them make decisions. More importantly, the organization must be capable of providing access to the existing knowledge base.

For example, in this application, an investment firm is required to keep track of the amounts and prices of securities which are purchased daily by their traders for clients. The securities are mortgage securities, such as GNMA and FNMA securities available on the open market, The system must be flexible enough to accommodate potentially large numbers of trades each day. The reports must be generated in a timely way, and provide an accurate computation of "positions" taken by the traders.

Users, such as analysts and portfolio managers, should be provided with adequate training in understanding the intent of the system. There will be tradeoffs dealing with these issues:

1. Who is responsible for checking the accuracy of the data?
2. What other parallel information systems are there?
3. How will data entry be accomplished?
4. How will data be corrected, problems identified, and requests for enhancements made?
5. What are the performance issues? What volume of transactions can be handled online, real-time, or in batch?

The answers lies not in the technology or in the database design, but in the way people in the organization interact. In short, it is a problem in teamwork and in motivation. As we all know, "the reports may be perfect, but someone has to want to read them."

This application will discuss further FOCUS reporting techniques. Some of the techniques are:

1. Manipulating dates.
2. Using HOLD files.
3. Passing options and parameters with DIALOGUE MANAGER variables.
4. Multiverb TABLE requests.
5. Using column notation in TABLE requests.
6. Cross-reference files.
7. Decode feature.

We shall not discuss the data-entry procedures used for entering daily trades. This is not so much a technical consideration, as it is logistical. Some of the questions related to data entry are:

1. How shall the trade transactions be validated.
2. What if TRADERS wish to enter their own transactions.
3. What if the trades are not entered due to computer problems or too much volume.
4. Is there a need for simultaneous entry of data into one database.
5. How shall corrections and revisions be made.
6. How shall old trades be removed from the database.
7. When can traders access reports and perform inquiries of today's trades.
8. What kind of security is required on trade data.

As shown in figure 9-27, the INVENT file is a single-path file with several segments. Each segment, except for the root, is a child segment, because it depends on its parent segment. A FOCUS file can have a large number of child segments — each child segment has a many-to-one relationship with its parent segment. In this MASTER description, the bottom segment contains the trade data, such as assigned sequence number, amount of the security purchased, price of the security, etc.

```
FILENAME = INVENT, SUF = FOC,$

  SEGNAME = PORT, SEGTYPE = S1,$

      FIELD = PORTFOLIO, PORT_ID, A04,$

  SEGNAME = SECURITY, PARENT = PORT, SEGTYPE = S1
      GROUP = IDENT, ALIAS = KEY, A16,$

          FIELD = SEC_LABEL, LABEL  , A04  ,$
          FIELD = MDATE     , MD    , I6YMD,$
          FIELD = COUPON    , CPN   , P6.3 ,$

  SEGNAME = LABELS, PARENT = SECURITY, CRKEY= LABEL, CRFILE= IN-
VLAB,
      SEGTYPE = KU,$

  SEGNAME = TRADE, PARENT = SECURITY, SEGTYPE = S1,$

      FIELD = SETTLE_DATE, SDATE, I6YMD,$

  SEGNAME = T_INFO, PARENT = TRADE, SEGTYPE = SH1,$

          FIELD = TRADE_NUM  , TNUM  , I03   ,$
          FIELD = TRADE_DATE , TDATE , I6YMD ,$
          FIELD = TRADE_PRCE , PRICE , P9.5  ,$
          FIELD = AMOUNT     ,       , P10.3 ,$
          FIELD = CUSTOMER   , CUST  , A8    ,$
```

**Figure 9-27  Trading Inventory MASTER file.**

We shall first describe how the segments are related to each other. When the database is defined in a hierarchical way, using parent-child segments:

## EACH SEGMENT MEANS LITTLE BY ITSELF

Daniel D. McCracken, in a book written on another fourth-generation language, says about hierarchical segments, "that it is hard to see how we would ever need to work with the data in a child segment by itself ..." For example, the data in the (bottom) trades segment is inherently about some security, and does not stand alone.

In this example, the trades are related to securities. A security, in our case, corresponds to mortgage securities and bonds. They are described by the following data:

1. Mortgage label, the coupon, and maturity date.
2. The date or month in which the security's ownership will change hands after it is bought or sold — this is also known as the settlement date. Note: The same security label, coupon, and maturity date may be traded over and over with different settlement dates.

For example, a trader may buy:

GNMA 8% COUPON WITH MATURITY OF 1/1/95,
AND THE TRADE SETTLES ON 9/30/87.
GNMA 8% COUPON WITH MATURITY OF 1/1/95
AND THE TRADE SETTLES ON 10/31/87.

GNMA 8% COUPON WITH MATURITY OF 1/1/95
AND THE TRADE SETTLES ON 11/30/87.

Settlement dates are common to trading other types of securities besides mortgage securities.

Lastly, the trader may make a number of different trades for the security before the settlement date. These trades are stored in the bottom segment. A positive quantity represents a "buy" of the security; a negative quantity represents a "sell" of the security.

Therefore, the best way to describe the securities traded is to use several segments. The top segment contains the code name of the trader (PORTFOLIO). The next segment will contain the label, coupon, and maturity date of the security. The next segment contains the settlement date. Notice in the MASTER description that the security segment has a SEGMENT TYPE S3, which indicates that there are three key fields — LABEL, COUPON, MATURITY. This makes sense since it is possible for two securities to have the same label and coupon, but not the same label, coupon, and maturity date. No security which is traded is without a trader portfolio id. This portfolio id is the root segment of the file.

There are other ways to design the MASTER description, but this best brings out the relationships between the data. With this hierarchical organization, we have related the data to each other in a natural way. Any data which has a many-to-one relationship with other data should be stored in a descendent segment.

All the related data is stored in the same path. The items in a TABLE print request may come from any segment, so long as they are in one path from a segment down throught a sequence of dependent segments. For example, to get a list of the trades of all GNMA securities on 9/1/87, the request is:

```
PRINT TNUM TDATE TAMT TPRICE
IF LABEL EQ GNMA
IF TDATE EQ 870901
```

or, to get a list of all traders who have traded GNMA 8 (i.e., label is GNMA, the coupon is 8%) on date 9/1/87, the request is:

```
PRINT PORTFOLIO
IF LABEL EQ GNMA
IF COUPON EQ 8
IF TDATE EQ 870901
```

or, to print the amounts traded of FNMA securities after date 8/31/87 by trader ZAF, with subtotals for each coupon,

```
PRINT TAMT
BY LABEL
BY COUPON SUBTOTAL
IF PORTFOLIO EQ ZAF
IF TDATE GT 870831
IF LABEL EQ FNMA
```

The INVENT file may also be related to other FOCUS files. For example, there may be another file containing only options trades executed by traders, or a cross-reference file may contain information on customers for which the trades were executed. As shown in the MASTER, we have included a cross-reference file, INVLAB, which contains data on each security label. As you will see in the reports, the field COL_HEAD in the INVLAB file is used to determine how security types should be sorted on the reports. Its MASTER is shown in figure 9-28. Notice that the field LABEL is indexed.

### Determining Net Position

With this design, we can be sure that the information is readily available for reports which may be requested. Before presenting several

```
FILE = INVLAB, SUF = FOC,$

   SEGNAME = LABELS, SEGTYPE = S1,$

         FIELD = LABEL       , LAB    , A04, FIELDTYPE = I,$
         FIELD = S_LABEL     , SLAB   , A04, FIELDTYPE = I,$
         FIELD = COL_HEAD    , CHEAD  , A24,$
         FIELD = MBSFLAG     , MBS    , A01,$
         FIELD = SORT_RANK   , SRANK  , I03,$
         FIELD = PRICED_TO   , PT     , A04,$
         FIELD = ADDIT_SVC   , AS     , P8.4,$
```

Figure 9-28   INVLAB MASTER file.

reports, we should define other terms which are relevant to securities trading. The terms BUY and SELL are used to indicate if a security is bought or sold for a client. (Keep in mind that these trades are done on behalf of clients.) If the buys exceed the sells, then the bank will be getting a net positive position in a security, and vise versa. It is important for the trading desk to maintain careful control of its position. If they have too much of a positive (long) position, they may incur losses if the price of the security declines due to changes in the interest rate. Every trade has a settlement date. A trader will usually make a number of trades of the same security, which settle on the same date. If the trader still has a net positive or negative position in the security on the day of settlement, then the trader (investment firm) will own an amount of the security. This establishes a "CASH" position in the security.

A report described below computes the net cash position of the firm at various points in time. The reports summarizes by label, by coupon, etc., the cash position, and positions on trades which settle next month, the following month, etc.

The first report, below, simply obtains a listing of trades which were made by the entire desk on any day or over a range of dates. The SEETRD FOCEXEC is shown in figure 9-29. It is usually executed at the start of the day to present a listing of trades which were made on the prior day. The output shown in figure 9-30 shows the trade listing for one trader portfolio. The report uses a PRINT command to list the trades, sorted by the key fields. The operator may select a single portfolio or all portfolios. Also, the range of trade dates is also selected. The operator may select if the report is sent directly to the

```
*******************************************************************
-* SEETRD FOCEXEC - LIST DAILY TRADES
-*
-*
-CMS FI OFFLINE DISK SEETRD LISTING A (LRECL 133 RECFM U
OFFLINE
-DEFAULTS &BRK = 'N'

-PROMPT &WHICH_PORT.A4.ENTER PORTFOLIO ID (OR 'ALL').
-IF &WHICH_PORT NE 'ALL' GOTO NOTALL;
-PROMPT &BRK.(Y,N).SEPARATE PAGES FOR PORTFOLIO (Y,N)?.
-NOTALL
-PROMPT &LOTUS.(Y,N).LOTUS FORMAT (Y OR N) ???.
-PROMPT &ANS.ENTER START TRADE DATE (YYMMDD) OR (* FOR ALL) =>.
-IF &ANS EQ '*' GOTO START;
-PROMPT &ANS2.ENTER END TRADE DATE (YYMMDD) =>.

-SET &PAGESKIP = IF &BRK EQ Y THEN 'PAGE-BREAK' ELSE 'UNDER-LINE' ;
-SET &FROM = EDIT(&ANS,'99')]'/' ] EDIT(&ANS,'$$99')]'/' ]
EDIT(&ANS,'$$$$99');
-SET &TO = EDIT(&ANS2,'99')]'/' ] EDIT(&ANS2,'$$99')]'/' ]
EDIT(&ANS2,'$$$$99');
-START

-IF &ONLY_OPT EQ 'N' GOTO TBLSTRT;
DEFINE FILE INVENT
 FLAG_LBL/I1 = IF OPTLAB EQ 'GCOS' OR 'GPOS' OR 'BFOC' OR 'BFOP' OR
               'BOC2' OR 'BOP2' OR 'BOC1' OR 'BOP1' OR 'GSFO' THEN
1
            ELSE 0;
END
-TBLSTRT
TABLE FILE INVENT
HEADING CENTER
"(SEETRD)<+25 C I T I C O R P   M O R T G A G E   F I N A N C E
<+25 &DATE"
" "
"TRADE INFORMATION REPORT"
-IF &ANS EQ '*' GOTO LOOP;
"TRADES FROM &FROM TO &TO    "
-LOOP
"-------------------------------"
" "
SUM   PRICE AMOUNT CUST
AND COMPUTE
BAR/A1 = ' '; AS ''
```

Figure 9-29  FOCEXEC for printing daily trade listing.

```
AND COMPUTE
LONG/P7.2S= IF AMOUNT GT 0 THEN AMOUNT ELSE 0; AS 'BUY'
AND COMPUTE
SHORT/P7.2S= IF AMOUNT LT 0 THEN AMOUNT ELSE 0; AS 'SELL'

BY TRADE_DATE BY PORT_ID BY LABEL BY COUP BY MD           BY SDATE
BY TNUM
-IF &ANS EQ '*' GOTO LOOP2;
 IF TRADE_DATE FROM &ANS TO &ANS2
-LOOP2
-IF &WHICH_PORT EQ 'ALL' GOTO  ALLPORT2;
 IF PORT_ID EQ &WHICH_PORT
-ALLPORT2
ON PORT_ID SUBTOTAL LONG SHORT AS 'LONG/SHORT'
ON PORT_ID &PAGESKIP
-IF &BRK EQ 'Y' GOTO SKIPNXT;
ON TRADE_DATE PAGE-BREAK
-SKIPNXT
ON TABLE NOTOTAL
-IF &LOTUS EQ 'N' GOTO NOPE1;
ON TABLE SAVE AS POS FORMAT LOTUS
-NOPE1
END
```

Figure 9-29     (continued) FOCEXEC for printing daily trade listing.

OFFLINE device (printer), or stored in a disk file. The formatting of the report is straightforward.

There is a PAGE-BREAK on portfolio. Column headings are specified using the AS option for each item.

There are two screening conditions which are controlled by dialogue manager variables.

1. The variable &PORT is prompted for a value. If all trader portfolios are to be listed, then a value of 'all' is provided. Otherwise, a single portfolio id is entered.
2. The trade date is also requested as a dialogue manager variable. The operator inputs a starting date and an ending date.

Instead of prompting for a single portfolio, a procedure may be set up to prompt for more than one portfolio to screen on. To do this for up to five portfolios, it is necessary to set up five variables with default values as follows:

```
-SET &PORT1 = '$$$$' ;
-SET &PORT2 = '$$$$' ;
....
-SET &PORT5 = '$$$$' ;
```

This "mask" can be used as a screening value if a portfolio value is not selected. Its presence means to skip the screening test. It is also necessary to prompt for five variables. This can be done with indexed variables, where an index variable is used as a counter:

```
-SET &N = 0;
-LOOP
-SET &N = &N + 1;
-IF &N GT 5 GOTO OUT;
-PROMPT &PORT.&N.ENTER ANOTHER PORTFOLIO &N OR 'X' TO END.
-IF &PORT.&N EQ 'X' GOTO OUT;
-GOTO LOOP
-OUT
```

In this example, &PORT is the indexed variable. &N is the index. As the index is incremented each time, a new variable is prompted. If not all five portfolios are entered, then the procedure jumps out, and the default values '$$$$' can be used. (Note that this indexing facility for variables is not available in PC/FOCUS.)

The screening condition in the TABLE request should be:

```
IF PORTFOLIO EQ &PORT1 OR &PORT2 OR &PORT3 OR &PORT4 
OR &PORT5.
```

Say, the values of "za1," "za2," and "za3" are selected, then the screening condition is:

```
IF PORTFOLIO EQ ZA1 OR ZA2 OR ZA3 OR $$$$ OR $$$$
```

Using this technique, any number of values in screening conditions can be generated.

The next report is called the "NET POSITION" report. It computes the cash position which traders have taken in each security. It dis-

```
1 PAGE    1                           M O R T G A G E   F I N A N C E                              11/30/

        (SEETRD)                            TRADE INFORMATION REPORT
                                        TRADES FROM 87/11/30 TO 87/11/30


TRADE_DATE  PORTFOLIO  SEC_LABEL  COUPON   MDATE     SETTLE_DATE  TRADE_NUM  TRADE_PRCE   AMOUNT   CUSTOMER   BU
----------  ---------  ---------  ------   --------  -----------  ---------  ----------   ------   --------   --
87/11/30    ZOOM       GNMG        8.500   88/01/31   88/01/16        1       90.06750    -9.000   HILL       --
                                   9.000   87/12/31   87/12/15       33       92.19750    -1.000   HILL       --
                                                                    34       92.12250     1.000   HILL       1.0
                                                                    35       92.18525     1.000   HILL       1.0
                                                                    36       92.19000     1.000   GARBAN     1.0
                                                                    37       92.20000     5.000   GARBAN     5.0
                                                                    38       93.06750    -5.000   GARBAN
                                                                    39       93.06250    -1.000   HILL
                                                    87/12/30        40       93.05750    -4.000   FILL
                                                                     6       93.05750     4.000   ZUF        4.0
                                                                     7       93.06250     1.000   ZUF        1.0
                                                                     8       93.06750     5.000   ZUF        5.0
                                   9.500   87/12/31   87/12/15       44       95.20000    -2.000   HILL
                                                                    45       96.00000    -3.000   RMJ
                                                    87/12/30        46       96.00000     1.000   WESTERN    1.0
                                  10.000   87/12/31   87/12/21       69       98.23750     3.000   ZUF        3.0
                                          88/01/31   88/01/25       23       98.30000    -1.000   HILL
                                                                                          1.000   INTERST    1.0
```

**Figure 9-30  Trade Information report.**

|  |  | 88/02/29 | 88/02/22 | 8 | 98.02000 | 1.000 | ATLANTIC | 1.0 |
|  |  |  |  | 9 | 98.01250 | 1.000 | JPC | 1.0 |
|  |  | 11.000 | 87/12/31 | 87/12/21 | 17 | 104.07000 | -1.500 | IMCO |  |
|  |  |  | 88/01/31 | 88/01/25 | 12 | 103.26000 | 1.500 | IMCO | 1.5 |
|  | NOTE | 8.875 | 97/11/15 | 87/12/01 | 1 | 98.21875 | -5.000 | GARBAN |  |
|  |  |  |  |  |  |  |  |  | 26.5 |

LONG/SHORT ZOOM

**Figure 9-30** (continued) Trade Information report.

plays the current position and the position for the following months according to label, coupon, etc. The report output is shown in figure 9-31.

As with the previous report, the operator may select a single portfolio for which the net position will be displayed. The operator also selects the date, at which the cash position is calculated. Remember that only trades which have settled prior to the input date are considered part of the cash position. The NETPOS FOCEXEC is shown in figure 9-32. The procedure must define several fields for computing the position on settled trades, and trades which will settle in the following months. A summary of total BUYS and SELLS is also computed.

The first step sums the trade amounts according to security and settlement date, and places the result in a HOLD file. The step also obtains the total amount for each security, by using a MULTI-VERB request:

```
SUM CASH BY SECURITY BY COUPON
SUM CASH BY SECURITY BY COUPON BY SECTYPE BY
COL_LABEL BY TRADERS
```

The techniques used in the FOCEXEC are described as follows:

1. The cash position is determined by defining the field CASH as the trade amount if the settlement date has past. E.g.,

   ```
   CASH = IF SDATE LE &ANS THEN AMOUNT ELSE 0;
   ```

   Also, the buys and sells are defined as CASHB and CASHS. The amount settling in future months are defined as MO1_$, MO2_$, etc. The trader name is obtained using the DECODE file — TRADERS DATA.

2. The first TABLE request creates a HOLD file containing the amounts summed by portfolio, security, coupon — to get the coupon total. The amounts are also summed by security type by trader — in the same TABLE request. The variable &PORT2 is used as a screening condition, if the report is for each portfolio.

3. The report is formatted in columns using the dialogue manager variables as column headings. The report is also sorted by trader. Total buys and sells are shown only in the subfooting.

M O R T G A G E   F I N A N C E                                                            10/30/87

NET POSITION REPORT FOR
MBS SECURITIES
FOR PORTFOLIO: ZOOM
AS OF OCT 29 87

| COUPON | SECTYPE | POSITION | CASH | OCT | NOV | DEC | JAN | FEB | SECURITY TOTAL |
|---|---|---|---|---|---|---|---|---|---|
| 8.000 | GNMA | REG. 30YR | 15.000 | --- | --- | --- | --- | --- | 15.000 |
| 8.500 | GNMA | REG. 30YR | (12.500) | | | | | | (12.500) |
| 9.000 | GNMA | REG. 30YR | 2.000 | | | | | | 2.000 |
| 9.500 | GNMA | REG. 30YR | 20.000 | | | | | | 20.000 |
| 10.000 | GNMA | REG. 30YR | 4.000 | | 30.000 | | | | 34.000 |
| 11.000 | GNMA | REG. 30YR | (3.000) | | | | | | (3.000) |
| *TOTAL SECURITY | | | 25.500 | | 30.000 | | | | 55.500 |
| *TOTAL PORTFOLIO ZOOM | | | 25.500 | | 30.000 | | | | 55.500 |
| *TOTAL TRADER JONAS | | | 25.500 | | 30.000 | | | | 55.500 |
| TOTAL BUYS: | | | 153.000 | | 30.000 | | | | |
| TOTAL SELLS: | | | (127.500) | | | | | | |

**Figure 9-31** Net Position report — output.

```
-**********************************************************************
-*  PROGRAM NAME - NETPOS FOCEXEC
-*  PROGRAM DESCRIPTION - PRODUCES NET POSITION REPORT
-*
-*

-SET &PORTID = 'ALL ';
-PROMPT &ANS.ENTER "AS OF" DATE (YYMMDD) =>.
-PROMPT &ANS2.(D,P).ENTER "D" FOR DISK "P" FOR PRINT =>.
-IF &ANS2 EQ 'P' GOTO NODISK;
-CMS FI OFFLINE DISK NETPOS    LISTING A (RECFM UA LRECL 133
-RUN
-NODISK
-PROMPT &ANS3.(Y,N).BY PORTFOLIO ??? ( Y OR N ) =>.
-IF &ANS3 EQ 'N' GOTO NOTIT ;
-PROMPT &PORTID.A4.ENTER PORT ID OR 'ALL' =>.
-NOTIT
-SET &PORT1 = IF &ANS3 EQ 'Y' THEN 'BY PORTFOLIO NOPRINT' ELSE ' ';
-SET &PORT2 = IF &ANS3 EQ 'Y' THEN 'BY PORTFOLIO' ELSE ' ';
-SET &PID   = IF &PORTID EQ 'ALL' THEN '$$$$' ELSE &PORTID ;
-SET &ANS3  = IF &PORTID EQ 'ALL' THEN &ANS3 ELSE 'Y';
-SET &MON =  EDIT(&ANS,'$$99$$');
-SET &DAY =  EDIT(&ANS,'$$$$99');
-SET &YR  =  EDIT(&ANS,'99$$$$');
-SET &MON1 = &MON + 1;
-SET &MON2 = &MON + 2;
-SET &MON3 = &MON + 3;
-SET &MON4 = &MON + 4;

-SET &MTN0 = DECODE &MON  ( 01 JAN 02 FEB 03 MAR 04 APR 05 MAY 06
JUN
-                          07 JUL 08 AUG 09 SEP 10 OCT 11 NOV 12
DEC
-                          ELSE ' ');

-SET &DATE0 = &MTN0 ] ' ' ] &DAY ] ' ' ] &YR ;

-SET &MTN1 = DECODE &MON1 ( 2 FEB 3 MAR 4 APR 5 MAY 6 JUN 7 JUL
-                           8 AUG 9 SEP 10 OCT 11 NOV 12 DEC 13 JAN
-                           ELSE ' ');

-SET &MTN2 = DECODE &MON2 ( 3 MAR 4 APR 5 MAY 6 JUN 7 JUL 8 AUG
-                           9 SEP 10 OCT 11 NOV 12 DEC 13 JAN 14 FEB
-                           ELSE ' ');

-SET &MTN3 = DECODE &MON3 ( 4 APR 5 MAY 6 JUN 7 JUL 8 AUG 9 SEP
-                           10 OCT 11 NOV 12 DEC 13 JAN 14 FEB 15
```

Figure 9-32   FOCEXEC for Net Position report.

```
MAR
-                            ELSE ' ');

-SET &MTN4 = DECODE &MON4 ( 5 MAY  6 JUN  7 JUL  8 AUG  9 SEP
-                          10 OCT 11 NOV 12 DEC 13 JAN 14 FEB 15
MAR
-                          16 APR ELSE ' ');
-*GOTO TEMP
-CMS FI TRADERS  DISK TRADERS  DATA A
DEFINE FILE INVENT
XMD/A6 = EDIT(MD);
XAMT/P8.3SB = IF SDATE GE &ANS THEN AMOUNT ELSE 0;
CASH/P8.3SB = IF SDATE LE &ANS THEN AMOUNT ELSE 0;
CASHB/P8.3SB = IF SDATE LE &ANS AND AMOUNT GT 0 THEN AMOUNT ELSE 0;
CASHS/P8.3SB = IF SDATE LE &ANS AND AMOUNT LT 0 THEN AMOUNT ELSE 0;
MO_OF/I2 = EDIT(EDIT('&ANS','$$99$$'));
DY_OF/I2 = EDIT(EDIT('&ANS','$$$$99'));
MO1/I2 = MO_OF;
MO2/I2 = IF MO_OF + 1 LE 12 THEN MO_OF + 1 ELSE (MO_OF + 1) - 12;
MO3/I2 = IF MO_OF + 2 LE 12 THEN MO_OF + 2 ELSE (MO_OF + 2) - 12;
MO4/I2 = IF MO_OF + 3 LE 12 THEN MO_OF + 3 ELSE (MO_OF + 3) - 12;
MO5/I2 = IF MO_OF + 4 LE 12 THEN MO_OF + 4 ELSE (MO_OF + 4) - 12;
XSDATE/A6 = EDIT(SDATE);
SETTLE_YR/I2 = EDIT(EDIT(XSDATE,'99$$$'));
SETTLE_MO/I2 = EDIT(EDIT(XSDATE,'$$99$$'));
SETTLE_DY/I2 = EDIT(EDIT(XSDATE,'$$$$99'));

MO1_$/P8.3SB = IF SETTLE_MO EQ MO1 AND SETTLE_DY GT DY_OF THEN XAMT
               ELSE 0;
MO2_$/P8.3SB = IF SETTLE_MO EQ MO2 THEN XAMT ELSE 0;
MO3_$/P8.3SB = IF SETTLE_MO EQ MO3 THEN XAMT ELSE 0;
MO4_$/P8.3SB = IF SETTLE_MO EQ MO4 THEN XAMT ELSE 0;
MO5_$/P8.3SB = IF SETTLE_MO EQ MO5 THEN XAMT ELSE 0;

MO1BUY/P8.3SB = IF SETTLE_MO EQ MO1 AND SETTLE_DY GT DY_OF AND XAMT
                GT 0 THEN XAMT ELSE 0;
MO2BUY/P8.3SB = IF SETTLE_MO EQ MO2 AND XAMT GT 0 THEN XAMT ELSE 0;
MO3BUY/P8.3SB = IF SETTLE_MO EQ MO3 AND XAMT GT 0 THEN XAMT ELSE 0;
MO4BUY/P8.3SB = IF SETTLE_MO EQ MO4 AND XAMT GT 0 THEN XAMT ELSE 0;
MO5BUY/P8.3SB = IF SETTLE_MO EQ MO5 AND XAMT GT 0 THEN XAMT ELSE 0;

MO1SEL/P8.3SB = IF SETTLE_MO EQ MO1 AND SETTLE_DY GT DY_OF AND XAMT
LT 0 THEN XAMT ELSE 0;
MO2SEL/P8.3SB = IF SETTLE_MO EQ MO2 AND XAMT LT 0 THEN XAMT ELSE 0;
MO3SEL/P8.3SB = IF SETTLE_MO EQ MO3 AND XAMT LT 0 THEN XAMT ELSE 0;
MO4SEL/P8.3SB = IF SETTLE_MO EQ MO4 AND XAMT LT 0 THEN XAMT ELSE 0;
MO5SEL/P8.3SB = IF SETTLE_MO EQ MO5 AND XAMT LT 0 THEN XAMT ELSE 0;
```

**Figure 9-32**   (continued) FOCEXEC for Net Position report.

```
SECURITY/I2 = IF MBS EQ 'Y' THEN 1 ELSE 2;

SECTYPE/A4 = IF LABEL EQ 'FCMO' THEN 'FCMO' ELSE
             IF EDIT(LABEL,'9$$$$') EQ 'G'  THEN 'GNMA' ELSE
             IF EDIT(LABEL,'999$$') EQ 'FPT' OR 'F15' OR 'FAR'
                OR 'FNV' OR 'FPM' THEN 'FPTI' ELSE
             IF EDIT(LABEL,'999$$') EQ 'FCMG' THEN 'FCMO' ELSE
             IF EDIT(LABEL,'999$$') EQ 'FPC' OR  'PC5' OR 'PG5'
                OR 'PAR' OR 'FPM' THEN 'FPCI' ELSE
                  IF LABEL EQ 'WC15' OR 'WCNO' THEN 'FPTI' ELSE
                  IF LABEL EQ 'WCGP' THEN 'FPTI' ELSE
                ELSE LABEL;

COL_LABEL/A15 = IF MBS EQ 'N' THEN  EDIT(XMD,'$$99$$') ]] '/' ]]
         EDIT(XMD,'$$$$99') ]] '/' ]] EDIT(XMD,'99$$$$') ELSE
               EDIT(COL_HEAD,'999999999999999');
CASHX/P8.3SB = CASH;
M1/P8.3SB = MO1_$; M2/P8.3SB = MO2_$; M3/P8.3SB = MO3_$;
M4/P8.3SB = MO4_$; M5/P8.3SB = MO5_$;
TRADER/A8 = DECODE PORTFOLIO  ( TRADERS ELSE ' ');
END

 TABLE FILE INVENT

 WRITE CASH MO1_$   MO2_$   MO3_$   MO4_$ MO5_$
 AND COMPUTE
 COUP_TOT/P8.3B = C1 + C2 + C3 + C4 + C5 + C6;
 &PORT2
 BY SECURITY BY COUPON

 WRITE CASHX M1  M2   M3   M4 M5  LABEL LST.SRANK
 CASHB MO1BUY   MO2BUY    MO3BUY    MO4BUY MO5BUY
 CASHS MO1SEL   MO2SEL    MO3SEL    MO4SEL MO5SEL
 AND COMPUTE
 SEC_TOT/P8.3B = C8 + C9 + C10 + C11 + C12 + C13;
 &PORT2
 BY SECURITY BY COUPON BY SECTYPE BY COL_LABEL BY TRADERS
 IF PORT_ID EQ &PID
 IF TRADE_DATE LE &ANS
 IF COUPON LE 18.00
 IF AMOUNT NE 0
 IF TRADER NE ' '
 ON TABLE HOLD AS NETPOS
 END
-RUN
-*EXIT
```

Figure 9-32    (continued) **FOCEXEC for Net Position report.**

```
OFFLINE
TABLE FILE NETPOS
HEADING CENTER
"NETPOS <+25 C I T I C O R P   M O R T G A G E   F I N A N C E <+25
&DATE"
" "
" "
" "
"NET POSITION REPORT FOR"
"MBS SECURITIES"
-IF &ANS3 EQ 'N' GOTO NOPORT;
"FOR PORTFOLIO: <PORTFOLIO>"
-NOPORT
"AS OF &DATE0"
"-----------------------"
" "
" "
  SUM MO1BUY NOPRINT   MO2BUY NOPRINT   MO3BUY NOPRINT   MO4BUY NOPRINT
      MO1SEL NOPRINT   MO2SEL NOPRINT   MO3SEL NOPRINT   MO4SEL NOPRINT
      MO5BUY NOPRINT   MO5SEL NOPRINT
      CASHB  NOPRINT   CASHS  NOPRINT
BY TRADER   NOPRINT
&PORT1

PRINT COL_LABEL AS 'POSITION'   CASHX AS CASH M1 AS '&MTN0' M2 AS
'&MTN1'
      M3 AS '&MTN2' M4 AS '&MTN3' M5 AS '&MTN4'
      SEC_TOT AS 'SECURITY,TOTAL'
AND COMPUTE
COUP_TOT/P7.3BS = IF LAST COUPON NE COUPON THEN COUP_TOT ELSE 0;
BY TRADER   NOPRINT
&PORT1
BY SECURITY NOPRINT
BY COUPON BY HIGHEST SECTYPE
BY SEC_LABEL NOPRINT
ON COUPON UNDER-LINE
ON SECURITY SUB-TOTAL
-*ON TABLE COLUMN-TOTAL
-IF &ANS3 EQ 'N' GOTO NOBRK;
ON PORTFOLIO PAGE-BREAK
ON PORTFOLIO SUBFOOT
" "
"<10 TOTAL BUYS:  <36 <CASHB   <48 <MO1BUY <60 <MO2BUY <72 <MO3BUY
 <84 <MO4BUY <96 <MO5BUY "
"<10 TOTAL SELLS: <36 <CASHS   <48 <MO1SEL <60 <MO2SEL <72 <MO3SEL
 <84 <MO4SEL <96 <MO5SEL "
-GOTO BRK1
```

Figure 9-32    (continued) FOCEXEC for Net Position report.

```
-NOBRK
ON TABLE SUBFOOT
" "
"<10 TOTAL BUYS:   <36 <CASHB   <48 <MO1BUY <60 <MO2BUY <72 <MO3BUY
 <84 <MO4BUY <96 <MO5BUY "
"<10 TOTAL SELLS:  <36 <CASHS   <48 <MO1SEL <60 <MO2SEL <72 <MO3SEL
 <84 <MO4SEL <96 <MO5SEL "
-BRK1

END
-DONE

FIN
```

Figure 9-32    (continued) FOCEXEC for Net Position report.

## Example 6: Working With External Files; Audit Trail Reports

This example discusses how the FOCUS report generating facilities can be used with several types of external files. We will present the basics of creating a MASTER DESCRIPTION for external files. Two FOCEXECS will be presented — one which creates an audit trail report, and another performing a MATCH file on two external files.

External files can be simple sequential files with a fixed format and one type of record, or they can have other formats, such as free format, ISAM, VSAM, etc. Most of the time you will deal with external files with one type of record, with a fixed record length.

These simple sequential files can come about in a number of ways:

1. Files created from the editor.
2. Files created from FOCUS as HOLD or SAVE files.
3. Files created from MODIFY procedures as LOG or TYPE files.
4. Files created as output of other COBOL, FORTRAN, ..., programs.
5. Tape files created as output of COBOL programs.

Most of the time the file will contain data in "text" format (i.e., alphanumeric format). This data is not stored in internal or binary format, it looks like readable alpha or numeric data. We will describe an application of creating a MASTER description for this type of file, created as an audit trail for a MODIFY procedure. Using FOCUS reporting techniques, the file can be analyzed and an audit trail report developed.

The other common situation which we shall discuss involves working with TAPE files. If a tape file is small enough, it can be moved into a disk file using the CMS MOVEFILE command. However, if it is large, or if you just don't feel like creating a disk file, you may still create a MASTER description and use FOCUS reporting on it. In either case, you will need to know if the records are in alphanumeric text format, or if they are in internal format. If they are in internal format, you should know the type of program used to create the file. We will present an example of creating a MASTER description for an output file of a COBOL program. Although there is an automatic procedure available from Information Builders Inc. to do this, it may not be ready when you need it. It is recommended that you have some familiarity with using COBOL files.

It is good to know that FOCUS can be used to manipulate and access external files. The power of defining fields, sorting records, formatting reports, etc., can be applied to external files — as long as a MASTER description is available. Although the MASTER description may contain declarations of the type of file, type of segments, and type of fields, most of the time you will only need a declaration of the fields in the file. Segment declarations are used when there are multiple data occurrences, which you wish to describe as a parent-child relationship.

In order to define external files and their location to FOCUS in CMS, you use the FILEDEF statement in your FOCEXEC or before executing the FOCUS procedure. For example, assume a file has been created from a MODIFY procedure, which contains a LOG of records. A FILEDEF for this file may look like:

```
-CMS FILEDEF TAPERR DISK FNMA TAPEERR A (LRECL 205 RECFM FB
```

The DDNAME TAPERR is the name used to refer to the file in FOCUS reporting procedures. The actual name of the file in CMS is FNMA TAPEERR on the A-disk. Before you can use the file with FOCUS reporting, you must have a MASTER description which tells FOCUS about the fields in the file. The DDNAME should be the same as the name of the MASTER. The MASTER in figure 9-33 shows one way to describe the fields in the TAPERR file. The SUFFIX = FIX indicates that it is a fixed format file (this is optional). The field names and aliases are like those for FOCUS files — up to 12 characters.

```
$* THIS MASTER DESCRIBES THE ERROR TYPE FILE CREATED BY BBTAPE
FOCEXEC
$*
$*    CALLED BY : TAPEERR FOCEXEC
$*
$***********************************************************************
FILENAME = ERROR,      SUFFIX = FIX,   $
   FIELD = FILL3 ,     F3,    A3,      $
   FIELD = PROGRAM,    PR,    A2,      $
   FIELD = FILLER,     FI,    A1,      $
   FIELD = POOL,       PL,    A6,      $
   FIELD = FILLER,     FI,    A1,      $
   FIELD = TYPE,       TY,    A3,      $
   FIELD = FILLER,     F2,    A2,      $
   FIELD = COUPON,     CP,    A6,      $
   FIELD = FILLER ,    FI,    A1,      $
   FIELD = ISSUE,      IS,    A8,      $
   FIELD = FILLER ,    FI,    A1,      $
   FIELD = MATURITY,   MT,    A8,      $
   FIELD = FILLER,     FI,    A1,      $
   FIELD = ORIGINAL,   OB,    A16 ,    $
   FIELD = FILLER,     FI,    A2,      $
   FIELD = WAM,        WM,    A4,      $
   FIELD = FILLER,     FI,    A1,      $
   FIELD = WAC,        WC,    A7 ,     $
   FIELD = ZIP_CODE,   ZC,    A5,      $
   FIELD = FILLER,     FI,    A1,      $
   FIELD = PTKEY,      PT,    A5,      $
   FIELD = FILLER,     F2,    A2,      $
   FIELD = YEAR,       YR,    A2,      $
   FIELD = FILLER,     FI,    A1,      $
   FIELD = MONTH,      MON,   A10,     $
   FIELD = FILL10,     FI0,   A10,     $
   FIELD = DPROGRAM,   DPR,   A2,      $
   FIELD = FILLER,     FI,    A1,      $
   FIELD = DPOOL,      DPL,   A6,      $
   FIELD = FILLER,     FI,    A1,      $
   FIELD = DTYPE,      DTY,   A3,      $
   FIELD = FILLER,     FI,    A2,      $
   FIELD = DCOUPON,    DCP,   A6,      $
   FIELD = FILLER,     FI,    A1,      $
   FIELD = DISSUE,     DIS,   A8,      $
   FIELD = FILLER,     FI,    A1,      $
   FIELD = DMATURITY,  DMT,   A8,      $
   FIELD = FILLER,     FI,    A1,      $
   FIELD = DORIGINAL,  DOB,   A16,     $
   FIELD = FILLER,     FI,    A1,      $
```

Figure 9-33    TAPEERR MASTER file.

```
FIELD = DWAM,      DWM,  A4,   $
FIELD = FILLER,    FI,   A1,   $
FIELD = DWAC,      DWC,  A7,   $
FIELD = FILLER,    FI,   A1,   $
FIELD = DZIP_CODE, DZC,  A5,   $
FIELD = FILLER,    FI,   A1,   $
FIELD = DPTKEY,    DPT,  A5,   $
FIELD = FILLER,    FI,   A2,   $
FIELD = DYEAR,     DYR,  A2,   $
FIELD = FILLER,    FI,   A1,   $
FIELD = DMONTH,    DMON, A10,  $
```

**Figure 9-33**  (continued) TAPEERR MASTER file.

Notice that these names are arbitrary, and the name FILLER has been used for fields which represent data which will not be used for anything. This is a good way to recognize the fields you need and don't need.

The formats shown next to the alias represent the ACTUAL FORMATS of the fields. It describes the type and length of the data as it exists in the file. The type will always be ALPHA (A), unless the file is in internal, binary format (output from other programs like COBOL or FORTRAN). Note that FOCUS HOLD files also contain data in internal formats, but we shall not discuss them here.

Each field may also have a USAGE format, which describes the way you wish to use the data in calculations, and have it displayed on reports. The usage format may also contain various edit options, such as zero suppress, YMD date displays, etc. These edit options are the same as fields in FOCUS files, and are described in the FOCUS manual section 2.3. The fields in the TAPERR MASTER do not have usage formats. In that case, they will be used as alphanumeric data. If we need to perform arithmetic calculations on the data, or if the data is to be SUMMED in a TABLE request, then a USAGE format must be assigned. For example, if the field COUPON is to be used as a numeric field in calculations, a USAGE format must be assigned such as:

```
FIELD=COUPON, CP, USAGE = F6.1, ACTUAL = A6, $
```

The usage format is first, then the actual format. You do not have to type the words "USAGE =" and "ACTUAL=." The usage format can have a length larger than the actual length. (This may be helpful to accommodate large summed values, or wide columns on reports.) Acceptable usage formats are:

A, D, F, I, P

The maximum length of an "A" field is 256.

Unless you need to use fields as numerics, or have some other good reason, it is easier to specify only the ACTUAL format, as we did in the TAPERR MASTER. The records can still be formatted into a report using the PRINT command. When creating the MASTER, you should be sure that the length of all the fields combined is equal to the record length specified in the FILEDEF. If not, FOCUS will issue an error message when a reporting request is made.

**COBOL to FOCUS Format Conversion**

Before presenting the audit trail example, we shall discuss how to convert a COBOL file, whose field formats are described within the OUTPUT FILE DEFINITION of a COBOL program, into fields in a FOCUS MASTER description. The fields are in COBOL internal format, described using the COBOL PICTURE formats. You should first refer to the conversion table in section 2.3 of the FOCUS manual. The table shows a few COBOL formats, and possible actual and usage formats. We shall not discuss the meaning of COBOL internal formats, since this is not necessary to convert one format into a FOCUS format. However, it is helpful to refer to the example which we shall present, if you must convert a COBOL file. The example shows not only the conversion into actual and usage formats, but also how to read through the fields in the COBOL file layout.

Figure 9-34 describes a COBOL file layout (NMD) for an aircraft parts inspection file. The file contains status codes on numerous aircraft parts which require special inspection. Only the first page of the file layout is shown. You should recognize that each field is assigned a PICTURE format, next to the name of field (or below it). The groupings of fields is by section (or "segment"), with each grouping starting with the level '05' or '10,' and associated fields grouped beneath each segment name. This grouping is not important to converting the format. The other parts of the layout to lookout for are the COMP FORMATS (COMP-1, COMP-2, COMP-3), and the OCCURS statement. COMP formats indicate either a computational integer,

RESPOND IMAGE DATABASE TAPE FILE DEFINTION

```
05  GEN-RESPOND-DB-COPY.
10  GEN-HISTORY-KEY.
    15  RCHIST-NMD-REF-DOC-CODE PICTURE 9(2).
    15  RCHIST-NMD-REF-DOC-NUMBER
            PICTURE X(15).
    15  RCHIST-NMD-REF-DOC-ITEM-NUMBER
            PICTURE 9(4).
    15  RCHIST-RECORD-LEVEL-CODE
            PICTURE X(01).
    15  RCHIST-DOC-LEVEL-CODE   PICTURE X(02).
    15  RCHIST-DOC-REF-DOC-CODE PICTURE 9(2).
    15  RCHIST-DOC-REF-DOC-NUMBER
            PICTURE X(15).
    15  TCHIST-DOC-REF-DOC-ITEM-NUMBER
            PICTURE 9(4).
10  RCNMDGEN-SEGMENT-DATA.
    15  RCNMDGEN-KEY.
        20  GEN-REF-DOC-CODE   PICTURE 9(2).
        20  GEN-REF-DOC-NUMBER PICTURE X(15).
        20  GEN-REF-DOC-ITEM-NO PICTURE 9(4).
    15  GEN-REF-DOC-DATE
            PICTURE 9(6)                COMP-3.
    15  GEN-REF-DOC-QTY
            PICTURE 9(6)                COMP-3.
    15  GEN-PART-NUMBER        PICTURE X(32).
    15  GEN-SERIAL-PART-NUMBER PICTURE X(10).
    15  GEN-REPAIR-PROJ
            PICTURE 9(4)                COMP-3.
    15  GEN-REPAIR-PRIM
            PICTURE 9(4)                COMP-3.
    15  GEN-REPAIR-SECN
            PICTURE 9(4)                COMP-3.
    15  GEN-UNIT-PRICE
            PICTURE 9(7)V9(3)           COMP-3.
    15  GEN-FINAL-DESTINATION  PICTURE X(7).
    15  GEN-EST-COMP-DT-REV-NO PICTURE 9(2).
    15  DOP                    PICTURE X(3).
    15  SIN                    PICTURE X(7).
    15  SMR-CODE               PICTURE X(6).
    15  GEN-DT-OF-LAST-CHANGE
            PICTURE 9(6)                COMP-3.
    15  GEN-REMARKS            PICTURE X(70).
    15  GEN-STATUS-CODES-DATES.
        20  GEN-STATUS-CODE-DATE-GROUP-1.
            25  GEN-STATUS-CODE-1
```

Figure 9-34   COBOL file layout.

```
                    PICTURE X(6).
               25   GEN-STATUS-DATE-1
                    PICTURE 9(6)                    COMP-3.
               25   GEN-STATUS-CODE-DATE-GROUP-2


                         ... MORE ..
```

**Figure 9-34**   (continued) COBOL file layout.


double precision, or packed field. The OCCURS indicates that there are multiple entries for the field, not just a single value. The MASTER shown in figure 9-35 is the FOCUS MASTER for the NMD COBOL file. There are quite a few fields which are FILLER fields, since they are not going to be used in FOCUS reporting. They have names F1, F2, F3, etc. Let's determine how the first several fields in the MASTER have been formatted:

1. The field F1 is filler and has length 24. By adding the formats of the first five fields in the NMD layout, you will arrive at length 24. These fields are not needed.
2. The field TYPEA has length 2, and corresponds to the next field (DOC-REF-DOC-CODE).
3. The field DOC_NUMA has length 15, and corresponds to the field (DOC-REF-DOC-NUMBER).
4. The field ITEMA has length 4 (DOC-REF-DOC-ITEM-NUMBER).
5. The field TYPE has length 2 (NMD-REF-DOC-CODE).
6. The field DOC_NUM has length 15 (NMD-REF-DOC-NUMBER).

The rest of the fields in the MASTER are obtained in the same way — by simply recognizing which COBOL fields to skip and which ones to include. Notice the filler F2 starts after the field PROGRAM (or NMD-MODEL on the COBOL layout). It has length 64 — the next field is PLANT.

After deciding on the names of the fields, you need to assign ACTUAL and USAGE formats to each field. The alphanumeric fields, such as DOC_NUM, are simple, since they have the same length as in the layout format. The hard part is to use the conversion table to as-

```
FILE=DMR, SUFFIX=FIX
SEGNAME=DMRDOC
 FIELD=F1               ,    ,A24,A24,$
 FIELD=TYPEA         ,ATY,I2,  A2,$
 FIELD=DOC_NUMA      ,ADC,A15,A15,$
 FIELD=ITEMA         ,AIT, A4,  A4,$
 FIELD=RECTYPE       ,03 ,A2,  A2,$
 FIELD=DOC_NUM       ,DOC,A15,A15,$
 FIELD=ITEM          ,IT ,I4,  A4,$
 FIELD=NMD_DATE      ,DT , P8,P4 ,$
 FIELD=QTY_DEF       ,QTY,    P8, P4,$
 FIELD=PART_NUM      ,PN ,A32,A32,$
 FIELD=SERIAL_NUM    ,SN ,A10,A10,$
 FIELD=PROGRAM       ,PRG,A7,  A7,$
 FIELD=F2            ,   ,A64,A64,$
 FIELD=PLANT         ,PLT,A3,  A3,$
 FIELD=DEPT          ,DPT,A4,  A4,$
 FIELD=F3            ,   ,A64,A64,$
 FIELD=REC_ACTION,RA,A3    A3,$
 FIELD=F4            ,   , A1,  A1,$
 FIELD=RESP_FAC      ,RF ,A7,  A7,$


 FIELD=F5            ,   ,A14,A14,$
 FIELD=AIRCRAFT,AC, A6,     A6,$
 FIELD=F6            ,   ,A194,A194,$
 FIELD=PO_NUM,PO,A19,       A19,$
 FIELD=F7            ,   ,A96, A96,$
 FIELD=CAUSE         ,CAU,A3,  A3,$
 FIELD=DEF_CODE      ,DC ,A3,  A3,$
 FIELD=CATEGORY,CAT,    A3,  A3,$
 FIELD=F8            ,   ,A50,A50,$
 FIELD=STAT_CODE1    ,SC1,A6,  A6,$
 FIELD=STAT_DATE1    ,SD1, P8,P4 ,$
 FIELD=STAT_CODE2    ,SC2,A6,  A6,$
 FIELD=STAT_DATE2    ,SD2, P8,P4 ,$
 FIELD=STAT_CODE3    ,SC3,A6,  A6,$
 FIELD=STAT_DATE3    ,SD3, P8,P4 ,$
 FIELD=STAT-CODE4    ,SC4, A6,  A6,$
 FIELD=STAT_DATE4    ,SD4, P8,P4 ,$
 FIELD=STAT_CODE5    ,SC5,A6,  A6,$
 FIELD=STAT_DATE5    ,SD5, P8,P4 ,$
 FIELD=STAT_CODE6    ,SC6,A6,  A6,$
 FIELD=STAT_DATE6    ,SD6, P8,P4 ,$
 FIELD=STAT_CODE7    ,SC7,A6,  A6,
```

Figure 9-35   MASTER description for COBOL external file.

sign formats for numeric fields. As an example, consider the field NMD_DATE. It has a format of

PICTURE 9(6) COMP-3

indicating it is a packed format. As in the table, the largest actual packed format for a COBOL field is P4. The usage format for this should be P8. Similarly, the format is the same for QTY_DEF. You should allow for more length in the usage format to accommodate the maximum possible number of digits in a value. For example, if the format of field were:

PICTURE 9(7)V9(2) COMP-3 has two digits after the decimal

the actual format is P4, but the usage format may be as large as P15.2, and as small as P10.2. Notice that the conversion table also indicates the equivalent formats for fields generated by programs written in FORTRAN, PL 1, ASSEMBLER.

**Creating an Audit Trail for a Modify Procedure**

A common type of external file are LOG files generated from MODIFY procedures. These are created when transactions are rejected or accepted. Refer to the FOCUS manual section 5.2.1 on how to LOG transactions. You may also use the TYPE command within a MODIFY to write out to a file certain text and/or data. This is described in detail in the FOCUS manual section 5.1.1. This is a powerful technique for formatting various types of records. These records can be displayed on the bottom of the screen, or written to a file. (Note that the maximum length of a TYPE record is 256 characters — including blanks and data values.)

In the FOCEXEC in figure 9-36, the MODIFY procedure uses the TYPE statement to write to a file when the data on an incoming transaction is different than the data in the database. Therefore, before UPDATING the value of any field in the database, the procedure writes out the values on the transaction to the file FNMA TAPEERR.

Notice that the TYPE record also consists of the values of the fields in the database — given by D.PROGRAM, D.COUPON, D.WAC, etc.

```
-*
-* PROGRAM :: BBTAPE FOCEXEC
-*
CMS FILEDEF FNMA   DISK FNMA DATA   *
CMS FILEDEF ERROR  DISK FNMA TAPEERR A ( LRECL 205 RECFM FB
CMS FILEDEF ZIPS   DISK ZIPS FOCTEMP * ( LRECL 6 RECFM F
-*
-SET &DT    = EDIT(&YMD1);
-SET &YEAR  = EDIT(EDIT(&DT,'99$$$$'));
-SET &MNTH  = EDIT(EDIT(&DT,'$$99$$'));
-SET &YM    = &YEAR | &MNTH ;
-SET &MONTH = DECODE &MNTH ( 01 'JAN' 02 'FEB' 03 'MAR' 04 'APR'
-                            05 'MAY' 06 'JUN' 07 'JUL' 08 'AUG'
-                            09 'SEP' 10 'OCT' 11 'NOV' 12 'DEC'
-                            ELSE 'AAA');
-TYPE UPDATING &MONTH FNMA ( FNMA1 )
-*
-RUN
MODIFY FILE FNMAFILE
START 1
STOP  *
 COMPUTE
SUFFIX/A1 =;
WAMKEY/A1 =;
XTYPE /A2 =;
JAN = -.1 ;
FEB = -.1 ;
MAR = -.1 ;
APR = -.1 ;
MAY = -.1 ;
JUN = -.1 ;
JUL = -.1 ;
AUG = -.1 ;
SEP = -.1 ;
OCT = -.1 ;
NOV = -.1 ;
DEC = -.1 ;
GOTO FNMA

 CASE FNMA
      COMPUTE
         PROGRAM  = 'FN';
         TYPE     = XTYPE | ' ';
         WAC      = WAC/10000.;
      GOTO CASEALL
 ENDCASE
```

Figure 9-36  File maintenance program with audit trail.

```
-*
-*
CASE CASEALL
     COMPUTE
          YEAR     = &YEAR;
          POOLX/A6 = EDIT(POOL);
          PRPOOL/A8= PROGRAM | POOLX ;
          ORIGINAL = ORIGINAL / 100.;
          ISSUE    = IF PROGRAM EQ 'FM' THEN ISSUE ELSE
                     EDIT(ISSUE,'$$$$99') | EDIT(ISSUE,'9999$$');
          MATURITY = IF PROGRAM EQ 'FM' THEN MATURITY ELSE
                     EDIT(MATURITY,'$$$$99') |
EDIT(MATURITY,'9999$$');
          MONISS/I4 = EDIT(EDIT(ISSUE, '9999')) ;
          MFISS/I4 = YM (MONISS, &YM, MFISS) ;
          &MONTH   = IF MONISS EQ &YM THEN 1.
                     ELSE IF MFISS LE 2 AND &MONTH LE .1 THEN -.1
                     ELSE IF (&MONTH LT .00000010) THEN 0 ELSE
&MONTH;
          WAMKEY   = IF WAM GT 180 THEN 'B'
                     ELSE IF WAM GT 0 AND WAM LE 180 THEN 'A'
                     ELSE ' ';
          PTKEY/A5 = PROGRAM | EDIT(TYPE,'99') | WAMKEY;
-*
     MATCH PRPOOL  YEAR
        ON NOMATCH INCLUDE
        ON MATCH GOTO CKVALUES
 ENDCASE
-*
 CASE CKVALUES
     MATCH PRPOOL YEAR
        ON MATCH IF TYPE NE D.TYPE GOTO ERROR;
        ON MATCH IF COUPON NE D.COUPON GOTO ERROR;
        ON MATCH IF ISSUE NE D.ISSUE GOTO ERROR;
        ON MATCH IF MATURITY NE D.MATURITY GOTO ERROR;
        ON MATCH IF ORIGINAL NE D.ORIGINAL GOTO ERROR;
        ON MATCH IF WAM NE 0 AND WAM NE D.WAM GOTO ERROR;
        ON MATCH IF WAC NE 0.0 AND WAC NE D.WAC GOTO ERROR;
        ON NOMATCH REJECT
        ON MATCH UPDATE &MONTH
 ENDCASE
-*
 CASE ERROR
   MATCH PRPOOL YEAR
       ON MATCH TYPE ON ERROR
" <PR <POOL <TYPE> <CP <ISSUE <MT <OB <WAM <WAC <ZC <PTKEY> <YEAR
```

**Figure 9-36**   (continued)

```
<&MONTH
<PR <PL <D.TY> <D.CP <D.IS <D.MT <D.OB <D.WM <D.WC <D.ZC <D.PT>
<D.YR <D.&MONTH"
ON NOMATCH REJECT
ON MATCH UPDATE TYPE CP ISSUE MT OB WAM WAC ZC PTKEY &MONTH
 ENDCASE
-*
DATA ON FNMA
END
-RUN
```

**Figure 9-36**   (continued)

When the MODIFY procedure is finished, the FNMA TAPEERR file will contain those records which were updated. The next step might be to create a formatted audit trail report of the records in the file. This is easily done once the TAPERR MASTER has been created. It only needs to be created once so that each time the MODIFY procedure is executed, an audit trail report procedure can also be executed. The programmer needs to be sure that the MASTER describes accurately the data on the file. See figure 9-33.

The TAPEERR1 FOCEXEC shown in figure 9-37 generates the audit trail report. It contains several useful techniques:

1. Several fields act as flags to check that only those records with changed values will be shown on the report.
2. Several fields (DTYPE, DCP, etc.) are redefined to have a value of BLANK (' ') if the database value has not been changed by the transaction.
3. The HEADER of the report is supplied using a -INCLUDE.
4. There are two separate reports:

    a. A count of the records indicating how many changes to each field.
    b. A listing of the records showing the values on the transaction and the value in the database (if they are different).

This type of audit trail report is easy to program, and quite effective for the user because it only shows records which have resulted in changes to the database. The report is shown in figure 9-38.

## 352 The Database Experts' Guide to FOCUS

```
-* THIS ROUTINE ANALYSES THE DB VALUES
-* VERSUS THE INCOMING VALUES FOR ERROR CONDITIONS.
-* CALLED BY TAPEERR EXEC
-*
OFFLINE

-CMS FI TAPEERR DISK &PROG      TAPEERR A ( LRECL 205 RECFM FB
-CMS FI OFFLINE DISK ERR&PROG LISTING A ( LRECL 132 RECFM FB
-SET &REPDTE1= EDIT(&BBDATE,'$$99$$') | '/' |
EDIT(&BBDATE,'$$$99');
-SET &REPDTE = &REPDTE1 | '/' | EDIT(&BBDATE,'99$$$$');
-RUN
DEFINE FILE TAPEERR
 TPERR/I6   = IF TYPE    NE DTYPE  THEN 1 ELSE 0;
 CPERR/I6   = IF CP      NE DCP    THEN 1 ELSE 0;
 ISERR/I6   = IF ISSUE   NE DIS    THEN 1 ELSE 0;
 MTERR/I6   = IF MT      NE DMT    THEN 1 ELSE 0;
 OBERR/I6   = IF OB      NE DOB    THEN 1 ELSE 0;
 WMERR/I6   = IF WM      NE DWM    THEN 1 ELSE 0;
 WCERR/I6   = IF WC      NE DWC    THEN 1 ELSE 0;
 ZCERR/I6   = IF ZC      NE DZC    THEN 1 ELSE 0;
 DTYPE      = IF TYPE    NE DTYPE  THEN DTYPE   ELSE ' ';
 DCP        = IF CP      NE DCP    THEN DCP     ELSE ' ';
 DISSUE     = IF ISSUE   NE DISSUE THEN DIS     ELSE ' ';
 DMT        = IF MT      NE DMT    THEN DMT     ELSE ' ';
 DOBP/A13   = EDIT(DOB,'9999999999999');
 OBP/A13    = EDIT(OB,'9999999999999');
 DOBP       = IF OBP     NE DOBP   THEN DOBP    ELSE ' ';
 DWM        = IF WM      NE DWM    THEN DWM     ELSE ' ';
 DWC        = IF WC      NE DWC    THEN DWC     ELSE ' ';
 DZC        = IF ZC      NE DZC    THEN DZC     ELSE ' ';
 ANYERR/I6 = IF   CPERR EQ 1 OR ISERR EQ 1 OR MTERR EQ 1 OR OBERR
EQ 1
            OR TPERR EQ 1 OR WMERR EQ 1 OR WCERR EQ 1 OR ZCERR EQ
1
            THEN 1
            ELSE 0;
END
-* NOTE: REPHDR IS A FOCEXEC CONTAINING THE REPORT HEADING
-*

TABLE FILE TAPEERR
-INCLUDE REPHDR
"    ERROR RELATING TO BB FACTOR INPUT FOR PROGRAM <PROGRAM "
"    BB INPUT : FACTORS FOR &REPDTE "
"      "
 SUM TPERR CPERR ISERR MTERR OBERR WMERR WCERR ZCERR ANYERR
```

Figure 9-37    FOCEXEC for creating Audit Trail report.

```
   BY TYPE
   END

   TABLE FILE TAPEERR
   -INCLUDE REPHDR
   "    ERROR RELATING TO BB FACTOR INPUT FOR PROGRAM <PROGRAM "
   "    BB INPUT : FACTORS FOR &REPDTE "
   "    COUPON ERRORS "
   PRINT POOL TYPE AS 'TP' DTYPE AS 'DT' IN +0 CP IN +0 DCP ISSUE
   DISSUE MT DMT
          OBP AS 'ORIG BAL' DOBP AS 'DB ORIG BAL' WM DWM WC DWC ZC AS
   'ZIP' DZC
   IF ANYERR EQ 1
   BY TYPE NOPRINT
   BY POOL NOPRINT
   ON TYPE SKIP-LINE
   END
   -RUN
   FIN
```

Figure 9-37 (continued) FOCEXEC for creating Audit Trail report.

## Example 7: Executing FOCEXECS Interactively; CMS EXECS

There are several ways to run FOCUS procedures. Depending on who the user is, you may wish to run FOCEXECS from a FOCUS created menu, from a CMS EXEC, or from native FOCUS. Sometimes, other types of programs such as FORTRAN, ASSEMBLER, etc., are executed in one CMS together with FOCUS programs. To handle this, you should recognize the steps in a CMS EXEC. EXECS will give you control over input and output files, error conditions, erasing files, linking to ids, setting up temp space, etc. EXECS also make it possible to run overnite BATCH procedures requiring several long steps.

FOCEXECS may also be executed from other FOCEXECS using the EXEC command. There are various reasons for wanting to do this, such as performing a sequence of tasks, or creating extract files, HOLD files, etc., which are used in several programs. Also, menus can be set up for reporting systems which run different report programs.

We shall present an example of a CMS EXEC which can invoke FOCUS programs, and outline some of its capabilities. This can be used as a guide for developing your own CMS EXECS. We shall also discuss how to pass parameters to FOCUS programs using local and

MORTGAGE RESEARCH
PRODUCT MARKETING & DEVELOPMENT

REPORT DATE : 09/05/87    REPORT TIME

ERROR RELATING TO BB FACTOR INPUT FOR PROGRAM FN
BB INPUT : FACTORS FOR 09/01/87

| TYPE | TPERR | CPERR | ISERR | MTERR | OBERR | WMERR | WCERR | ZCERR | ANYERR |
|------|-------|-------|-------|-------|-------|-------|-------|-------|--------|
| AM   | 0     | 20    | 0     | 0     | 0     | 0     | 0     | 6     | 20     |
| AS   | 0     | 293   | 0     | 0     | 0     | 0     | 0     | 23    | 293    |
| CL   | 0     | 0     | 0     | 0     | 0     | 0     | 0     | 0     | 0      |
| GL   | 0     | 0     | 0     | 0     | 0     | 0     | 0     | 0     | 0      |
| VL   | 0     | 61    | 0     | 0     | 0     | 0     | 0     | 2     | 61     |

1 PAGE    1

PRODUCT MARKETING & DEVELOPMENT

REPORT DATE : 09/05/87    REPORT TIME

ERROR RELATING TO BB FACTOR INPUT FOR PROGRAM FN
BB INPUT : FACTORS FOR 09/01/87
COUPON ERRORS

**Figure 9-38  Audit Trail report.**

| POOL | TP | DT | COUPON | DCP | ISSUE | DISSUE | MATURITY | DMT | ORIG BAL | DB ORIG BAL | WM | DWM | WC | DWC | ZI |
|---|---|---|---|---|---|---|---|---|---|---|---|---|---|---|---|
| 9776 | AM | | 9.073 | 9.095 | 84/11/01 | | 14/03/01 | | 38,252,782 | | 352 | | 13.357 | | 91 |
| 9777 | AM | | 9.073 | 9.095 | 84/11/01 | | 14/04/01 | | 13,111,220 | | 353 | | 13.357 | | 91 |
| 9778 | AM | | 9.073 | 9.095 | 84/11/01 | | 14/05/01 | | 16,503,865 | | 354 | | 11.500 | | 91 |
| 9779 | AM | | 9.073 | 9.095 | 84/11/01 | | 14/06/01 | | 4,811,499 | | 355 | | 11.500 | | 91 |
| 9780 | AM | | 9.073 | 9.095 | 84/11/01 | | 14/09/01 | | 6,627,134 | | 358 | | 11.750 | | 91 |
| 9781 | AM | | 9.073 | 9.095 | 84/11/01 | | 14/10/01 | | 40,152,257 | | 359 | | 12.000 | | 91 |
| 9782 | AM | | 9.073 | 9.095 | 84/11/01 | | 14/11/01 | | 2,985,850 | | 360 | | 12.000 | | 91 |
| 12494 | AM | | 8.880 | 8.800 | 86/09/01 | | 08/03/01 | | 1,200,000 | | 258 | | 9.880 | | 91 |
| 20130 | AM | | 8.750 | 7.230 | 85/06/01 | | 14/08/01 | | 1,080,797 | | 350 | | 12.200 | | 91 |
| 20155 | AM | | 8.823 | 8.845 | 85/04/01 | | 14/08/01 | | 39,414,708 | | 352 | | 12.717 | | 91 |
| 20156 | AM | | 8.823 | 8.845 | 85/04/01 | | 14/09/01 | | 44,274,461 | | 353 | | 12.717 | | 91 |
| 20157 | AM | | 8.823 | 8.845 | 85/04/01 | | 14/09/01 | | 5,544,426 | | 353 | | 12.967 | | 91 |
| 20158 | AM | | 8.823 | 8.845 | 85/04/01 | | 14/10/01 | | 11,497,329 | | 354 | | 12.967 | | 91 |
| 20160 | AM | | 8.823 | 8.845 | 85/04/01 | | 14/12/01 | | 19,258,668 | | 356 | | 11.750 | | 91 |
| 20161 | AM | | 8.823 | 8.845 | 85/04/01 | | 15/01/01 | | 45,813,793 | | 357 | | 11.750 | | 91 |
| 20437 | AM | | 8.750 | 7.230 | 85/08/01 | | 14/08/01 | | 7,257,731 | | 348 | | 12.200 | | 91 |
| 20444 | AM | | 8.750 | 7.230 | 85/10/01 | | 15/08/01 | | 5,019,616 | | 358 | | 11.000 | | 91 |
| 20445 | AM | | 8.750 | 7.230 | 85/09/01 | | 14/08/01 | | 3,865,116 | | 347 | | 10.950 | | 91 |
| 20448 | AM | | 8.750 | 7.230 | 85/10/01 | | 15/08/01 | | 2,934,339 | | 358 | | 11.000 | | 91 |
| 20451 | AM | | 8.700 | 7.270 | 85/09/01 | | 15/02/01 | | 2,802,997 | | 353 | | 11.910 | | 91 |

**Figure 9-38** (continued) Audit Trail report.

global dialogue manager variables. This is essential for many applications where the values of certain parameters are selected by the operator at execution time. Note, our treatment applies to both local and global variables.

Passing parameters is done using dialogue manager variables. Within a FOCEXEC, these variables must be resolved with values in order for FOCUS commands to be run. Consider the TABLE request contained in a FOCEXEC (REP1):

```
TABLE FILE HISTORY
PRINT LABEL COUPON MATURITY DATE BID ASK
IF DATE EQ &TDATE
END
```

When running this interactively from FOCUS, you must supply the value of &TDATE. This can be done in a few ways. If the REP1 FOCEXEC has a PROMPT statement, it will prompt you for the value of &TDATE. If there is no PROMPT or CRTFORM, then FOCUS will look if you have supplied the value in some other way:

1. On the EXEC line, e.g., EXEC REP1 TDATE = 870901.
2. Using A DEFAULTS statement in the FOCEXEC to supply a default value for the variable.
3. Using a SET, or READ statement.

These are described in detail in Chapter 6 of the FOCUS manual. DEFAULT statements are useful since the default value is assigned only if no value appears on the EXEC line. Note that prompt statements, set statements, and read statements will assign values which override the value assigned by the default statement.

A useful application of DEFAULT is to facilitate switching between CRTFORM assignment of values and non-CRTFORM assignment of values. For example,

```
-DEFAULTS &OPT = N , &TDATE = 870901, &LABEL = GNMA
-IF &OPT EQ N GOTO SKIPCRT ;
-CRTFORM
-" ENTER VALUES FOR THE FOLLOWING: "
-" "
-" .... "
-SKIPCRT
```

```
TABLE FILE HISTORY
PRINT LABEL COUPON MATURITY DATE BID
IF LABEL EQ &LABEL
IF DATE EQ &TDATE
END
```

When the FOCEXEC is executed from native FOCUS or from another FOCEXEC, the operator may supply a value of 'Y' for the variable &OPT on the EXEC line:

```
EX REP1 OPT = Y
```

If this is done, the program shall ignore the default values and display a CRTFORM for entering the other values. If no value of OPT is supplied, then the default values will be used. There are variations on using the DEFAULT in this manner.

When using implied prompting or direct prompting of values, the operator will have to wait until a prompt message is issued by FOCUS. The only way around this is to execute the FOCUS program from a CMS EXEC. When you do this, you may stack the values which are required by the FOCEXEC. For example, the following CMS EXEC invokes FOCUS and executes the REP1 FOCEXEC.

```
&CONTROL OFF
&TYPE ENTER THE DATE OF THE REPORT (YYMMDD)
&READ VARS &REPDATE
&STACK EXEC REP1
&STACK &REPDATE
&FIN
EX FOCUS
-EXIT
&EXIT
```

The concept of stacking commands applies to all types of EXECS such as EXEC II, REXX, etc. We shall not discuss the variations here. Any number of values can be stacked in this way. The above EXEC invokes FOCUS, and places in the console stack the EXEC statement and the value of the variable which will be supplied to the prompt. This is a standard way to run FOCUS procedures from a CMS EXEC. Notice also the command FIN is stacked to leave FOCUS after the procedure is completed. (FIN can also be placed in the FOCEXEC it-

### 358 The Database Experts' Guide to FOCUS

self.) You may want to execute the FOCEXEC within the CMS EXEC sometimes, or execute it from native FOCUS other times.

The sample CMS EXEC shown in figure 9-39 is a sophisticated procedure for performing a number of tasks at once. The steps are outlined as follows:

1. The command DAILY runs the exec from CMS. If the operator needs clarification on the procedure, a HELP section is displayed by running DAILY HELP.
2. The filemode is determined for various files using the exec variable &FM.
3. The operator enters the date; the date is checked as a valid date. The type of files to be extracted is selected. FILEDEFS for various files used in the FOCEXEC are issued.
4. The DAILY FOCEXEC is executed from FOCUS, along with values for several variables. A log of the steps is maintained using another EXEC LOGIT (shown in figure 9-40); the log messages are stacked.
5. If the process successfully extracted a file, a SYNCSORT procedure is executed on the file to sort the records. Other messages are sent to the log file using LOGIT, and the EXEC is completed.

Using this technique, it is possible to set up procedures which can run a number of programs, manipulate data files, and go in and out of FOCUS to run FOCEXECS.

### Example 8: Processing Employee Expense Vouchers

This example illustrates how to use DIALOGUE MANAGER to set up preliminary data required in a MODIFY procedure. In some maintenance procedures, it is necessary to locate records in other FOCUS files before starting the MODIFY procedure. This is usually required in more sophisticated applications, where the operator should not begin data entry unless certain employee or project information has been retrieved first. In this example, an operator processes expense vouchers submitted by employees in a large organization. An employee usually submits several vouchers over a period of time. After the voucher information is entered into a FOCUS file, other FOCUS procedures may be used to print the voucher forms, and to ob-

```
&TRACE OFF
*
PRO00060
* THIS EXEC CONTROLS THE EXECUTION OF THE DAILY FOCEXEC, WHICH
WILL       PRO00070
* PRODUCE SEVERAL SECURITY FILES FOR A PARTICULAR DATE.
PRO00080
*
PRO00060
*
&FLAGERR = 0
*
&IF   &INDEX = 0  &GOTO -START
&IF   &1 = ?       &GOTO -HELP
&IF   &1 = HELP   &GOTO -HELP
&TYPE
&TYPE IF YOU NEED HELP TYPE ====== > DAILY HELP
&GOTO -ERR
*
-START
 USERID
 &READ VARS &TRASH1 &PRINTID &TRASH2 &PRINTDT &PRINTTI &TRASH3
&TRASH4
*
&FM = B
&IF &PRINTID ^= PDM3 &FM = A
&IF &PRINTID ^= PDM3 &GOTO -OVER
SET CMSTYPE HT
CP DET 203
CP LINK PDM3   191 203 RR RPDM3
ACC 203 D
*
-OVER
CLRSCRN
&BEGTYPE 8

     DAILY EXEC


======================================================================

    ENTER THE DATE FOR DATA EXTRACTION (MMDDYY) :
         OR QUIT TO EXIT

&READ VARS &REQ_DATE
&IF .&REQ_DATE  =  .    &GOTO -OVER
&IF  &REQ_DATE  = QUIT &GOTO -EXIT
```

**Figure 9-39**   CMS EXEC procedure.

**360** The Database Experts' Guide to FOCUS

```
&CTYPE             = &DATATYPE OF &REQ_DATE
&IF  &CTYPE       ^= NUM  &GOTO -OVER
&YY = &SUBSTR OF &REQ_DATE 5 2
&MM = &SUBSTR OF &REQ_DATE 1 2
&DD = &SUBSTR OF &REQ_DATE 3 2
&IF &MM GT 12 &GOTO -OVER
&IF &DD GT 31 &GOTO -OVER
&IF &YY LT 80 &GOTO -OVER
*
-AGAIN
CLRSCRN
&BEGTYPE 8

        DAILY EXEC


======================================================================
        DO YOU WANT TO EXTRACT
           (B) BOND FILE  OR  (M) MBS FILE  OR  (A) ALL ? ( B/M/A )
              OR QUIT TO EXIT
&READ VARS &ALLFILES
&IF  &ALLFILES   = A     &GOTO -ASTART
&IF  &ALLFILES   = B     &GOTO -ASTART
&IF  &ALLFILES   = M     &GOTO -ASTART
&IF .&ALLFILES   = .     &GOTO -AGAIN
&IF  &ALLFILES   = QUIT &GOTO -EXIT
&GOTO -AGAIN
*
-ASTART
CLRSCRN
*
*
FI BOND      DISK BOND     &REQ_DATE &FM ( LRECL 102 RECFM F DISP
MOD
FI FUTURE    DISK FUTURE   &REQ_DATE &FM ( LRECL 102 RECFM F
FI MBS       DISK MBS      &REQ_DATE &FM ( LRECL 160 RECFM F DISP
MOD
*
&STACK DAILY EXEC : EXECUTING AND FILEDEFS COMPLETE
&STACK DAILY EXEC : DATE = &REQ_DATE : FM = &FM : OPTION =
&ALLFILES
EXEC LOGIT
DESBUF
&STACK EX DAILY
&STACK &FM
&STACK &REQ_DATE
```

**Figure 9-39**   (continued) CMS EXEC procedure.

```
 &STACK &ALLFILES
 EX FOCUS
 &IF &RC = 0 &GOTO -GOODFOC
 &FLAGERR = 1
 &STACK DAILY EXEC : ENTRY TO FOCUS FOR DAILY FOCEXEC FAILED
 EXEC LOGIT
 &GOTO -WRAPUP
-GOODFOC
*
-MBSEND
 STATEW MBS &REQ_DATE &FM
 &IF &RC = 0 &GOTO -SORTMBS
 &FLAGERR = 1
 &STACK DAILY EXEC : MBS FILE - EXTRACT PROCESS FAILED
 EXEC LOGIT
 &GOTO -WRAPUP
-SORTMBS
 DESBUF
 &STACK   115,5,CH,A 20,7,CH,A 29,7,CH,A 15,4,CH,A
 SSORT MBS &REQ_DATE &FM
 &IF &RC = 0 &GOTO -GOODMBS
 &FLAGERR = 1
 &STACK DAILY EXEC : MBS FILE - SORT PROCESS FAILED
 EXEC LOGIT
 &GOTO -WRAPUP
-GOODMBS
 &STACK DAILY EXEC : MBS FILE CREATED / SORTED OK
 EXEC LOGIT
 &GOTO -ENDMBS
-ENDMBS
 &IF &ALLFILES = M &GOTO -WRAPUP
*
-BBEND
 STATEW BOND &REQ_DATE &FM
 &IF &RC = 0 &GOTO -GOODBB
 &FLAGERR = 1
 &STACK DAILY EXEC : BOND FILE - EXTRACT PROCESS FAILED
 EXEC LOGIT
 &GOTO -WRAPUP
-GOODBB
 &STACK DAILY EXEC : BOND FILE CREATED OK
 EXEC LOGIT
 &IF &ALLFILES = B &GOTO -WRAPUP
*
*
-WRAPUP
SET CMSTYPE RT
```

**Figure 9-39**  (continued) CMS EXEC procedure.

## 362 The Database Experts' Guide to FOCUS

```
CLRSCRN
&BEGTYPE 7

    DAILY COMPLETE -

*
&IF &FLAGERR EQ 1 &GOTO -ERR
&STACK DAILY EXEC : SUCCESSFUL COMPLETION OF DAILY EXEC / FOCEXEC
EXEC LOGIT
&RC = 0
&GOTO -EXIT
*
-ERR
  &RC = 99
&STACK DAILY EXEC : FAILURE IN DAILY EXEC / FOCEXEC PROCESS &RC
EXEC LOGIT
&GOTO -EXIT
*
-HELP
SET CMSTYPE RT
CLRSCRN
&BEGTYPE 10
* ROUTINE TO SPLIT PRICES FILE INTO DIFFERENT DATA SETS.
*
*            THE TAPE DATE PROMPT WILL BE IN YYMMDD
*
*            THE PRICES IN ALL FILES ARE IN DECIMAL(S).
*
*
*
*
*
```

**Figure 9-39**  (continued) CMS EXEC procedure.

tain summary reports of expenses incurred by each department. The voucher forms, themselves, are sent to managers for approval.

The MASTER description of the VOUCHER file is shown in figure 9-41. It contains several segments:

1. EMPDATA: the key field is SSN, representing the SOCIAL SECURITY NUMBER of the employee. Each employee may submit many vouchers during the course of the year, which will be entered in the VOUCHER file. Segment also contains employee name.

```
&TRACE OFF
&NOW =
&NOWDATE =
&FILL = &STRING OF =================
SENTRIES
&LINES = &RC
Q T (STACK LIFO
&READ ARGS
&READ ARGS
&NOW = &3
&NOWDATE = &6
&STACK LIFO &FILL &NOW &FILL &NOWDATE &FILL
&NUM = &LINES + 1
EXECIO &NUM DISKW DAILY LOG A (FINIS
&EXIT
```

**Figure 9-40    LOGIT procedure — CMS EXEC.**

2. IDINFO: the key field is ID_CODE, representing the voucher number or ID code. The segment contains employee name, employee information, business purpose, and approval information.
3. LINEINFO: the key field is ACCOUNT, representing various types of expenses incurred (meals, lodging, etc.).
4. ITEMINFO: the key field is ITEM_NO, representing the itemized expenses incurred for each account type. The segment contains the date, dollar amounts, description, etc.

There is also an employee cross-reference file, PERSON, which contains detailed information on the employees in the organization. This file may be useful in reporting, as well as maintenance procedures.

The maintenance procedure can be designed in a number of ways. Using FIDEL, the operator can perform data entry on various types of expenses. Validations can be built in to verify account codes, dollar amounts, etc. We shall describe how one might set up the procedure to verify that employee information is accurate. Dialogue manager techniques are useful for this procedure. We shall not get into the details of the FIDEL procedure.

In order to assure that the operator processes vouchers only for employees contained in the PERSON file, it is necessary to verify that an employee exists in the file before proceeding with data entry. If the employee is found in the PERSON file, then the employee data such as address, phone number, etc. will be extracted and displayed later

```
FILENAME=VOUCHER   ,SUFFIX=FOC
SEGNAME=EMPDATA  , SEGTYPE=S1

  FIELDNAME=SSN             ,ALIAS=SSN       ,FORMAT=A9        ,$
  FIELDNAME=NAME            ,ALIAS=NM        ,FORMAT=A28       ,$

$    ****************************************************
$    *      IDENTIFICATION INFO SEGMENT               **
$    ****************************************************

SEGNAME=IDINFO   , SEGTYPE=S1,      PARENT = EMPDATA,  $

  FIELDNAME=BLDG_CODE       ,ALIAS=BCD       ,FORMAT=A4        ,$
  FIELDNAME=VB_ADDRESS      ,ALIAS=VBADR     ,FORMAT=A24       ,$
  FIELDNAME=VB_CITY         ,ALIAS=VBCITY    ,FORMAT=A20       ,$
  FIELDNAME=VB_STATE        ,ALIAS=VBSTATE   ,FORMAT=A2        ,$
  FIELDNAME=VB_ZIPCODE      ,ALIAS=VBZIP     ,FORMAT=A5        ,$
  FIELDNAME=VSAL_RANGE      ,ALIAS=VSRNG     ,FORMAT=A3        ,$
  FIELDNAME=VTITLE          ,ALIAS=VTTL      ,FORMAT=A18       ,$
  FIELDNAME=VDEP            ,ALIAS=VDEP      ,FORMAT=A15       ,$

$    ****************************************************
$    *      COMMON FIELDS                             **
$    ****************************************************

  FIELDNAME=SERIAL_NOF      ,ALIAS=SNOF      ,FORMAT=I07       ,$
  FIELDNAME=SERIAL_NOT      ,ALIAS=SNOT      ,FORMAT=I07       ,$
  FIELDNAME=CASH_ADV        ,ALIAS=CADV      ,FORMAT=P9.2C     ,$
  FIELDNAME=BUS_PURP        ,ALIAS=BP        ,FORMAT=A48       ,$

$    ****************************************************
$    *      LINE INFORMATION SEGMENT                  **
$    ****************************************************

SEGNAME=LINEINFO, SEGTYPE=S1,      PARENT = IDINFO   ,$
  FIELDNAME=ACCOUNT         ,ALIAS=ACT       ,FORMAT=I07       ,$
  FIELDNAME=ATOTAL          ,ALIAS=ATOT      ,FORMAT=P9.2C     ,$
  FIELDNAME=HELP_DESC       ,ALIAS=HDESC     ,FORMAT=A40       ,$

$    ****************************************************
$    *      ITEM INFORMATION SEGMENT                  **
$    ****************************************************

SEGNAME=ITEMINFO, SEGTYPE=S1,      PARENT = LINEINFO ,$
  FIELDNAME=ITEM_NO         ,ALIAS=INO       ,FORMAT=I02       ,$
  FIELDNAME=DATE            ,ALIAS=DT        ,FORMAT=I6YMD     ,$
  FIELDNAME=TRSP_AMT        ,ALIAS=TAMT      ,FORMAT=P8.2C     ,$
```

**Figure 9-41**   Voucher MASTER file.

```
FIELDNAME=MEALS_NO    ,ALIAS=MLNO    ,FORMAT=I2      ,$
FIELDNAME=MEALS_AMT   ,ALIAS=MLAMT   ,FORMAT=P8.2C   ,$
FIELDNAME=LODGING     ,ALIAS=LDG     ,FORMAT=P8.2C   ,$
FIELDNAME=OTHER       ,ALIAS=OTH     ,FORMAT=P6.2C   ,$

SEGNAME=EMPINFO , SEGTYPE=KU,    PARENT = LINEINFO ,
   CRKEY = SSN ,    CRFILE = PERSON, $
```

**Figure 9-41** (continued) Voucher MASTER file.

on in the MODIFY FIDEL procedure. As shown in the focexec, the data is extracted from the PERSON file and written to a SAVE file.

There are several steps in developing such a procedure. As shown in figure 9-42, the VOUCHER FOCEXEC uses dialogue manager extensively to perform the preliminary screening. The steps required are:

1. The operator enters the employee social security number, or the last name of the employee. The operator may also enter the first name and inital if there may be more than one employee with the same last name.
2. The employee data is extracted from the PERSON file based on the SSN, if entered, or on the employee's name. If there are more than one employee with the same last name, the names are displayed to the operator so that he may select one.
3. The employee data is read (using -READ) as dialogue manager variables, to be displayed later using FIDEL.
4. The last voucher number is extracted from the voucher file, and the current voucher number is determined by incrementing it by one.
5. The MODIFY procedure starts; Before displaying the current voucher number and employee data on the screen, the values of employee fields, such as SSN, ADDRESS, DEPT, LEVEL, are obtained from the dialogue manager variables using a COMPUTE.

This FOCEXEC demonstrates the use of dialogue manager in controlling the execution. Depending on the operator's selection, the process will display messages requesting further operator input.

The following describes the techniques used:

```
-* PROGRAM VOUCHER1: DATA ENTRY FOR EMPLOYEE EXPENSE VOUCHERS.
-*

-SET &QUIT = OFF;
-STARTV
-CMS FILEDEF SAVE2 DISK SAVE2 DATA A (LRECL 138 RECFM FB

SET MSG = OFF
SET PAGE = OFF

-SET &HEADDSC =
-'       OUR ELEVATOR COMP. SERVICES DIVISION'|' ;
-SET &HEADDSC1 = '          DATE: '|&DATE ;
-SET &HEAD_DSC = &HEADDSC | &HEADDSC1 ;
-SET &HEAD_DSC1 =
-SYS:BUDREP                          VOUCHER ENTRY             PGM:
BRVFA';
-SET &SSN = '            ';
-SET &LNM = '                 ';
-SET &FNM = '            ';
-SET &MI  = '  ';
-SET &FINI = ' ';
-SET &INVMSG = '  ';
-*
-START
-CRTFORM
-"<D.&HEAD_DSC> "
-"<D.&HEAD_DSC1>"
-"                          EMPLOYEE DATA ENTRY      "
-" "
-" PLEASE ENTER THE FOLLOWING EMPLOYEE DATA:     "
-" "
-"              SOCIAL SECURITY NUMBER <T.&SSN> "
-"        OR"
-"              LAST NAME     <T.&LNM> "
-"              FIRST NAME    <T.&FNM> "
-"              INITIALS      <T.&MI> "
-" "
-"                        TYPE 'Q' TO EXIT ===> <T.&FINI> "
-" "
-"<D.&INVMSG> "
-IF &FINI EQ 'Q' GOTO ENDPROC1 ;
-IF &SSN NE ' ' GOTO START1 ;

-SET &INVMSG = IF &LNM EQ ' ' AND &FNM EQ ' ' AND &MI EQ ' ' THEN
-      AT LEAST EMPLOYEE LAST NAME MUST BE ENTERED' ELSE ' ' ;
-IF &LNM EQ ' ' AND &FNM EQ ' ' AND &MI EQ ' ' GOTO START ;
```

Figure 9-42   FOCEXEC for processing vouchers (1st step).

```
-* CHECK IF FIRST NAME WAS ENTERED. CHECK IF MASK ($) IS USED.
-* SET UP SCREENING CONDITION FOR FIRST NAME, IF ENTERED.

-SET &FNMX   = IF &FNM CONTAINS '$' THEN ''''  | &FNM || '*' || ''''
-              ELSE &FNM ;
-SET &FNMSCR = IF &FNM NE ' ' THEN 'IF FIRST_NAME EQ ' ELSE ' ';
-SET &MISCR  = IF &MI NE ' ' THEN 'IF MID_INIT EQ' ELSE ' ';

-* FIND EMPLOYEE IN PERSON FILE USING THE NAME ENTERED.

TABLE FILE PERSON
PRINT SSN ORGCD
    B_ADDRESS B_CITY B_STATE BZIP_CODE TITLE LOC COMP NORGCD
    BY LN BY FN BY MI BY SSN NOPRINT
IF LAST_NAME EQ '&LNM'
&FNMSCR &FNMX
&MISCR  &MI
ON TABLE HOLD
END
-RUN

-* IF AT LEAST 1 EMPLOYEE FOUND, BRANCH TO SKIPMSG1.

-IF &RECORDS NE 0 GOTO SKPMSG1 ;
-SET &INVMSG = 'THE EMPLOYEE NOT FOUND ...PLEASE RE-ENTER';
-GOTO START

-* FIND EMPLOYEE IN PERSON FILE USING SOCIAL SECURITY NUMBER.
-*
-START1

TABLE FILE PERSON
PRINT LN FN MI
    SSN ORGCD
    B_ADDRESS B_CITY B_STATE BZIP_CODE TITLE LOC COMP NORGCD
IF SSN EQ &SSN
ON TABLE SAVE AS SAVE2
END
-RUN
-IF &RECORDS EQ 1 GOTO STREAD ;
-SET &INVMSG = 'THE EMPLOYEE NOT FOUND ...PLEASE RE-ENTER';
-GOTO START
-*
-* EMPLOYEE FOUND, CHECK IF THERE ARE MORE THAN 1 WITH THE SAME
NAME.
-*
-SKPMSG1
```

Figure 9-42    (continued) FOCEXEC for processing vouchers (1st step).

```
-SET &OPT = '    ';
-IF &RECORDS EQ 1 GOTO SKPMSG2 ;

-* MORE THAN 1 EMPLOYEE WITH THE SAME LAST NAME
-* DISPLAY THEM AND LET OPERATOR SELECT ONE.

-SET &INVOPT = ' ';
DEFINE FILE HOLD
OPTION/I5 WITH SSN = OPTION + 1;
END
-STARTEMP
-CRTCLEAR
TABLE FILE HOLD
HEADING
"&HEAD_DSC "
"&HEAD_DSC1 "
"                       EMPLOYEE NAME SELECTION "
"OPTION                 FIRST           SOCIAL "
"NUMBER   LAST NAME     NAME       MI   SECURITY # "
"------   ----------------   ---------  --   ---------- "
PRINT OPTION AS '' E01 AS '' IN 9 E02 AS '' E03 AS '' E04 AS ''
END
-RUN
-TYPE &INVOPT
-TYPE PLEASE SELECT ONE OF THE ABOVE OPTIONS (TYPE 'Q' TO EXIT).
-READ SYSIN &OPT.A2.
-IF &OPT EQ 'Q' GOTO ENDPROC ;
-IF &OPT GE AND &OPT LE &RECORDS GOTO SKPMSG2 ;
-SET &INVOPT = '* INVALID OPTION ...' ;
-GOTO STARTEMP

-SKPMSG2
-SET &OPTMSG = IF &OPT EQ ' ' THEN ' '   ELSE 'IF OPTION EQ ';
-* RETRIEVE THE ONE SELECTED INTO A SAVE FILE.
TABLE FILE HOLD
PRINT E01 E02 E03 E04 E05
B_ADDRESS B_CITY B_STATE BZIP_CODE TITLE E11 E12 E13
&OPTMSG &OPT
ON TABLE SAVE AS SAVE2
END
-RUN

-* THIS PROGRAM USES FIDEL TO ACCEPT DATA ENTRY FOR AN EMPLOYEE
-* VOUCHER. EMPLOYEE INFO, SUCH AS ADDRESS, CITY, STATE, ETC.
-*           IS FIRST READ FROM THE PERSON FOCUS FILE .
-*           THE VALUES ARE READ FROM A SAVE FILE AS DIALOGUE
MANAGER
```

Figure 9-42    (continued) FOCEXEC for processing vouchers (1st step).

**Designing FOCUS Applications: Case Studies** 369

```
-*                 VARIABLES. IN THE MODIFY, THESE VALUES ARE DISPLAYED
-*                 USING FIDEL AND INCLUDED IN THE VOUCHER FILE.
-*
-STREAD
-SET &A = '                          ';
-SET &T = '                      ';
-SET &C = '                       ';
-SET &S = '    ';
-SET &Z = '           ';
-SET &L = '         ';
-SET &P1 = '      ';
-SET &O  = '          ';
-READ SAVE2 &FIL1.A28. &SSN.A9. &ORGCD.A8. &A &C &S &Z &T &L &P1 &O
-RUN
-SET &P = IF EDIT(&P1,'$$$9') EQ ' ' THEN EDIT(&P1,'999') ELSE &P1
;
-START2
-*
-* RETRIEVE LAST VOUCHER ID NUMBER FROM THE VOUCHER FOCUS FILE.
-SET &MY = EDIT(&MDY,'99$99');
-SET &MAXIDCD1 = 0;
-SET &MINSERNO = 0;
-SET &MAXSERNO = 0;

DEFINE FILE VOUCHER
IDCD1/A7 = EDIT(ID_CODE);
S_NOF/A7 = EDIT(SNOF);
S_NOT/A7 = EDIT(SNOT);
END
TABLE FILE VOUCHER
SUM MAX.IDCD1 MAX.S_NOF MAX.S_NOT
ON TABLE HOLD
END
-RUN
-IF &RECORDS EQ 0 GOTO NOIDCD ;
-READ HOLD &MAXIDCD1.A7. &FIL9.A1. &MINSERNO.A7. &FIL9.A1. &MAXSER-
NO.A7.
-RUN
-NOIDCD
-SET &MAXIDCD = IF &MAXIDCD1 LT &MINSERNO THEN &MINSERNO ELSE &MAX-
IDCD1;
-SET &MSG = IF &MAXIDCD GE &MAXSERNO THEN
- '     *** PLEASE ENTER A NEW BLOCK OF SERIAL NUMBERS ***' ELSE '
';
-IF &MSG = ' ' GOTO STARTVOUCH ;
-TYPE
-TYPE
```

**Figure 9-42** (continued) FOCEXEC for processing vouchers (1st step).

```
-TYPE
-TYPE &MSG
-CMS CP SLEEP 9 SEC
-EXIT
-*
-* AT THIS POINT, THE MODIFY PROCEDURE IS ABOUT TO START.
-* FIRST, READ IN ACCOUNT NUMBER CONTAINED IN THE HELPDATA FOCUS
FILE.
-*
-STARTVOUCH
DEFINE FILE HELPDATA
SDSC1/A3 = EDIT(SDSC,'999');
END
TABLE FILE HELPDATA
PRINT SDSC1
IF HDESC EQ 'ACCOUNT'
ON TABLE SAVE AS SAVE9
END
-RUN
-SET &ACCOUNT = '    ';
-READ &SAVE9 &ACCOUNT
-RUN

DEFINE FILE VOUCHER
END

-*START MODIFY

MODIFY FILE VOUCHER
-* CASE TOP
COMPUTE
SSN = '&SSN' ;
DBADDR/A24 = '&A' ;
DCITY/A20  = '&C' ;
DSTATE/A2  = '&S' ;
DZIP/A5    = '&Z' ;
DTTL/A18   = '&T' ;
IDCD = 0;
MAXIDCD/I7 = &MAXIDCD ;
CYMD/I6    = &YMD ;
DACCT/A3   = '&ACCOUNT' ;
GOTO MOD1

CASE MOD1
MATCH SSN
ON MATCH GOTO MOD2
```

Figure 9-42    (continued) FOCEXEC for processing vouchers (1st step).

```
ON NOMATCH INCLUDE
ENDCASE

CASE MOD2
MATCH SSN
ON MATCH COMPUTE
IDCD/I7  = MAXIDCD + 1;
DLV/A2   = D.LV ;
DBCD/A4  = D.BCD ;
DLNM/A17 = D.LN ;
.....
```

**Figure 9-42** (continued) FOCEXEC for processing vouchers (1st step).

1. Several variables &HEAD_DSC and &HEAD_DSC1 contain headings which are displayed in the -CRTFORM, and also in the display of employees who have the same last name.
2. If a first name has been entered, then a screening condition is created using the variable &FNMSCR; similarly for the middle initial. These screening conditions are used in the TABLE request which tries to find the name in the PERSON FOCUS file. If no employee is found (&RECORDS EQ 0), a message is set in variable &INVMSG, and displayed on the CRTFORM.
3. If only one employee record is found with the given last name or SSN, the process extracts the address, city, state, etc. and stores it in a SAVE file, SAVE2. Using -READ, values from the SAVE file are read into the variables &SSN, &A, &C, &S, etc. Note that the format length of the variables &A, &S, etc. are determined using a SET statement such as:

   ```
   -SET &S = '   ' ;
   ```

   Using COMPUTE in the MODIFY, these values are assigned to temporary fields and displayed on the first FIDEL screen.

   If more than one employee is found, they are displayed to the operator so that one may be selected. The field OPTION is defined to contain sequential numbers. (1, 2, 3, ...) which facilitates the operator's selection.
4. The last voucher number is retrieved from the VOUCHER file using the direct operation MAX. I.e.,

```
TABLE FILE VOUCHER
SUM MAX.IDCD1 MAX.S_NOF MAX.S_NOT
ON TABLE HOLD
END
```

The alphanumeric value is read from the HOLD file using READ. (Note that integer or other numeric formats cannot be read from HOLD files using READ.) Note: The fields S_NOF and S_NOT represent a range for the block of voucher numbers.

The FOCUS file HELPDATA contains account numbers for various departments. The account number is read as the variable &ACCOUNT from a SAVE file. This is a useful technique if each department has a different account code.

# Appendix

## Using FOCUS in the Operating Systems: VM/CMS, MVS/TSO, PC/DOS, VAX/VMS

All of the FOCUS features which have been presented in this book are available in each operating environment. There are differences in setting up FOCUS applications to run in the different envirnoments. These differences are due mostly to:

1. How files are identified in different environments.
2. How FOCEXECS are stored and organized.
3. How operating system commands are issued from FOCEXECS.
4. How space and CPU resources are used by FOCUS.
5. Internal considerations — such as accessing cross-reference files, and pointer resolution.

In this section, we shall present the terminology which is relevant to each operating system, and discuss several examples of setting up applications in each environment. The details of each operating environment will not be described here — and you should refer to the FOCUS users manual available for each environment to obtain specific information. We assume that you are familiar with the basic requirements of your particular operating system.

## Operating FOCUS Under VM/CMS

### Setting Up the Environment

The FOCUS system is installed by the mainframe operations group on a virtual disk. All users ids may link to this disk in order to access FOCUS. All FOCUS system files are included on the FOCUS disk — except for the library of user-written subroutines which is accessed by issuing the CMS command:

```
GLOBAL TXTLIB FUSELIB
```

To send output to a file when the OFFLINE command is in use, assign the file to DDNAME OFFLINE. This is done using a FILEDEF statement. First, you should close the current offline. For example,

```
OFFLINE CLOSE
-CMS FILEDEF OFFLINE DISK MAIL LISTING A (RECFM F
LRECL 132
```

This statement sends the output to the file MAIL LISTING on the A disk. It has a fixed record format and a record length of 132 bytes. The record length of CMS offline files may not exceed 133 bytes.

FOCUS will initially allocate the OFFLINE to the local printer when the FOCUS session starts. Therefore, any reports sent to OFFLINE will be sent to the local printer.

In order to issue CMS operating system commands from within dialogue manager, you may use the -CMS command. Any statement in a FOCEXEC having a -CMS at the start is executed directly within dialogue manager. You may check if the operating system command executed properly by checking the system variable &RETCODE. If there is no error, the value of &RETCODE is returned as zero.

When executing a FOCEXEC from FOCUS, you can issue an interrupt to stop execution of some commands. To issue an interrupt, type either KT, KX, RT, or ? and press enter. The command KX causes the FOCUS execution to halt, and returns to the FOCUS command level. The command KT causes all output to be suppressed on the screen, but the command will continue to execute. The command RT is used after the KT command to resume display of output on the screen. The

## Using FOCUS in the Operating Systems: VM/CMS, MVS/TSO, PC/DOS, VAX/VMS

command ? displays statistics on reports or file maintenance procedures that FOCUS has processed.

Within a FOCEXEC, all messages and output to the screen may be suppressed using the CMS command:

```
-CMS SET CMSTYPE HT
```

To resume the display of messages, use:

```
-CMS SET CMSTYPE RT
```

Many other CMS commands may be issued within a FOCEXEC (or within the FOCUS environment). For example, to erase files (such as temporary HOLD or SAVE files), from a FOCEXEC, use the command

```
-CMS ERASE filename filetype filemode
```

To issue a CMS command within the FOCUS environment, use the CMS prefix. For example, to edit a FOCEXEC using XEDIT, you may issue the command

```
CMS XEDIT filename FOCEXEC A
```

The CMS command COPY should not be issued within a FOCEXEC, or within native FOCUS — it might cause some addressing problems when other FOCUS procedures are executed.

FOCUS issues its own FILEDEFS for work space required for sorting and retrieving records. Normally, it will write work files to the A disk, unless the SET TEMP parameter has been set to another filemode (or unless there is more available space on another writeable disk which has been linked — see example 8 in the last chapter).

### FOCUS Databases and MASTER Descriptions

FOCUS files have a filename that matches the filename of its MASTER file description, and a filetype of FOCUS. The FOCUS file, as well as the MASTER file, may reside on the A disk or on any virtual disk which is linked to your id. If the MASTER file resides on more than one virtual disk, then the version on the lowest letter disk will be used. If two FOCUS files with the same name reside on more than one disk, then the one on the A disk will be used in FOCUS commands — unless overridden with a USE statement.

The USE command indicates the names and locations of FOCUS databases. See the last chapter for a detailed discussion of the command. For example, if the SALES FOCUS file is on the C disk, and it is to be used in a FOCEXEC, the following USE command should be issued from within native FOCUS or from within the FOCEXEC:

```
USE
PERSON FOCUS C
END
```

The FOCUS file may also have a name different from the MASTER file. In that case, issue the USE command to associate the filename with the description name. For example, to read the CMS file SALES001 FOCUS A described by the MASTER description SALES, enter the USE command:

```
USE
SALES001 FOCUS A AS SALES
END
```

FOCUS also permits files to have different MASTER descriptions — where two or more alphanumeric fields are combined into one field. This feature is called the "alternate MASTER" technique — because several MASTERS may be used with a single FOCUS file (depending on the application).

### External Files

There are several kinds of external files (or sequential files) which are used for various purposes:

1. External files which are read by FOCUS TABLE commands for reporting purposes.
2. HOLD and SAVE files which are extracted from other files.
3. LOG files which are created for logging transactions in a MODIFY procedure.
4. DECODE files which contain decoded pairs of data values.

5. Transaction files which contain FIXFORM or FREEFORM records used as input to MODIFY procedures.
6. Files from other kinds of database systems — such as QSAM, ISAM, VSAM, IMS, IDMS, ADABAS, TOTAL, S2K, M204, and SQL. FOCUS is able to retrieve records from these files. See the FOCUS manual Chapter 3 section 7 for describing these files to FOCUS.

External files must be defined to the operating system using FILEDEF statements. These statements may appear in a FOCEXEC, or within a CMS exec. They may also be issued within the FOCUS or CMS environment before executing a FOCEXEC. You must issue a FILEDEF to identify external files to FOCUS. However, in some cases, you can let FOCUS issue default FILEDEF statements for data files which have a record length of 80 and a fixed record format. Furthermore, FOCUS will automatically issue a FILEDEF after creating a HOLD or SAVE file. The syntax for a FILEDEF is:

```
FILEDEF ddname DISK fn ft fm (LRECL _ RECFM _
```

The blocksize is sometimes added as a parameter if the records are blocked at some factor. Once a FILEDEF has been issued for a file, it remains in effect until cleared or the file is erased. The following is used to clear all FILEDEFS:

```
FILEDEF * CLEAR
```

A list of all the active FILEDEFS may be obtained from the FOCUS environment by issuing the command:

```
? FILEDEF
```

**Space Requirements**

In CMS, every user id is allocated an amount of space which may be used for FOCUS files, data files, programs, external files, report files, work files, etc. By issuing the CMS command Q DISK, you can view the total amount of space allocated to your id, the amount which is used, and the amount which is still available. Since FOCUS requires work space for various activities such as sorting records, it may be necessary to allocate TEMP SPACE for running procedures on large files. Considerations on using TEMP space with FOCUS have been discussed in the last chapter.

FOCUS supplies a utility for estimating the amount of space which will be required for a FOCUS file. This program, called CALCFILE, is discussed in separate IBI documentation. In general, the following formula is useful for converting blocks into bytes of storage.

150 BLOCKS = 1 CYLINDER
4096 BYTES = 1 BLOCK

or, approximately 600,000 BYTES are in each cylinder. Therefore, if your id has been allocated a total of 10 cylinders, it will store a total of 6 million bytes.

There are limitations on the size of a FOCUS file. A FOCUS file may not require more than 256 megabytes of storage, or be larger than one VM disk pack. Also, a FOCUS file which is cross-referenced or joined to another file should not exceed 32K FOCUS pages. (The number of pages can be determined using the command ? FILE.) In order to avoid a file getting too large, you may use the LOCATION feature to relocate one of the segments on another disk, or in another file. (see the FOCUS manual Chapter 4 section 5.)

## CMS EXECS

It is often useful to execute various FOCUS procedures by invoking them from an EXEC. Currently, the exec language which is supported by IBM for its mainframe operating systems is called REXX. Its predecessors, EXEC and EXEC 2, are still very much in use — and perhaps more popular among FOCUS users. EXECS can be used for a number of purposes (See example 8 in the last chapter for a detailed treatement of EXECS):

1. EXECS permit the user to run FOCUS systems directly from CMS — so that they do not have to enter the FOCUS environment to start the process.
2. EXECS are used to run "batch" procedures — where more than one type of program makes up one procedure. For example, one

EXEC can execute several FORTRAN programs, and then execute several FOCEXECS. A batch EXEC can also be set up to start execution when a data file is received, or at a certain time each day.
3. EXECS are sometimes used to preprocess data files before using them as transaction files for MODIFY procedures. By sorting large files first, reports may be quickly created in FOCUS using the TABLEF command — since no further sorting of records is required.
4. EXECS are used when your CMS id must obtain read or write access to other ids. This is accomplished using the CP LINK command.

An example of an EXEC is shown below (written in EXEC 2). The user is prompted to enter the year and month of the report. This value is stacked as a value passed to the SALESREP FOCEXEC (assume that the SALESREP FOCEXEC requires a value for the dialogue manager variable &YYMM).

```
&TRACE OFF
&TYPE ENTER THE DATE FOR THE SALES REPORT (YYMM)
&READ VARS &YM
&STACK EXEC SALEREP
&STACK &YM
EXEC FOCUS
&IF &RETCODE = 99 &GOTO -EXIT

RENAME SALESREP OUTPUT A SALESREP &YM A
-EXIT
&EXIT
```

In this EXEC, after control passes to FOCUS, it is necessary to stack commands and data to FOCUS — since FOCUS will expect to read them from the program stack. (Any number of FOCEXECS may be executed in this way.) Also, the FOCEXEC may pass to the EXEC a special return code if it did not execute properly. This is done within the SALESREP FOCEXEC with the -QUIT FOCUS command. See the FOCUS Manual Chapter 6 section 2.5.4. If the FOCEXEC does not execute successfully, a return code of 99 is passed to the EXEC, and stored in the variable &RETCODE.

## Rebuilding FOCUS Files

The REBUILD command allows you to change the layout of a FOCUS file, or compress space within a file, after the file has been created. Examples of when the REBUILD command is appropriate are:

1. If transaction records have been loaded into a FOCUS file in a disorganized manner — where the records have not been presorted in the same order determined by the key fields in each segment.
2. If many segment instances have been deleted from the FOCUS file, rebuilding the file may be necessary to compress the FOCUS pages.
3. If the MASTER file description is changed to accommodate additional fields, or to remove fields.
4. If fields should be indexed.
5. If a large number of records must be removed from the file — based on simple screening conditions.

The process of using the REBUILD/REORG command is described in the FOCUS manual Chapter 12 section 7. In CMS, you usually do not have to allocate work space prior to using the REBUILD command. FOCUS automatically creates a sequential output file containing the dumped records — it is allocated as REBUILD FOCTEMP x4, where "x" is a temporary disk letter. You may have to attach temporary space if there is not enough on your A disk. You may also want to mount a scratch tape for work space during the DUMP phase (of the REORG command).

Instead of using the FOCUS sorting routine, you may improve the speed of performing a REBUILD by using the CMS package SYNCSORT. (See example 8 in the last chapter.) This is done by referring to SORTLIB in a CMS GLOBAL command.

## Operating FOCUS Under MVS/TSO

### Setting Up the Environment

There are two ways to execute FOCUS programs in the MVS/TSO environment:

1. From the native FOCUS environment, using the regular online 'execute' command.
2. From TSO batch operation, where the MVS user can initiate jobs directly, or submit them for batch processing using the TSO SUBMIT command.

Before executing any FOCUS procedure, your TSO logon procedure should allocate the FOCUS load module (residing in the partitioned dataset FOCLIB.LOAD) to the DDNAME STEPLIB, and then enter FOCUS. Alternatively, you may enter the CALL from the TSO command line, or through a CLIST. A convenient way of allocating frequently used datasets is in the TSO logon procedure. For example,

```
//TSOLOGIN EXEC PGM = IKJXT01
/*
//STEPLIB DD DSN=FOCUS.FOCLIB.LOAD,DISP=SHR
//ERRORS DD DSN=FOCUS.ERRORS.DATA,DISP=SHR
//USERLIB DD DSN=FOCUS.FUSELIB.LOAD,DISP=SHR
//OFFLINE DD SYSOUT=A
/* ... OTHER TSO LOGON DATASETS FOLLOW */
```

This is usually coded by a systems programmer involved in TSO operations. You do not have to allocate all FOCUS-related files prior to using them, because FOCUS will dynamically allocate certain files. However, if FOCUS does not allocate enough space for these files, you may allocate them yourself using CLISTS. The permanent files which may be allocated by FOCUS or in your own CLISTS are:

1. FOCUS databases.
2. MASTER file descriptions.
3. FOCEXE files.
4. ERRORS files (containing the text of error messages).
5. Input data files.

In addition, there are temporary datasets which may be allocated in the same way. These are HOLD, SAVE, and SAVB files; FOCUS work files like FOCSORT, FOCSTACK; OFFLINE, SYSIN, and SYSPRINT files. There are four files which are required by FOCUS whether executing online or in batch. These are:

**382** The Database Experts' Guide to FOCUS

1. ERRORS — contains the text of error messages.
2. SYSPRINT — the destination of all FOCUS output. In batch, this is usually a SYSOUT dataset. All output is sent here unless you use the FOCUS OFFLINE command to send output to an offline printer or file.
3. SYSIN — the input file for FOCUS commands. It may be a dataset, the card input stream, or the terminal.
4. OFFLINE — the default OFFLINE file is the terminal, for on-line programs; it is the printer for batch jobs. You may reallocate it within a FOCEXEC after issuing OFFLINE CLOSE.

The following is an example of JCL for a batch run:

```
//FOCUS    EXEC PGM = FOCUS
//STEPLIB  DD DSN=FOCUS.FOCLIB.LOAD,DISP=SHR
//ERRORS   DD DSN=FOCUS.ERRORS.DATA,DISP=SHR
//SYSPRINT DD SYSOUT=*
//OFFLINE  DD SYSOUT=*
//MASTER   DD DSN=MASTER.FILES,DISP=SHR
//FOCEXEC  DD DSN=FOCEXEC.FILES,DISP=SHR

//SALES    DD DSN=SALES.FOCUS,DISP=SHR
//SYSIN    DD *
.....
..... FOCUS commands
.....
/*
```

The library of user-written subroutines should be allocated as a USERLIB. For example,

```
ALLOC F(USERLIB) DA(FUSELIB.DATA) SHR
```

Any other arbitrary library of user routines is also allocated as USERLIB:

```
ALLOC F(USERLIB) DA(USER.PROG.DATA) SHR
```

Both libraries may be referred together with:

```
ALLOC F(USERLIB) DA(FUSELIB.DATA USER.PROG.DATA) SHR
```

## Issuing TSO Commands From Within FOCUS

TSO commands can be issued from within FOCUS or from within FOCEXECS. This capability applies only to online FOCUS sessions. FOCUS ignores TSO commands when running in batch mode. In batch mode, you must add JCL statements to replace any TSO allocate statements which may be embedded in a FOCUS procedure. An example of an allocate statement within a FOCEXEC is:

```
TSO ALLOCATE F(SAVE10) SPACE(5 5) TRACKS
```

This allocates five primary tracks and five secondary tracks to the filename SAVE10 — a SAVE file.

There are four TSO commands which are commonly used within the FOCUS environment. The four commands are TSO COPY, TSO LIST, TSO LISTDS, and TSO RENAME. From within FOCUS, you may refer to datasets either by actual dataset names or by DDNAMES. For example, to rename the file, SALES10.FOCUS (allocated as DDNAME SALES), to dataset name SALES20.FOCUS, enter:

```
TSO RENAME SALES SALES20.FOCUS
```

or, alternatively,

```
TSO RENAME SALES10.FOCUS SALES20.FOCUS
```

You may also refer to a member of a PARTITIONED DATASET (PDS) in any TSO command — by including the member name within parentheses after the DDNAME of the PDS. You may refer to the file by its DDNAME or actual name. This includes members of PDS for MASTER files and FOCEXECS. Note that in order to save a temporary dataset, you must use COPY, since RENAME does not catalog a temporary dataset.

When SAVE or HOLD files are created, they usually will not be retained after the session is over. Typical allocations for HOLD and SAVE files are:

```
ALLOC F(HOLD) SP(20 10) TRACKS
```

or, for batch:

```
//HOLD DD UNIT=SYSDA, SPACE=(TRK,(20,10))
ALLOC F(HOLDMAST) SP(1 1) TRACKS DIR(1)
ALLOC F(SAVE) SP(5 5) TRACKS
```

HOLDMAST files contain temporary MASTER files for HOLD files specified with (HOLD AS holdname). FOCUS will automatically create the member MASTER files when the HOLD file is created. If not allocated by you, FOCUS will automatically allocate HOLDMAST as a temporary dataset with five primary and five secondary tracks.

There are several ways to retain HOLD, HOLDMAST, and SAVE files. The TSO COPY command will keep the file it is copied to. This is useful for SAVE, HOLD, and SAVB files. Another way is to allocate the DDNAME with the name of a PDS, and assign a disposition (DISP). This is useful for HOLDMAST files. In some installations, you may also have to catalog the file to a permanent volume. Note: The command

```
? TSO DDNAME
```

lists all the currently allocated files and their dataset names. It can be issued from FOCUS to view the names of HOLD files, SAVE files, FOCUS files, MASTER files, OFFLINE files, etc. Also, the command

```
? TSO DDNAME ddname
```

is used to list the attributes of particular filenames.

Because of the option to allocate files as temporary or permanent datasets, you need to carefully consider how various SAVE and HOLD files are to be used in TSO. This does not need to be carefully planned in VM/CMS.

### Interrupting FOCUS Programs

To signal an interrupt of any FOCUS command, press one of the following function keys: PA1 or ATTN. FOCUS will issue the message:

```
FOCUS INTERRUPTED..ENTER KX,KT,RT, OR ?
```

The effect of each of these is the same as in VM/CMS.

KX — kill execution, return to native FOCUS.
KT — kill display of output to the terminal.
RT — resume display of output to the terminal.
? — display run-time statistics.

## FOCUS Databases, MASTER Descriptions, and FOCEXECS

You can execute a FOCEXEC by typing:

```
EXEC filename
```

where filename is the name of the procedure to be executed — and corresponds to the member name in a partitioned dataset (PDS) whose DDNAME is FOCEXEC. You may use TED to create FOCEXECS, or alternatively use the SPF editor. DDNAME FOCEXEC should be given the following DCB attributes: RECFM=FB, LRECL=80, BLKSIZE=nxLRECL. An example of an allocation for FOCEXEC is:

```
ALLOC F(FOCEXEC) DA(PRO.FOCUS.FOCEXEC) SHR
```

FOCEXECS may also be stored as sequential files — with a DDNAME that matches the name of the procedure. FOCUS will check for a sequential file, if the name of the procedure is not found in the FOCEXEC PDS. This is useful when a program is undergoing many changes. If stored as a member of a PDS, the PDS will need to be compressed often — since the FOCEXEC is edited often. A typical allocation of a sequential file used as a FOCEXEC is:

```
ALLOC F(SALESREP) DA(SALES.FOCEXEC.DATA) SHR
```

However, at the writing of this book, there are certain restrictions on using sequential files as FOCEXECS — they should not contain any -RUN statements, or any dialogue manager statements because unpredictable results may occur.

FOCUS files are allocated to a DDNAME that matches the member name of the MASTER file located in a PDS for MASTER. There are two types of MASTER files: permanent MASTER files allocated to

DDNAME MASTER, and temporary ones allocated to DDNAME HOLDMAST. Typical TSO allocations for a MASTER file are:

```
ALLOC F(MASTER) DA(PROD.FOCUS.MASTER) SHR
```

The PDS members must correspond to the FOCUS file names. MASTER file descriptions may created using TED or SPF editors. For example, if the database's MASTER description has the member name SALES, then the FOCUS file will be allocated to the DDNAME SALES. You may issue the USE command to change the default FOCUS file DDNAME. The syntax of the USE command is:

```
USE
DDNAME AS filename
END
```

where,

DDNAME is the DDNAME that the file is allocated to
filename is the name of the MASTER file description.

For example, to use a FOCUS file allocated to DDNAME SALES10 and described by MASTER file SALES, enter the USE command:

```
USE
SALES10 AS SALES
END
```

TSO FOCUS also supports other features in the USE command, such as simultaneous users, protecting files, concatenating databases.

FOCUS files should be allocated with a DISP = SHR. FOCUS automatically protects the file from being modified by two different users. However, multiple users may have the database open for read-only purposes at the same time. If a TSO user tries to modify a FOCUS file currently being modified by another user, the result is a message stating that the file is being modified — and the MODIFY routine ends.

FOCUS files are formatted as 4096-byte pages. FOCUS uses primary space until it is exhausted, and then extends the size of the file based on the secondary allocations. (Up to 15 secondary allocation

# Using FOCUS in the Operating Systems: VM/CMS, MVS/TSO, PC/DOS, VAX/VMS

extensions may be requested.) Usually, the space is requested in cylinders. Once the file is allocated, the space requirement is not needed. An example of an allocation for a FOCUS file is:

ALLOC F(PERSON) DA(PERSON.FOCUS) SHR

TSO FOCUS requires that you must first initialize a FOCUS file by issuing a CREATE command, before loading data into it. The syntax is

CREATE FILE filename

If the file already exists (and has been allocated), FOCUS issues a warning message and asks for approval to erase any existing data in the file. For example, in order to create the MAIL FOCUS file, with description in the MAIL MASTER, you may use:

TSO ALLOC F(MAIL) DA(MAIL.FOCUS) NEW SPACE(5,5) TRACKS
CREATE FILE MAIL

FOCUS responds with:

NEW FILE MAIL ON 10/01/87 AT 12:01:30

When allocating files for production purposes, the dataset should have a prefix in front of its name indicating that it is a production file. For example, PRO.MAIL.FOCUS may identify the file as a production file — while TST.MAIL.FOCUS may identify it as a test file. (This convention is also useful for PDS's containing MASTERS, FOCEXECS, etc.)

## Using CLISTS

A typical way to start the main menu of a FOCUS application is to execute a CLIST, which allocates the files and resources of the FOCUS session, and which invokes the FOCLIB.LOAD to start FOCUS and execute the PROFILE FOCEXEC. The CLIST will normally allocate the FOCUS files, the MASTER, the FOCEXECS, SYSIN, SYSPRINT, OFFLINE, and SAVE. The PROFILE FOCEXEC is automatically executed when FOCUS is entered — and it may execute the "main menu" of the application. You may locate the PROFILE FOCEXEC in the FOCEXEC PDS, or as a separate file with DDNAME PROFILE. An example of a CLIST to run a menu in the MAIL0 FOCEXEC is:

```
FREEALL
ALLOC F(MASTER) DA(PRO.FOCUS.MASTER) SHR
ALLOC F(FOCEXEC) DA(PRO.FOCUS.FOCEXEC) SHR
ALLOC F(SAVE) SP(5 5) TRACKS
ALLOC F(MAILSVE1) SP(5 5) TRACKS
ALLOC F(SYSIN) DA(*)
ALLOC F(SYSPRINT) DA(*)
ALLOC F(OFFLINE) SP(10 5) TRACKS
ALLOC F(MAIL) DA(PRO.MAIL.FOCUS) SHR
ALLOC F(REGN) DA(PRO.REGN.FOCUS) SHR
/* FOCUS PROFILE TO START MAIN MENU ***
ALLOC F(PROFILE) DA(PRO.FOCUS.FOCEXEC(MAILPROF)) SHR
CALL 'PRO.FOCLIB.LOAD(FOCUS)'
```

**Space Requirements**

The number of available pages for storing FOCUS files can be determined by the formula:

pages avail = total blocks — focus pages.

where,

total blocks = blocks per track X total tracks
focus pages = number of 4096 byte records indicated by the command ? TSO DDNAME ddname.

For fixed-block datasets, use the formula:

available blocks = total blocks — blocks written.

where,

blocks written = no. of records/records per block
records per block = blksize/lrecl

## REBUILD and REORG

FOCUS automatically allocates a work file as a dataset when you execute the REBUILD command. The DDNAME is REBUILD. Also, if the INDEX option is used, a set of SORT files must be allocated: SORTIN, SORTOUT, SYSOUT, SORTWK01 — 06, SORTLIB. SORTIN and SORTOUT may be allocated to disk or to tape.

## FOCUS in the VAX/VMS Environment

### Setting Up the Environment

The VAX environment is a relatively new one for FOCUS. It is structured in a way which is similar to PC/DOS FOCUS. All FOCUS features are available in the VAX environment — with very few differences from FOCUS on IBM mainframes. Information Builders Inc. (IBI) makes available a separate user's manual for VAX FOCUS.

There are several differences in features available on VAX and VM/CMS which should be noted:

1. The VAX represents characters and numbers in ASCII format, while the IBM uses EBCDIC format. This has a slight effect on several FOCUS techniques.
2. The VAX user id is structured very differently from the IBM mainframe user id. While the IBM user has access to files on his virtual disk, and on disks he is linked to, the VAX user has access to files in his directories, and on other users' directories which give him access.
3. The VAX environment does not use EXEC language to invoke batch procedures, or to preprocess files before invoking FOCUS. Operating system commands, and file manipulation can be accommodated in procedures called DCLs. The DCLs do not offer the same range of programming flexibility offered by EXECS.
4. The IBM FOCUS user may execute FOCEXECS which are located on other user ids, by linking to the id. The VAX FOCUS user must specify a "path" to other ids using the VAX DEFINE command. This command may be invoked before entering FOCUS. It makes it possible for many users to report from and

maintain data in files from several directories without needing to issue FILEDEF or USE commands. This is similar to the PATH command used in PC/DOS.

FOCUS may be installed on the VAX "system" directory, where all VAX users will have access to it. Alternatively, it may be installed in other ways so that only some users have access to it. This depends on your installation procedures.

FOCUS uses work files for sorting and retrieving records. These work files are written to the current directory, unless the TEMPDIR parameter has been set to a different directory using the command:

```
SET TEMPDIR = directory
```

VAX FOCUS allows you to set the CRT terminal to a 132-character mode in order to view report output which exceeds 80 characters in width. This is done by issuing the command:

```
SET WIDTH = 132
```

To set the CRT to the regular 80-character mode use:

```
SET WIDTH = 80
```

You may send reports to an OFFLINE file, by closing the OFFLINE and reallocate it using the VMS FILEDEF command (within a FOCEXEC):

```
OFFLINE CLOSE
-VMS FILEDEF OFFLINE DISK filename
```

In some installations, the OFFLINE file will not get overwritten the next time a report is written to it. Instead, the report output will be appended to the end of the file. In that case, you should erase the file from the directory before the report is created. This may be done within your FOCEXEC using the DELETE command. For example,

### Using FOCUS in the Operating Systems: VM/CMS, MVS/TSO, PC/DOS, VAX/VMS

```
-VMS DELETE SALESREP.LIS;*
```

Notice that all VMS operating system commands start with VMS. Depending on your installation, your VAX id may or may not be connected to a local printer. This can be done using the DEFINE command before entering FOCUS. If the printer is connected, you may direct output to it using the FOCUS command:

```
SET PRINT = LOCAL
```

To view the output online, use

```
SET PRINT = ONLINE
```

While in a FOCUS session, you may exit to VMS without interrupting your FOCUS session, by entering the command VMS. To return to your FOCUS session, type RET.

FOCUS user-written subroutines are provided in the file

```
FUSELIB.EXE
```

This file may be located in a central directory for everyone to access, or it may be located in a local directory. Also, you may add your own user-written routines to this library by following the instructions in the FOCUS VAX Installation Guide. To access the FUSELIB, a DEFINE command may be issued before entering FOCUS. For example:

```
DEFINE FUSELIB DISK10:[MTGP01.SOURCE]FUSELIB.EXE
```

There are several ways to configure the editor available to VMS users. The VMS editor may be used as a full-screen editor, or as a line editor. This depends on how your VMS id has been set up. Usually, the FOCUS editor TED is a good way to edit all your VMS files — since it is the same as TED on the IBM mainframe.

When executing a FOCEXEC from FOCUS, you can issue an interrupt to stop execution of some commands. The standard VMS interrupt key is CTRL-Y or CTRL-C. This interrupt is trapped by FOCUS. Then you may issue either KT, KX, RT, or ?. The command KX causes the FOCUS execution to halt, and returns to the FOCUS command level. The command KT causes all output to be suppressed on the screen, but the command will continue to execute. The command RT is used after the KT command to resume display of output on the screen. The command ? displays statistics on reports or file maintenance procedures that FOCUS has processed.

**FOCUS Databases, FOCEXECS, and MASTER Descriptions**

The following extensions are used in VMS to identify FOCUS-related files:

FEX: FOCEXEC procedures
FOC: FOCUS files
MAS: MASTER file descriptions
FTM: Extract files, such as HOLD or SAVE files

For example, the command

```
TABLE FILE PERSON
```

will cause FOCUS to search for a MASTER description called PERSON.MAS. The database file is assumed to be called PERSON.FOC (unless a USE has been issued).

Many users will need to access FOCUS files, and FOCEXECS which are located on other user directories. VAX FOCUS provides four logical names which may be assigned to any four directories: FOC$DIR1, FOC$DIR2, FOC$DIR3, FOC$DIR4. When FOCUS searches for a FOCUS file, MASTER file, or FOCEXEC file, it will search the current user directory first, then search the directories assigned to the above four logical names, followed last by the IBI$FOCUS directory. These are assigned before entering FOCUS, using a DEFINE command. For example,

```
DEFINE FOC$DIR1 DISK10:[MTGP01.SALES]
```

The above assignment indicates that FOCUS should search the directory DISK10:[MTGP01.SALES] when searching for files. You do not need to issue a FILEDEF or USE command to access FOCUS files in directories assigned in this way. However, FILEDEFS and USE commands may be issued to override this search sequence or to specify additional files.

Generally, the MASTER file description and the FOCUS file reside on the same directory, but this is not necessary. The MASTER files may be placed in a separate directory, so that many users may share the same set of MASTER files. This directory may be defined as one of the four logical FOCUS directories to be searched. Similarly, FOCEXECS may be located on the user's directory, or on another directory. If placed on another directory, this directory can be assigned as one of the FOC$DIR directories. The FOCUS directory IBI$FOCUS is searched last of all. FOCEXECS (like MASTER files) should not contain lines which exceed 80 characters in length. When entering a FOCUS session, FOCUS will first execute the FOCEXEC named PROFILE.FEX — if it has been created. This FOCEXEC is useful for starting main menus, setting up FOCUS DEFINE commands, selecting passwords, etc. FOCUS searches only the user default directory for PROFILE.FEX.

FOCUS files can also be located on other directories. They may be identified in a user's session:

1. By assigning the directory as a FOC$DIR directory.
2. By specifying the database with a USE command.

VAX FOCUS also allows a database to be accessed by more than one user via the Simultaneous Users feature. (Refer to the Simultaneous Users reference guide for VAX.)

**The USE Command**

FOCUS files may be located on the user's default directory, or on other directories. If on other directories, they will be located if the directory has been DEFINED as a FOC$DIR directory. Alternatively, they can be accessed in the user's FOCUS session if the USE command is issued.

The USE command specifies the names and locations of FOCUS files. This command is usually intended to specify files:

1. Which are not located on directories defined as FOC$DIR directories.
2. Which have a non-standard name or filetype.

3. Which should be protected as read-only files.
4. Which need to be concatenated to other FOCUS files.
5. Whose filename does not correspond with the name of its MASTER file.
6. Which are used in the simultaneous users mode.

The syntax of the USE command is:

```
USE [ADD]
filename [READ] [AS mastername]
  [NEW]
END
```

where:

filename is the VMS file id of the FOCUS file. (filename.filetype)
mastername is the FOCUS MASTER file description name.

You can specify several FOCUS files in one USE command, each with different parameters. For example:

```
USE
PERSON.FOC
DEPT1.FOC AS DEPT
ACCOUNT.FOC ON MULTIDS
END
```

The USE command may also refer to the node, id, and directory where the FOCUS file is located. For example,

```
USE
[MTGP05.MAIL]MAIL.FOC
[MTGP05.MAIL]REGION.FOC
END
```

A list of all USE commands which are in effect during your FOCUS session is obtained by entering:

```
? USE
```

FOCUS will search for databases having the filetype of FOC. To instruct FOCUS to search for databases having different filetypes, issue the USE command. For example:

```
USE
PERSON.NEW
END
```

This indicates that the PERSON.NEW file is a FOCUS file whose MASTER is the PERSON.MAS file. Note that by changing the default filetype, as above, all other FOCUS files are assumed to have the same filetype (.NEW). If you need a FOCUS file with filetype FOC, then add it to the USE command. For example:

```
USE
PERSON.NEW
DEPT.FOC
END
```

The first file in the list determines the default filetype of other FOCUS files which may be referenced in your FOCUS session.

### External Files

FOCUS procedures sometimes refer to external files when reporting or maintaining FOCUS files. If the external file has a MASTER description which describe the fields on the records of the file, then FOCUS will be able to use reporting commands to retrieve records and create reports. External files are also used in the following:

1. LOGGING transactions in a MODIFY procedure.
2. TYPING records in a MODIFY procedure.
3. Using -WRITE, -READ, to write records or read records.
4. As DECODE files.
5. As HOLD and SAVE files.
6. As input files to MODIFY procedures.

In all cases, the external file must be identified to FOCUS using a FILEDEF. The only exceptions are when FOCUS issues its own

FILEDEF, or if the filetype is .DAT. The syntax for the FILEDEF is (within a FOCEXEC):

```
-VMS FILEDEF ddname DISK filename [APPEND]
```

where:

> ddname is the ddname which you want to identify the file.
> filename is the VMS filename (including directory info.).

> APPEND appends records to the end of the file. Otherwise, FOCUS writes over the file.
> FOCUS will issue its own FILEDEF when HOLD or SAVE files are created; otherwise, you should issue them. Some examples of the FILEDEF command are:

```
-VMS FILEDEF SAVE DISK ACCOUNT.DAT
```

This enables a TABLE request to save a report extract in the file ACCOUNT.DAT.

```
-VMS FILEDEF OFFLINE DISK MAIL.LIS
```

This assigns the OFFLINE file to the file MAIL.LIS — to which report output will be written.

```
-VMS FILEDEF MAILLOG DISK MAILLOG.DAT
```

This enables the MAILLOG.DAT file to be assigned to the ddname MAILLOG. This file may be used for LOGGING transactions, TYPING records, etc.

In order to display the current ddnames assigned for various files, enter:

```
? FILEDEF
```

Note: In some installations the [APPEND] option, which allows data to be appended to a file, instead of overwriting it, does not work properly. In this case, you may use the VMS COPY command (with APPEND) to accomplish the same thing. For example, if the file

## Using FOCUS in the Operating Systems: VM/CMS, MVS/TSO, PC/DOS, VAX/VMS

SALESTOT.DAT already exists, and other records should be appended to it — from a TABLE request with HOLD, the following code might be used:

```
-VMS FILEDEF SALESTOT DISK SALESTOT.DAT
-VMS FILEDEF HOLD1 DISK HOLD1.DAT

TABLE FILE SALES
PRINT AMOUNT COST
BY SALESMGR BY REGION
ON TABLE HOLD AS HOLD1 FORMAT ALPHA
END
-RUN
-VMS APPEND HOLD1.DAT SALESTOT.DAT
-VMS DELETE HOLD1.DAT;*
```

Above, we have accomplished an append to the file SALESTOT.DAT using the VMS APPEND command. Then, the file HOLD1.DAT is erased — since it is no longer needed.

### Other FOCUS VAX Considerations

The following is a list of features which should be considered by VAX FOCUS users. Some of these point out differences between VM/CMS FOCUS and VAX FOCUS.

1. In a VMS FILEDEF or STATE command (STATE command is used to check the existence of a file), only three characters can be used for the filetype extension. All other characters are ignored (i.e., SALES.871005 will be interpreted as SALES.871.)
2. The FILEDEF for OFFLINE is treated as an automatic APPEND. Report output will be appended to the end of the file if it already exists. Delete the file before the report request is issued.
3. If too many characters are equated to a DEFINED alphanumeric field, there will be a format error. For example,

```
DEFINE FILE PERSON
NEWACCT/A3 = 'AAAA' ;
END
```

will produce an error message. On VM/CMS FOCUS there will be no error — as FOCUS will take only the first three characters as the value.
4. Alphanumeric fields assigned in a MASTER file cannot be redefined in a DEFINE with a different format — this will give an error.
5. To run a FOCEXEC from a VMS command file (.COM), you must use the following instructions to permit entry of data via PROMPT or CRTFORM (in the COM file):

```
$ ASSIGN 'F$LOGICAL("TT")' SYS$INPUT / USER
$ FOCUS "EXEC focexec "
```

COM files may use the VAX command language DCL to perform various tasks before entering the FOCUS session. The DCL command language is limited in applications — compared to the VM EXEC language. A good use of COM files is to assign the FOC$DIR directories for applications needing access to files on other directories.

## FOCUS in the PC/DOS Environment

### Setting Up the Environment

All FOCUS features are available in the PC/DOS environment — with very few differences from FOCUS on IBM mainframes. Information Builders Inc. (IBI) makes available a separate user's manual for PC/DOS FOCUS.

There are several differences in features available on DOS and VM/CMS which should be noted:

1. The DOS represents characters and numbers in ASCII format, while the IBM uses EBCDIC format. This has a slight effect on several FOCUS techniques.
2. The DOS user id is structured very differently from the IBM mainframe user id. While the IBM user has access to files on his virtual disk, and on disks he is linked to, the DOS user has access to files in his directories, or on other disk drives.
3. The DOS environment does not use EXEC language to invoke batch procedures, or to preprocess files before invoking FOCUS.

### Using FOCUS in the Operating Systems: VM/CMS, MVS/TSO, PC/DOS, VAX/VMS

Operating system commands and file manipulation can be accommodated in procedures called BAT files. BAT files are used in simple ways to set up the envirnoment.

4. The IBM FOCUS user may execute FOCEXECS which are located on other user ids, by linking to the id. The DOS FOCUS user must specify a "path" to other directories using the DOS PATH command. This command may be invoked before entering FOCUS. It makes it possible for you to use FOCEXEC stored on other directories.

FOCUS may be installed on the DOS "root" directory on the hard disk C: drive.

FOCUS uses work files for sorting and retrieving records. These work files are written to the current directory, unless the TEMP parameter has been set to a different directory using the command:

```
SET TEMP = directory
```

You may send reports to an OFFLINE file, by closing the OFFLINE and reallocate it using the DOS FILEDEF command (within a FOCEXEC):

```
OFFLINE CLOSE
-DOS FILEDEF OFFLINE DISK filename
```

Notice that all DOS operating system commands start with DOS. Depending on your installation, your DOS id may or may not be connected to a local printer. This can be done in a BAT file before entering FOCUS. If the printer is connected, you may direct output to it using the FOCUS command:

```
SET PRINT = OFFLINE
```

To view the output online, use

```
SET PRINT = ONLINE
```

FOCUS user-written subroutines are provided with PC FOCUS. You may add your own user-written routines by loading the routine into high memory. This is done by giving the argument FUSE =

routine name — upon entering FOCUS. See the PC/DOS FOCUS users manual for details.

There are several ways to configure the editor available to DOS users. This depends on how your DOS id has been set up. Usually, the FOCUS editor TED is a good way to edit all your DOS files — since it is the same as TED on the IBM mainframe.

When executing a FOCEXEC from FOCUS, you can issue an interrupt to stop execution of some commands. The standard DOS interrupt key is CTRL-C. This interrupt is trapped by FOCUS. Then you may issue either KT, KX, RT, or ?. The command KX causes the FOCUS execution to halt, and returns to the FOCUS command level. The command KT causes all output to be suppressed on the screen, but the command will continue to execute. The command RT is used after the KT command to resume display of output on the screen. The command ? displays statistics on reports or file maintenance procedures that FOCUS has processed.

## FOCUS Databases, FOCEXECS, and MASTER Descriptions

The following extensions are used in DOS to identify FOCUS-related files:

FEX: FOCEXEC procedures
FOC: FOCUS files
MAS: MASTER file descriptions
FTM: Extract files, such as HOLD or SAVE files

For example, the command

```
TABLE FILE PERSON
```

will cause FOCUS to search for a MASTER description called PERSON.MAS. The database file is assumed to be called PERSON.FOC (unless a USE has been issued).

You will sometimes need to access FOCEXECS which are located on other directories. PC/DOS provides the PATH command to set up connections between two or more directories which would enable a user in one directory to access command files (.EXE or .COM) in another directory. Starting with release 1.5 of PC FOCUS, the PATH command can be used so that from within the FOCUS environment users can now obtain command files (.EXE and .COM), MASTER files, and FOCEXECS. Below is an example of how this feature can be used:

The PGM directory contains the FOCEXECS REPORT1.FEX and REPORT2.FEX and the MASTER file SALES.MAS. The FOCUS directory contains the FOCUS file SALES.FOC. Before getting into FOCUS, issue the PATH command:

```
PATH \PGM
```

This sets up a path to your program directory. Then enter FOCUS from the FOCUS directory:

```
CD \FOCUS
FOCUS focus
```

At the PC/FOCUS command level, execute the report REPORT1.FEX:

```
EX REPORT1
```

FOCUS will first search the current directory (FOCUS) for the FOCEXEC, and then it will search the PGM directory — as directed by the PATH command. The MASTER file can be located in the same way.

When entering a FOCUS session, FOCUS will first execute the FOCEXEC named PROFILE.FEX — if it has been created. This FOCEXEC is useful for starting main menus, setting up FOCUS DEFINE commands, selecting passwords, etc. FOCUS searches only the current directory for PROFILE.FEX.

FOCUS files can also be located on other directories. They may be identified in a user's session by specifying the database with a USE command.

### The USE Command

FOCUS files may be located on the user's current directory, or on other directories. If on other directories, they can be accessed in the user's FOCUS session if the USE command is issued.

The USE command specifies the names and locations of FOCUS files. This command is usually intended to specify files:

1. Which have a non-standard name or filetype.
2. Which should be protected as read-only files.
3. Which need to be concatenated to other FOCUS files.
4. Whose filename does not correspond with the name of its MASTER file.

The syntax of the USE command is:

```
USE [ADD]
filename [READ] [AS mastername]
 [NEW]
END
```

where:

filename is the DOS fileid of the FOCUS file. (filename.filetype)
mastername is the FOCUS MASTER file description name.

You can specify several FOCUS files in one USE command, each with different parameters. For example:

```
USE
A:PERSON.FOC
A:DEPT1.FOC AS DEPT
END
```

The USE command may also refer to the directory where the FOCUS file is located. For example,

```
USE
/OURMAIL/MAIL.FOC
/OURMAIL/REGION.FOC
END
```

A list of all USE commands which are in effect during your FOCUS session is obtained by entering:

? USE

FOCUS will search for databases having the filetype of FOC. To instruct FOCUS to search for databases having different filetypes, issue the USE command. For example:

```
USE
PERSON.NEW
END
```

This indicates that the PERSON.NEW file is a FOCUS file whose MASTER is the PERSON.MAS file. Note that by changing the current filetype, as above, all other FOCUS files are assumed to have the same filetype (.NEW). If you need a FOCUS file with filetype FOC, then add it to the USE command. For example:

```
USE
PERSON.NEW
DEPT.FOC
END
```

The first file in the list determines the current filetype of other FOCUS files which may be referenced in your FOCUS session.

## External Files

FOCUS procedures sometimes refer to external files when reporting or maintaining FOCUS files. If the external file has a MASTER description which describes the fields on the records of the file, then FOCUS will be able to use reporting commands to retrieve records and create reports. External files are also used in the following:

1. LOGGING transactions in a MODIFY procedure.
2. TYPING records in a MODIFY procedure.
3. Using -WRITE, -READ, to write records or read records.
4. As DECODE files.
5. As HOLD and SAVE files.
6. As input files to MODIFY procedures.

In all cases, the external file must be identified to FOCUS using a FILEDEF. The only exceptions are when FOCUS issues its own FILEDEF, or if the filetype is .DAT. The syntax for the FILEDEF is (within a FOCEXEC):

```
-DOS FILEDEF ddname DISK filename [APPEND]
```

where:

ddname is the ddname which you want to identify the file.
filename is the DOS filename (including directory info.).

APPEND appends records to the end of the file. Otherwise, FOCUS writes over the file.

FOCUS will issue its own FILEDEF when HOLD or SAVE files are created; otherwise, you should issue them. Some examples of the FILEDEF command are:

```
-DOS FILEDEF SAVE DISK ACCOUNT.DAT
```

This enables a TABLE request to save a report extract in the file ACCOUNT.DAT.

```
-DOS FILEDEF OFFLINE DISK MAIL.LIS
```

This assigns the OFFLINE file to the file MAIL.LIS — to which report output will be written.

```
-DOS FILEDEF MAILLOG DISK MAILLOG.DAT
```

This enables the MAILLOG.DAT file to be assigned to the ddname MAILLOG. This file may be used for LOGGING transactions, TYPING records, etc.

In order to display the current ddnames assigned for various files, enter:

```
? FILEDEF
```

## Other PC/DOS FOCUS Considerations

The following is a list of features which should be considered by DOS FOCUS users. Some of these point out differences between VM/CMS FOCUS and DOS FOCUS.

1. In a DOS FILEDEF or STATE command (STATE command is used to check the existence of a file), only three characters can be used for the filetype extension. All other characters are ignored (i.e., SALES.871005 will be interpreted as SALES.871).
2. The FILEDEF for OFFLINE is sometimes treated as an automatic APPEND. Report output will be appended to the end of the file if it already exists. Delete the file before the report request is issued.
3. If too many characters are equated to a DEFINED alphanumeric field, there will be a format error. For example,

```
DEFINE FILE PERSON
NEWACCT/A3 = 'AAAA' ;
END
```

 will produce an error message. On VM/CMS FOCUS there will be no error — as FOCUS will take only the first three characters as the value.
4. Alphanumeric fields assigned in a MASTER file cannot be redefined in a DEFINE with a different format — this will give an error.
5. Because of limited CPU resources on the PC, it is best to precompile your large MODIFY procedures — using the COMPILED MODIFY feature described in the PD/FOCUS users manual.
6. Place as many COMPUTES as possible on a single line.
7. When specifying the panel and page parameters for an offline report, place the OFFLINE command before the SET command.

BAT files may be used to perform various tasks before entering the FOCUS session. The BAT command language is limited in applications — compared to the VM EXEC language. A good use of BAT files is to assign the printer port, and the PATH command.

# Index

aborting FOCUS requests, 75
activating fields in a Modify, 253, 255
actual format, 49–51, 347
aged trial balance, 128–138
alphanumeric transaction formats, 238
audit trail example, 348–353

by phrase, use of, 60–62

CASE logic and CRTFORMs, 252, 253
CASE logic examples, 256–276
CASE logic uses, 249–252
casual programmer, 5–8
CLEAR/NOCLEAR option, 246–247
clearing screen in FIDEL, 246
client mailing list system example, 308–314
CMS EXECS, 353–358
CMS filedef, 48–50, 237–238
CMS State command, 231
COBOL, 2, 4
COBOL files, 48, 52–53, 340–342
column positional notation, 90–91
COMPUTE in Modify command, 239–241, 250–252, 273–274
Compute in TABLE request, 96–102
Compute statement, 88–90
concatenate feature, 85–86

conditional fields, 223–225
contract file, 54–57
converting COBOL file, 344–348
Count verb, 68–74
cross referencing, 37–43, 291
CRTFORM, 235–248
CRTFORM statements, 236–239

database language, 1
database fields, 243–246
database fields in a Modify, 247
database management, 11–21
dates, 34, 142, 239
debugging CASE logic, 254
debugging features, 281–283
debugging programs, 290–292
DEC VAX, 4
Decode, 87–88, 93–95, 139, 230–231, 316–317
Decode table, 125
Defaults statement, 354
Define and compute statements, 80–83
Define techniques, 84–85
Define, use of, 75–76
defined field, 61
Define statements for screening, 83
deleting segments instances, 228–229
design efficiency, 26–29, 204
designing FOCUS files, 32–48, 203–204, 322–325

407

dialogue manager, 118–124,
    133–138, 168–171, 207, 243,
    345–348, 352, 366
dialogue manager variables,
    151–153, 271, 313–314, 325–330
dialogue manager CRTFORM, 239
direct calculation, 93–95, 102–104,
    113, 150, 198, 293–294
direct operation, 101–102
display fields, 243–246
documentation program sample,
    12–13
driver FOCEXEC, 124–129
driver program, 133–138
dummy fields in Modify, 236

echo feature, 138
end user, working with, 277–278
EXEC language, 54
expense voucher processing
    example, 358–372
external files, 44–53, 335–340
external files example, 340–344

FIDEL, 235–248
FIDEL data entry, 239–240
FIDEL features, 236
FIDEL formatting, 240–242
field declarations, 33
file design, 32–37
file maintenance, 185–187
file structure, 27–30
financial modeling language,
    210–212
find feature, 232
Fixform, 200–208, 262–263,
    265–266
Fixform formats, 209–210
Fixform from Master, 222
Fixform statement, 202
FOCEXECS, 50, 53–56, 118–124,
    146–150
FOCEXECS execution, 353–358
FOCUS database, 223
FOCUS research, 4

FOCUS techniques, reuse of,
    146–150
FOCUS utilities, 278–279
footing, 109–110
formatting reports, 104–125
formatting FIDEL screens,
    240–242
FORTRAN, 1–2, 4–7
fourth-generation languages, 1–5

global variables, 311, 351–353
GOTO statements, 253–256

headings, 109–110
headings, formatting of, 99–101
Hold files, 17–20, 44, 220–223, 303
    extracting records into, 19

If statements, 253–256
income tracking system, 115–118
Includes, 186, 200–201
indexed fields, 156–158, 174,
    177–179
indexed dialogue manager
    variables, 285–286
Information Builders Inc. (IBI),
    2, 11
input transaction file sample,
    205–208
internal formats, 48–51, 246–247
internal format records, 218–220
internal format records, use of,
    220–223
invalid transactions, logging of,
    228–230

Joins, 174, 189–190, 207, 325
Joins, use of, 170–175

key fields, 35, 226

Last command, 92–93, 99–102
learning aids, 10–11
Line option, 247–248
loading FOCUS file, 213–220

# Index

logging transactions, 242, 259–260
logical records, 237
lookup feature, 232–234

Mailing Labels Program, 27
mask feature, 85
masking 91–92
Master file description, 14–15, 32–38
Match command, 296–304
match logic, 222–229, 289–290
member enrollment application example, 284–287
methodology, 4–5
Modify elements, 224
Modify file, 195–196
multipath files, 37–38
multiple CRTFORMS in FIDEL, 247–248
multiverb table requests, 71–73, 78–81

net position, 327–340
Next command, 285, 306

offline, 64, 144–145, 162
offline command, 58–59
online commands, 58–59
one-to-many relationship, 11
Over command, 106–110
overflow conditions, 47–48

pagebreak, 101, 106–108, 110, 123, 316–318, 327
parent-child relationship, 34–38
physical records, 237
pointers, 35
price history example, 153–156
Print verb, 23–25, 69–70, 74–75
Print verb, limitations of, 76–77
project tracking system example, 314–321
Prompt command, 225
protected areas, 237

Read statement, 276–286
recap, 117–123
record-by-record processing, 210–214
records, counting of, 62–68
repeating groups, 265–267
report preparation features, 108–111
report request basics, 54–58
reporting requests, 21–27
reports, formatting of, 95–99
REXX language, 54
root segment, 34–35, 43–45, 128, 204, 223
rounding error, 83–84

sales tracking systems example, 287–308
Save files, 17–18, 186, 216–218, 244–245
screening conditions, 73–77, 81–83
segments, 14, 34–38, 226–227
    relating of, 21
segtype, 36
security trading system example, 321–327
self-documenting, 55
separate segments, 25
short path segments, 129, 145–146
single path files, 37, 128, 362
sort fields, 22–27
sort order, 204–205
sorting transactions, 232–233
subfooting, 112–116, 334–335
subheadings, 102–104, 112–116, 316–319
subtotals, 104–108, 114–118, 316–318
Sum verb, 23–25, 65–67
summarize, 117–123
syncsort package, 233
system messages, suppressing of, 204

Table command, 22

TABLEF command, 70–71
Temp space, 283–284
terminating data entry, 240
tape files, 336
transaction file, 192–194, 203,
    220–222, 230–238
transactions, logging of, 214–216
transaction values, matching of,
    194–201
transaction values, validation of,
    225–228
turnaround fields, 243–246

unique segment, 29, 41–44,
    229–230
unique segments, modifying of,
    201–202

usage format, 49–51, 337
use command, 279–281
user-friendly language, 6–8
use of book, 8–10

validating transactions, 226–229
validation features, 230–234
virtual segment, 39–43
VM/CMS operating system, 49–50,
    58–60
    status inquiry, 50–51
    working in, 51–54

wild card feature, 53
wild card screening conditions, 84,
    338
within feature, 305
Write statement, 276–286